Major General
Maurice Rose

Major General Maurice Rose

World War II's Greatest Forgotten Commander

Steven L. Ossad

and

Don R. Marsh

Foreword by
Martin Blumenson

TAYLOR TRADE PUBLISHING
Lanham • New York • Boulder • Toronto • Oxford

Published by Taylor Trade Publishing
An imprint of The Rowman & Littlefield Publishing Group, Inc.
4501 Forbes Boulevard, Suite 200, Lanham, Maryland 20706

Distributed by NATIONAL BOOK NETWORK

The Library of Congress has cataloged the hardcover edition of this
book as follows:
    Major General Maurice Rose : World War II's greatest forgotten commander /
Steven L. Ossad and Don R. Marsh.
        p.   cm.
    Includes bibliographical references and index.
    1. Ruhr Pocket, Battle of the, Germany, 1945. 2. Rose, Maurice,
    1899–1945. 3. Generals—United States—Biography. I. Marsh, Don R.
II. Title.
    D756.5.R8 O77 2003
    940.54'1273'092—dc21
                                                                    2002155778

    ISBN-13: 978-0-87833-308-0 (cloth : alk. paper)
    ISBN-13: 978-1-58979-351-4 (pbk. : alk. paper)
    ISBN-10: 0-87833-308-8 (cloth : alk. paper)
    ISBN-10: 1-58979-351-X (pbk. : alk. paper)

♾™ The paper used in this publication meets the minimum requirements of
American National Standard for Information Sciences—Permanence of
Paper for Printed Library Materials, ANSI/NISO Z39.48-1992.
Manufactured in the United States of America.

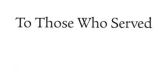

To Those Who Served

Contents

I shall lack voice: the deeds of Coriolanus
Should not be utter'd feebly. It is held
That valor is the chiefest virtue, and
Most dignifies the haver: if it be,
The man I speak of cannot in the world
Be singly counterpoised. At sixteen years,
When Tarquin made a head for Rome, he fought
Beyond the mark of others: our then dictator,
Whom with all praise I point at, saw him fight,
When with his Amazonian chin he drove
The bristled lips before him: be bestrid
An o'er-press'd Roman and i' the consul's view
Slew three opposers: Tarquin's self he met,
And struck him on his knee: in that day's feats,
When he might act the woman in the scene,
He proved best man i' the field, and for his meed
Was brow-bound with the oak. His pupil age
Man-enter'd thus, he waxed like a sea,
And in the brunt of seventeen battles since
He lurch'd all swords of the garland. For this last,
Before and in Corioli, let me say,
I cannot speak him home: he stopp'd the fliers;
And by his rare example made the coward
Turn terror into sport: as weeds before
A vessel under sail, so men obey'd
And fell below his stem: his sword, death's stamp,
Where it did mark, it took; from face to foot
He was a thing of blood, whose every motion
Was timed with dying cries: alone he enter'd
The mortal gate of the city, which he painted
With shunless destiny; aidless came off,
And with a sudden reinforcement struck
Corioli like a planet: now all's his:
When, by and by, the din of war gan pierce
His ready sense; then straight his doubled spirit
Re-quicken'd what in flesh was fatigate,
Run reeking o'er the lives of men, as if
'Twere a perpetual spoil: and till we call'd
Both field and city ours, he never stood
To ease his breast with panting.

—*Coriolanus*, Act II, Scene 2

Foreword

Maurice Rose was an outstanding leader in World War II. He served in North Africa, Sicily, and northwest Europe. He showed his aptitude and skill at the head of an armored division's combat command. He gained legendary status as commander of the 3rd Armored Division.

Like Manton Eddy, who commanded a corps, Maurice Rose was neither a West Pointer nor a college graduate. An armor officer like George S. Patton Jr., Rose knew how to use effectively in combat tanks and their supporting arms—infantry, artillery, and the rest.

Rose had a brief but telling contact with Patton. During Patton's last few weeks as commanding general of the 2nd Armored Division at Fort Benning, Georgia, before Patton assumed command of the I Armored Corps, some time between December 7, 1941, and January 15, 1942, Maurice Rose was Patton's Chief of Staff.

The relationship between a commander and his chief of staff is something special. The persons involved must be very close to and in tune with each other. The burden of accommodation rests with the chief of staff. He must know and understand at once what the commander, his boss, needs and wants in order to function. Thus, he oversees the staff members who are competent in a variety of areas, who are planners, administrators, information gatherers, bridge builders, regulators of supplies and communications, and who do other necessary tasks.

Patton could have chosen any number of officers for this important position. It is significant that he selected Maurice Rose. For a fleeting moment they fulfilled the demands of their respective posts. In the process

Rose learned how Patton practiced his profession as a soldier and how he directed his division. This was Patton's intention.

When Rose took the reins of the 2nd Armored Division's Combat Command A, he exhibited his own mastery of armored warfare. His elevation to command the 3rd Armored Division was no surprise to the senior authorities in the European Theater of Operations.

The 2nd and 3rd Armored Divisions were structured according to an early and outmoded scheme of organization. They were thus different from those armored divisions formed later, the 4th, 5th, 6th, and so on. The 2nd and 3rd had twin Combat Commands A and B. They were also heavier, that is, had more troops and tanks—about 15,000 men and 254 Shermans in each division as compared to the 10,000 and 154 tanks in the subsequent triangularized armored divisions. The latter had Combat Commands A, B, and R (Reserve) to facilitate mobility. Because the 2nd and 3rd were overseas when the shift in organization took place, they remained unchanged. Maurice Rose's appointment as division commander of the 3rd occurred in part because he was familiar with how these two older units operated.

Rose's 3rd Armored Division operated in Courtney Hodges's First Army, and Rose's aggressive style of warfare made him a favorite tank commander. His performance allowed First Army veterans to claim equal proficiency and speed of advance with Patton's Third Army, normally regarded as the premier armored force among the U.S. armies in the field. Rose's division was part of J. Lawton Collins's VII Corps, and Rose's leadership contributed much to the success of the corps, often judged to be the best and most effective American corps in Europe.

The death of Maurice Rose shortly before the end of the war in Europe was a tragic event on two levels. The first was a feeling of personal loss of a cherished colleague. The second was the setback suffered by the U.S. Army at large, for the high-ranking officers had counted on Rose to be one of the giants of the postwar period.

Steven L. Ossad and Don R. Marsh have charted with sensitivity and skill the professional growth and achievements of Maurice Rose. They have made Rose come alive. Their biography is a moving tribute to the qualities and the behavior of a rabbi's son who turned himself into an American military legend.

Martin Blumenson
Washington, D.C.
December 2002

" . . . and he drove out the inhabitants of the mountains,
but could not drive out the inhabitants of the valley
because they had chariots of iron."

—Book of Judges, Chapter 1:19

Preface

For men like Maurice Rose, war is the window through which we can peer at their true being because the destiny of such men is written in the clash of arms. There is no way to really know them except in the world of battle, a world that exists by itself, and which offers only momentary portals of insight into its terrible reality.

Such men offer only fleeting glimpses into their true natures. They are often closed and not given to easy conversation, or the exchange of personal details of their lives. A letter, a remembered comment, a photo, a vignette recounted by an acquaintance—these are our only avenues into their souls. Had Rose left a mountain of documents, a diary, or a host of men who claimed to have known his moods and thoughts, we would still be mostly in the dark. He is revealed most fully in his deeds on the battlefield, through the witness of others. Time and the fog of war both hide and reveal his nature.

This, then, is a story about a very great, yet now unknown, American hero. It is a tale that begins with the stuff of legend, the symbols and language of myth, and is covered by the embellishments of old men's dreams of lost and courageous youth. If the story were placed in a genre of literature, it would probably be closest to the tradition of the "saga"—grand in scale, passed on in the oral tradition by men who were there, and many who were not, but all agreed on the power of the saga's hero. Each storyteller stands in awe of his deeds and the pathos of his end.

It is in that end, after the sun had fallen on a day that saw the hero's greatest triumph, that the story reaches an almost unbearable crescendo. Cut down in the darkness in cold blood by the faceless enemy after raising his hands in surrender—so close to the war's end—the hero's tale gains its full power, and its most enduring myths. In unraveling the strands of time that bind the imagination, we see many things about how legends are born and how the truth is often obscured, or even brushed aside, by opinions, and by what well-intentioned people think sounds good.

As an effort of military biography, telling the story in a traditional way has been a daunting task, mostly because there is virtually no written record upon which to rely. Because of the circumstances of Maurice Rose's death, and his family history, there is a paucity of papers, letters, journals, or other primary material. All that apparently survives of the written record are a few short documents: the general's last letter to his son, two technical articles separated by a decade, and penned for professional journals (one of which is probably not even his work), and a letter to the SHAEF Commander, Gen. Dwight D. Eisenhower, about the strengths and weaknesses of American equipment. A few memos and reports; that is all there is. His many letters to his wife—the best portal into the soul of the man—apparently did not survive.

The rest is based on a sparse cache of official documents, newspaper accounts, what men saw, or thought they saw, what they heard from others, or read somewhere. Many personal mementos, including the physical relics of the Warrior—his sword, collection of weapons, decorations, and even his pen and Zippo lighter were reported "lost in a flood in Kansas" by his widow. What remains is the flag that flew over Cologne in early March 1945 when the city was conquered by the hero, a bronze bust of Hitler, a General Officer's Colt .380 pistol, a typewriter, and a plaque taken from the wardroom of a U.S. Navy attack transport renamed in his honor. These war trophies are all that remain of the warrior's physical legacy to his descendants and to us.

The photographic record is more extensive, including official U.S. Army Signal Corps photos of the World War II period, many of which, along with a few old family snapshots, are in an album started by Rabbi Samuel Rose, the general's father, and now kept by his grandnephew Jeff Rose, MD. But, the most intriguing truly personal item of all is his widow's photo album of their life together. It spans the time from when they met in Panama in the early 1930s until the time her husband went to war in 1942. It is filled with the small 1-inch square black and white images typical of the period. But even the album is a torment for the biographer, and more problematic than revealing. There is no one left to discuss the pictures, to identify the people and places, to remember the occasion that caused the smile, or to describe the locale of the horseback ride, or the pleasant cruise down a river.

No one remains to give intimate substance to the reality of the man as he was in the fullness of life before he became wrapped in the cloak of legend and the visions of the aged storytellers. Maurice Rose was born a century ago and died just fifty-eight years ago, but it is as if one set out to write a biography of Achilles, or Ajax, or some other mythic ancient hero, centuries after their deaths, when only fragments of their lives remained.

To this day, those who fought through Europe with him as young men speak his name with quiet respect, pride, and honor. Most still regard him not as some distant, or remote figure, but as one of them, a frontline soldier who did what they did, and suffered the same as they. The story of his death—cut down in the darkness and "fog of battle" by a blast from a Schmeisser machine pistol—became the focus of persistent myths, embellished after the fact, never corrected, and magnified by the telling of the tale over many years.

It is the enigma at the heart of the story. How could this "bullet proof" warrior of undeniable courage, who was oblivious to sniper rounds and who crossed bridges that should have blown up under him, get himself shot while surrendering? What is the answer? And not just to the question, how, but also why? Perfidious adversary? Cold-blooded killer? Friction of war? Nervous soldier with an itchy trigger finger? A sudden jolt of a tank that triggered an accidental stream of bullets?

The actual circumstances are best revealed in the official ETO War Crimes Investigation, the only such inquiry into the death of an American general in our history. The officer responsible, Colonel Leon Jaworski, decided that no atrocity had taken place, but that is still not clear. The recollections and testimony of the only surviving eyewitness—T/4 Glenn H. Shaunce, Rose's longtime jeep driver—are not as dramatic as the many stories, but do not obscure the essential truth about the man. His name was, according to Martin Blumenson, one of the authors of the U.S. Army's Official History of World War II, "already wrapped in legend even in his own time."

Maurice Rose was the quintessential professional, the living embodiment of a warrior, and in the words of Major General Roderick R. Allen, his friend and confidante, godfather to Rose's son, and future successor as Commander of 3rd Armored, "a real soldier's soldier."

This is also the story of a great military unit. The 3rd Armored Division that Maurice Rose led was one of an elite few whose like will never

be seen again. Third of a series of sixteen armored divisions that were created for a unique task at a unique moment, its history and greatest deeds
on the battlefield are intermingled with the last year of the hero's life. In
fact, if a military unit can be said to have a kind of independent life with
different stages, then the *Rose Period* was unquestionably the most important historically.

Further, for a great number of the thousands of men who belonged
to the 3rd Armored and wore its patch, this period was the most intense of
any that preceded it, and for the survivors, any that would follow. More
than 2,000 of them never returned; thousands of others bore the wounds
of battle on their bodies and in their spirits. All great units are proud, and
many have longer years of tradition, are richer in lore and their flags hold
the streamers of more campaigns, but none was greater than the 3rd
Armored—the "Spearhead" of "Lightning" Joe Collins' VII Corps, batter-
ing ram and "fer-de-lance" of the U.S. First Army—and none contributed
more to the final victory over Hitler's Third Reich.

This is also the story of at least one truly great victory, and like the
hero who was in command, it too is virtually unknown. The second Battle
of Mons remains a footnote to other great battles, never studied in depth
in the great military academies, or by any of the great historians, professional or citizen, in the more than five decades since VE Day. It was a battle that can be compared to the highest achievement of arms, and echoes
the fabled victory of Hannibal over the Romans at Cannae on August 2,
216 B.C. It was a campaign of agile maneuver and innovative tactics, an
engagement of encirclement and annihilation. Martin Blumenson and
other great historians first thought it was simply a successful meeting
engagement, in fact, an "accident." Even after the disclosure of the *Ultra
Secret*, which illustrated why it happened and its strategic importance, it
received scant attention.

Finally, this is a story of a deep friendship between two men—one,
now old, who was there and who rode with the hero, and the other who
was born afterwards into the generation of the children of ". . . *those who
served*." From totally different worlds, by accident or by destiny, they
became united in friendship, and in a mission to tell a great tale of what
those who were there call the Brotherhood of War. The two men were
haunted by an untold story. The younger was pursuing the rediscovery of
a lost hero of childhood over a winding, eerie trail of thirty-five years. The
veteran was unable for more than fifty years to exorcise the heroic image
of his battlefield commander, and viscerally incapable of accepting the

"official" explanation of his death. Each came to realize that only together could they tell the story.

Bred in America on the threshold of a new century, the son of hard-working immigrants, and raised on romantic tales of valor in a time of unabashed patriotism, Maurice Rose was prepared and molded by war and by long years of lonely and hard service. Toiling unknown, like thousands of others to whom we owe our lives and our freedom, he could not have known for what the preparation had been. Perhaps, he sensed at some point that a great test still lay ahead, but that would have been small consolation against the isolation and disappointments of twenty years of solitary service on dreary army posts all over our country.

But, when the ultimate test came, when the stakes were survival, he was ready, and the men he led were ready, and up to the terrible ordeal that none willingly chose. In the unforgiving and merciless crucible of war, the hero was found to be possessed of a fierce determination to succeed, and a drive for excellence, and victory, no matter what the odds, and regardless of the cost in men, machines, and most of all, to himself.

This then is the story of the life and the death of Major General Maurice Rose, one of only three American fighting division commanders to be killed in action during World War II. He was one of the greatest battlefield leaders ever produced by our country, and possibly our greatest armor commander. Often decorated, always at the front of his columns, he fell on March 30, 1945, near a castle at Hamborn, Germany. Just a few miles up the road, his 3rd Armored Division would, a few hours later, close the Ruhr Pocket, thus ending the greatest encirclement battle in American history, and renamed the *Rose Pocket* in the Commander's honor.

He was a man who, in John Keegan's phrase, wore the "Mask of Command" tightly. On the battlefield, however, his was the face and form of the pure warrior. There, he appeared like a modern day Caesar, who wrapped himself in a red cloak so all could see him, or an Alexander, surrounded by faithful companions who fought at his side. In combat along with his men, Rose was a soldier who by his physical courage, personal appearance—and even his garb—matched the very image of the heroic leader risking death with his troops. At the very edge of the front lines, in the company of soldiers with whom he personally engaged the enemy hand-to-hand, he was cut down at the pinnacle of his career. Like thousands of others whom he led to glory, he sleeps under a marble cross on foreign soil drenched and liberated by the blood of Americans, some of whom—fewer every day—still walk amongst us unrecognized as giants.

Introduction

Major General Maurice Rose was the youngest of three fighting division commanders to fall in battle in World War II, out of thirty generals and admirals lost, and the only armored division commander ever killed in action. To put this in perspective, our Civil War claimed a total of 160 general officers killed in action, split equally—ironically—between the Union and Confederacy. In just one single encounter at the Battle of Antietam on September 17, 1862—still counted as the bloodiest day in American history—three division commanders fell, out of a total of seven general officers lost on that day alone.

Perhaps it is not surprising that Rose should have met his end on the battlefield at the very "tip of the lance." In the age-old debate about the proper place of a combat commander, Rose came down firmly as an advocate of leading from the front, and that is where he could always be found. The top Allied commanders, even admirers who thought his behavior somewhat reckless, viewed him as an effective, aggressive commander—fearless and hard on himself and his men—and this doubtless was a consideration in his rapid promotions once the war began.

Generals Omar Bradley and Dwight D. Eisenhower supported Rose's advancement to general, and he was hand picked to command the 3rd Armored Division right after the Normandy Breakout. He had already attracted attention in Tunisia, where in May 1943, Rose negotiated and accepted the first large-scale German unconditional surrender to an American during World War II. It is not difficult to see why the senior commanders chose him. His record during the first two months of the European Campaign was a model of battlefield success.

As leader of Combat Command A, 2nd Armored Division, at the Battle of Carentan on June 13, 1944, Brigadier General Maurice Rose played a major role in holding that crucial beachhead position, thereby saving the 506th Parachute Infantry Regiment (of "Band of Brothers" fame) from being overrun by German armor. It can be argued, based on subsequent evaluation of the German plan, that he might very well have saved the entire Normandy beachhead from a catastrophic German counterattack. What was not known at the time—and remained hidden for more than twenty-five years after the war—was that Allied code-breakers had provided the crucial intelligence that led to the victory. Rose thus became one of the first ground commanders to effectively exploit *Ultra* intelligence tactically. He would do so again later in early September at the Battle of Mons, where he won even greater recognition and his second general's star.

Rose's performance during the oft-celebrated *Operation Cobra* in late July 1944 was even more impressive. His daring breakthrough of the German defenses was not fully appreciated at the time, or in the postwar studies. Famed Army Historian Martin Blumenson, however, credits Rose as the catalyst of Bradley's decision to move towards Avranches. His successful attack was the " raw material" that military academies turn into history. When the senior commanders—Omar Bradley and "Lightning Joe" Collins—realized what was happening, they changed the plan and made the decision to head south immediately. As Blumenson concludes, *"One could, I am sure, say that Rose propelled the Cobra's fangs."*

But while we can credit Rose's success largely to his leadership, he knew—as every true warrior knows—that in the attack, ultimate success or failure is determined down at the battalion and company levels. The men there follow orders, but they also can instinctively recognize a commander whom they would follow into hell. During *Cobra*, Rose did not wait safely in the rear for radio reports of the situation; he took position just behind the lead vehicles. In essence, he acted as his own scout and forward observer, and rode into battle alongside his troops in his thin-skinned jeep starting at the line of departure. There he went into combat with the men of the 66th Armored Regiment in their Sherman tanks and the soldiers from the 22nd Infantry Regiment riding on the rear decks, as he had trained them to do. While other high-ranking officers in the rear heard the thunder of the heavy artillery at a distance, Rose, ever the cavalryman, "rode to the sound of the guns." There he personally observed the action up close; disregarding danger, his own casualties, and driving his tired and hard-pressed men—and himself—while constantly issuing radio orders, "Keep pushing. Keep moving" to crush the enemy opposition. It was because of this that Rose became the greatest, most decorated, battlefield Armor commander ever produced by our country, recognized as the American Rommel in the Armored Forces.

It was as the commander of the 3rd Armored Division that Rose became in Blumenson's words, "a legend in his own time." The selection of Rose was not without irony. General Bradley was gently pressed by his corps commander, MG J. Lawton Collins, to replace Bradley's West Point classmate and friend, Leroy Watson, who had not performed to Collins's expectation. The decision to select Rose, an "old" cavalryman who never attended college, had enlisted as a private in the National Guard, and had come up from the ranks, was daring and somewhat unconventional. The "Mustang" general had arrived at the pinnacle of command, and neither Bradley nor Collins ever had second thoughts. Under Rose, the 3rd Armored Division earned a reputation as the "Spearhead" of the VII Corps and the U.S. First Army. Veterans of that outfit still feel that while George Patton's Third Army got the headlines, they earned the victory.

The division drove across France and Belgium, broke the Siegfried Line, suffered through the static battles in the fall of 1944 and the terrible ordeal of the Bulge, and captured Cologne in March 1945. Under Maurice Rose's command the division made the longest, enemy-opposed armored drive in history—more than 150 kilometers—on March 29, 1945—a record that still stands. This resulted in the greatest encirclement battle in American history, the "Ruhr Pocket"—with over 350,000 enemy troops captured—renamed the "Rose Pocket," the only major battle in World War II to be named for an American General. These achievements were heroic, but they came at a very high price. Rose's division led all other American armored divisions in total casualties and loss of equipment.

Rose, like thousands of his men, paid the highest price, and it was in his death that his story truly becomes compelling and full of pathos. Rose was the only American division commander ever to be killed while a prisoner of war and the only American general to be the subject of a war crimes investigation. What actually happened on March 30, 1945, has been the subject of speculation, hearsay, educated and misinformed opinion, and much debate. This book is the first critical attempt to piece together the events of that night with as much detachment as authors passionately pursuing the dispassionate truth can summon.

Finally, while the debate about Rose's death has generated much controversy, the questions related to his religion, burial, and fund-raising for the hospital named in his honor have also raised tempers and voices. One thing however, remains true. Whatever Maurice Rose decided about himself and his beliefs, he was born the son and grandson of rabbis, and became the highest-ranking American Jewish combat officer to serve in World War II, and the highest-ranking American Jewish officer ever to be killed in action.

CHAPTER One

March 30, 1945 (I)

"The devil was loose on the road."
Hauptmann Wolf Koltermann, CO, 507 Sch.Pz.Abt.

T he early morning was silent and calm, almost peaceful, but every man in the outfit, everyone except the general, was troubled. The dawn had broken cold, grey, and damp, with the sky heavily overcast. Fog and low clouds stretched from the ground to the far horizon. Such conditions contained an element of danger. Unless the day cleared, the P-47 Thunderbolt fighter-bombers would be unable to help the columns if they ran into trouble.

The general started his day with the practiced routines and rhythms of more than twenty-five years of military service. He shaved closely, dressed with his usual fastidiousness, and quickly drank a single cup of coffee.[1] (A) Before he strapped on his belt and holstered .45 automatic, he checked to make sure he had a round chambered, a full magazine, and the safety on; his weapon was cocked and locked. Next, he lit a Camel. He was ready for whatever the day would bring.

A Second Lt. "Bud" Bressler joined the 2nd Armored Division in May 1943 as an aide to Brig. General Isaac D. White, CG, Combat Command B. He fought in Sicily and Normandy, where he frequently observed Rose, who "looked like he just stepped off a bandstand, even during the breakout in Normandy." This same description appears in many veterans' recollections.

Regardless of the weather and the Germans, Major General Maurice Rose felt optimistic. His elite 3rd Armored Division—the organization he had named "Spearhead"—had the day before carried out a spectacular achievement.[2] **(B)** A sixteen-hour drive north from Marburg, Germany, resulted in a more than ninety-mile advance, the longest forward movement ever gained against enemy opposition in history. **(C)**

The record brought a sense of deep pride, but no satisfaction to Rose. Almost as soon as the march from the Rhine began on March 25, his boss, VII Corps Commander Major General "Lightning" Joe Collins, had been needling him about the achievements of Patton's Third Army, 4th Armored Division, the heroes of Bastogne. **(D)** Three days later,

---

B According to the Semi-Official History, General Rose authorized the use of the flash "Spearhead" under the standard Armored Force patch "after his Division had brilliantly led many of U.S. First Army's drives in France, Belgium, and Germany during 1944 and 1945," pg. 30. Actually, the first mention of "Spearhead" is in a newspaper article appearing on August 22, 1944, and before the division entered either Belgium or Germany (see chapter 10, footnote 113).

C *Spearhead in the West* records the distance as "more than 90 miles, cross country, from Marburg to Niedermarsburg," pg. 142. The *3rd Armored Narrative Battle Report, March 1945* (May 4, 1945), pg. 6, says that "When the advance ended that night, leading combat elements had covered 75 miles of road distance, other elements had covered over 90 miles of the distance to Paderborn." Omar Bradley, in his memoir, *A General's Life*, describes the drive as "one of the most electrifying of the war. In one day, Rose covered 90 miles, exceeding even Patton's longest drive," pg. 420. John Toland's *The Last 100 Days* puts Lt. Col. Walter B. Richardson's (lead column Task Force Commander) odometer at 102 miles by midnight, pg. 311. Charles Whiting's *The Battle of the Ruhr Pocket* puts the number at 109 "odometer miles." Numerous other secondary sources describe the distance as being in a range of 90 to 110 miles, as for example the *Newsweek*'s April 16, 1945, issue which put the record at "101 miles in 24 hours"; pg. 33. Whatever the source, and however the length is measured, it is generally acknowledged that the 3rd Armored record still stands.

D J. Lawton "Lightning Joe" Collins (1896–1987) was Rose's Corps Commander during most of the campaign in Northwest Europe. He was born in Algiers, Louisiana and attended Louisiana State University before entering the U.S. Military Academy at West Point. He graduated in 1917, and spent the World War I years in the United States. After service in the Army of Occupation, he spent the next twelve years as both student and instructor at the Army's schools, including West Point, Army Industrial College, and the Army War College. He was a classmate of Maurice Rose at the Infantry School, returning as an instructor during

Collins playfully reminded Rose once again of the rival 4th's progress. The division was drawing a lot of attention in the press for having gone more than fifty miles in fifty-eight hours, and the commanders in the First Army, like Collins, were starting to bristle at the lack of publicity for their efforts.[3]

The comparison stung Rose. The subtle suggestion that 3rd Armored was somehow slacking off annoyed him greatly. He had been pushing his men—himself too—harder than usual since the jump-off on March 25. Having rushed more than fifty miles in forty-eight hours, as an experienced campaigner he could sense that the drive was about to intensify still more.[4] Of course, as a division commander, he didn't know exactly how, but he found out soon enough.

On the morning of March 28, the American strategy had abruptly changed. The 12th Army Group, headed by Lt. General Omar N. Bradley, ordered First Army, commanded by Lt. General Courtney H. Hodges, to halt its easterly advance, pivot 90 degrees, and attack to the north.[5] The top American brass, especially Bradley, was now obsessed with making large encirclements to capture thousands of Germans. Politics, especially competition with the Soviet forces operating to the east of Berlin, no doubt played a part. The goal was now to close the "Ruhr Pocket."[6] **(E)**

To do so, Hodges' First Army and Lt. General William Simpson's Ninth Army would aim at a link up at Paderborn, more than 100 miles

---

George C. Marshall's tenure as asst. commandant. After Pearl Harbor, he was promoted to major general and took command of the 25th Infantry Division, which relieved the 1st Marine Division on Guadalcanal late in 1942. During his South Pacific tour, Collins picked up the nom de guerre "Lightning Joe," taken from the lightning bolt on the shoulder patch of the 25th, or "Tropic Lightning" Division. After the New Georgia campaign, he went to England and assumed command of VII Corps for the Normandy invasion. He led that unit through Five Campaigns.

E Capturing large bodies of enemy troops—"bagging" or "pocketing" them—rather than fighting them head on, has always been one of the highest aims of the military operational art. By the end of World War II it had reached the level of obsession among several top officers, especially Omar Bradley. Some critics argue, however, that closing the Ruhr Pocket, actually prolonged the war, and that capturing large numbers of troops in the closing days of March and April 1945 was a costly diversion of resources better employed in seizing the final significant geographical objectives.

away. **(F)** Leading the First Army advance and forming the right pincer of the encirclement would be Collins' VII Corps. Leading VII Corps would, as usual, be Maurice Rose's 3rd Armored Division, the spearhead of the advance. At Paderborn, Rose would join hands with his old outfit, the 2nd Armored Division, commanded by Maj. General Isaac D. White, and a part of the Ninth Army's XIX Corps. There was more than a little rivalry in the line up. Back in Normandy, White had led Combat Command B when Rose led Combat Command A. Now each had his own armored division.

During an afternoon conference on March 28 at Rose's HQ near Marburg, senior officers from VII Corps, IX Tactical Air Force, and the division gathered to coordinate the shift to the north. Among them was the IX Tactical Air Commander, Maj. General Elwood R. "Pete" Queseda, **(G)** an old friend of Maurice Rose, who was responsible for providing close air support to First Army and its components.

Once again, Collins publicly needled Rose about the 4th Armored Division's exploits. On the surface, Collins was indulging in a bit of school-boy jostling—as if division commanders were football captains. Rose, always the respectful subordinate, had endured the previous needling in

---

F Paderborn is a small industrial city lying on the banks of the Pader River, whose source flows from under its Cathedral, and from which it takes its name. Located in the State of North Rhine-Westphalia, it was the spiritual birthplace of the Holy Roman Empire, when, in 799 a.d. Charlemagne met Pope Leo III there to discuss the founding of a Germanic empire. In that regard, it holds a place in German history similar to Aachen, Charlemagne's capital, and scene of another important battle waged by Rose's 3rd Armored Division along the Siegfried Line in mid-September 1944. Because of its airport, road, and rail junctions, Paderborn was selected as the site of the *SS* Panzer Officer Training School, as well as other military schools, thus giving rise to its American sobriquet as "the Fort Knox" of Germany.

G Elwood Richard "Pete" Queseda (1904–1993) was born in Washington, D.C., and enlisted in the U.S. Army in 1924, receiving his wings and commission in 1926. He was one of Rose's closest friends, dating from their year together at the Command and General Staff School at Leavenworth, Kansas. They reconnected during the North African Campaign, when Queseda was deputy commander of the Northwest African Coastal Air Force. Queseda assumed command of the IX Fighter Command & IX Tactical Air Command late in 1943. Responsible for close air support of the U.S. First Army in Europe, he earned a reputation as forceful, innovative, and a fierce advocate of effective air support of infantry and armored forces. Queseda, working with Bradley, Collins, and Rose essentially developed the basic tenets of close air support that have guided U.S. forces since then. He retired as a Lt. general.

silence, but this time he couldn't restrain himself. Especially embarrassed in front of Queseda, and in a moment of stung pride, Rose boasted aloud in front of the senior officers, including Collins, that he would be in Paderborn by midnight of the next day![7]

The officers at the conference were stunned and immediately fell silent. Paderborn was more than 100 miles from Marburg! Later that evening, at a gathering with several news correspondents, Rose repeated the claim. To those at the gathering, he seemed obsessed. Within just forty-eight hours, what had started out as friendly banter and competitive boasting would have terrible consequences for Rose and the men of his division.

As March 30 began, he had missed the boastful deadline, but not by much. Rose's leading column, Task Force Richardson (Lt. Colonel Walter B. Richardson) was only a dozen miles short of the tactical objective: the high ground around Paderborn's airfield.[8] The early morning mood at 3rd Armored headquarters remained upbeat in spite of the stiffening enemy resistance and overcast skies. As he reviewed the overnight intelligence and operations reports, radio messages, and situation maps, General Rose felt good. The 2nd Armored Division was moving steadily towards Paderborn; so was his outfit. He was sure that by the end of the day—it was Good Friday—the "Ruhr Pocket," holding Field Marshal Walter Mödel's Army Group B, would be surrounded.

With the war in Europe drawing to a climax, the pocketing of the Ruhr would be the crowning achievement of Rose's career. There could even be another Presidential Unit Citation for the 3rd Armored Division. **(H)** Of course, the victory would be total if his division reached the objective one step ahead of his old command. To the long list of "firsts" and great feats of battle racked up by his men, would be added one more success: the largest encirclement battle in our history, an American Cannae. In this classic battle in 216 B.C., Hannibal encircled and annihilated a much

---

H Various units of the division received a total of seven Distinguished (Presidential) Unit Citations during World War II. This citation is the highest decoration awarded to a field unit and is equivalent to the Distinguished Service Cross, our second highest battlefield decoration for an individual. The Headquarters of 3rd Armored Division had been awarded a Presidential Unit Citation (PUC) for its actions at Mons, Belgium, in early September 1944. Only one other armored division headquarters was awarded a PUC during World War II—the 4th Armored—for its performance during the Battle of the Bulge.

larger Roman force sent to intercept him. **(I)** After closing the "Ruhr Pocket," Rose and his men could move on to the next prize, reaching the Elbe River ahead of everyone else, and maybe even Berlin.

On the "other side of the hill," the Germans were exhausted, but not yet finished. Paderborn had joined the long list of bombed-out cities on March 27, when more than 250 British Lancaster Heavy Bombers unloaded 1,200 tons of high explosive and incendiary bombs on it. The town was devastated, and the medieval cathedral was severely damaged. As soon as the bombers departed, the Germans emerged from the rubble and started to fortify their positions in preparation for the inevitable attack.

The Paderborn area was the site of a number of military installations. Sennelager, to the northwest, was a major *Panzer* training center and tank testing ground (Henschel, the manufacturer of the turret atop the King Tiger II tank, had an experimental station nearby at Haustenbeck). The village of Augustdorf housed the *Waffen SS Panzer* Training and Replacement Center. **(J)** Personnel from these facilities marched out to join the men holding the defensive line south of Paderborn.

I On August 2, 216 B.C., at Cannae, Italy, the Carthaginian General Hannibal Barca encountered the Consuls Varro and Paulus, who were sent to stop his march through Italy. In the cataclysmic battle that followed, more than 50,000 Romans perished in a ghastly slaughter that lasted just one afternoon. It is written in the ancient sources that as Hannibal walked through the human wreckage, he watched his men collect gold Senatorial rings by the bushel basket. Ever since then, the Battle of Cannae has been studied by every generation of commander and student and viewed as a paradigm of the classic encirclement battle and the penultimate example of the application of tactical military genius.

J Augustdorf was the headquarters of the *SS Panzer Reconnaissance Training and Replacement Regiment* (CO, Stuermbannfuehrer Holzer) and the *SS Junior Leaders School* (CO, Oberstuermbahnfuehrer Stern). *SS Pz.Bde.Westfalen* was deployed as follows:

Sector	West	Center	East
Area	Wewer/Borchen	Dorenhagen/ Eggeringhausen	Scherfelde
Infantry	*SS Pz Recce Bn 1*	*SS Pz Recce Bn 2* (1,000 men)	*SS Pz Recce Bns 3 & 4*
Armor	*Pz Bn 501* (no tanks)	*Pz Bn 507*	None
Commander	Meyer	Holzer	Unknown

Source: JRW Graves, et. al., (British Army of the Rhine), *Battle of Paderborn, March/März 1945*, 1985, pg. 4.

At first light on March 30, 3rd Armored was ready to move. The engines of hundreds of tanks, guns, armored cars, half-tracks, trucks, utility vehicles, and peeps roared or sputtered to life. "Peep" was the Armored Force term for the more commonly used "jeep" to describe the ubiquitous quarter-ton utility vehicle. Thousands of men stirred, and steeled themselves to face another day of deadly peril along the gauntlet of fire and hell that lay ahead.

In the Headquarters Company area, T/Sgt. John T. Jones, of the Operations Section (G-3) was just finishing breakfast when he felt a tap on the shoulder.

It was Lt. Col. Wesley A. Sweat, my boss, and head of G-3 of the 3rd Armored Division. He said to me, "Sarge, the General wants you to join our advance group today as we may need a stenographer." Members of G-3 had been on these missions before and they were usually long days, full of danger and excitement. Our leader, Major General Maurice Rose, always wanted to be at the head of his troops, and sometimes this meant that we would be at the front line quite close to the enemy.

I felt a premonition that something bad was going to happen that day, but since I had no choice, I grabbed an apple and an orange from the table, and quickly joined the general's party. It consisted of one peep with Shaunce, the driver; Major Bellinger, the general's aide; and General Rose. The other peep contained Col. Frederick Brown, Division Artillery, his driver (A. C. Braziel), and another soldier unknown to me (Lt. Col. George Garton). Finally our scout car, driven by a headquarters soldier named Henderson or Richardson, I believe, (actually, Pvt. James E. Stevenson of HQ Service Company), a radio man, name unknown, Lt. Col. Sweat, and myself, armed with a .45 pistol and a sub machine gun.[9] **(K)**

K Lt. Colonel Wesley A. Sweat, a Florida native and graduate of the University of Florida, entered the Army in 1941, graduated from the 5th Special Command and General Staff College Course on December 6, 1941, and was one of the original cadre of officers assigned to the 3rd Armored Division. He was division G-3 (Operations), a member of the General Staff, or "G" Section, responsible for the operational aspects of combat, as well as training, deployment, etc. He was awarded the Legion of Merit, Silver Star, Bronze Star with two Oak Leaf Clusters (OLC), Presidential Unit Citation, and Purple Heart. He was the last survivor of the men aboard the M-20 on March 30, 1945, and passed away in 2001.

Jones was known as "Africa Jones" because he had been in an advance 3rd Armored party that observed the fighting in North Africa, and also to distinguish him from another Sgt. Jones in the G-3 section. He had one last chore before boarding the M-20. **(L)** He went to see Master Sgt. Frank A. Koukl, the senior enlisted man in Colonel Andrew Barr's G-2 (Intelligence) section. **(M)** Koukl, a former musician and infantryman, was about to get an incredibly lucky break.

> I was awakened by someone (probably a guard) and told to eat an early breakfast as Col. Barr and I were to accompany the general's party. On the way back to get ready, Jack T. (Africa) Jones informed me that a mistake had been made and that it was G-3 personnel that were to go with Rose.[10]

The 3rd Armored Division was poised for battle and ready to resume its march north. Jones's presence in the M-20 was no accident. Rose, always mindful of the value of publicity and eager to make sure his achievement was recorded, wanted a stenographer along to chronicle the triumph about to be achieved. First Army intelligence officers estimated that as many as 125,000 German troops might be trapped between the converging pincers of the American forces. The actual total turned out to be closer to 350,000 enemy soldiers.[11]

By 0600 the four columns of 3rd Armored were positioned along parallel roads all converging on the Rhine-Westphalia town of Paderborn. **(N)**

L The six-wheeled M-20 was a variant of the rubber-tired M-8 armored car (called the *Greyhound*). It was developed in 1942 by the Ford Motor Company, which began production in 1943. The vehicle was built in larger numbers than any other American armored car. The M-20 is based on the chassis and hull of the M-8, but with the turret removed and replaced by a superstructure mounting a 12.7mm machine gun on a ring mount. It had frontal armor of 320 mm and could accommodate four to six men.

M Lt. Colonel Andrew Barr (1918–1997) had already enjoyed a distinguished career as chief accountant of the SEC before entering military service in 1941. He served as G-2, head of Intelligence throughout all five campaigns. He was decorated with the Legion of Merit, Bronze Star (with OLC), and Presidential Unit Citation. He endowed the Andrew Barr Archive of the 3rd Armored Division at his Alma Mater, the University of Illinois (Champaign) before his death. It is the only archive of its kind in the United States.

N The twenty-four-hour system, i.e. 0600 is 6:00 a.m.; 1300 is 1:00 p.m., is standard military usage and will be used throughout.

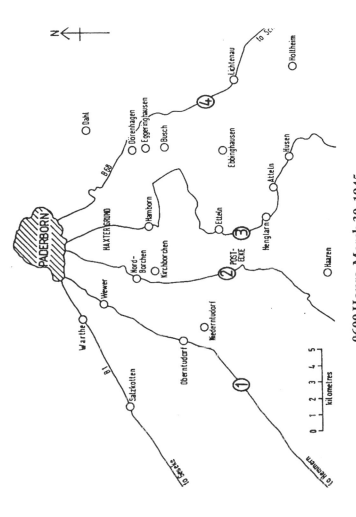

0600 Hours, March 30, 1945

Axes of advance of Third Armored Division

Source: The Battle of Paderborn [British Army of the Rhine, 1985].

To the left were the two main striking arms of Combat Command Reserve. **(O)** Task Force Richardson (Lt. Colonel Walter B. Richardson) moved out first along Route #2. Rose was on the radio almost immediately urging Richardson on, "Roll 'em! Load your doughs! . . . OK, men, let's move out."[12]

The spirited exhortations didn't work. Richardson bogged down quickly. As the column neared the hamlet of Kirchborchen, it was hit by

---

O The central organizational concept guiding the operations of the two "heavy" American armored divisions in 1945 (the 2nd and 3rd) was a dual command structure with both administrative and tactical components. The general scheme had already proven itself in battle, as practiced by the German panzer units in the opening campaigns of World War II. The 3rd Armored Division entered the war with two complementary and parallel lines of command authority. In the terminology of modern business, one could be characterized as having "direct line" relationships to established organizations and the other was characterized by "dotted line," or ad hoc and semi-permanent, relationships.

The "direct line" organization was built around the traditional tactical military units, regiments, battalions, and companies, which retained their normal administrative infrastructure, including headquarters, staffs, support units, etc. The responsibility, procedures, and authority of this structure were deeply rooted in the Army's traditions.

As illustrated in the Table of Organization chart (see Appendix A) the 3rd Armored Division was built around two Armored, or Tank Regiments: the 32nd (its motto was: "Victory or Death") and the 33rd (motto: "Men of War"), and one Armored Infantry Regiment: the 36th (motto: the "Orioles"). The division also included a Reconnaissance Battalion (83rd); Division Artillery, controlling three permanently assigned Armored Field Artillery (AFA) Battalions of self-propelled 105mm guns (the 67th, 54th, and 391st) and one Battalion each of Engineers (23rd); Medics (45th); Anti-Air Artillery (486th); and Tank Destroyers (703rd). In addition, there were support elements attached to every level of command, including Service, Supply, Maintenance, and Signals (143rd Company), and a divisional General Staff, or "G," section, headed by the Chief of Staff and responsible for Personnel (G-1), Intelligence (G-2), Operations (G-3), Logistics (G-4), and Military Government (G-5).

The "dotted line" organization was loosely based on the German system of *Kampfgruppe* (translation: "fighting group"), a unique concept arising from their "blitzkrieg" innovation—namely the use of fast moving, hard-hitting, combined-arms teams to exploit breaks in the enemy's front achieved by tanks. The fluid, constantly changing nature of armored warfare inspired the structure. The American version was somewhat more fixed, and the formations were called (in descending order) Combat Commands (CC), Task Forces (TF), and Battle Groups (BG). The first was roughly equivalent to a Brigade, the second to a reinforced

murderous anti-tank fire that destroyed the lead vehicles. Fighting raged all day, and the hard-pressed men—facing the fanatic Hitler Youth and *SS* men armed with deadly *Panzerfausten* and backed by tanks—soon had a new name for the village: "Bazooka-town."[13] **(P)** Task Force Hogan (Lt. Colonel Samuel E. Hogan), moving to Richardson's left along Route #1, fared little better, and it was stopped cold at the village of Wewer.

Farther to the right, the two main units of Combat Command B (Brig. General Truman E. Boudinot) were approaching Paderborn from the east. Task Force Welborn (Col. John C. Welborn) moved out on Route #3, a serpentine road that ran north through several towns before passing through the small village of Etteln. There it turned northeast, traversing heavily wooded terrain before turning north once again towards Paderborn. On the extreme right flank, Task Force Lovelady (Lt. Colonel William B.

Battalion, and the third to a reinforced Company. There were two permanent Combat Commands with staffs ("A" and "B"), each built around an Armored Regiment, and a Reserve ("R") led by the commander of the organic Armored Infantry Regiment. The composition of forces and assignments of each formation depended on the requirements of the mission, terrain, and the state of intelligence about the enemy, but after a certain time, the units became semi-permanent. The chronic shortage of infantry was addressed by attaching units (usually Regiments) from Infantry divisions. The staff of the TF or BG was drawn from the traditional headquarters units of the Regiments, Battalions, or Companies assigned.

The designations of the more or less permanent formations eventually took the names of the Commanders; for example, 3rd Armored's Combat Command A was referred to as Combat Command Hickey (CG, BG Doyle O. Hickey). There were usually two Task Forces in each Combat Command, TF X and TF Y were the designations for CCA, and TF 1 and TF 2 were used for CCB. This gave way to using the commanders' names. Many of the leaders were flamboyant, and after surviving a few encounters frequently became well known, thanks to the group of newsmen who traveled with the division. Thus, the readers of *Stars and Stripes* and the home town papers soon became familiar with the exploits of Task Force Doan, Task Force Lovelady, and Task Force Hogan, all of which were led by fighting Regimental and Battalion Commanders. This established, and combat-tested system was highly flexible and also made it possible to easily attach and control other units (especially infantry and artillery) to the division, which often approached or exceeded Corps size. We will follow the convention of using abbreviations as well as the names of commanders in identifying fighting units.

P The *Panzerfaust* and *Panzerschreck* were extremely effective, infantry-borne anti-tank weapons (like our "bazooka"), which were highly effective against virtually all Allied armor, especially at close range.

Emblem of the 507th Heavy Tank Battalion

Lovelady) had barely moved out on Route #4 before it had been stopped in the Wrexen area, southwest of the town of Scherfede. The units of Combat Command A (Brig. General Doyle O. Hickey) were in reserve behind Combat Command B, and were far from the action.

Meanwhile, the Germans were also on the move. Army Group B had organized a *Kampfgruppe,* or Battle Group, called *SS Panzer Brigade Westfalen* on March 29 to defend the area around Paderborn. It was placed under the command of *Oberstuermbahnfuehrer* Stern, a tough, stocky, and battle-hardened thirty-eight-year old *Panzer* officer who had won the Knight's Cross for bravery in Russia. Since January 1944 he had been Commandant of the *SS Panzer Junior Leaders School* at Sennelager. In addition to the School's faculty and students, his forces included the *SS Panzer Training and Replacement Regiment* (comprising two Reconnaissance and two *Panzer* Battalions), *Panzer Battalion 501* (without tanks), and the main striking power of his unit—the crack 507th Heavy Tank Battalion *(Schwere Panzer Abteilung 507)*. Altogether, Stern had fifty-five tanks, mostly Mark V Panthers and Mark VI Tigers, including some late model King Tigers of the 507th. At this stage of the war, this was an incredibly powerful formation and his tanks were more than a match for the American armor believed to be in the area.[14] **(Q)**

Q There is a misconception that in the Battle of Paderborn the 3rd Armored encountered old men and boys, walking wounded, or inexperienced, "green" soldiers. This is totally incorrect. The armor units, especially, were veterans of the eastern

Starting early in the morning hours of March 30, the Germans had been busy organizing their defense of Paderborn. Two hundred *Waffen SS* infantrymen dug in at Kirchborchen and 600 more fortified the road from the Borchen hamlets east toward Lichtenau. The King Tiger tanks of the 507th took positions on the high ground between Dahl and Nordborchen/Kirchborchen, where they could command the main access roads to Paderborn.

The *507th Battalion HQ,* including a security platoon of Tiger I tanks under the command of *Leutnant* Dieter Jähn, was at Dorenhagen and the Second Company (CO, *Hauptmann* Wirschig) was based at Lichtenau. By 1500 hours, the Third Company, led by *Hauptmann* Wolf Koltermann, was in position about one mile east of Kirchborchen (near Kuhlenberg). It took position close to the fork in the road leading to Hamborn. Koltermann quickly sent out scouts who reported that the enemy had occupied parts of Kirchborchen and that fighting was also raging in Nordborchen.[15]

The *507th Battalion* was well equipped, having just received more than a dozen brand new late model King Tiger II (Mark VIE) tanks to supplement their formidable Panthers (Mk V's).[16] They were supported by several 128mm self-propelled *Jagdpanzers* (Tank Destroyers) as well as highly motivated young foot soldiers from the *Waffen SS Reconnaissance Training Regiment.* The men of the 507th were tough, experienced veterans of armored warfare on the eastern front, where they had destroyed more than 600 tanks. On the battlefield that day were six holders of the coveted *RitterKreuz* (Knight's Cross of the Iron Cross), including both of the 507th's Company Commanders. **(R)**

---

front, and were led by experienced and brave tank commanders. The infantry, drawn from the Hitler Youth and trainees, were young, but highly motivated, and were led by tough non-coms and officers from the SS Schools nearby. The main armor unit that engaged TF Welborn, *Schwere Panzer Abteilung* 507 (507th Heavy Panzer Battalion) was formed on September 23, 1943, and attached to Army Group Middle (Eastern Front) in March 1944. Ordered to return to Germany on February 6, 1945, it began conversion to King Tiger IIs at Sennelager training camp later that month. During the Battle of the Ruhr it was under the command of Major Schoeck and was attached to *SS-Pz.Brig.Westfalen* from March 29, 1945 until April 17, 1945, when it was designated as a tank destroyer (*Jagdpanzer*) unit.

R Among these decorated tank aces was *Hauptmann* Wolf Koltermann (see note 26).

**Hauptmann Wolf Kolterman, Commander, 3rd Company,
507th Heavy Panzer Tank Battalion**
(*Source:* Dr. Dieter Jähn)

As his peep weaved north through the columns of Task Force Welborn, General Rose instructed his aide, Major Robert M. Bellinger, to radio each of the of the Task Force Commanders to ascertain their positions. **(S)** Bellinger had been a platoon commander in the 32nd Armored Regiment and later an aide to MG Leroy Watson, Rose's predecessor. He had a well-earned reputation as both efficient and discreet and that was why Rose decided to keep him when he took command. Major Haynes W.

S Major Robert M. Bellinger (1914–1979), a native New Yorker, was tactical Aide-de-Camp to General Rose. Just two weeks before (March 12, 1945) General Rose had personally pinned the Silver Star on Bellinger's chest for gallantry in action.

Dugan, the division Assistant Intelligence Officer (G-2) had many opportunities to observe Bellinger in discharging his duties. **(T)**

> What kind of fellow was Bellinger? I found aides tended to take on the character of their masters. Bellinger was tight lipped, observant, one step to the left and behind the general. He had a hell of a lot of details to take care of, but not like a peacetime aide concerned with the social calendar, arrival of laundry (he didn't have to do it, just see that it was *done*), etc.
>
> He went where the general went, unlike Wes Sweat (G-3) or Frederick Brown (Divarty) who accompanied the general in the field. He was also known for what he did not do, such as lord it over anyone. I think he was useful in getting information from some who would not be so open with the general.[17]

T/4 Glenn H. Shaunce, the general's driver, maneuvered along the narrow roads and dirt tracks and finally ended up just behind the half-tracks carrying the infantrymen of F Company, 36th Armored Infantry, at the end of Welborn's column. Shaunce, a twenty-eight-year old farmer from Minnesota, had spent his war years driving generals and high-ranking staff officers. **(U)**

T Major Haynes W. Dugan was born in Texas in 1913 and graduated from Texas A&M in 1934, when he was commissioned a 2nd Lt. of Cavalry in the Reserves. He received an MS degree from Columbia School of Journalism in 1936. He reported for active duty in February 1941 and was assigned to the 2nd Armored Division. He was transferred as one of the original cadre to the 3rd Armored and served as Asst G-2 (Intelligence) and Public Relations Officer (PRO) throughout the entire war. He was decorated with the Bronze Star and Presidential Unit Citation for his heroism at Mons. He retired from the Army with the rank of Lt. Colonel and was employed as a petroleum landman before retiring. He serves as the Historian of the 3rd Armored Division Association.

U T/4 Glenn H. Shaunce, born October 1916, is a native of Minnesota. He was drafted in 1942 and was a driver for several generals and staff officers while serving with Headquarters Service Company, 3rd Armored Division, during his entire period overseas. Holder of two Purple Hearts (both "won" while driving General Rose), the general personally pinned the Bronze Star on his jacket. He is the only living American eyewitness to the events that engulfed Maurice Rose late on the night of March 30, 1945. The authors taped his recollections over a three-year period, 1995 to 1998.

**Robert M. Bellinger (left) and Col. John Smith (right)
at dedication of the *USNS Maurice Rose*, February 26, 1948**
(*Source:* Rose Family Album)

As their driver, you get to know them better than most people. And sometimes they let their hair down a bit and talk about things they would not otherwise. I think he was quite a man and he knew his stuff. I drove for about four other generals off and on, and he had them all beat. The other ones were over the hill for World War II. I could tell you a few stories about some of them. It's a good thing some of them got sent back so they could take care of horses, as they were still fighting the wars when they rode horses.[18]

Shaunce had been Rose's driver from the middle of August 1944, when he took command, except for a brief convalescence in England after Shaunce had been wounded near Stolberg. **(V)** While he and the general could hardly be described as close, he knew his commander's moods as well as anyone in the division. No one actually spent more time with him, except maybe Bellinger. The general wasn't a man given to idle chatter or easy banter, nor was he one to show emotion, especially fear, but every once in a while he smiled, or offered a word of encouragement. On a very few occasions, he came close to real conversation with his driver.

Shaunce thought back to the day the general decorated him with the Bronze Star and was sure he saw a smile as Rose pinned the ribbon on his chest and shook his hand firmly with words of personal congratulations. Mostly, though, the general was quiet, professional, checking his maps, or talking on the radio, and drinking lots of coffee from the thermos that Shaunce kept full. The general was a chain smoker and always seemed to have a Camel cigarette in his hand.

It didn't take very long for everyone in the command group, including "Africa" Jones and the other men "buttoned up" in the M-20 Armored Scout Car to realize that March 30 was going to be a long and difficult day.

> The Germans fought ferociously from cellars, trenches, and buildings, and our forces could make little headway. All morning Col. Sweat would ride with Gen. Rose toward the head of our column to observe the action. They would call in our Air Force to bomb German strongholds; then our tanks and infantry would follow and clean out the town. We sat in our scout car most of the day without actually seeing much real action. This type of fighting took place all morning and afternoon, and the Task Force had cleaned out two towns (names unknown).[19]

V General Rose was wounded in both shoulders in the same mortar attack.

T/4 Glenn H. Shaunce and MG Maurice Rose
(*Source:* Personal Collection of Glenn H. Shaunce)

Major Bellinger was jammed into the jump seat of the general's peep, trying to find a comfortable way to sit in the midst of the radios, maps, and other equipment packed around him. It wasn't easy as the ¼-ton vehicle bucked and rocked along the rutted dirt roads. After a relatively routine morning drive, the radio traffic reported increased activity after noon. Bellinger started to feel a curious mixture of anxiety and confidence.

A call on the radio indicates that the afternoon will be aggravating and exasperating. Resistance is being met by "Task Force Welborn," at the point of the column.

We are riding in an open peep, with only small arms for protection, and no armored steel between us and the enemy fire.

This is a general who loves combat. This is a general who scorns anything but a bold front in the sight of the enemy. As we speed to the troubled spot, he is wearing a gray shirt, riding breeches, and highly polished boots. As usual, he is in complete command. We are moving through a wooded area, toward the cutting edge of the Division.

Now a conference with his Task Force Commander, and the general is returning to the peep with a half-smile on his face. He has done it again—prodded a stalled column into action. We are now in that column, here at the point, riding along where the action is the hottest. The general likes it here. In this position "brass" from higher headquarters never bothers him. They visit his rear command post, and leave him to direct his troops up front

When I am up here, I run my own show, the general frequently comments.[20]

What Bellinger didn't know was that the hazing and embarrassment that Rose had suffered at the hands of Joe Collins was still weighing on his mind. The promise to reach Paderborn in record time, regardless of the price, was now almost a compulsion. It dominated Rose's thinking, even on the battlefield, where emotions were dangerous.

By 1400 hours, the small Forward Echelon command group had reached the village of Etteln. Located along a forested ridge, it was six miles due south of Paderborn. They halted there while establishing contact with the various columns moving up the roads around them. Enemy resistance, which had initially been scattered, stiffened as the main elements of Task Force Welborn bypassed the town and moved north on Route #3 toward Paderborn.

Still focused on reaching Paderborn with the first men to enter the city, Rose tried to gauge which column he should join. After looking at his maps, and listening to the radio traffic, he concluded that Task Force Richardson, now fighting on the outskirts of Kirchborchen, had the best chance to get to Paderborn first. Rose was on a parallel road about five miles to Richardson's right and before joining him wanted to make sure that the lateral route was secure. Bellinger radioed Richardson to ask for a peep and a CCR Liaison Officer to guide them to his Task Force. Richardson, however, was in a fierce firefight twelve miles south of Paderborn and the last thing he needed (or wanted) was the general showing up. He radioed back that he couldn't spare a man or a peep, "Don't send Big Six this way," he warned and got off the radio.[21] **(W)**

It was another indication that resistance was increasing, but Rose wasn't deterred. He studied the maps again. Task Force Hogan was hung up at Wrexen and Task Force Lovelady was blocked far to the rear just south of Scherfrede. Neither looked likely to reach Paderborn soon. Instead of waiting for the combat picture to become clearer, and for the resistance to be overcome, Rose decided to push on. There was one choice left: to stay on Route #3 with Task Force Welborn all the way into the city.

Maurice Rose had a lot of respect for Jack Welborn. He was the sort of man a commander could rely on to get the hard jobs done. **(X)** Like Rose, Welborn began his career as an infantry officer, transferred to the cavalry, and joined the Armored Force at its birth. He had, according to intelligence officer Lt. George Bailey, "a real obsession" about killing Germans. His aggressiveness probably had something to do with living up to his father's reputation. Ira Welborn had been a distinguished soldier, an early advocate of armor, and during the Spanish–American War had won the Medal of Honor. **(Y)**

At the head of Task Force Welborn were four combat companies, two of Sherman medium tanks (M4) and two of infantry mounted on M-3 armored half-tracks. Colonel Welborn was in a peep a few vehicles back

---

W In military radio code "Six" is the Commanding Officer. "Big Six" is an unofficial variation on Rose's actual radio call sign, which would have been "Omaha Six." Omaha was the Code name for the 3rd Armored Division. Each of its organic units began with the letter "O."

X Colonel John C. Welborn was born at Fort Sam Houston, Texas, on May 15, 1909, graduated from West Point (1932), and was commissioned into the infantry. He soon transferred to the cavalry and in 1940 transferred again to the newly organized Armored Force. He participated in the fighting in North Africa, Sicily, and was in the first wave at Utah Beach on June 6, 1944, in command of the 70th Tank Battalion. He took command of the 33rd Armored Regiment in early September 1944 and led Task Force 1, the larger of the two Task Forces of CCB. Often decorated for bravery, he was awarded the Distinguished Service Cross, Silver Star w/OLC, Legion of Merit w/OLC, Presidential Unit Citation w/OLC, French Croix de Guerre (with Palm), and Legion of Honor. He retired in 1959 as a Colonel and died in Portland, Maine, on March 15, 1995.

Y Second Lieutenant Ira C. Welborn, 9th Infantry Regiment, was awarded the MOH for rescuing one of his men while under fire on July 2, 1898, near Santiago, Cuba.

from the front. Close behind him were the Battalion and Regimental Headquarters and the attached guns of the 703rd Tank Destroyer Battalion.[22] **(Z)** Also riding in Col. Welborn's column was Combat Command B Liaison Officer Lieutenant Walter W. May. He had the greatest respect for Welborn, whom he described as "one of the finest, ablest, and bravest commanders of the War."

> As we moved along a gentle tree-lined slope with a right turn at the bottom, I saw our Division Commander, Major General Maurice Rose, across the narrow road. He passed me while wending his way through the column on-and-off the road and well into the forward elements just before dark.
>
> I had met the general when he pinned the Bronze Star with oak leaf cluster on me in a small ceremony in Stolberg, Germany, in October 1944. He gave a short "morale-boost" talk to our "loose" military formation. It was "loose" because the front line was just yards ahead in Stolberg.
>
> General Rose's face as he passed me in the column was without expression and he was dressed in what appeared to be a plain GI raincoat. At the time I thought his attire looked different from other times I had seen him. I wondered why he was so close to the hostile front. Later I read somewhere he had promised some higher ranking general that he would leave Marburg and be in Paderborn by nightfall! I thought that was a hell of a brag to make at our expense.[23]

Lieutenant May expressed what many others felt. While there was universal respect for the general among the troops, not everyone appreciated his aggressiveness and the price in blood that it sometimes entailed. Sure, there was a common sentiment that "the sooner it's over, the sooner we'll be back home," but no one wanted to volunteer to pay the price of shortening the war. There was some grumbling that having Rose close by was dangerous, and that he was too willing to gamble their lives to make a big splash. The casualty rate at headquarters provided some evidence that this viewpoint was close to the mark, and that

---

Z I Company, 33rd Armored was in the van, followed by E Company, 36th Armored Infantry; then came F Company, 33rd Armored; with F Company, 36th Armored Infantry bringing up the rear of the forward combat elements.

being at the *"fer de lance"* ('tip of the spear') with Maurice Rose was perilous. **(AA)**

The Germans were also moving. At 1515 hours, or an hour after Rose reached the village of Etteln, Koltermann's *3rd Company, Pz. Bn. 507* was just one half mile east of Kirchborchen. From their well-concealed positions, the tanks immediately opened fire on Task Force Welborn, stalling their advance. By 1600 the skies had cleared sufficiently for Rose to call in an air strike. The men in Welborn's column—Walter May among them—watched, and silently cheered, as the P-47s roared in at tree top level unloading what appeared to be 500-pound "tank-buster" bombs on the third platoon of Koltermann's *3rd Company, Pz. Bn. 507*.[24]

> Most important to our survival and mission were the P-47 Thunderbolts (called "Jugs") that buzzed like angry hornets at tree top level. Those brave pilots saved our skins more than once by knocking out enemy tanks or strong points, roadblocks, machine gun emplacements, etc. On occasion they strafed so closely in front of us that the belt links from their 50-caliber machine guns sprinkled down on us, pelting our helmets and backs. That is called "close air support."
>
> As dusk came upon us the "Jugs" had to leave and return to base. After they left it seemed as if the entire German *Panzer* force descended from the higher ground. King Tigers, Panthers, and other tanks must have turned everything available against us. We lost vehicles in column formation, along and off each side of the road. In a very short time it appeared that everything was on fire. The noise of combat was in the air and it was just plain Hell![25]

Welborn's column remained stalled for about an hour when, at 1700, Lt. Dieter Jähn's security platoon spotted another American armored column advancing from Eggeringhausen, in a westerly direction, and coming up on the rear of Kolterman's *3rd Company*. General Rose and his party were in this second group of vehicles, which had passed through Etteln as the sun was setting. Exercising care to preserve security and not

---

AA The casualty rate for the 3rd Armored Division Headquarters and Headquarters Company was very high. The placards displayed at the 3rd Armored Division Association Reunions list nineteen men killed in action. In addition, many others were wounded and/or captured, including General Staff Officers Jack Boulger, G-1, and Wesley Sweat, G-3, both wounded and captured in late March 1945.

reveal his location, Major Schoeck radioed an alert to the whole *507th Battalion*.[26]

The picturesque North Rhine-Westphalia village had been reduced to rubble and ashes. In the march across Europe, Jones had seen the sight many times before.

> Like all towns where battles were fought Etteln was demolished. We slowly drove down a street and then to an open area that looked like a public square. After the square we proceeded up a steep hill into some forest, took a left turn through these woods, then a sharp left out of the forest where the road went down grade. It opened into a large field and I can still remember saying to Col. Sweat: 'look at that beautiful sunset! You would never imagine a war was going on.' And he replied, 'Yes, and it is appropriate because today is Good Friday.'[27]

As Rose passed the intersection of the road from Etteln and the road to Kirchborchen, Col. Welborn was preparing to move once again along the Eggeringhausen road before turning north toward Paderborn. He had received reports that the few German tanks still visible on the high ground to his front had been knocked out by the air strikes.[28] In fact, the reports were wrong; one enemy tank had been hit with negligible damage. The cost of this misinformation would be very high.

At 1800 hours, Koltermann issued orders for his *3rd Company* to redeploy. The second platoon, straddling the road, remained in place and opened up a covering bombardment, designed to conceal the redeployment from the enemy. The first and third platoons wheeled around, taking up new positions facing east, the new front direction. *Hauptmann* Koltermann personally reconnoitered the terrain right up to the edge of the forest, calculating the firing ranges. By 1900 hours, when twilight descended on the field, the movement was complete.[29] Just a few minutes later, as the last rays of daylight were fading, the Americans appeared.

Task Force Welborn was now traveling west on the road toward Nordborchen, advancing in column. Because the U.S. Army Air Force had reported the destruction of the tanks they had attacked a few hours earlier, the Americans in the column were unconcerned as they advanced up the road. They hadn't sent out scouts to reconnoiter the road or the woods. As the German veterans in their concealed positions watched in amazement, the enemy approached almost as if they were on parade, "offered up like food on a platter." The Americans were perfect targets for the *Panzers* and

SS infantry. Welborn turned at the intersection, but as his men approached the barn nearby they sensed trouble and began to deploy. It was too late.[30]

Welborn's peep and the first three Shermans rumbled forward, concealed by a depression in the road, and were untouched. Within a few minutes after the Germans received the order to open fire, however, seven tanks in the first wave were ablaze. The supposedly "disabled" King Tigers of the *3rd Company, Pz. Bn.* 507 had engaged Task Force Welborn at a range of 850 meters with deadly accuracy. Koltermann's personal reconnaissance had zeroed in the road and led to a near perfect ambush. Welborn and a small group of survivors barely made it to a large stone chateau near Hamborn (*Schloss Hamborn*), where he set up a perimeter defense and makeshift command post. Welborn ordered that a group of pregnant women housed in the chateau be escorted to safety in the basement.[31]

As Welborn's tiny vanguard took cover, the rest of the stalled column was hit by an inferno of fire from well-concealed German tanks occupying the high ground. The SS infantry opened up with small arms fire from their positions all along the thin corridor running through the rapidly darkening forest.

General Rose was about a half mile behind the burning tanks when he learned that communications with Welborn had been cut. He was concerned, but still didn't yet realize how precarious his own situation was. He and his companions had been cramped in the peep a long time that day and were tired and edgy. The sounds of battle were sharp, and while still off in the distance, they now seemed to be coming from every direction.

In the back of the peep, Bellinger sat uncomfortably, his limbs aching from the rough ride and from bumping into all the radio gear around him. His discomfort, however, distracted him somewhat from a growing feeling of nervousness. At least, he thought, now that it was getting dark, the advance would probably stop pretty soon. He was right, but not for the reason he thought.

At 1900 hours, just as the overwhelming force of enemy tanks moved to cut Route #3 in multiple locations, Rose's tiny Forward Echelon headquarters group passed through the intersection of the Etteln road with the east-west route to Nordborchen. The small group numbered just fifteen men (five officers and ten enlisted), three peeps, two motorcycles, and a single M-20 armored car. The .50 caliber machine gun normally fitted to the M-20 on a ring mount had been removed to better accommodate the larger than usual number of passengers. All they had to defend themselves were pistols, rifles, and a few submachine guns.

After traveling several hundred feet towards Nordborchen, Shaunce stopped the general's peep so that the officers could check their maps. At this moment, Rose—who was cradling a Thompson submachine gun in his lap—was himself cut off by intense small arms fire.[32] The *Second Company of the 507th*, under command of *Hauptmann* Wirsching and supported by SS infantry, had moved south to cut the Eggeringhausen road behind Rose. It happened with a suddenness that threw every man into shock and some into near panic. Shaunce had been sitting in the peep waiting for the order to move.

> We were setting along the road in column and something ahead held up the column. They were getting quite a little opposition up ahead I guess. We sat there for about fifteen minutes and then they started to open up with small arms fire from both sides of the woods.[33]

Bellinger had been following the action during the day by closely monitoring the radio and observing the impromptu battlefield conferences. His senses were more sharply attuned to the surrounding terrain than usual.

> It is late afternoon; the sun is beginning to fade. The forest to our left and right seems to close in tighter.
> "Paderborn must be only about two miles head, Major. Will you check your maps?"
> We jerk to a halt; crossfire rakes our vehicles. We are completely exposed to searing fire from both sides.
> Where the Devil did this fire come from?
> My God, we've been cut off front and rear by German tanks and self-propelled guns! Many vehicles following us burst into flame. Some GIs caught in their vehicles will never dismount. We return fire with our meager small arms.
> Hit the ditch!
> Never was a command more welcome.[34]

The fire intensified and soon it was obvious that enemy tanks had joined the battle. A gap had opened between the last half-track holding infantrymen of F Company and a repair vehicle just to the front of General Rose's party. As soon as this vehicle was hit, the rear of the column was engaged by a detachment of tanks from the *507th Battalion Headquarters Company,* under the command of *Leutnant* Dieter Jähn, positioned on the forward edge of Eggeringhausen.[35] Jähn's *Panzers* shot down a tree, which then blocked the vehicles still in the Etteler Ort woods south of the intersection.[36]

All along the American column, men frantically jumped out of their vehicles and took cover along the road. T/4 Wesley D. Ellison was among the passengers in Lt. Col. Sweat's M-20 armored car just behind General Rose's peep. The twenty-one-year old Texan had grown up quickly while serving as one of General Rose's personal radio operators. He was accustomed to being close to and sometimes actually in combat.

> At about dusk anti-tank fire opened up on us and cut off about the first 75 vehicles in our column. Our 75 vehicles were then grouped together to protect themselves, and upon investigation we found that there was a road running perpendicular to the four roads that that our four columns were riding on. It was then planned that the general and his aide, Major Bellinger, the command car commanded by Lt. Col. Wesley Sweat (who was Division G-3 Officer) would go forward to this road and attempt to cut to the west a distance of some three or four miles in an effort to contact either Column A (Task Force Hogan) or Column B (Task Force Richardson).[37]

The infantrymen, riding in their half-tracks, were particularly vulnerable to the tidal wave of gunfire that suddenly engulfed them. Sgt. L.D. McQuade, already a seasoned veteran, was serving in F Company, 2nd Battalion, 36th Armored Infantry, and was in a group of vehicles just ahead of General Rose when the action began.

> I was on point and in the lead half-track. We had entered a wooded area and took some intense small arms fire and returned same. We stopped to evaluate the situation when General Rose and his group passed us. They continued on down the road and entered another wooded area. I had just told my driver to move out, when "all hell broke loose." The small arms fire from the rear started up again and small arms fire from the front, where the general had gone. We dismounted and took off to the left into a field that had small stacks of hay in it.[38]

Colonel Fred Brown, the division artillery commander, was riding, with his driver, PFC. A.C. Braziel, in a peep just in front of the general. **(BB)** Brown was a Regular Army officer who had come to the Armored Force with extensive experience in the Field Artillery. He had participated in the mechanization experiments of the thirties and during one summer exercise, he had met a foreign officer whom he would have occasion to remember, *Oberst* Heinz Guderian, father of German *Panzer* doctrine.

M/Sgt. Angelo Cali, assigned to G-2's Order of Battle Team #9, witnessed Brown's harsher side during the drive across France right after the closing of the Falaise Gap. Cali was sitting on a couch in a farmhouse when he saw Brown talking on a field phone. A group of about twenty Germans were cornered in a barn and wanted to surrender. Brown screamed into the phone, "lay it on them, I don't give a God-damn if they're finished, plaster 'em." Then he turned to Cali and said, "Don't worry, they're not going to do it."³⁹

Riding in another peep was one of Brown's Battalion Commanders, Lt. Colonel George G. Garton of the 391st AFA, heir to the great New England fishery fortune whom everyone called "Seafood." **(CC)** Garton, a tough-talking, plump, balding, cigar-chomping, whiskey-drinking professional,

---

BB Colonel Frederick J. Brown, Jr. (1905–1971) part Sioux Indian, was born in Britton, South Dakota, graduated from West Point (1927), and was commissioned into the Field Artillery. He joined 3rd Armored shortly after its formation in 1941, initially commanding the 54th Field Artillery Battalion. Like a number of commanders within the division, he had the unique experience of receiving his men still dressed in civilian clothes, training them, leading them in combat, burying some, and sending the survivors home after the war was over. He was decorated for bravery many times and after a distinguished post-war career, retired as a Lt. General in 1965, after commanding the U.S. Sixth Army. He died on March 31, 1971, in Washington, D.C.

CC Lt. Colonel George Goodrell Garton (1906–1970) was born in Iowa on Christmas Eve 1906. He graduated from West Point (1930) and was commissioned in the Field Artillery. He also held an MS degree from MIT (1935). From 1943 until the end of the war, he commanded the 391st Armored Field Artillery Battalion. The 391st provided support to Combat Command B, the major element of which was Task Force Welborn. Garton enjoyed the confidence of his boss, Col. Frederick Brown, with whom he frequently traveled, and he was generally responsible for coordination of attached artillery units. He was awarded the Silver Star, Bronze Star, Legion of Merit, Air Medal, and Purple Heart.

Colonel Frederick J. Brown, Jr., Germany, 1945
(*Source:* Lt. General Frederick J. Brown, III [retired])

often rode up front with Brown, where the two men were instantly available to coordinate the artillery firepower of the division.

Shortly after bailing out of their peep, Rose, Bellinger, and Shaunce were joined at the makeshift emergency command post by Brown, Garton, and Sweat, who rushed over from the M-20, along with several of the enlisted men. The fire that erupted to their front and rear had forced the hasty evacuation from most of the vehicles that weren't hit in the first salvos. The rest of the men took cover as best as they could while the mayhem mounted around them. Not every one of them made it unscathed. Just as the M-20 came out of the forest, "Africa Jones" heard a loud explosion in the field in front of him.

Quickly more explosions followed, our column stopped and everyone jumped out of their vehicles and lay in a ditch. The firing continued and suddenly a burst from a tank shell hit a tree above me, and a large piece of shrapnel landed on my back just above the belt. I thought a whole hill had fallen on me and the pain was excruciating. I yelled, 'I'm hit,' and in a minute, Col. Sweat crawled to me and tore open my clothes and picked off a large piece of hot metal. He said he thought I was O.K. as the piece landed flat and did not tear open my skin with a lot of blood, but if it had come down vertically, I would never have survived. Then he crawled back to the general. I remember not being too scared even when wounded, as I kept thinking—I'm with a major general who ought to be able to get us out of this.[40]

Also lying in the ditch along the south side of the lateral road was PFC William T. Hatry, a Signal Company code-clerk, and frequent passenger in Lt. Colonel Sweat's M-20.

We were in the column that was cut off from both sides. We lay in the ditch for over an hour under intense tank fire. When they got around to trying to hit the armored car (which they never did do), the shells that missed were ricocheting off the road by our heads, finally landing in the field on the other side of us.[41]

In a peep just a few vehicles back was PFC William T. Whitten, a twenty-year-old Virginian of the forward observer section of Battery A, 391st Armored Field Artillery (AFA), Garton's Battalion. It was about 1900 hours and just around twilight when he was jolted into a terrible reality.

We were in the vicinity of Paderborn when our column was cut by knocking out a medical half-track on one end, and an M-4 tank on the other. We were being fired upon by Mark VI's (Tigers). I hit the ditch, and the tank in front of us was hit. Fragments from that hit me in the side. A medic patched me up. At about the same time, Lt. Plummer, who was our forward observer officer, was standing by our peep when an 88mm shell hit the peep and Plummer.

The Germans were out on top of their tanks yelling like a bunch of drunken Indians. As I was trying to find some cover, I was crawling down the ditch and came upon General Rose and his party. The general had a submachine gun with him. I remember seeing one or two motorcycles, and I knew this was the general's party. I finally found my way into a patch of woods and it was dark by this time. I worked my way through the woods to get back to the battalion. An MP stopped a tank and put me on it back to headquarters.

I was questioned by all the officers about the condition of General Rose. I told them that the last time I saw him, he was alive and in the ditch with his submachine gun and that was just before dark.[42] **(DD)**

Private Whitten was not the only one to suddenly find himself alone, desperately trying to escape from the slaughter. In the confusion and mayhem many men were cut off and lost contact with their units. PFC Jim Omand, a motorcycle rider with General Rose, had lost his bike earlier that day and was hitching a ride in the M-20.

The night we ran into those German tanks we stopped, and I jumped out of the armored car thinking that someone would hand me a bazooka, but instead they drove off leaving me standing on the road in front of the German tanks. They started firing at me so I jumped into the ditch. I made my way back along the burning column, cut across to the left where we were laying in the ditch before we moved out. The Germans spotted me and gave me a good peppering; they did not hit me so I crawled into the forest and stayed until our men picked me up.[43]

Farther up the line with Task Force Welborn, Sgt. Edward S. Boyden was riding in the command half-track of 1st Battalion, 33rd Armored Regiment.

They cut the column as our medic half-track got to the bend in the road. There were one Tiger and two Panthers that fired on us. We were behind the medic track and the artillery half-track—a Sherman tank was behind us—"Plenty Tough II"—and it fired on the German tanks. We got out of our vehicles and ran into the woods. We stayed there all night.[44]

DD This manuscript forms the basis for the description of March 30, 1945, contained in the updated division history, *Spearhead in the West, 3rd Armored*, Turner Publishing, Paducah, Kentucky, 1991. The statement of William T. Whitten (postmarked November 29, 1990) was inserted into the updated manuscript. The *Battle History of A Battery, 391st Armored Field Artillery Battalion* by H. Glen Jenkins and Colonel Brown (see note 41) confirms that the group of vehicles in Rose's immediate vicinity before the column was cut included one from the 391st AFA Battalion.

General Rose decided to wait for the fire to subside so that he could regain control of the situation. Shaunce was lying next to him in the roadside depression trying to get as close to the earth as possible.

> We all got down in the ditch and stayed there for about twenty minutes, and then went up and got the two peeps and run them down in the ditch for radio communication. Then we started getting direct fire from the tanks to the front and they knocked out a peep ahead of mine (probably LTC Garton's vehicle) and some more vehicles along the column. Then we got word from Lt. Keown that we were cut off ahead also. By that time it was getting pretty dark and they were starting to throw flares in and still firing small arms. Colonel Brown was also there calling for artillery and directed it himself from his own peep right there in the ditch.[45]

In the immediate aftermath of the action, Colonel Brown remembered those moments with the eye of a critical observer and trained engineer, and a dispassionate appreciation for the professionalism of his adversaries.

> Late in the afternoon, tanks were reported in our vicinity. MG Rose had directed that air be diverted to bomb these tanks, as they seemed to be directly along Highway #3. At about 1730, we turned the corner and from there could plainly see the tanks on the high ground covering the route of approach on Highway #3. We watched the second flight of fighter-bombers attack the tanks, and thought at the time that two or three of the tanks were left burning.
>
> At this time we were in the column in rear of the first double company. When we moved down the road the tanks on the high ground opened fire, hitting a vehicle, setting it afire, and blocking the road. We could not see the column ahead of the burning vehicle due to defilade.
>
> Gen. Rose and I pulled our vehicles into the ditch on the left-hand side of the road and took cover there. The German tanks methodically searched the length of the column with fire hitting with AP (armor piercing) or HE (high explosive) shells about every third vehicle in the column. We noticed shortly after the tanks in front opened fire that fire was also coming from our rear, and there were vehicles on fire in back of us. We realized at that time that the column was cut.[46]

As a result of Brown and Garton's efforts in directing their artillery, the tank fire slowed down a bit. Lt. Colonel Roberts, Welborn's executive officer, arrived on foot and reported that he had lost contact with Welborn after the column had been cut in the rear and had lost all communication with his outfit.

Staff Sgt. Leonard Y. Kunken, F Company, 36th Armored Infantry, was in the forward part of Task Force Welborn when Rose was trapped in the ditch. As Colonel John A. Smith, Jr., the division Chief of Staff, was desperately trying to reach General Rose, Sgt. Kunken was standing in the turret of his half-track.

> We had stopped on the road awaiting further orders. The men were aware that Paderborn was considered the Fort Knox of the German Army and the resistance was great. No one seemed to know what to expect next.
>
> Suddenly a peep appeared to the left of my half-track and stopped. We could hear the constant calls on their radio "Big Six, come in Big Six"! This peep was apparently part of General Rose's entourage, and was trying to make contact with the general. The fact that this peep stopped alongside me was an exciting experience in itself. I knew there was a problem when they couldn't make contact with him.[47]

Rose knew that he had to get back in touch with his command. During the brief lull, he ordered Shaunce to get the peep into the ditch and then instructed Bellinger to get Colonel Smith on the radio. **(EE)** Smith, back at division headquarters, and unaware of Rose's situation, had been trying, without success, to reach his commander for nearly an hour. He already knew that Welborn's column had been cut ahead of Rose and was starting to get worried. When the general finally contacted him, he could plainly hear the sounds of battle in the background, and knew immediately that his earlier fears had been justified.[48]

> He contacted me on his radio and in battlefield jargon to maintain radio security, informed me of the situation and ordered the next unit following to close up, take the German tanks under fire, and to restore the continuation of the forward movement.[49]

EE The radio mounted in the rear of Rose's peep was a SCR-506, with both transmitter and receiver.

In a taped interview more than a quarter century later, Colonel Smith recalled General Rose's last radioed words, "Smith, send somebody to close up this column. We have been cut. Two of our ambulances have been shot up."[50]

> I issued the necessary orders and then attempted to contact General Rose over the radio net. I could get no answer from him; however, I could hear the hum of his radio, indicating that his transmitter was turned on, but I got no reply from my call signal "Omaha Five to Omaha Six." Omaha was our Division code name and "Six" indicated the Commander while "Five" indicated the Chief of Staff.[51]

Colonel Smith ordered Task Force Doan (Col. Leander A. Doan) of Combat Command A, which was in the Boddeker forest well behind Welborn, to break through the roadblocks to the rear of Rose's isolated vehicles. In spite of Smith's reassurances that Doan would relieve them from their pinned down position, Bellinger, who was monitoring the radio, heard the increasingly serious reports of strong resistance to Doan's attempt to seal the breach.[52] The *2nd Company of the 507th* under *Hauptmann* Wirsching had moved south from Lichtenau through Busch and blocked the road, knocking out an M-18 tank destroyer and several half-tracks.[53] Doan tried hard, but couldn't break through.

Up ahead, Welborn's command was being methodically destroyed. Cut off with only a few men, and with enemy tanks maneuvering in his rear, supported by large numbers of SS infantry in the woods all around, Welborn's position was hopeless. At 1930 hours Koltermann radioed headquarters and requested permission to advance from his present location to complete the destruction of the enemy. Fifteen minutes later, at 1945 hours, he got the go-ahead and issued new orders. With the second platoon holding its position in reserve, the other two platoons were to move forward along the open ground between the woods and the stalled American column to finish it off.

It was slaughter, a bloodbath. Over the next two hours the Germans destroyed the remnants of Welborn's command. Even as darkness descended, the Tigers continued their work. By the light of the burning Shermans and half-tracks, they shot at every target they could identify. The Americans were brave, resisting bitterly in small groups with hand grenades and submachine guns.

> What vehicles that weren't burning along that stretch they shot up. One brave guy had stayed on a 'fifty' in one of the half-tracks and opened up on the tanks, with the bullets hitting the turret.[54]

The Americans fired from the edge of the forest, but with little effect, and the *Panzers* pushed aside the abandoned vehicles from the road.[55] Before it was over, at least seventeen M4 Sherman tanks; seventeen armored half-tracks; and numerous other vehicles had been destroyed, and dozens of peeps, trucks, ambulances, and other vehicles lay on the road in a terrible tangle of death and destruction. Task Force Welborn had been annihilated.[56] The Germans knew they had killed many men on that terrible stretch of road. Forty years later, Koltermann described the horror of it, almost sorrowfully, by observing that during that night "the Devil was loose (*Der Teufel los!*) on the road."[57]

Meanwhile, Rose's situation was worsening. Shaunce looked up and down the column and as far as he could see in each direction, he was witness to a flaming cauldron. Vehicles were on fire all around, the explosions fed by gasoline and ammunition, and he could clearly hear the screams of the burning and dying men. He could see that the lead and rear vehicles had been knocked out and knew how serious their situation was just by looking at the commanders. They were shook up worse than he had ever seen, and they had been in some bad scrapes before. He thought to himself, "We wuz cut off, that's for sure."

While they were pulled off the road, and huddling close together in the wet ditch, Shaunce heard Rose order Brown to call artillery in "on top of us." The awful spectacle reminded Fred Brown of a scene from Dante's *Inferno*, which he had read as a young West Point cadet. He continued to radio instructions for "neutralization" artillery fire, and "during that time General Rose personally directed stragglers back to their tanks." Machine gun fire came from every direction, and Brown realized that the Germans were methodically "mopping up" the column. Garton's driver reported that nine enemy tanks were moving west on the road to their front. Brown could himself see at least three tanks moving east on the south side of the road.[58]

Shaunce figured sooner or later they'd make a run for it, so he asked Rose if it was OK if he ripped off the general officer's red plate with the two silver stars from the front of their peep. He got no objection and flipped it in the rear of their peep. To Bellinger it appeared as if the entire column had been destroyed.[59]

With every man except Rose flinching and ducking low as the tank rounds rocked the ground in a constant crescendo of terrific explosions, the general turned to Sweat and said, "We're in a hell of a fix now." It wasn't spoken with any obvious fear, but Sweat's reply, "we'll get out of it," was offered as much for self-reassurance as to maintain a positive demeanor before his fearless commander. Sweat remembered feeling somewhat reassured when recalling that they had been in plenty of tight spots before and had always gotten out of them. The incessant staccato of small arms fire, along with the exploding vehicles, roar of cannons, and the terrible cries of wounded men were not encouraging.[60]

The senior officers discussed their personal situation and quickly debated their options. They knew that German infantry were moving in the woods, and they could hear small arms fire all around them. Colonel Brown advised that they abandon the vehicles, take cover, and lay low until Doan arrived. Major Bellinger agreed.

> We believe we have two peeps, one armored car, and two motorcycles in which to make our run to safety. I suggest we leave all vehicles and move out on foot—otherwise our escape will not go unnoticed. The general agrees to leave only the two motorcycles, because of the noise factor.
>
> Col. Brown's peep will lead the way. I will follow in my peep. Mount up and let's go.[61]

General Rose was determined to find Welborn and get to Paderborn. Nothing would stand in his way. He had concluded that their only hope for survival was to go cross-country, evade the enemy, and get to the main road. There wasn't any firing to their front, so he concluded that the Tigers had withdrawn after destroying Welborn's column.[62] Actually, they were redeploying in accordance with *Hauptmann* Kolterman's new orders to concentrate further east. Brown radioed one of his forward observers to find out where the tip of Welborn's column was located, and he confirmed that it was on Route #3. Garton's peep had been destroyed, so he and his driver crowded in with Col. Brown, who, in a highly unusual move, took the wheel of the vehicle himself.

> During the time we were in the vehicles General Rose had asked me to lead with my peep, which I was driving, and in it was Colonel Garton, who had been over the route as far as Point D and seen the

country forward to that point. Also in the vehicle were Colonel Garton's and my drivers. [63]

The men in Sweat's group, except for the "deserted" Jim Omand, ran back to their M-20. Jones, still hurting from his back wound had lain

> in the ditch for some time, and the shooting continued. Many of our vehicles were on fire, and screams of the wounded filled the evening air. I never learned how many men we lost, but it must have been very many. By this time it was getting dark, and General Rose ran to his peep, got on the radio, and I could hear him calling for tanks to clear the area. But he got no reply. After a few minutes a call came along for the general's party to mount their vehicles. We all ran to our scout car.[64]

Major Bellinger got back to the peep.

> There was a prayer on everyone's lips that the motors will turn over.
>   I mount to my jump seat, sitting high and exposed. Thank God for the darkness of night! Exploding ammunition in the burning half-tracks to our rear helps to cover our dash for safety.
>   Driver Shaunce has our peep moving. We are on our way toward life or death . . .[65]

Just after 1930 hours, with the last traces of daylight rapidly fading, the small command caravan moved out in the direction where they thought Task Force Welborn had gone. At virtually the same moment, the four King Tiger tanks of the *3rd Platoon, 3rd Company*, were directed by their aggressive commander *Hauptmann* Wolf Koltermann to move down the same road toward the Hamborn intersection. There they would render the *coup de grace* to the remnants of Colonel Welborn's column. The inexorable rendezvous with destiny was now set into motion. When the two unsuspecting groups collided, the tragedy to follow would transform the story of Major General Maurice Rose into legend. He could not know, nor could his companions know, that he had less than a quarter hour left to live.

CHAPTER Two

Early Life (1899–1916)

"I'm going to make good."

Private Maurice Rose

As the sun started to set, Sam Rose began the ritual. His wife Katy and two-year old son Arnold were at his side. Slowly moving the burning candle towards the *Menorah*, his concentration was broken by the cry of Maurice, his newborn son. **(A)** For a brief moment, he paused, looked lovingly at his child, and then continued to chant the ancient Hebrew prayer of thanksgiving and remembrance.

Maurice Rose was born on Sunday, November 26, 1899, at his parents' rented home at 508 Main Street in the South Farms district of Middletown, Connecticut.[1] **(B)** He was the youngest (and last) of four children, only two

---

A The *Menorah* is an eight-branched candelabra with a holder in the center for the candle used to light each of the others. It is used to celebrate the eight-night Festival of Hanukkah, which marks the victory of Judah Maccabeus ("the Hammer") over Antiochus, ruler of the Seluccid Empire, in 164 B.C. After the liberation of Jerusalem, it was discovered that a very small amount of oil was available for the lamps that would purify the ancient temple. The pitifully small amount lasted eight days—a miracle—giving rise to the duration of the festival, and the number of branches on the *Menorah*.

B Rose's birth certificate lists his home address as 424 Main Street. Research conducted by Vic Damon, New Haven, Connecticut—who served in the Public Information Office (PIO) of the 3rd Armored Division during the mid-sixties—

of whom survived infancy. **(C)** According to the Jewish calendar, it was the eve of Hanukkah, the Festival of Lights. Virtually the first sound that the infant heard was joyful singing in celebration of the only Jewish holiday to celebrate—at least in part—a military victory. It was a fitting day for the birth of a warrior.

Maurice Rose came from a family of distinguished rabbis. His grandfather was born in 1802 in the White Russian town of Borisov. Located at the confluence of the Berezina and Skha Rivers, the city was an important stop on the Moscow-Warsaw railway line and a significant lumber mill center. It was home to a vibrant Jewish community for centuries. **(D)** In the early nineteenth century, the profession of "rabbi" was far from the modern conception and was closer to the literal translation of the Hebrew word, "teacher." Teachers, especially Jews, did not make much money and Rabbi Rose established a lumber business to support his family. Eventually he moved to Warsaw, where for forty years he was the spiritual leader of one of Poland's most famous centers of Jewish learning. **(E)** He also continued his lumber business in the Polish capital.

Samuel, his first-born son, was born on May 15, 1855, and was reared in the Orthodox traditions of his forefathers. **(F)** He was tall, with a distinctly erect bearing, and was a star pupil and athlete at the private Jewish school run by his father. The regimen was severe, and the study of the ancient sacred texts was unrelenting and rigorous. There was no time for play, and the ener-

---

established that during the early part of the century, Middletown renumbered all the buildings on Main Street. Today the building is 508 Main Street.

C In spite of numerous references citing a middle initial (variously reported as "B," "C," "D," "E," and "G"), Rose's birth certificate, as well as other official documents, and his Army grave marker, establish conclusively that he had no middle name or initial.

D On October 20, 1941, the entire Jewish population of Borisov, including relatives of Maurice Rose, was forcibly marched to a field outside the town and was murdered by elements of *SS Einsatzgruppe* B and the German *Order Police*.

E This world famous center of learning and prayer, the *Chevra Medrosh*, survived for hundreds of years until destroyed by the Germans during the Holocaust.

F Maurice Rose's birth certificate (dated December 6, 1899, and signed by D.A. Nolan, MD) describes his parents' birthplace as Poland, but in the "State or Country" of Russia. Further, Sam and Katherin's birth-dates are subject to some confusion. Sam is described as thirty-nine years old (which would put his date of birth at 1860, not 1855) and Katy as thirty-six (that would put her birth year at 1863). These dates are inconsistent with those reported in each respective obituary.

getic and imaginative child chafed under the iron discipline. It was always assumed that he would continue the family tradition of a life of learning and service to the community. Sam found it hard to concentrate on his studies, however. His rich imagination and adventurous spirit carried him far beyond the boundaries of his seemingly pre-ordained life.

Of all his boyhood dreams, one always stood out. He wanted to be a soldier, and specifically a cavalryman. As a small boy walking the bustling streets of Warsaw, he often observed the officers in their colorful uniforms, with sabers at their sides, and crowned with plume-topped helmets. He watched them descending from their carriages and escorting beautiful young women into the fashionable tearooms full of wonderful pastry smells. He could hardly control his excitement and envy.

His father, who had probably seen first hand the torment wrought by the Czar's soldiers on Jews, especially Cossacks on horses, abhorred the very idea of a man in uniform. He mocked Sam's dream of a soldier's life, reminding him of his duty and family responsibilities. The arguments continued, but finally more practical considerations intervened and stilled the angry voices. As his father got older, his business began to suffer and he feared that the source of the family's livelihood would disappear. The pressure mounted on Sam. In 1870, he left school, also abandoning his military dreams, and entered his father's business. It would be many years before Sam would be able to fully return to the family tradition of learning and service to the community.

He labored for thirteen years, but found neither satisfaction in his work nor commercial success. There were very few other options. Prospects for Jews in Poland were not attractive, with access to education and most professions severely restricted. The one idea that sustained the miserable and poor Jews of Eastern Europe was the promise of a better life in the "Golden Land" of America. The prospect of freedom and a fresh start called strongly to young and adventurous spirits like Sam Rose. In 1883, the tall, handsome bachelor sailed for the New World.

On arrival at Ellis Island in New York's harbor, the entry point for millions of immigrants, and in the very shadow of the Statue of Liberty, his family name was changed from "Rauss" to Rose.[2] There was irony in the change; the German root word for "Rauss" is vernacular for "get out." **(G)**

G The word "Rauss," screamed at Jews to roust them violently from Ghettos, labor camps, and the barracks of concentration camps, is still remembered by Holocaust survivors as a sound of terror.

Whether the name "Rose" was Sam's choice or the quick notation of a clerk who didn't hear his real name or didn't really care—as was so common at the moment of entry—is unknown. Immediately after arrival, through the Hebrew Immigrants Aid Society (HIAS), Sam got a job as a clerk. Like ambitious immigrants before and since, he quickly learned English and rapidly assimilated the dress and customs of a young American.[3] **(H)**

Ten years after arriving in the United States, he courted and married Katherin Brown (née Bronowitz), who was called Katy. She was a twenty-six-year-old dark-eyed fellow immigrant from Warsaw, and a seamstress. Mrs. Rose was shy and quiet, although a strong matriarchal figure. Her great-grandson, Jeff Rose, describes a woman who, even in old age, managed to exert a strong influence over her family.

> My memories of my great-grandmother were childishly fond—she always brought two dollar bills for my brother and me, which she dispensed early in the visit. As the evening progressed, she would remain piercingly quiet until the time came for her to grasp her dark wooded cane, rise from her chair onto her thick soled orthopedic shoes (which elevated her stature to at least five feet), and wobble with Arnold at her elbow to the door. There, a cab seemed to magically appear in front of our suburban home to transport her and her son to their home in old Denver.[4]

In 1897, the year their son Arnold was born, the family moved to Middletown, Connecticut, a mill town on the Connecticut River. Sam moved there because the mills offered opportunities for tailors, especially those who also had skill as clothing designers. **(I)** Sam did well, and he soon moved his business out of his apartment, but in 1901 he decided to move his shop back home to save money.[5]

H Other sources, including his obituary (July 11, 1945, *Denver Post*) report that Samuel Rose came to the U.S. in 1885, and that his first stop was Savannah, Georgia, where he met and married Katy Rose. Her obituary (October 3, 1965, *Denver Post*) makes no mention of Savannah, however, and cites New York as the place where she and Sam met and were married.

I The *Middletown Business Directory* lists several commercial and residential addresses for Samuel Rose from 1900–1902, describing his occupation as "Merchant Tailor." There is no entry for 1903.

The next year, the Rose family moved to Denver, almost certainly because of Sam's health problems.[6] Like many immigrants from Eastern Europe, it is quite likely that he suffered from "consumption," or tuberculosis. The choice of destination offers some circumstantial evidence of that possibility. Denver was, by that time, the site of several well-known hospitals especially built for consumptives and sponsored by an active, accepting, and rapidly growing Jewish community. Among the inhabitants of the tenements and sweatshops of the Lower East Side of Manhattan and similar locales, the clean mountain air of Denver was viewed as medicine, almost in a miraculous light.

The Jewish community had deep roots in Colorado, and a small group of pioneers had been among the first to settle in Denver, as well as other communities. During the first decades of immigration to Colorado in the mid nineteenth century, several "utopian" settlements had been established, and although they eventually failed, the experience gained by these intrepid souls led to their later success as cattlemen, miners, and ranchers. These hardy survivors formed the first organized Jewish communities in Colorado.

Captain Cecil Oppenheim, a World War II Denver veteran who served under General Rose in the 3rd Armored Division, proudly traced his family back 100 years to these early settlers and ranchers. His own grandfather had been a gold miner.[7] Only a decade after Sam Rose had moved to Denver, the Jewish population had grown to 15,000, or about 90 percent of the state's Jewish residents.[8] By the time Captain Oppenheim returned home in 1945 to recover from his wounds and receive the Bronze Star, there were more than 20,000 Jews in the Western States (not including California), most of them in Denver. **(J)**

The Jewish community established a Burial & Aid Society as one of its first communal acts, and later sponsored the construction of a hospital established specifically for the treatment of tuberculosis. The support of hospitals, and a strong commitment to nonsectarian medical care, were a major part of the Denver Jewish community's activities from its very beginnings. The National Jewish Hospital for Consumptives (NJHC) was opened in

J The *Intermountain Jewish News*, an English language weekly then serving 20,000 people in five Western states, provided comprehensive coverage of Maurice Rose, especially after his death, in a series of articles, and was the principle source of syndicated information provided to the national Jewish press. In addition, it provided extensive coverage (and support) to the Maurice Rose Memorial Hospital project that was initiated almost immediately after General Rose's death.

1899, and became a major factor in the wave of immigration that began at the turn of the century and continued through the onset of World War I.

Thus, it is very likely that the NJHC, or one of Denver's other tuberculosis institutions, was Sam Rose's main reason for moving to Denver. The city was a welcoming community on several levels. It was known especially to be friendly to Jews from Eastern Europe, who were often treated as "second class citizens" by their more affluent and more assimilated co-religionists from Western Europe, especially Germany. While most people arrived in Colorado directly from Europe through the Texas port of Galveston, many also came overland, especially those, like Sam Rose, who needed a healthier environment.

Sam was soon able to open a dress design shop downtown at 1317 Broadway. The store gradually developed a reputation as a "fashionable" establishment and began to attract a more socially prominent clientele. In a chance encounter in the shop just five years after arriving in town, Sam met and quickly befriended Frederick G. Bonfils (1860-1933), the influential publisher of the *Denver Post*. The midwestern "FG" was—like Sam—tall, handsome, and dapper, as well as a transplanted citizen building a new life in a country without limits. The meeting established a lasting friendship that strongly influenced Sam and the Rose family. Over the next four decades, the *Denver Post*, and later the *Rocky Mountain News*, covered the Rose family. It reported on Sam's accidental fall from a tram in 1927, his birthday celebrations, honorary dinners at the synagogue, as well as Sam and Katy's first prize in the community waltz contest.

Later, of course, the papers covered extensively the exploits, and especially the death, of Maurice Rose—its pre-eminent "native son" soldier and the highest-ranking Colorado combat general. These papers—and to a lesser extent, the *Intermountain Jewish News*—were major factors in the creation of the "legend" of Maurice Rose.

"FG" Bonfils and his partner Harry H. Tammen (1856-1924) had purchased the *Denver Post* in 1895, and reestablished it as a crusading newspaper dedicated to "the service of the people." Above the door of their building they inscribed this legend: "O Justice, when expelled from other habitations, make this thy dwelling place."

Bonfils, who had attended West Point for three years, shared an interest in military affairs with Sam, whose dreams of wearing a uniform were not entirely forgotten. Through his friendship with the powerful newspaperman—his "nearest and dearest friend"—Sam got an appointment as a park policeman in 1907. Almost forty years later, he recalled that FG thought he would look good in the braided uniform of a Denver peace

Sam Rose shortly after moving to Denver
(*Source:* Rose Family Album)

officer. Almost as a joke, Sam went to the office of the mayor and repeated
their mutual friend's suggestion. Mayor Robert Speer was a man who
knew full well the importance of spreading favors to all segments of the
rapidly growing Denver community. The city had already had a Jewish
mayor and the benefit of cultivating influence with a politically aware
minority was certainly not lost on Speer. **(K)** He also appreciated the value
of doing a relatively painless favor for the influential (and muckraking)
newspaper publisher.

K Wolfe Londoner, a well known pioneer, merchant, landowner, and celebrated
host whose "Cyclone Center" was a rendezvous for Denver's prominent citizens,
was mayor from 1889–1892.

Along with his new uniform, the tall police rookie was also issued a .38 caliber handgun. When eight-year-old Maurice learned where it was kept, he took it out to the back yard. He held the gun in his hands. He handled it carefully, savoring the moment. This was no toy; it was the real thing. He took out the bullets, examined them carefully, and then reloaded the revolver. Next, he gathered up tin cans, placed them on the fence, and marked off a proper distance for target practice. He aimed carefully and fired. The first can went down as the sound of the shot rang through the neighborhood.

His terrified mother ran out of the kitchen and saw her younger son holding his father's gun. She screamed, "Mauri, what are you doing? Put that gun down. You'll kill yourself." He calmed her down and then surrendered the gun. It became an apocryphal story. General Rose repeated later that his first target practice whetted his appetite for the life of a soldier, and he never lost his appreciation of weapons. In what was probably the last letter he wrote to his son, he described in detail his collection of trophy firearms with great pride.[9]

But even earlier, in an oft-described childish prank, he had displayed a remarkable indifference to personal danger and a kind of reckless courage. During 1905, in order to accommodate the rapid growth of the East Denver neighborhood where the Rose family lived, city engineers excavated the local streets and started to lay new water mains. Buried deep in a trench was a giant, twisting pipe. The kids dared each other to crawl all the way through it, a full city block distance. Six-year-old Maurice was the only one to accept the challenge.

Seemingly unafraid, he crawled into the darkness, and while his friends and older brother waited fearfully (and for what seemed an eternity) he made his way through the long tube. With a shout of victory, he emerged at the other end; filthy, soaking wet, shivering, and covering his eyes as he suddenly emerged into the daylight. Like the "gun" story, the "pipe" story assumed great importance in family lore. These tales became parables of how Rose's life subsequently unfolded, and offered a glimpse into the kind of character that governed his actions even in childhood. After the gun episode and the long crawl in the terrifying unknown, those who knew him best described him as becoming increasingly serious at school and at play. But, they hastened to add, he still maintained a friendly and likable demeanor.

As far back as anyone in the family could remember, Maurice, like his father, dreamed of being a soldier. During recess at the elementary

Whittier School, Arnold and Maurice divided their classmates into rival teams and played games of mock warfare. For 'Mauri,' the playground was a battlefield, an arena where his natural aggressiveness, dreams of glory, leadership abilities, and spirit of adventure were displayed in embryonic form. He played soldier with his friends, riding and hiking in the hills, dreaming of cavalry charges and fighting Indians. His interest in things military was deep, however, and went beyond games. It governed his reading and shaped his experience in school and extracurricular activities.

He consumed books about American history, especially about our wars and our war heroes. Many veterans of the recent conflicts—the Civil War and Spanish–American War—were still alive, and the spirit of patriotism was fervent and fed by their writings and reunions.

He read biographies of Washington, Jefferson, and the other founding fathers; Lincoln was a special hero. The more he read, the more he identified with their ideals, and the more commitment he felt to protecting the guiding precepts of our democracy. Like many others born at the beginning of the century, the young Rose was passionate about our history, and patriotic in a way that many can now hardly understand. America had emerged from the war with Spain at the turn of the new century as a global power, victorious, and confident, and for those like Maurice Rose, born into that time, the call to service was compelling.

Like many others, his first experience with community service was through the Boy Scouts. In 1910, he joined his local troop and, embracing its challenges fiercely, rose rapidly to the highest level of Eagle Scout, his merit badges literally covering his uniform blouse. For him, the oath to honor God and country, to help other people, and to be "physically strong, mentally awake, and morally straight," was not an abstraction, but almost a living thing. His scout picture shows a proud, ramrod straight, handsome, and unsmiling boy: the very image of a serious young officer in training.[10]

Maurice and his brother Arnold grew up in an religiously observant, yet rapidly assimilating family, in a city that offered success to natives and newcomers alike in school, houses of worship, and on the athletic fields. By all accounts, Maurice Rose had a happy childhood and was active in all these venues. If he felt any discomfort in reconciling his life as a native-born American kid with the Old World heritage and practices of his family, he didn't show it to outsiders.

He did very well in school, played sports actively, and tried to excel in every pursuit. But, while living the American dream, he continued to honor the traditions of his family and performed the rituals and routines of a

Jewish boy. The language spoken in his home (and quite possibly the first he learned) was Yiddish, the distinctive East European melange of German and Hebrew. Lt. Colonel Wesley A. Sweat, G-3 (Operations) of 3rd Armored Division, personally observed General Rose speaking and reading German, almost certainly related to his upbringing and fluency in Yiddish.[11]

By the time of his appointment to the park police, Sam Rose had become an active and visible member of the small, but highly vocal, Eastern European Jewish community. He had a strong affiliation with the leading conservative synagogue that lasted for more than forty years. **(L)** Led by Rabbi Charles E. H. Kauvar, Sam's close friend, and for fifty years a nationally known spiritual leader and spokesman for the Denver community, the synagogue was central to the Rose boys' early experience. Both graduated from its Hebrew school, both were proficient in Hebrew, and conversant with the important texts of Judaism, and both were valued members of the choir. In fact, Arnold Rose remained the lead bass in the choir for the rest of his life.

Sam was a well-known lay leader of religious services and active in synagogue affairs. He was a teacher in the Hebrew School for many years and was remembered as a stern disciplinarian, apt to react harshly to raucous outbursts or other inappropriate behavior.[12] Years later, after the synagogue moved to a new location, Sam maintained his membership at the old site even though it was reorganized as an Orthodox synagogue. **(M)** On April 13, 1925, at the age of seventy, he was named a rabbi in that congregation, with special responsibility for performing weddings. **(N)** This is the source of the reference to Samuel Rose as a rabbi. In fact, it was more of an honorary title, in keeping with the original role and meaning of the term rabbi (or, teacher) signifying respect for his service and learning, rather than a formal title reflecting completion of a formal ordination process. Sam had fulfilled the destiny that his father had envisioned for him and that seemed inevitable when he was a boy in Warsaw.

L *Beth Ha-Medrosh Hagodol* (BMH) Synagogue, Denver.

M The *Beth Joseph* Congregation, Denver.

N The original synagogue document is in the Rose family album. The album was started by Sam Rose, passed to Arnold, then Herb (Arnold's son), and is now held by Jeff Rose, MD, Sam's great grandson and General Rose's grandnephew. It contains both family and Signal Corps photos, newspaper clippings, a few letters, and other documents. The late Mrs. Virginia Rose's photo album belongs to Maurice Roderick Rose, of San Antonio, her only child by General Rose.

Because of the special significance of the day of his birth in the Jewish calendar, and the strong traditions of his family, it is quite likely that Maurice's *Bar Mitzvah* **(O)** would be scheduled around Hanukkah. In an interview given after General Rose's death, Rabbi Kauvar remembered him as an alert and ambitious student whose *Bar Mitzvah* speech before the congregation had been impressive and had left his friends and family brimming over with pride.

It is obvious that as the grandson of a renowned rabbi, and the son of a very observant and scholarly father, much was expected of him. He viewed the Jewish ritual of passage into adulthood as a very important occasion. It also seems likely that the military significance of Hanukkah was not lost on him, and he could not have thought the timing of his birth was anything other than another sign of his ultimate destiny. The story itself—a band of desperate, fiercely loyal, guerrilla fighters, outnumbered, outgunned, yet defeating three armies of a sophisticated power through guile and superior tactics—has stirred the hearts of Jewish boys for more than 2,000 years.

In the event, he was sufficiently encouraged by the very positive reception to his speech to go further. After entering high school, he joined the debating team and sharpened his skill at public speaking. He was a serious student, but also found time for other activities. Because of his parents' very modest means, and his desire to help out, he earned spending money riding a paper route for the *Denver Post*.

His high school classmates recalled years later that Maurice Rose eventually developed into a powerful orator. His speeches were passionate and filled with references to the founding fathers and our highest ideals as a nation. Further, he combined an excellent memory (some described it as near photographic) with a power and ease of expression that held the attention of his audience. As a debater, he used the vast reservoir of historical facts that he had accumulated through his voracious reading. That habit (and hunger) remained with him for the rest of his life. Major Haynes W. Dugan, Asst. G-2 (Intelligence), who served under him in the 3rd Armored, remarked that he "soaked up knowledge as a sponge takes water."

Lt. Colonel Boulger (G-1) was a frequent attendee at the senior staff dinners at HQ and recalled that the conversation often turned abruptly to

---

O Hebrew for "Son of the Commandment." A religious coming-of-age ceremony for Jewish boys of thirteen years, at which time they formally assume the responsibilities and obligations of adulthood in the community.

something the general had read or heard. **(P)** God help the man who couldn't hold his own in the discussion that followed. Sometimes, the subject had nothing to do with the war. One of Boulger's most vivid memories was a visit by Rose's friend, Admiral Richard Byrd, during which the conversation ranged over a broad range of topics and issues.[13] Given Rose's grueling schedule and pace, no one could understand where he found the time to read.

His writing ability was recognized early, and he was an editor of the school newspaper. His ultimate dream of military service, however, was never far from his mind, nor from his behavior. To his classmates, it was clear what he wanted to be. In the annual school yearbook, a cartoon depicting the newspaper staff shows Maurice Rose carrying a rifle.[14] Socially, the tall and athletic young man was somewhat aloof, but likable. Handsome, intense, and with piercing eyes, girls found him attractive, but also somewhat serious and unapproachable. In 1916, he graduated from East High School with honors.

What he did next is not entirely clear. His father apparently did not have enough money to send him to college, although some evidence suggests that he went to the University of Colorado at Boulder with the intention of matriculating.[15] Other accounts say that he was already enrolled when the continued patriotic fervor unleashed by Pancho Villa's murderous raid into Columbia, New Mexico on March 9, 1916, changed his plans.[16] There is no firm evidence, however, that he ever enrolled in the university or attended classes there, or at any other civilian college.

He was convinced that the trouble in Mexico was the opportunity he had been waiting for his whole life. The rising crescendo of excitement surrounding the proposed expedition, to be led by San Juan Hill hero Brigadier General John J. Pershing, sparked his next decision. He made plans to enlist in the 1st Volunteer Cavalry Regiment, Colorado National

---

P Jack A. Boulger, born in 1917 in North Dakota, and graduated from North Dakota Agricultural College in Fargo, ND. He was commissioned in the U.S. Army Reserve and served as G-1, or Personnel Officer, for 3rd Armored Division, after serving as a Company Commander in the 36th Armored Infantry Regiment. Wounded and captured just before the drive on Paderborn (March 25, 1945), he was liberated several weeks later. During World War II, he was awarded the Silver Star, Presidential Unit Citation, Legion of Merit, Bronze Star, and Purple Heart. After service in Vietnam, he retired from the U.S. Army as a Colonel.

Guard. The state militias were being federalized and, if all went well, he would be sent to the border quickly. There, on horseback he would chase the murderous outlaws and live out his dream.

But before he could make the dream a reality, he had to overcome a major problem. At sixteen, he was underage, so at first he tried to convince his parents to give him permission to "join up." He might logically have assumed that his father would understand and react sympathetically. After all, they had both shared a childhood dream of serving in the military, as well as a deep love of their country. But his father was now past sixty, and like his father before him, had mostly practical considerations on his mind. He wanted his son to get a college education and "make something of himself." Both parents were united in their opposition and refused to sanction his enlistment.

Maurice Rose decided to take matters into his own hands. On June 24, 1916, he hitchhiked to the rifle range on Golden Road, in sight of the Rocky Mountains, where the National Guard cavalry was then encamped. He told the recruiting officer that he was eighteen and signed up on the spot.[17] He was one of the first Denver boys to volunteer for service on the Mexican border.[18] Private Maurice Rose was assigned to Troop B, issued a uniform, a blanket, and a spot to sleep in a tent. He was, finally, a soldier, but the exhilaration of the moment was short-lived. The next day his mother arrived at the camp and was escorted to the rifle range where he was practicing.

There, once again, and under strained circumstances, she found him shooting at targets, but no longer a boy, and dressed in the uniform of a soldier. She was introduced to Captain Lawrence, the Commander of B Troop. Far from anxious to lose such a good recruit, he told Mrs. Rose "if all my boys were as apt and as good soldiers as Maurice, things would be easier for us."[19] Still, Lawrence couldn't keep an underage boy against the wishes of his parents. Mrs. Rose returned home alone.

Maurice threw himself into the soldier's life with the same intensity and desire to succeed that he brought to all his endeavors. One might even characterize his behavior as zealous. He exhorted his fellow soldiers, especially the older men, who were often goldbricking. He talked to the men in the guardhouse, urging them to reform, reminding them of their duty and responsibility as men and soldiers. He must have seemed downright grim to his comrades, most of whom, one can assume, were not as altruistically motivated or sincere as the very young but enthusiastic patriot.

The next visitor was his father. The discharge papers had still not arrived, and Sam was increasingly concerned that Maurice would be shipped out before he could get him released.

> Maurice, is this the kind of life you want to lead? Look how you sleep in these tents. Look at your meals. Do you like them better than your mother's cooking? Let's talk sense. If I can get you out of this, will you go back to college?
> "Dad, I made my bed and I'm going to sleep in it. And, I'm going to make good."[20]

Finally, the discharge papers came through. Maurice Rose was honorably discharged on August 8, 1916. His official record lists this six-week period as his first service in spite of his underage enlistment. Rose's experience in the National Guard, short as it was, may have had some small influence on the perceptions of his fellow officers during his career. It was a common view, and somewhat justified by events, that the Colorado National Guard, including the cavalry regiment, were "strike-breakers," especially useful in brutal environments, like the mines. **(Q)**

This reputation was common in other states as well, including Pennsylvania, where Rose later served as an instructor to the 103rd Cavalry Regiment, Pennsylvania National Guard, which was also involved in strike breaking. While men who began their service in the Guard certainly rose to high command in the U.S. Army during World War II and after, there was a hierarchy in the American officer corps, based on date and type of commission, military education, and other factors. No officer who began his career in the National Guard has ever risen to Chief of Staff of the Army.

Still determined to become a soldier and still not ready (or able financially) to attend college, Rose bided his time for a year, and went to work at the Hendrie & Belthoff Manufacturing Co, a meat-packing plant, where his brother Arnold was already employed. The military fever inspired by the Pancho Villa expedition (and the rapidly escalating events in Europe) remained strong. In addition to formally established "civilian"

Q In a famous incident on April 14, 1914, a coal miners' strike in Ludlow, Colorado, was suppressed violently by Rockefeller interests with active help from the Colorado Guard, resulting in the deaths of twenty-six people, including a dozen women and children.

training programs, spontaneous employee-inspired paramilitary efforts also appeared. Rose organized and took command of the first such effort in Denver at his plant.[21]

At lunchtime the men, "armed" with wooden rifles, practiced marching in a parking lot across from the Union Station, learned the manual of arms and other drills, all under the guidance of the energetic, would-be soldier. His efforts went beyond just drilling, however. Drawing on his other talents, he conducted lectures and classes on the meaning and responsibilities of service and patriotism. The daily headlines, like the sinking of the *Lusitania*, continued unrestrained submarine warfare, and finally the Zimmerman Telegram affair suggested that America's entry into the Great War was almost a certainty. On April 6, 1917, Wilson's efforts to avoid armed conflict ended in failure. The Congress declared war on Imperial Germany and her allies.

This time, Maurice Rose had no doubts, nor would his parents try to stop him. Although still underage, this time he got his parent's permission and went directly to Camp Logan, just outside Denver, where he was among the first of the city's sons to enlist in the U.S. Army.[22] He applied for an officer's training program, took the required tests, scored near the top of the list, and was accepted.

His destiny seemed fulfilled. But, his childhood dreams of glory were about to give way to the cruel reality and terrible ordeal of war. Maurice Rose was about to experience the horror of trench warfare, including gas attacks and "going over the top" facing machine guns and the German Army, rites of passage that had already decimated an entire generation of young men. His feet were now firmly set on a path that would lead to both glory and tragedy

CHAPTER Three

The Young Officer (1917–1920)

"Well Pop, I'm going to France."

First Lieutenant Maurice Rose

When Maurice Rose entered the U.S. Army it was already in the midst of a dramatic expansion. On New Year's Day of 1917, it had a total strength of about 110,000 men, not including the National Guard. By the Great War's end, more than 4.7 million Americans had served in the armed forces (3.7 million in the U.S. Army alone), and more than 2 million troops (forty-two divisions) had reached France, where 1.4 million men (twenty-six divisions) had actually been in combat.[1]

Almost at the same time that Rose and thousands of other young men began to arrive at their designated Officer Training Camps, the Selective Service Act of 1917 (signed by President Wilson on May 18, 1917) was passing into law. This was the first true conscription law in our history. With the first large-scale draft scheduled for September, the top command had already begun to address the question of where to find the large numbers of officers that would be necessary to keep pace with the flood of draftees.

It had become apparent early in the expansion process that major efforts would be needed to meet the huge requirement for leaders, especially for company-grade officers (lieutenants and captains). They would be needed to staff a field army that was scheduled to reach eighty divisions by the middle of 1919. Assuming a basic 20:1 ratio of enlisted men to officers, the proposed ground army would need about 200,000 officers quickly.

The Regular Army and National Guard between them could muster just 10,000 officers! The original idea of sprinkling the new draftee divisions with Regular Army men soon proved impractical due to the shortage of regulars, the requirement for officer instructors, and the pressure to use the few available regulars for a token American commitment to France as soon as possible.[2]

The most important of the new initiatives was the First Officers Training Camps (FOTC). When Maurice Rose boarded the train at Denver's Union Station bound for Kansas in the spring of 1917, the FOTC at Fort Riley was his destination. It was his entry point into the life of the professional soldier. These encampments traced their roots back to the Plattsburg Camps, which had, by the Declaration of War, already trained thousands of young civilians, mostly for service in the National Guard.[3] **(A)**

The FOTC program started with fourteen locations and eventually expanded to sixteen nationwide sites. By the end of the war, these had trained and commissioned more than 80,000 officers, mostly in the infantry, or roughly two thirds of the total number of line officers in the U.S. Army. The FOTC graduates (including staff officers and other specialists) represented roughly half of the total number of officers who served in the American Expeditionary Force (AEF).[4] **(B)**

Maurice Rose was a splendid example of the kind of men produced by the program. Healthy, literate, and highly motivated, he represented the best of American youth. The level of professional competence achieved by the young graduates was widely respected, especially by their battle-hardened French and English instructors. The level of training achieved was all the more impressive considering the short duration of the main course and the pressures of wartime.[5]

The entry of America into the Great War led to many rapid and dramatic changes in the Army's infrastructure. In addition to officers, there was a critical need for training facilities and bases. Fort Riley, Kansas, had

---

A The effort to train civilians and increase preparedness was named for Plattsburg, New York, site of a summer civilian training camp that attracted broad press coverage because of its wealthy and well-known graduates. Training was also conducted at Gettysburg, Pennsylvania, and the Presidio of Monterey, California. The National Defense Act of 1916 provided the authorization for the First Officers Training Camps.

B More than 40,000 officers, or 20 percent, were doctors, clergymen, and other specialists commissioned directly from civilian life.

been selected early as a site for a First Officer's Training Camp and training ground for the 89th Division. Traditionally regarded as the home of the cavalry, Fort Riley had been an army post since the mid-nineteenth century and the days of the Indian Wars; Custer's 7th Cavalry Regiment had been stationed at Fort Riley.

The Great War put serious strains on the facilities of the old base, and plans were quickly made to build a new cantonment. During the summer and fall of 1917, as Rose was being trained at Riley, a new camp (named for Major General Frederick Funston, a hero of San Juan Hill and the 1906 San Francisco earthquake) was built five miles east of the permanent post. **(C)** This training site was a model for the others established across the country, and could accommodate from 30,000 to 50,000 men, or a single army division, with its supporting infrastructure.

Like thousands of other fervently patriotic young men, Maurice Rose applied and was quickly accepted for the First Officers Training Camp program shortly after the declaration of war. **(D)** Because of his service in the National Guard and the civilian drilling program at the meat plant (and probably his father's influence), his name was placed at the top of the list of officer applicants from Denver.[6] After a battery of rigorous physical and mental examinations, he was assigned to Fort Riley, the closest FOTC to his home. The candidates were organized into the 14th Provisional Training Regiment, and Rose was assigned to the 5th Company, one of its nine infantry companies.[7] In addition, the regiment had two cavalry troops, three field artillery batteries, and an engineering company attached.

Rose underwent a rigorous ninety day course that included the basic drills of a typical enlisted man, as well as the rudiments of platoon and company command. The instructors included non-commissioned officers (NCOs) and officers from the Regular Army and National Guard, as well as veteran British and French soldiers. The latter taught basic tactics, as

---

C Major General Frederick Funston (1865-1917), a native of Kansas, won the Medal of Honor while leading the 20th Kansas Volunteer Infantry during the Philippine Insurrection. As the senior officer at the Presidio during the San Francisco earthquake of 1906, he earned high praise for his command of the situation. He was in overall command on the Mexican border in 1916 during Villa's raid, and was responsible for dispatching Brig. General John J. Pershing in pursuit. Had he not died of a heart attack at age fifty-one, he would have been the logical choice to lead the American Expeditionary Force.

D By the end of the war, four FOTC programs had been completed.

Maurice Rose after enlisting in the U.S. Army in 1917
(Sam Rose, Maurice, Katy Rose, Arnold Rose)
(*Source:* Rose Family Album)

well as more specialized subjects, like the reduction of enemy strong points and the use of hand grenades, machine guns, and other weapons. They did their best to impart their hard-gained experience to the Americans, who seemed to the Europeans to be unduly "cocky."[8]

Special emphasis was placed on the use of the rifle, including marksmanship and bayonet drill. This presented some early problems, as the enthusiasm of the men was counterbalanced by the lack of just about all the necessary accouterments of war. The shortage of essential weapons, including rifles (fewer than 300,000 were on hand at the beginning of 1917) meant that the men of Rose's division had to "whittle mock weapons from pieces of wood."[9]

His training course—the first one conducted—ran from May 15, 1917 to August 11, 1917. About 30,000 civilians and 8,000 Reserve Corps officers were initially admitted to the first class nationwide, with just over 27,000, or 70 percent, receiving commissions.[10] Upon graduation, Rose and the other men of the First Officer's Training Camps became "Gentlemen by Act of Congress." Supplemented by regulars and guardsmen, including experienced NCOs, they were earmarked for assignment to the new National Army, then being formed from the large pool of draftees. Just three weeks after Rose and his fellow junior officers had completed their initial training, the first men they would command, part of a group of 280,000, started to report to the fourteen nationwide cantonments. **(E)**

On August 15, 1917 (just about three months before his eighteenth birthday), Maurice Rose was commissioned a 2nd Lieutenant of Infantry in the Officer Reserve Corps (ORC). Thus, with a handshake, certificate, and smart salute, Maurice Rose became one of the very first "Ninety Day Wonders," a group of men that has led Americans in some of their most desperate struggles on every battlefield since then. **(F)** After spending a brief furlough back home, he returned to the newly constructed Camp Funston for more advanced infantry training with the draftees who would make up his platoon. It did not take long, however, for the young officer to attract the attention of his superiors and to distinguish himself.

While on routine guard duty in the late fall of 1917, 2nd Lt. Rose led a detachment of men that captured an escaped prisoner. After personally chasing down and collaring the escapee, he sat down to write his parents about his achievement. The young officer didn't know that the incident had already received press coverage and had already reached the newspapers in his hometown. When Sam Rose received the letter from his proud son, he wrote back, "Maurice, when you write me, tell me something I don't know. I read about the incident in the papers."[11] It was just the kind of response from father to son that sharpens the desire to do just that.

Rose soon got his chance. His role in the successful conclusion to the guardhouse escape, and his obvious abilities and affinity for leadership,

---

E The divisions of the United States Army in World War I fell into three categories based on their origin. The first were units in the Regular Army (Divisions 1–20), the second were National Guard (Divisions 26–42), and the third category was the National Army (Divisions 76–93). Regimental designations paralleled these three categories. Regiments numbered below 100 were in the Regular Army, National Guard Regiments were assigned numbers over 100, and the National Army Regiments (those raised as a result of the Selective Service Act of May 1917) had numbers over 300.

F The term was later applied to the hundreds of thousands of graduates of the World War II Officers Candidate Schools (OCS).

**Maurice Rose after receiving his
Officers' Commission**
(*Source:* Rose Family Album)

led to early promotion. On December 31, 1917, he was advanced to the
rank of 1st Lieutenant (temporary) in the National Army. His next letter
took Sam by surprise and must have been sweet satisfaction for the eigh-
teen-year old officer.

> Dear Pop: You asked me to tell you something you don't already
> know. Well, this is something you don't know. I have been promoted
> to first lieutenant!

As a favorite son, this too was dutifully reported in the *Denver Post.*[12]
  A short time after returning from his first visit home, he was assigned
to the 353rd Infantry Regiment, which was a part of the 89th Division,
National Army.[13] The 89th Division, called the "Middle West Division,"
was the first of three to be formed and trained at Camp Funston during
the Great War. **(G)** It was organized on August 15, 1917, under the command of Major General Leonard Wood, who trained it until he was
detached as an observer in France. **(H)** After being severely wounded,

---

G The others were the 10th Division, a Regular Army outfit, which was formed
too late to see service in Europe, and the largely African-American 93rd Division.
  H Leonard Wood (1860–1927) graduated Harvard Medical School and joined the
Army in 1885 as a surgeon, winning the Medal of Honor fighting against Geronimo.
He was White House physician at the outbreak of the Spanish–American War and,

Wood returned in April 1918, and oversaw the division's final preparations for war when in May 1918, he released the 89th—reportedly with tears in his eyes—to the AEF for combat duty. Because of his unpopular political views, he never held a combat command in World War I.[14] **(I)**

The 89th Division was organized under the Table of Organization and Equipment (TOE) published in September 1917, and had an authorized strength of 28,000 men, or twice the size of comparable units in either the Allied or Central Power armies.[15] **(J)** It consisted of two infantry brigades, each one made up of two infantry regiments (hence the appellation "Square" division) as well as an artillery brigade, several machine gun battalions, and other supporting units. **(K)**

For Maurice Rose, it was the regiment that shaped his early military experience. Since the earliest days of the infantry, in armies where the geo-

---

with Teddy Roosevelt, recruited the 1st Volunteer Cavalry (Rough Riders), later assuming command of the 2nd Cavalry Brigade at San Juan Hill (July 1, 1898). He served as military governor of Cuba, during which time yellow fever was brought under control, and was Army Chief of Staff (1910–1914). Even though he was the most senior officer in the Army, he never held a fighting command during World War I.

I As a vocal advocate of U.S. preparedness during his tenure as Chief of Staff, Leonard Wood had frequently clashed with President Woodrow Wilson, but he was able to effect some positive changes before the outbreak of war. He was a strong believer in training civilians and was the chief architect of several such efforts, including the Citizen Military Training Camps (CMTC) and the Plattsburg camps. In a real sense, then, he was directly responsible for the training programs that ultimately led to the commissioning of Maurice Rose. The civilian training efforts, vindicated by events, continued during the interwar period, and Maurice Rose served as an instructor in the CMTC camp established at Fort Logan, Colorado.

J The average strength of the division during June–November 1918 was actually about 20,000. The divisions of the French, British, and German armies numbered about 12,000 men.

K The 353rd Infantry Regiment was constituted on August 7, 1917 (a week before Rose's graduation), formally organized on August 27, 1917 (when Rose and the rest of the first crop of junior officers was returning from their furloughs), and established on September 5, 1917. Except for a few brief periods, Colonel James H. Reeves (1870–1963), an already oft-decorated and highly experienced officer who was destined to achieve even more glory in France, commanded it throughout the war. The 353rd, along with the 354th Infantry Regiment and 341st Machine Gun Battalion, formed the 177th Infantry Brigade. BG Frank L. Winn, a West Point graduate (1896) and veteran of the Indians Wars, Cuba, the Pershing Expedition,

graphical origin of the manpower defines the character of units, it is in the regiment that a soldier first finds identity, comradeship, and a home. In the National Army of 1917, the manpower was drawn from specific state drafts, and so there was a kind of local character to each unit. Rose's regiment, the 353rd Infantry, while still stationed at Camp Funston, received a great deal of publicity as the "All-Kansas Regiment," since it contained men from nearly every county in the state. In fact, the subtitle of the official regimental history is "They're from Kansas!"[16]

Near the end of his training, Rose was given a final furlough before heading overseas. Late one evening just before returning to Camp Funston he sat with his father in the parlor. The conversation was strained. Each knew that it might be the last time they would be together, yet the son was exuberant. After the abortive enlistment in the Guard, and a year of waiting, events were right for him to realize his dream. He was wearing the uniform of an officer in the United States Army. His images of battle, nurtured by his reading, the stories of old soldiers, and the nights around the campfire during his brief time in the Guard, were about to become reality. His opportunity to fight was drawing near. He couldn't restrain himself and blurted out his excitement with the bravado of youth.

Well, Pop, I'm going to France. Now for the real shooting.[17]

Sam Rose had been nervous and worried since his boys had left home, and he was torn apart by his son's cavalier words. His older son, Arnold, had enlisted in the Marines when war broke out and was already gone, maybe even in harm's way. Perhaps Sam took some satisfaction in the fact that the dream that had sustained him during his difficult youth in Poland was about to be fulfilled by his boys. But like any loving father, he was also terrified of what the future might hold. His own dreams of "soldiering for the Czar" had long ago given way to the painful realities of life. His son's excitement could not still his own worst fears or prevent him from speaking the deepest of them aloud.

---

and the Philippines, commanded it throughout the Great War. The 178th Infantry Brigade (BG Thomas G. Hanson) consisted of the 355th and 356th Infantry Regiments and the 342th Machine Gun Battalion. The 164th Field Artillery Brigade was made up of three field artillery regiments, the 340th (75mm), 341st (75mm), and 342nd (155 mm), and the 314th Trench Mortar Battery. In addition, the 314th Engineer Regiment, 314th Trains, 314th Field Signal Battalion, 340th Machine Gun Battalion as well as other units were attached to the division.

Emblem of the 353d Infantry Regiment (L)

What are you talking about, Maurice? Do you know what you're say-ing? Do you know where you're going? You're likely to be killed in battle.

But Maurice Rose knew what he was about and what he wanted.

But Pop, that's why I went into the army—to fight. If the general wouldn't send me over, I'd be mighty disappointed.[18]

L The crest atop the shield is the same as that used for all the regiments and battalions of the U.S. Army Reserve, and is a depiction of the statue of Minuteman Captain John H. Parker, which stands on the commons in Lexington, Massachusetts. The shield is painted blue, the traditional color of the infantry. The Red Cross of Lorraine (France) in the upper left quadrant commemorates the regiment's prin-cipal service in the Great War from September 1917 to November of 1918, first at St. Mihiel and then in the Meuse-Argonne Campaign.

The sunflower at the lower right of the shield is the State Flower of Kansas, home of the regiment, source of many of its soldiers, and its final stop after the Great War, where it was assigned as part of the Reserve. The motto of the regiment, "To the Stars through Difficulties," is the translation of the Latin motto of the State of Kansas. In a very real sense, and as is evident in his career, the motto might also be applied to one of its most distinguished veterans, Maurice Rose.

Each man knew there was nothing more to say. The young officer arranged his affairs, just in case the worst did happen, and said his good-byes to friends and family. On May 25, 1918, less than nine months after the 353rd Infantry was created, 1st Lt. Maurice Rose shipped out with his infantry company. **(M)** Crossing the country by railroad, he arrived at Camp Mills, Long Island, New York, several days later. He spent a few days there, as did most of the Europe-bound doughboys, before departing from Hoboken, New Jersey, aboard the British vessel *HMS Karmala*. On June 1, 1918, the regiment shipped out.

As he passed the Statue of Liberty heading for war, he could not have helped thinking that it was through the same waters that his mother and father had arrived to start their lives in America. His voyage back to help save the Old World was a fitting repayment of the debt he felt to his country. The 89th Division, thanks to the successful convoy escort achievement of the U.S. Navy, made the Atlantic crossing without losing a single man, arriving safely in Liverpool on the evening of June 15.

By June 22, Rose was in France and a few days later was at the division's final destination of Manois, having traveled via Southampton, England, and the port of Le Havre. Consistent with Pershing's practice of further training for the newly arrived divisions in quiet zones, Rose's regiment was posted to the Reynel Training Area, a relatively peaceful sector on the Lorraine front between late June and early August 1918.

On July 14, 1918, Bastille Day, Rose marched with the 1st Battalion in review before General Pershing at Caumont, France, the AEF Headquarters. The American Commander "commended the men highly for the showing they made" and remarked on the men's "fine appearance, soldierly bearing, and excellent work."[19] Their final training was a period of acclimation during which the American units were assigned to veteran British and French outfits close to the front. Just like the training in the states, the focus was on offensive warfare, especially the use of rifle and the bayonet.

This was consistent with Pershing's belief that the only way out of the bloody, stagnant, stalemate of the trenches was to inculcate in America's fighting men the spirit of the offensive. Such a philosophy was perfectly

---

M The unit roster in the 353rd Regimental History (Charles F. Dienst) lists 1st Lt. Maurice Rose in both Companies A and B. These companies (along with "C" and "D") were part of the First Battalion. It is likely that Rose served in one before St. Mihiel and the other after returning from hospital. There is no listing for dates of service in the regimental history.

suited to Rose's aggressive nature. He had already developed a reputation as an expert marksman, not surprising given his early enthusiasm for weapons. His willingness, even eagerness, to lead men into danger was apparent to everyone who met him.

In early August 1918, Rose's division started to move forward, the first American unit to be transported to the front by trucks. It relieved the 82nd Division in the Lucey Sector, northwest of Toul, and was assigned to Lt. General Joseph T. Dickman's IV Corps, a part of the newly formed U.S. First Army. **(N)** The 353rd Regiment moved quietly into the Limey sector on August 6 without alerting the enemy, and Rose's battalion dug in along the road to Metz. Almost immediately, they began actively patrolling and raiding the enemy's trenches to the north.

The movement of the division was preparatory to the St. Mihiel Offensive, scheduled to begin on September 12, 1918. For some generations of soldiers, there are pivotal, formative battles where junior officers destined to fight even greater battles receive their first baptism of fire. On these battlefields they cross paths with men with whom they will continue to serve and sometimes confront men against whom they will once more fight. **(O)**

For the generation of generals that commanded in the Civil War, it was the stirring capture of Mexico City at the end of the Mexican War. **(P)** For Maurice Rose, and many others who served in World War I, and later commanded major forces in World War II, those formative battles were the St. Mihiel and Meuse-Argonne Offensives. For the rest of his life, Rose spoke of his service in the Great War with quiet pride.

N The First U.S. Army was established on August 15, 1918, and was at that time directly under the command of General John J. Pershing.

O A quarter century later, Maurice Rose, fighting once more through France near these same battlefields, would again serve in a reconstituted First U.S. Army commanded by Lt. General Courtney Hodges, a hero of St. Mihiel.

P In that battle, Lt. George Pickett grabbed the 8th Infantry Regimental flag and charged the heights of Chapultepec after Lt. James Longstreet and Lt. Lewis Armistead both fell with bullet wounds. In the field close by were Captain Robert E. Lee, a brilliant engineer, and an artilleryman named Jackson, as well as Sam Grant, Longstreet's best friend, and George McClellan, the star of the West Point class of 1846. At Gettysburg, Armistead was killed commanding a Brigade in Pickett's Division during the charge made by Longstreet's I Corps. Facing them were many men who were with them in the field below the Chapultepec bastion.

By August 1918, both the German-held Marne and the Amiens salients had been eliminated, and only one major threat to lateral rail communications behind the Allied lines remained: the four year old St. Mihiel salient near the Paris–Nancy railroad line. This modest threat offered Pershing an ideal opportunity. In his first offensive action, he could show what the Americans were capable of under their own command in a large operation, but one where both the objective and risks were limited.

Under pressure from his allies, Pershing agreed to reduce his attacking forces to the minimum required to reduce the salient in three or four days, and to simultaneously prepare his troops for the much more important Meuse-Argonne drive. But, while the St. Mihiel attack was subordinated to the larger offensive scheduled for late September, Pershing resisted the Allies' desire to put American units under British and French command and managed to keep the First Army intact. Pershing was confident he would be able to mount both offensives, partly because of excellent logistics staff work, largely under the direction of a brilliant General Staff aide, Colonel George C. Marshall.

The total Allied force involved in the St. Mihiel offensive numbered 650,000 men, including 550,000 Americans. In support of the attack, the First Army had over 3,000 guns (mostly French), 1,500 airplanes, and a detachment of French-built tanks under Col. George S. Patton. Col. William "Billy" Mitchell directed the heterogeneous air force, composed of American, British, French, and other units, in what proved to be the largest single air operation of the war.

The battle plan was based on a three-pronged assault. Two American Corps would make the main attack against the southern face of the salient. On the right was I Corps (Liggett), covering a front from the village of Pont-à-Mousson on the Moselle River westward to Limey; on the left would be IV Corps (Dickman) with its divisions deployed along a line between Limey westward to Marvoisin.

The secondary thrust by V Corps (Cameron) was directed against the western face of the salient, which ran along the heights of the Meuse River from the village of Mouilly north to Haudimont. A holding action was to be mounted by the French II Colonial Corps against the apex, in order to keep the enemy pinned in the salient. First Army reserve would consist of three American divisions.

Dickman's IV Corps was deployed north of the Gironville–Pont-a-Mousson Road, with the 89th Division on the extreme right flank and

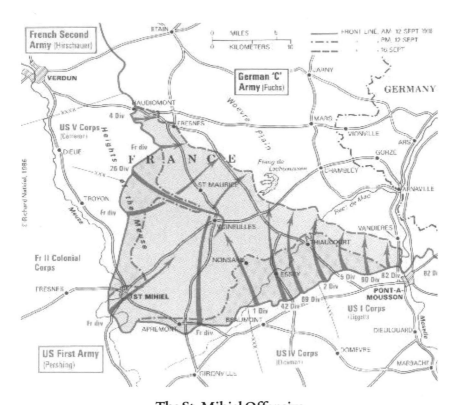

The St. Mihiel Offensive
Source: Atlas of American Military History

next to the 2nd Division, which was itself on the left of I Corps. The 42nd "Rainbow" Division, with the brilliant Brigadier General Douglas MacArthur now commanding an infantry brigade, was in the center. The 1st Division was on the left.

Defending the salient was German *Army C* (Fuchs), consisting of eight divisions and a brigade in the line, with two divisions in reserve. Directly opposite the trench lines of the 89th Division were the German *77th* and *10th Divisions*. The Germans had actually begun a step-by-step withdrawal from the salient only the day before the offensive began, but American intelligence hadn't picked up the movement.

The plan called for the 89th Division, now commanded by Major General William Mason Wright, a highly respected officer, to attack east past the town of Essey to a point northeast of Thiaucourt. **(Q)** The division's 177th Infantry Brigade, commanded by Brig. General Frank Winn, was to lead the advance from the right with Rose's outfit, the 353rd Regiment, spearheading the attack.

As the order to attack drew near, Rose cautiously crawled up to the top of the trench dug close to the road and peered through his binoculars. By the moonlight, he surveyed the terrain. To his right was the village of Limey and directly ahead, just past the wheat field, was the Mort Mare forest, strongly fortified and considered one of the St. Mihiel salient's key defensive positions. To the east of the woods was a high bare ridge, known as the Promenade des Moines, and beyond his line of sight and along the planned line of advance were the Bois de Euvezion and the Beau de Beau Vallon, both dense wooded areas. Out in the open and within plain view were two heavily fortified and well-defended enemy machine gun positions at the Ansconcourt and Robert Menil Farms.

As his platoon prepared for battle, the final plans that would decide Rose's fate and that of thousands of others, were being made at 177th Brigade headquarters. Considering the history of bloody frontal assaults that had characterized most of the war so far, Winn's plan was inspired. It called for an advance to the right of the Mort Mare position, putting his men in position to outflank the enemy from the east and clear out the trenches from the rear. Two battalions (the 2nd and 3rd) of the 353rd Regiment would lead the advance over the open ground, with Companies B, C, and D of the 1st Battalion following and then peeling off to clear each of the three lines of enemy trenches. Company A would maintain contact with the 2nd Division on the left of I Corps.

The "big picture" and plans of the high command meant little to Rose and his men. They were by now fully drawn into the horror of the trenches. Their lives were defined by the rhythms of the Western Front: artillery bombardment, trench raids, snipers, and their constant companions: mud, rats,

---

Q Major General William Mason Wright (1863–1943) dropped out of West Point, enlisted in the Army, and served in the Philippine Insurrection and the Spanish American War. He was appointed a Major General in the National Army on August 5, 1917. He commanded the 35th Division from its formation in September 1917 until June 1918, including combat in the Vosges Campaign under British command, before taking command of the 89th Division. At war's end he led I Corps in the drive to the Rhine. He was highly regarded by Leonard Wood, as well as by the Allies, especially Field Marshal Sir Douglas Haig, OC, British Expeditionary Force.

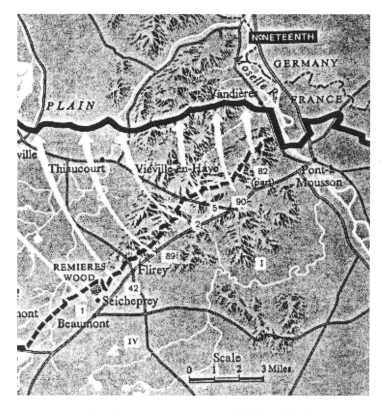

I and IV Corps Sectors, St. Mihiel Offensive

Source: American Heritage, World War One

lice, and fear. The men covered up their lack of actual combat experience
with the normal bravado and the recklessness of youth. They mocked death
in the trenches and tried to hide the horror, but they were also able to see
the moments of humor in their miserable predicament.

As the regiment moved up to occupy the front line trenches, in some
places they discovered "treasures" left behind by the previous owners: the
Germans. Corporal Andrew Hess and his buddies of I Company discovered
several kegs of carrot beer in the abandoned dugouts.

> We rolled the kegs up the hill and took our hatchets and knocked the
> bung out, took our mess kits and caught the damned stuff as it came
> out. It was pretty good beer, but we were only 28 miles from the

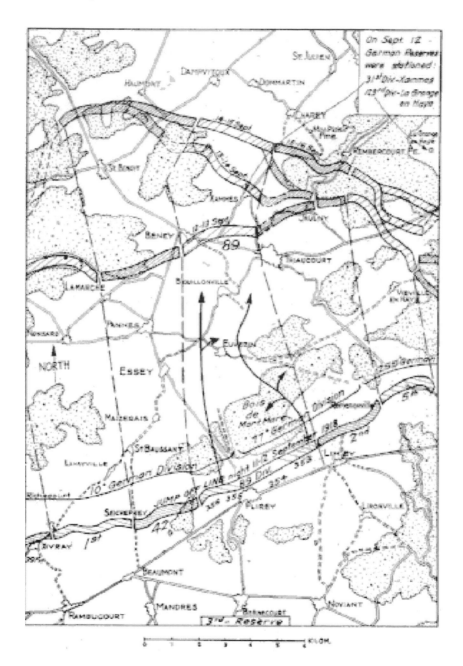

89th Division, St. Mihiel Offensive
Source: History of the 89th Infantry Division

Germans that we'd run out of there, and they knew every foot of ground, so our dugouts didn't do us much good. And Bradshaw, my buddy, and I had nailed on to a feather bed that we put in our dugout, and then we went back to drink beer, and there was a direct hit, goddam, and the feathers just flew. And the boys said, "There goes Hess and Bradshaw." And we said, "No they're here drinking beer with you." We made as much fun out of it as we could. Which wasn't fun, by a hell of a ways.[20]

Pretty soon the joking and laughing stopped. At 0500 hours on September 12, 1918, after a devastating four-hour artillery bombardment, Maurice Rose was crouching in his trench right in front of the village of Limey. Huddled among his men, he moved among them, checking their equipment and speaking quiet words of encouragement, calming their nerves as well as his own. The 1st Battalion, commanded by Captain Clay Crump, was ready to jump off. Company A was on the extreme right of the regiment, the right-flank guard of the entire division. Company B would "mop up" the trenches along the south edge of the Mort Mare woods in the first wave of the attack, while Company D would clear the center of the woods in the second wave. Company C would clear out the upper portion of the Mort Mare and the western part of the Bois de Euvezin in the third and final wave.[21]

At the appointed moment, the barrage suddenly lifted. For a few moments an eerie silence settled over the battlefield and was suddenly broken by four loud blasts from the company commander's whistle. It was the signal to move forward. With a wave of his arm, and clutching his Colt .45 automatic, Rose screamed over the din of battle "follow me!" and led his frightened men "over the top" and into no man's land. The St. Mihiel offensive was underway.

Each company moved forward in order, veering off to clean out the trenches. The enemy's 77mm guns and trench mortars exploded among the advancing men with high explosives, and as they crossed the ground in front of the enemy trenches, the deadly rattle of machine guns and sharp cracking sound of rifle fire could be heard over the shell explosions. Rose maintained the line of advance, leading his doughboys forward even as men fell around him or disappeared in the explosions. As they reached the trenches and infiltrated them from the rear, there was heavy hand to hand fighting, and large numbers of prisoners and machine guns were captured. Pershing's emphasis on "open warfare," the aggressive use of rifle and bayonet, was paying off.

There were many acts of heroism in the advance, and numerous soldiers of the 353rd were cited for exceptional bravery on that first day. Among them was 2nd Lt. J. Hunter Wickersham; mortally wounded by shell fragments, he refused to be evacuated and kept firing at the enemy until he collapsed. He was awarded the Medal of Honor, posthumously.[22] **(R)** Rose was Wickersham's friend; they had enlisted together in Denver, graduated from the same First Officer Training Camp at Camp Funston, were in the same infantry training company, and had both been assigned to the same battalion of the 353rd Regiment when it was first organized.

The momentum of the initial attack carried the Americans to their first day's objectives very quickly, and Rose's battalion then assembled at the north edge of the Bois de Euzin to support the 3rd Battalion. Company A was still anchoring the flank of the whole division, while Company B moved up to the front line of the regiment. Every outfit in the 177th Brigade moved out toward the village of Xammes, the First Army's initial objective. After midnight, Rose and his men moved into the town, which had been evacuated but was still on fire, and made contact with the 3rd Battalion, which had led the advance.

The first day's attack went so well that Pershing ordered a speedup in the offensive. By the morning of September 13, the 1st Division, IV Corps, advancing from the southern face of the salient had linked up with the 26th Division, V Corps, moving in from the west. Before evening, all objectives within the salient had been captured. At this point Pershing halted further advances so that the position could be consolidated and the bulk of the American units could be withdrawn for the coming offensive in the Meuse–Argonne sector.

The battle was declared a victory, with the Americans bagging 16,000 prisoners and 250 guns at a cost of 7,000 casualties, about the same number they inflicted on the enemy. Pershing had eliminated the long-standing threat of an attack on the rear of the Allied fortifications at Nancy and Verdun, greatly improved the security of Allied lateral rail communications, and opened the way for a possible future offensive to seize Metz and the Briey iron fields.[23]

While this first major operation of the twentieth century by an American Army under its own command met its goals in less than thirty-six hours, it was not quite the easy stroll that some descriptions suggest.

R A second officer of the regiment, 1st Lt. Harold A. Furlong, won the Medal of Honor for actions on November 1, 1918, during the Meuse–Argonne Offensive.

At various places, especially on the IV Corps front—where Rose's regiment was engaged—the fighting was intense and at very close quarters.

The fighting was fierce on the second day as well, and the artillery and mortar fire was especially heavy, causing most of the American casualties. While many Germans had already been withdrawn, the enemy guns had not been pulled out of the salient. While the German guns would soon be war booty, on the second day they were still taking a terrible toll. During the two-day battle, the 89th Division suffered 833 casualties, including 217 men killed in action. The losses in Rose's 353rd Regiment from September 12 to 16 reached 150, with 88 men killed in action, or more than 40 percent of the division's dead.[24]

But whatever the official or popular assessment, for Maurice Rose the battle of St. Mihiel, and his Great War experience generally, was a profound and defining event, both professionally and personally. During a furious mortar and artillery barrage on September 13, 1918, Maurice Rose was wounded by shrapnel, also suffering a concussion. At first, he refused to be evacuated, directing the stretcher-bearers to remove others more seriously wounded than he was.

It was one of the first examples of his life-long conviction that it was only by visible acts of personal courage and public demonstrations of bravery that a leader can inspire his men and imbue them with fighting spirit. Eventually, however, he collapsed and was evacuated to the rear. More than twenty-five years later, in command of 3rd Armored Division and close to the front, he was hit a second time by shrapnel and again refused to be treated until all those who had been wounded were treated or evacuated.[25]

At the front-line first aid station, the medics were overwhelmed with the volume of wounded men. They looked quickly at the bloody officer and told him that his injuries would keep him out of action for at least a few months. They dressed his wounds, tagged him, and eventually he was evacuated to the 89th Division Base Hospital behind the village of Flirey.

Unlike most soldiers, however, who dream of clean sheets, the company of nurses, warm food, and what, in the next World War was called the "million dollar wound," Rose was unable to accept the idea that he would be out of action. Perhaps sensing that the war was moving to a rapid close and his chances for glory were slipping away, and hearing that his outfit was headed back to the front, he left the hospital in late September and rejoined his regiment.

While he was later rebuked for this headstrong action, apparently it left no permanent blemish on his record. After getting back to the front, he fought with his regiment in the second stage of the bloody Meuse–Argonne Offensive, when the 89th Division, now assigned to V Corps (Ligget), was brought in the line at the beginning of November. The role of the 1st Battalion in this battle was relatively minor, and it was mostly held in reserve.

Sometime between the time he was wounded (September 13) and the date it was reported (September 16), or, sometime after he left the hospital without authorization, his parents received the dreaded official War Department telegram.[26] It began with the shattering, simple phrase, "We regret to inform you that your son, Lt. Maurice Rose, has been killed in action." Rose's parents were devastated. Sam replayed in his mind the words he had spoken to his boy on their last night together: "You'll probably be killed." It was as though he had passed sentence on his own son.

Arnold was serving in the Marines and could not be present, and his parents were already in the midst of the thirty-day mourning period, when they received another telegram informing them of the terrible mistake.[27] Maurice was back in action, and while that was far from assurance of his safety, at least he was still alive just as the war was winding down. But something had changed—although it would be decades before anyone knew fully what had happened.

As terrible as it is to suffer wounds, and as important as one's first battle is to a professional soldier, these were not the only dramatic events in Maurice Rose's life during the last two weeks of September 1918. Sometime after being wounded at St. Mihiel—or perhaps even before—he had made a major decision that would alter the course of his life and lead to questions, confusion, and even bitterness, after his life was over.

While still in the hospital, and either voluntarily, or possibly in response to some routine inquiry which was dutifully recorded, on September 26, 1918, at the Base Hospital, Maurice Rose declared to Captain D.A. Thom of the Medical Corps that he was a Protestant. The statement, along with five others about his religious preferences spanning two decades over the course of his career, became part of his official Medical Record File #55A. **(S)**

S The six declarations vary as to specificity of stated denomination. The first (9/28/18), third (1/8/27), fourth (11/16/30), and fifth (6/16/31) entries simply say "Protestant." In the second (6/22/23) he describes himself as "Methodist," and the final entry (2/11/41) records his religion as "Episcopalian," which was the denomination of his wife Virginia. The "official" investigation into Rose's religion resulted from several inquiries made in 1949, including a request from his brother

It is quite possible that he was making his first "official" declaration of Christian faith at the same time that his parents were mourning, sitting in grief on low stools, their garments torn, the mirrors in their home covered, while their many friends, both Jews, and Gentiles, stopped by to offer words of condolence.[28] **(T)** The irony of such a coincidence is overwhelming; among some very orthodox Jews, when a child leaves the faith, parents go into mourning. While that did not happen in the Rose family, it is not difficult to imagine the mixture of pain and relief Sam and Katy would have felt had the correcting telegram and news of their son's statement of Christian faith arrived simultaneously. As it was, we don't know when (or if) his parents ever learned of his formal statements.

The history of battlefield conversion is long, and World War I in particular is rich in examples of men changing their faiths for all kinds of reasons. The history of Jews professing Christian belief is also long, and the reasons for the pretense are equally diverse. But put simply, there are only two possible explanations: one, that his "official" statement was related to his career ambitions, and two, that the statement of belief was sincere. It is impossible to know exactly what was in the mind of Maurice Rose on September 26, 1918, what his true motivation might have been, or how deep this stated change of faith really was. He left no written explanation or description of these declarations. If he ever shared his feelings about religion with those closest to him—apart from his parents or brother—we have no evidence about what he said.

While the Rose family could hardly be described as objective, their anecdotes, especially those recalled just after Maurice's death, support the first view. While no one could describe Rose's life after joining the Army as a model of traditional Jewish observance, it appears certain that he retained at least a minor connection to his religious past. His father, mother, and brother each told interviewers and friends that during his long and solitary years of service, Maurice's letters home included Hebrew

---

Arnold and his widow, asking for clarification about the status of Rose's final resting place and the type of religious marker over his grave. The citations about his religion quoted in the correspondence were taken directly from Rose's 201 file, the original of which is now lost.

T The "correcting" telegram arrived approximately two weeks after the first had been received. Assuming the first telegram was sent between the time Rose was wounded and the time it was reported (September 13–September 16), the second would have reached Denver around September 28, the date of the first declaration of Rose's Protestant faith.

and Yiddish greetings, especially at holidays and festival times. They especially remembered that he quoted from the *Haggadah*, the text celebrating freedom from slavery read during the *Seder*, or Passover Dinner.

Besides the testimony of his family, Rose's public actions (or lack thereof) also speak to an equally minor commitment to Christianity. There is no evidence, except hearsay, that he ever underwent any type of formal conversion process. The use of several different Christian denominations in his "official" declarations of faith over a twenty-year period, especially use of the term "Protestant" suggests, at a minimum, an indifference to (or ignorance of) the subtleties of denominational differences. The last description as "Episcopalian" is almost certainly related to his wife's background. But it is striking he did not discuss religion during courtship, or even inform his bride that he had been born Jewish until their wedding day![29] In the event, it had no apparent impact on their very strong marriage. In fact, when he married Virginia Barringer in 1934, the Protestant Chaplain at Fort Davis, Panama, married him.

In later years, Rose displayed no particular preference for religious service attendance as a Commander. Lt. Colonel Wesley A. Sweat, G-3 (Operations) of the 3rd Armored, and a frequent companion, recalled that he and Rose "often attended religious services on the front lines, regardless of the denomination, and we attended all manner of services." Sweat did not know Rose's religion at the time but remembers that after the war, Lt. Col. Andy Barr, G-2 (Intelligence) said he knew that Rose had been born Jewish.[30] Still, he never revealed that fact before his officers, even when one might have reasonably expected some kind of reaction.

At the division HQ at Prym House in Stolberg, Germany, during the long stay in late 1944, the General Staff officers often gathered for dinner with their Commander when possible. Lt. Col. Boulger recalls that the Chief of Staff sometimes passed anti-Semitic remarks and jokes. As the senior member of the staff, this officer worked more closely with Maurice Rose than anyone else. Yet Rose never betrayed any emotion, nor did he ever rebuke the officer, or in fact, say anything. No one else made any comment, and the conversation would then turn to something else. The officer served loyally throughout the whole war, and Rose apparently never held the comments against him.[31] Maurice Rose had long before inured himself to overheard anti-Semitic jokes and other slurs.

But the most intriguing piece of evidence of all is his reported decision to have his son circumcised, calling in a rabbi from Louisville, Kentucky, even though, as the son of a Christian woman, he knew his son was not

Jewish.[32] **(U)** At the same time, he gave that son his own first name, something that practicing Jews almost never do. **(V)**

Perhaps the answer is simple and without psychological dimensions. It must have already been clear to the eighteen-year-old Rose that the Regular Army Officer Corps was, as Patton biographer Carlo D'Este describes,

> . . . all white, strongly upper middle class, overwhelmingly Anglo-Saxon Protestant, conservative in its political views, and tainted by an institutional anti-Semitism and racial bias."[33]

Rose was not the only young man to conclude that identification as a Jew was inimical to advancement in the Army. West Point Cadet Mark Clark, whose mother was Jewish, made a more dramatic gesture than Rose. He had himself baptized as an Episcopalian in the Academy Chapel. As his biographer, Martin Blumenson, observed,

> This dispelled trifling or troublesome ambiguities, for military men were far more comfortable when they could firmly categorize people and things. He perceived, whether vaguely or clearly, the structure of American society and the advantage of being Protestant with an Anglo-Saxon name.[34] **(W)**

Prejudice and open hostility against Jews and blacks were common in both the Regular Army and the general society in the early twentieth century and were often aggravated by outside events, like the Dreyfus Affair in France. It was not unusual in the officer's mess for idle dinner table talk (like that at Prym House) to include racial insults and jokes. There were even more insidious attitudes present in the Officer Corps, comparable to the worst anti-Semitic attitudes of European soldiers.[35] In such an environment, Rose no doubt realized quickly—as did Clark—that his prospects for advancement

---

U The children of Gentile women are not Jewish unless formally converted according to Jewish law.

V The traditional practice among Jews is to name children after deceased family members, especially before the full emergence of a Reform movement in Judaism during the last half of the twentieth century.

W Mark Clark rose to four star rank and commanded the 5th Army in Italy during World War II.

and promotion would be minimal if he were to continue to practice his religion openly, or publicly acknowledge that he was a Jew. He had already intentionally lied about his age to pursue his military ambitions, so he apparently was prepared to make false statements to enhance his career.

Years later, after reaching the pinnacle of his career, he was still sensitive about his press coverage and how he was characterized. During late 1944, Major Haynes W. Dugan, in his role as Division publicity officer, was often a witness to Rose's PR savvy. While he was aware that the Denver papers described him as a "Jewish" General, Rose did nothing to support that portrayal. On at least one occasion, he avoided a one-on-one interview by correspondents from the Jewish Press and left the reporters—who had journeyed from the United States for the interview—cooling their heels in his outer office where Dugan gave them a standard briefing.[36]

The bulk of evidence, then, supports the notion that the verbal statement of faith was not based on any strong religious beliefs. There is no significant or tangible support for the idea that Rose underwent a true, transforming conversion to Christianity. There are no surviving letters or journals that describe his innermost thoughts, and he was not a man to easily share such deep confidences. The only witness who could shed light on his deepest beliefs, his widow, never spoke about the subject to her son, or anyone else that we know of during her lifetime, nor did she leave behind any written account. **(X)**

Still, Maurice Rose was a soldier, and he knew that soldiers often die in battle. The only evidence we have—circumstantial though it may be—that his statement of Christian faith was sincere is as simple and as stark as death. He knew that if he fell, he would sleep forever under a cross on foreign soil. But that is not entirely compelling either for there are still two interpretations: First, that is what he sincerely wanted if he was killed, or second, he was indifferent to what symbol marked his grave.

He probably had no strong feelings about death itself and viewed it merely an "occupational hazard." If he were buried on foreign soil his family (especially his parents if they survived him) would be spared the pain of praying over a grave marked by a cross, so what did it matter what symbol marked his resting-place? He was wrong—tragically wrong—about that judgment. As it turned out, even the marker over his grave would give rise to controversy and pain to those who survived him. What seems most likely is that, like Mark Clark, he cared very little for formal religion of any sort.

X Mrs. Virginia Barringer Rose passed away in San Antonio in February 1997 at the age of eighty-three.

After the Armistice on November 11, 1918, Rose served in the Army of Occupation and probably remained with his regiment until June 19, 1919, when he was honorably discharged. His official record suggests that he was separated from his regiment while still in Europe, although that would be highly unusual. It specifically says he "returned to the United States in January 1920," so, if true, he probably spent some time touring the Continent, perhaps visiting the battlefields of the recent struggle and enjoying the remaining pleasures of the war-weary capitals and cities of the Old World.

Maurice Rose's first experience of war was in a division that earned great credit on the battlefield. The high level of training, fighting spirit displayed, and the competence of the 89th Division was exemplary. Of the ninety Medals of Honor awarded to men in Army ground units during World War I, nine were awarded to men of the 89th Division, including six posthumously. No National Army division received more. Among the officers who served in the division were several who later achieved very high command, including Colonel John C.H. Lee, division Chief of Staff, who later ran the Services of Supply in the European Theater of Operations during World War II. **(Y)**

As a model for a future brigade and division commander, Rose's experience with the 89th Division was perhaps the best he could have hoped for.**(Z)** The achievements of his first regiment were no less glorious. In addition to the three American Campaign Streamers awarded for service in World War I, the 353rd Regimental flag also carried a French Streamer embroidered with the legend *St. Mihiel*. The 353rd Regiment was the only one of the four regiments assigned to the 89th Division to be so honored.[5] Finally, for its service in World War I, the entire regiment was awarded the French *Croix de Guerre* with Palm. In addition, two members of the regiment were awarded Medals of Honor, one posthumously.

Y Lt. General J.C.H. Lee graduated from West Point in 1909. He was quite possibly the least popular officer to serve in World War II, earning the nickname "Jesus Christ Himself," for his absolute dominance—some might say arrogance—in his handling of the Services of Supply in the ETO.

Z Other statistics of war earned for the 89th Division a place of honor in the final calculation of the American contribution to victory. It ranked third in the number of enemy soldiers captured (5,061), fifth in the distance advanced against the enemy (twenty-eight miles), thirteenth in the number of days in combat (twenty-eight), and fourteenth in the total casualties suffered (7,291, including 1,433 killed in action).

Emblem of the 89th Infantry Division

Maurice Rose had also forged a lasting connection with Kansas. Several times during his career he returned to Ft. Riley as both student and teacher and was reminded of many of the early defining moments of his life as a soldier. Kansas was his first "professional" home in a career that spanned almost three decades. While an officer in the 353rd Regiment, he experienced the terrors and exhilaration of combat for the first time, witnessed the devastating impact of poison gas, and led a platoon of men in two pivotal battles in American military history.

In the first major war fought by Americans on the world stage, he had suffered wounds and the terrible loss of men under his command. In addition to the Mexican Service Ribbon, on his blouse he now wore the Purple Heart, the World War I Victory Medal with three clasps (Lorraine 1918, St. Mihiel, and Meuse–Argonne), and the Army of Occupation medal. These were all clear signals within his profession that he had "gone over the top" with honor and had experienced the horror of no man's land.[38] For his bravery in the trenches, and his leadership on the offensive, he had already developed a reputation among his peers as the "shavetail who fights."[39]

And there was something else. He had decided somewhere in the maelstrom of war to cut himself off from his past and the expectations that others had for him. He would set out on his own path. Taking that journey, he would make it possible to realize his dream, a dream out of his father's reach because of his faith and the stagnation and prejudice of the country of his birth. Even as the Army was shrinking, Rose resolved that somehow he would remain a professional soldier.

And he had made another crucial decision. He already knew instinctively that in order to succeed it would be easiest to leave behind the traditions of his ancestors and the outward observance of their faith. They would be impediments to promotion and prevent him from being accepted as a member of the "club."

It would never be enough for Maurice Rose to be an ordinary soldier. It was his character to seek excellence; that had always marked his efforts and drove his ambitions. An outsider cannot rise to the pinnacle in a profession where only insiders succeed. It would be hard enough without a West Point ring, a college diploma, and the lower status of a Reserve commission, but it was certain that an openly practicing Jew could not hope to be a fighting general. In that regard, at least, the New World was the same as the Old. There was only one way. To the outside world, then—whatever the truth lodged deep in his soul—he would no longer be a Jew.

CHAPTER Four

Peacetime Officer (1920–1930)

"The advantages of training for citizenship."
Captain Maurice Rose

B y the time Maurice Rose returned to America, nearly 4 million men had already returned to civilian life, and the Army had shrunk back to its pre-war level. The twenty-year old veteran, like so many others returning from war, had no clear idea of what his future might hold. He still wanted to be a soldier, but the circumstances didn't seem advantageous. Besides, he had already been demobilized.

The mood in the country had changed dramatically, and the patriotic fervor that had carried him and millions of others off to "save the world for democracy" was spent. The human cost and the physical devastation wrought by the Great War had left people apathetic about the military. President Wilson was focused on his visions of world peace and universal brotherhood, and was locked in a battle of wills with a Congress determined to turn inward. Few could envision a future that would require a large, standing army.

Rose's dream of a professional military career, passed down from his father, held since early childhood, and enhanced by service in the Great War now seemed more remote than ever. Pondering his options, Rose couldn't imagine sitting quietly in a college classroom after all he had been through, but neither did he have any firm notion of what else he could do.

These were the things that weighed on his mind as he neared Denver on the last leg of his long journey back from the battlefields of Europe.

It had been nearly two years since he had been home. A lifetime, it seemed, had passed since his parents kissed him goodbye as he left to face the perils of war. He was still not yet able to vote, but the teenager had been transformed by war into a man far older than his years. Like any combat veteran, his eyes looked far beyond the horizon to a place most of us cannot imagine.

Perhaps to escape from thoughts about his future, or the terrible images from his recent past, he headed to the railroad bar car for a smoke. It was a habit he had picked up in the trenches, and one he would indulge heavily for the rest of his life. **(A)** Glenn H. Shaunce, his peep driver, remembers that there were periods when Rose chain-smoked Camels and seemed to live on coffee. This was the extent of his substance abuse. No surviving staff officer ever saw him take an alcoholic drink.

In a chance encounter in the bar car, the general manager of his former employer, the Hendrie & Belthoff Manufacturing Company, recognized him. The older man struck up a conversation with the returning soldier. Perhaps he remembered that Maurice had organized and led the workman's drilling group at the plant, but neither man mentioned it. Maybe both realized that after the brutal reality of war, the civilian drills didn't merit any discussion. The businessman was very impressed by the demeanor and bearing of the tall, proud young man and listened intently to his war experiences. His words must have taken Maurice completely by surprise.

> How would you like to go to work for me as a traveling salesman? You can see the country, and you'll have a good chance to advance in my organization.[1]

For a man without any plans for the future, or money in his pocket, it sounded like a pretty good offer. After all, he had worked in the meat plant before the war and his brother Arnold was already back at his old job there. The sales position did offer an opportunity for travel and promised the chance to make more money than he had ever seen. Rose accepted on the spot. After visiting with his family and a brief rest, he went right to work. He underwent a short period of product and sales training, and then took his first major road trip. He was encouraged, as his customers were receptive and his prospects were good.

A Many of the photographs of him in combat or at his desk, or relaxed and at ease, show him holding a cigarette.

He must have seemed the ideal salesman, handsome, enthusiastic, and articulate with a good war record. His sales territory included Salt Lake City, where he spent a considerable amount of time. With limited funds, like other neophyte salesmen working out of a suitcase, he followed the accepted practice of seeking lodging in a private home. He soon found suitable accommodations at the home of Mr. and Mrs. John Hanson at 1365 Emerson Avenue, Salt Lake City. There, early in 1920, the twenty-year-old met the dark-haired and attractive Venice, twenty-four, who was living with her parents, both pillars of the Mormon community. **(B)**

In spite of their age difference, the relationship blossomed and the couple was soon discussing marriage. Rose continued to travel his territory but was increasingly troubled. He found little satisfaction in the salesman's routine and found it difficult to forget that it was the soldier's life that had brought him the greatest satisfaction. Still, it seemed he had no choice.

But another chance meeting soon ended his business career before it really got started. After several months on his sales route, he bumped into an officer from the 353rd Infantry who had gone "over the top" with him at St. Mihiel and was still in the service, wearing the oak leaf of a major. The officer took one look at his one-time comrade, now dressed in a civilian suit, and made a simple and only faintly critical comment:

Why, Maurice! I'm surprised that a soldier like you would wear that kind of garb.[2]

The remark struck at Rose's pride and was a stinging reminder that he was out of place in any "garb" but that of an officer in the U.S. Army. The fact was that he had never really been comfortable as a traveling salesman. It certainly wasn't the ideal way to begin married life. His fiancé wasn't happy with the idea of him crisscrossing the country and spending long periods of time away. That evening he returned to Salt Lake City and had a long conversation with Venice.

He told her that at one of his visits to the Fort Douglas quartermaster, he found out that there were several openings for company grade officers in the three regiments that had units stationed there. He had already made inquiries and found that it would be possible for him to rejoin the Army

---

B Venice Hanson was born March 14, 1895, in Fillmore, Millard County, Utah. Her parents were John Marius Hanson and Maude Payne.

as a captain and be based near home. She agreed with the idea, although she probably had ambivalent feelings about the life of an officer's wife. What was clear was that her husband-to-be was not happy.

They made decisions. They would marry immediately and he would return to the Army. Together they would build a life together. On June 12, 1920, the couple was married in Salt Lake City by Venice's uncle, Judge William Greenwood.

The newly married Rose went back to Denver, dropped off his sample case at H & B's main office, and said his good-byes to his family. He returned to Salt Lake City and after his honeymoon, boarded the train to New Mexico, where the Army was accepting the enlistment of experienced veterans into the Regular Army officer corps.[3]

On July 1, 1920, Maurice Rose received his second commission in the U.S. Army, this time as a 2nd Lieutenant of Infantry in the Regular Army. On that same date, in an administrative adjustment, he was promoted to 1st Lieutenant and on the following day he was promoted to Captain. These promotions reflected his combat experience and distinguished service during World War I. The postwar records of many of the officers with, and under whom, Rose served over the next quarter century reflect a similar process of administrative adjustment to permanent rank. **(C)** The exhilaration of his recommissioning and promotion would soon pass, however. Maurice Rose remained a captain for the next sixteen years!

What had changed to make Maurice Rose's dream of a soldier's life once again possible? Just before he arrived in New Mexico to "sign-up" for the third time, Congress had passed an amendment to a crucial piece of military legislation. It opened the door for Maurice Rose. The National

---

C The service records of the officers directly above Rose in the chain of command make the point dramatically:

Officer	Unit Commanded	Date	Rank	Time in Grade
D.D. Eisenhower	SHAEF	August 2, 1920	Major	16 years
O.N. Bradley	12th Army Group	June 25, 1924	Major	12 years
C.H. Hodges	First Army	July 2, 1920	Major	14 years
J.L. Collins	VII Corps	June 25, 1919	Captain	13 years
M. Rose	3rd Armored	July 2, 1920	Captain	16 years

Defense Act of 1916, passed on June 3, 1916, was one of the most important legislative initiatives affecting the military in U. S. history. As amended, the National Defense Act of 1920 (the "Act"), signed into law by President Wilson on June 4, 1920, shaped the Army for three decades. It was the foundation upon which the country mobilized for World War II. In fact, it is arguable whether we could have reacted to the German and Japanese threats in time had it not been in place.

Maurice Rose was among the very select group of men chosen from the non-regulars who had served with distinction during the war and were recommissioned. This group made up half the total of newly commissioned officers. The Act also provided that the promotion of officers, except for doctors, chaplains, and other specialists would henceforth be made from a single list, a step that largely equalized opportunity for advancement throughout the Army.

During his first five years back in the service, Rose moved through a succession of postings in the three Regular Army Infantry regiments stationed at Fort Douglas. The newly married couple was not required to move from Salt Lake City, and they enjoyed an atypical period of stability. The disruption in his life was mostly organizational and resulted from the demobilization that followed the war.

His first postwar duty was with the 21st Infantry Regiment, which was then stationed at Fort Douglas, Utah. After just one year, that outfit was transferred to Hawaii, but Rose did not accompany it and was transferred to the 53rd Infantry in October of 1921. Less than one year later, that regiment was disbanded, and during July 1922 Captain Rose joined the 38th Infantry. He remained with this regiment for nearly four years—the longest period he served with any one unit during his entire military service. **(D)**

Consistent with the new structure and expanded mission of the Regular Army, military education—of both soldiers and civilians—became much more important than it had ever been. In a very real sense, then, the interwar period was for Maurice Rose a time of intense professional education, both as student and teacher. For a man like Rose, whose formal education was limited compared to his colleagues (especially the ROTC and West Point graduates among the Regulars), the Army's educational system was a kind of "equalizer." One had only to excel in one school to pass on to the next. In addition, during the interwar years, he was often in

---

D The 38th Infantry called "The Rock of the Marne" won battle honors in World War I and survived the cuts of the interwar years.

academic settings that stimulated his strong passion for reading and learning in both general and professional subjects. **(E)**

The structure of the Army's training and education efforts was a multi-level edifice. At the base were the schools and programs responsible for selecting, educating, and training the professional officer caste. The main burden was borne first of all by West Point and the Reserve Officers' Training Corps (ROTC) programs at various colleges, including some that were essentially military academies. **(F)** Clearly, the graduates of West Point were the "first among equals." But even those newly graduated second lieutenants were far from ready to assume field responsibilities. They were especially inexperienced in actual field tactics and lacked familiarity with many modern weapons, especially airplanes and tanks.

Thus, the next level was a group of schools aimed at the continuing "vocational training" of already commissioned officers. This was the task of the more than thirty Special Service schools that offered advanced, largely tactical training specific to the requirements of the individual branches of the service. These schools, i.e. Infantry, Cavalry, Field Artillery, etc., trained both officers and enlisted men, as well as civilian reservists at Army posts and via extension courses. There was some crossover (Marines attended the Infantry School, for example) but most of the attendees were from the branch of the Special Service school.

At the highest level of the system were the three General Service schools, regarded as the pinnacle of the Army's educational system, the equivalent of civilian "graduate schools." The apex of the pinnacle was the Command and General Staff School, oldest of the three, and located at Fort Leavenworth, Kansas. It educated both company and field grade officers in the principles of division-level command and the responsibilities of General Staff duty. The attendees had already completed their respective Special Service school courses; many also had been instructors, and the student body came from many branches of service. Many of the CGSS graduates—including Eisenhower, Patton, and Maurice Rose—considered it to have been the most demanding, thought-provoking, and rewarding educational experience of their lives.[4]

E During 1920–1940, Maurice Rose spent nine years in the Army's schools or in training or professional education programs, including assignments as both student and instructor. This was typical of the interwar Officer Corps.

F The Citadel, Norwich University, and VMI are several examples of institutions which offered commissions to its graduates, including some—for those who graduated with high honors—in the Regular Army.

The service records of Maurice Rose and his comrades who served in the interwar period and rose to high command in World War II all have a striking similarity. There is a kind of pattern in each record: posting with units in the field—both in the U.S. or overseas—punctuated by stints as students and teachers at the Army's schools, the ROTC, and National Guard units.

For a man like Maurice Rose, the emphasis on education was a real gift, as it both stimulated and fed his hunger for learning, filled the gap in his formal education, and gave him a chance to excel. He was, in many ways, a product of the Army's educational system. As he had never attended college—a potential major drawback to his career—he probably viewed the Army schools as his way to demonstrate that he was as smart as any one of his colleagues. The fact that he attended two out of the three General Service schools, after excelling at his two branch Special Service schools, testifies to his competitive performance.

In the first signal that Rose's abilities had already been recognized, and that he had been marked for higher command, he was selected to attend the Infantry School at Fort Benning, Georgia, during the 1925-1926 academic school year. By the time Maurice Rose arrived at the Infantry School, its reputation as "the place to be" was already well established. While it was just over six years old, its history can be traced back to 1881 when General William T. Sherman supported the establishment of a "School of Application for the Infantry and Cavalry" at Fort Leavenworth. In 1907, Lt. Gen. Arthur MacArthur, concerned by the decline of marksmanship in the Army, helped establish the School of Musketry at the Presidio of Monterey, California. These were the direct antecedents of the Infantry School.

Fort Benning eventually became known as the "Home of the Infantry." It was understood throughout the ranks that a foot soldier could not expect to advance without completing at least one of the two year-long courses offered: the Company Officer's Course or the Advanced Class (attended by senior Captains, Majors, and Lt. Colonels). Between the years of 1925 and 1927, coinciding with the time Rose was at the school, Col. Frank S. Cocheu was Assistant Commandant, the officer directly responsible for the academic program. **(G)** While the reputation of the school

---

G Col. Frank Sherwood Cocheu (1871-1959) was born in New York and graduated from West Point in 1894. He served in the Cuban Campaign, the Philippine Insurrection, and was a member of the War Department General Staff during 1907-1911 and 1914-1917. During World War I he commanded an Infantry Regiment and Infantry Brigade, and was awarded the Distinguished Service Medal.

reached its pinnacle during the tenure of his successor, Lt. Colonel George C. Marshall, it was Cocheu who established the framework upon which its excellence was built.[5]

One of his greatest achievements was recruiting the finest instructors available, both officers and enlisted men, especially in the weapons and tactics sections. Some students felt that the quality of the instruction, educational methods, and motivation of the students at Benning was in fact better than what they had experienced at West Point.[6] The policy of supporting excellence in teaching was matched by the administration's interest in identifying and nurturing rising stars, like Rose. These practices were continued by Marshall, who drew heavily on his experience at Fort Benning in selecting the men who would hold the highest commands during World War II. Among the exceptional teachers present during the period Rose was a student was Major Courtney H. Hodges, captain of the Infantry Rifle Team. Among his classmates was Captain J. Lawton Collins. The former would later lead the U.S. First Army. **(H)** Collins would command VII Corps, First Army's principal striking force, and become Rose's direct superior and most important sponsor during the campaign in Europe.[7]

When Rose arrived at Fort Benning at the beginning of September 1925, the Infantry School was in the midst of a major expansion. Although funding remained tight in the immediate aftermath of the Great War, barracks for enlisted men, officers' quarters, warehouses, a headquarters building, and other facilities were under construction. Student housing was almost nonexistent, however, especially for married junior officers.[8]

Rose faced more than the usual difficulties. Venice was seven months pregnant. After the formalities, he found lodging in nearby Columbus. Conditions were Spartan and many of the flats were unheated. The road between the town and the school meandered over a nine-mile stretch of a

---

H Courtney H. Hodges (1887–1966) was a member of the West Point class of 1908 but failed mathematics in his first year. In 1906 he enlisted in the 17th Infantry Regiment, receiving an officer's commission in a competitive examination in 1909. During World War I he served with the 6th Infantry Regiment rising to lieutenant colonel and winning the DSC and Silver Star. In February 1943, he was promoted to Lieutenant General, and assumed command of the Third Army. When George Patton was chosen to lead the Third Army, Hodges became Omar Bradley's Deputy. Bradley described him as "a military technician" with "faultless techniques and tactical knowledge." Hodges spent most of his time with the corps and division commanders and when Bradley activated 12th Army Group, he took command of the First Army, leading it until VE Day and afterward.

"ghastly . . . old dirt washboard road" and was described as the "Daily Risk."[9] In spite of the difficulties, Rose was exactly where he wanted to be. His personal life was also on track, and on December 29, 1925, his first son, Maurice ("Mike") Rose, was born at Fort Benning, Georgia.

It was a hard year of field and classroom work—the daily commute stretched the average day past twelve hours—but Rose excelled. He did especially well in the Weapons Section due to his extensive experience with the infantry weapons to be mastered. **(I)** One of his instructors was Omar Bradley, a major who had missed out on combat during World War I, but who was highly respected among his colleagues and superiors. **(J)** Rose was also stimulated by the classroom studies of tactics and strategy. Consistent with Pershing's principles, the emphasis was on "open warfare" and the spirit of the attack, not the static trench warfare that characterized most of the fighting World War I.

Rose, whose most important battlefield experience was on the offensive at St. Mihiel, however, was already thinking about the future. He undoubtedly noticed that the field at Maxwell Air Base was only a few minutes flying time by Jenny and probably wondered why working with airplanes was not part of the training. Similarly, the primitive armored vehicles—mostly leftovers from World War I—were not utilized in the field exercises. Clearly, there were limits to the Army's ability (or willingness) to push experiments too far, and he was frustrated with the rigidity of the instruction.

Still, Rose had completed his first assignment as a student in the Army's educational system, and acquitted himself well, particularly in the areas

---

I The weapons section, whose goal was to qualify each student in every standard issue weapon in the Army, was staffed by a group of very respected NCOs (led by Sgts. Woolf and Magonis). These weapons included the .45 automatic pistol, 1903 Springfield rifle, Browning Automatic Rifle (BAR), Lewis machine gun, 81mm mortar, and 37mm towed field gun.

J Omar Nelson Bradley (1893-1981) was born in Clark, Missouri, graduated from West Point in 1915 (with Eisenhower), and was commissioned in the infantry. During the interwar years Bradley's career followed a pattern typical for officers of his generation. While serving as an instructor at the Infantry School, he attracted the attention of the deputy commandant, Lt. Col. George Marshall. In 1941, he became commandant of the Infantry School, and in 1942 took command of 82nd Division. In 1943 he was promoted to Lt. General and took over II Corps from George Patton. He led II Corps in the conquest of Sicily and in October 1943 took command of First Army for the invasion of Europe. In August 1944 Bradley took command of the 12th Army Group.

where he was strong, like the use of weapons. He attracted the notice of both his instructors and his classmates and, in the tightly knit fraternity of the professional officer corps, that was as important as one's actual academic performance. Rose had done well in his first competition with men whose paths he would continue to cross for twenty years.

After graduation from the Infantry School in May 1926, Rose was reassigned to the 38th Infantry, which was stationed at Fort Logan, Colorado, as the Regimental Plans and Training Officer, responsible for operations (S-3). It was his first major staff job. Just four months later, he was named Post Adjutant at Fort Logan. This type of rapid rotation through a broad range of functions was typical during the interwar period. Major Haynes Dugan, Asst. G-2 of 3rd Armored remarked that the reason Rose was so familiar with the various responsibilities of the men under his command was that "at one time or another he had had every one of their jobs."[10]

As adjutant, Rose was the principal administrative assistant of the post commander, responsible for all paperwork not specifically the responsibility of the line officers. **(K)** His duties included general correspondence, personnel matters, and the operation of the base postal service. Among his daily routine tasks were authoring, authenticating, and disseminating orders—except those pertaining to "combat" or field operations. Essentially, the post's office manager, Rose also prepared expense reports, daily rosters, and supervised all base publications, except for ciphers and codes.

Among his personnel responsibilities was securing replacements, as well as job classifications, transfers, and promotions. Finally, he was responsible for the welfare of the men (not including religious matters) including sports and other recreation. As part of his responsibilities Rose was also the officer principally responsible for Fort Logan's annual summer Citizens' Military Training Camp (CMTC), one of the elements of the Army's system of civilian military training.

Like the other officers' training activities of the period, this program traced its roots back to the Plattsburg movement. Each summer, it offered tens of thousands of young volunteers four weeks of training on military posts. Those who completed four years of CMTC training became eligible for a reserve commission. That supplied the Army of the United States (AUS) with another source of men for the Officers' Reserve Corps and the National Guard.

K An "adjutant" should be distinguished from an "aide," whose responsibilities to the commander are more personal, rather than administrative.

The relationships established during these summer sessions sometimes lasted a lifetime, and the program was another underpinning to the evolution and coherence of the American Officer Corps. For example, H.M. Forde, who served with Rose in the 2nd Armored Division during World War II had strong memories of him that went back to the CMTC.

> In 1921 the War Department began annual one-month Citizen Military Training Camps to increase interest in the Army. I attended the first one at Fort Logan (south of Denver) and my Company Commander was Captain (Inf.) Maurice Rose. In 1930 as a 2nd Lt. (Cavalry) I attended the troop officer's class at the Cavalry School (Fort Riley, Kansas) and my platoon leader was the newly transferred Cavalryman: Captain Maurice Rose.[11]

During the 1927 summer session at Fort Logan, Maurice Rose attracted the attention of the *Denver Post* for his extensive efforts to organize activities for the 576 young men training at the base. Crediting Logan with establishing "one of the most attractive programs of games, athletics, movies, and dancing ever arranged for citizen soldiers" it noted that Capt. Maurice Rose was the "man largely responsible for the camp program."

Reminding its readers that Rose had enlisted at Fort Logan—he was, after all, a "hometown" boy—the article then reviewed the main elements of Rose's career, also noting that he was "the only officer left behind when the 1st Battalion of the 38th Infantry entrained for Fort Sill, Oklahoma." Rose's approach to the program was based "on the theory of a man for every game and a game for every man" and aimed at offering "diversion during all the waking hours of the young soldiers in addition to the military drill. Every type of game from golf to baseball is offered, with the latter most popular."

The patriotic spirit that first motivated him in his boyhood games and civilian drills was not gone, however. He still saw the unbreakable link between citizenship and service.

> "I am happy to see the increasingly large numbers of Denver boys at the camp this year," said Captain Rose. "It is an indication they are seeing the advantages of this training for citizenship."[12]

While Rose expected to rejoin his Battalion at Fort Sill at the close of the Camp in July, his career took another turn in the summer of 1927. He was actually looking forward to the change. His relationship with Venice was strained. No doubt the move back to Denver, close to his family and the strains that must have caused, aggravated the situation. Venice was far away from her supportive family and had the responsibility of bringing up a child almost alone. Perhaps she was beginning to face the very real hardships imposed on an officer's wife, especially the wife of a rising star whose career could lead literally to almost anywhere.

In September of 1927, Maurice Rose, equipped with a high school diploma, nearly a decade of active service, and a fierce intellectual curiosity, became a professor in the Reserve Officers Training Corps (ROTC). Ten years after graduating from the first large-scale officer training program in our history, Maurice Rose headed back to Kansas, virtually at the doorstep of Fort Riley, the original and current "home" of his old Regiment, and site of the Cavalry School. By that time, his first military "school"—the massive Camp Funston cantonment—had been torn down, and all that remained was a monument.

The Reserve Officers Training Corps predated the National Defense Act of 1920. It was centered in three major locations: military colleges, like Norwich University; state land-grant schools set up under the Morrill Act of 1862 (like Kansas State); and private colleges and universities. For decades before the entry of America into the Great War, the Army had appointed 100 regular officers each year as instructors, along with the necessary equipment, for military training of college students. After passage of the Act, the dependence on the civilian components for Army expansion, and the establishment of the Officers' Reserve Corps as a way of retaining college graduates in the Army of the United States, stimulated a larger and better organized college-based program.

By the second year of Rose's tenure, there were some 325 ROTC units enrolling 85,000 students in colleges and universities all over the country. Regular Army officers, like Maurice Rose, were the instructors, and each year more than 6,000 men were commissioned in the Officers' Reserve Corps.[13] A large number of the field grade officers in the 3rd Armored Division were graduates of leading ROTC schools, like Texas A&M, illustrating the rich professional dividends reaped by this relatively inexpensive program.

As the senior line officer instructor of the ROTC program at Kansas State Agricultural College (Manhattan, Kansas), Rose held the title of Professor of Military Science and Practice. In addition, he was head of the department and, consistent with general practice, he held the same academic rank as any department head. In academic matters, therefore, he reported directly to the civilian institutional authorities; in strictly military matters, he reported to the corps area commander.

In performing the duties of his new office, his training as adjutant would prove to be very useful. As at Fort Logan, he was responsible for the preparation of academic and other reports, the keeping of records and other administrative requirements, and was responsible for supervision of the other members of the department as well as their course work. Rose was fully in charge, able to draft rules, regulations, and orders governing his local program and appoint, promote, and reduce in rank cadet officers.

He was required to live on or near the campus. While his opportunities for actually pursuing his own formal course of study were limited, it is logical to assume that he immersed himself in the academic and cultural offerings of the campus.[14]

Still, he was restless. Maybe it was the sight, sounds, and even smell of the horses. Maybe it was the nostalgia of being back at Fort Riley. Certainly his personal life was a major factor. It was at this time that he and Venice separated in late 1928 or early 1929. Taking young Maurice with her, Venice moved back to her parents in Salt Lake City, where her uncle, Judge Greenwood, expedited divorce proceedings.

After this painful choice, Maurice Rose was soon facing another crucial decision. As he neared the end of his tenure as a professor, he changed his career dramatically. After ten years in the infantry, he took a major step back to his roots. Still hearing the call of the boy dreaming of service on the Mexican border, as the new decade dawned, he transferred to the cavalry.

CHAPTER **Five**

The Cavalry Officer
(1930–1935)

"The horse will always get through."

Captain Maurice Rose

O ne month before the beginning of the 1930 academic year at
Kansas State, Maurice Rose received official notification that his
request for transfer to the cavalry had been approved. The paperwork had been expedited by Major Roderick R. Allen, head of personnel at
Cavalry Headquarters in Washington, D.C. **(A)** Thanks to Allen, Rose's first
assignment was to the Cavalry School for the year-long Troop Commander's
course. The two men would remain close for the next fifteen years and
would continue to influence each other's decisions and paths.

It was an indication that Rose's career was progressing well that the
assignment to the Cavalry's Special Service school was approved, rather

---

A Roderick Randorn Allen (1894–1970) was born in Texas and attended the
Agricultural and Mechanical College of Texas. He was commissioned a 2nd Lt. of
Cavalry on November 19, 1916. After service in France during World War I and
in cavalry units and at numerous schools during the interwar period, he was
among the first officers (along with Rose) to transfer to the Armored Force. He
was Rose's predecessor as executive officer of the 1st Armored Brigade and commanded the 12th Armored Division in combat during World War II. After the war,
he also commanded the 3rd Armored Division.

than drawing a field or staff assignment in a line regiment. This was in contrast to his earlier experience, when, after rejoining the infantry, he spent more than five years in various units before attending the prestigious Infantry School. This time, however, he was a mature, experienced thirty-year-old officer with a fine combat record, some modest cavalry duty (albeit in the National Guard), and more than a decade of exemplary Regular Army service. Apparently, his divorce was not a factor in his unfolding career.

The actual logistics of his physical move were easy and there was a minimum of disruption. The Cavalry School was located on the main Fort Riley base, only a few miles from the Kansas State campus where he had lived for the previous three years. He could not have failed to notice the seeming "recurrence" in his situation. He had begun his army service in the Infantry at Camp Funston, also at Fort Riley. The place where he had first been an army instructor was just down the road. Now he was about to begin his career in the regular cavalry at the same place where he first became an officer. If the mountains of Colorado and the streets of Denver had largely molded Maurice Rose's early life, then it was also true that Kansas would leave a mark on him as well.

Service in the cavalry was a renewal of dreams and drew him back to his childhood. The image of men on horses, riding to the sound of the guns, was lodged deep in Maurice Rose's consciousness, planted there in no small part by his father. But the appeal was not purely emotional. He realized early that the wars of the future would be based on rapid movement, large-scale mechanization, and indirect strategy. The cavalry, even the horse cavalry, was the place to prepare. **(B)**

The infantry, strongly conservative, was slow to realize the importance of the independent employment of the powerful new weapons that had appeared during the last war but had not been decisive. Many officers saw tanks and airplanes in purely support roles. They wanted to use tanks, especially, to support the traditional infantry-led attack to break the enemy's front. At this stage of development, very few officers publicly supported the idea of a "separate" armor-based branch because such advocacy could be dangerous to one's career. This was especially true in the infantry.

B Colonel George H. Cameron, designer of the Cavalry School crest and shield, translated the motto of the Cavalry School, *Mobilitate Vigemus*, as "We Thrive by Mobility."

Consequently, many officers, including Rose, concluded that the innovations in thinking and tactics that would be necessary to fight the next war would likely find their most fertile ground in the cavalry. While resistance to change and professional rigidity existed in the cavalry as well, there were officers—men like Chafee, Voorhis, and George Patton—who were already quietly pioneering the concepts and evolving the doctrine that would guide the American armored formations of the future. Of course, excessive zeal without obeisance to the horse could exact a painful price. Brad Chynoweth, an outspoken proponent of mechanization, found that his promotions were slower and his assignments were less than choice compared to his 1912 West Point classmates. Patton, who was more circumspect in his public statements in favor of an independent armor branch, suffered no such sanctions.[1]

The Cavalry School, like its infantry counterpart, traced its roots back to the late nineteenth century letter written by General Sherman in support of a "School for Application of Infantry and Cavalry." In 1884, the Commander of the Army and Civil War Cavalry hero General Philip H. Sheridan called for a more specialized school for men in the mounted service. An Act of Congress passed on January 29, 1887, provided for the establishment of "a school of instruction for cavalry and light artillery" at Fort Riley, Kansas. In 1907 the name was changed to the Mounted Service School and the institution attended by Maurice Rose was by then called the Cavalry School. It had been organized under War Department General Order No. 112 on September 25, 1919, which also established a full complement of other Special Service schools.[2]

There is romanticism surrounding the cavalry and its institutions that has always held a powerful place in the American historical imagination. The popular literature—and even the first motion pictures—is rich in images of the horse soldiers of the Civil War and the great Indian campaigns of the western plains. *Harper's Weekly* and the Hearst newspapers—to name just a few examples—were filled with heroic tales of heroes on horses conquering the West and battling the Great Plains and desert Indians. In 1876, more people probably knew George Custer's name than that of the president of the United States.

The Cavalry School was the very embodiment of these images. When Rose arrived in 1930, with its twilight fast approaching, it was in its golden age. In spite of the early experiments in mechanization of the late 1920s and the unspoken realization that the days of the soldier on horseback were numbered, the cavalryman reigned supreme at Fort Riley. Much of the school's routine was based on that fact and had changed little over the previous half century. Rose loved the rhythms, caring for the horses, the drills, the exercises, the games, especially polo, and the use of weapons while mounted.

The leadership of the school during Rose's attendance was excellent. The commandant, Brig. General Abraham "Abe" Lott, was a distinguished combat veteran and West Point graduate (1896) and was ably assisted by Col. Bruce Palmer, who as a tank commander distinguished himself on many battlefields during World War II. Col. Charles L. Scott, also a West Pointer (1905), was Director of Instruction and had beneath him a group of skilled and motivated professionals.

Among them was Captain Lucian K. Truscott, Jr., whom Rose first met and befriended at the school. Later, as a brigadier general in Sicily commanding CCA, 2nd Armored, Rose was attached to the 3rd Infantry Division, then under Major General Truscott. In his World War II memoir—one of the best to emerge from the war[3]—Truscott referred to Rose as "a close friend."[4] In another memoir of his earlier, pre-war experiences in the Army, Truscott, better than anyone else, captured the spirit, atmosphere, and daily life of what it was like during that last decade of the horse cavalry.[5]

At the school, Rose encountered others whose careers and lives became intertwined with his own. One was Robert L. Howze, a young, well-connected 1st Lieutenant and West Point graduate (1925) and a student in the Advanced Equestrian course. **(C)** There was a competitive edge to their relationship. The newly divorced Rose and the young lieutenant both courted a woman named Peggy, who eventually became Mrs. Howze. Almost a decade and a half later, then Colonel Howze reported to the Headquarters of 3rd Armored as the new commander of the 36th Armored Infantry Regiment. Lt. Colonel Jack Boulger, G-1 or Personnel Officer, knew of the earlier rivalry between the men and thought it might be a problem,

---

C Robert Lee Howze, Jr. (1903–1983) was born in Washington, D.C., and was commissioned in the cavalry on graduation from West Point in 1925. He came from a long line of distinguished army officers, and his father was a Medal of Honor recipient and well-known cavalry commander. "Bobby" Howze took command of the 36th Armored Infantry Regiment in September 1944 and led it for the remainder of the war. He was awarded the Silver Star (with OLC), Distinguished Service Medal, Legion of Merit, and Bronze Star. After the war, he commanded the Armor School and the 1st Armored Division, as well as holding several high-level staff positions. He retired in 1962 as a Major General and died at Monterey, California, in 1983.

but he was mistaken. Both men were happily married by then, and whatever personal feelings remained were subordinated to the demands of war.

After graduation in September 1931, Rose was assigned to Fort Bliss, Texas, as a troop (company) commander in the 8th Cavalry, which was then a part of the 1st Cavalry Division. The commander was Howze's father. The motto of the 8th Regiment—"Honor and Courage"—quickened Rose's blood and commanding a troop in such a famous outfit was the ideal line assignment. **(D)** The routine consisted of constant training and long rides along the shores of the Rio Grande on lonely Mexican border patrols. This was the same terrain over which Pancho Villa had ridden. Maurice Rose had once again returned to a landscape from his past. Years later some correspondents asked him what he wanted to do when the war was over, and in a kind of dream-like reverie, he replied, "Oh, I'd like to go back to Fort Bliss and command a horse cavalry troop."[6]

His stay at Bliss, however, was brief. After one year's service in Texas, Captain Maurice Rose's name came up on the list of available officers for transfer to the Panama Canal Zone, as Post Adjutant of Corozol. A two-year foreign duty posting was a common assignment for Regular Army officers during the interwar period. These locations had much to commend them from a career and personal point of view. Some of the bases were in physically beautiful locations and offered numerous amenities, like Schofield Barracks on Oahu, Hawaii. Others, while not glamorous, had in the past offered a taste of danger, like the Philippines, and the prospect of combat experience and faster promotion. In almost every case, however, overseas assignments were considered a necessary rite of passage.

The foreign stations also had practical professional benefits, especially the opportunity for realistic and extensive training exercises. This activity had been severely curtailed by the Great Depression and the resulting cuts in military appropriations, including funds for field training, which reduced the overall readiness and morale of the army. This, and the disruptions to normal civilian life in heavily populated areas, made it very difficult to organize large-scale field maneuvers in the continental United States. In fact, during the interwar period, the best opportunities for training and maneuvers involving larger units occurred overseas in the fairly sizable garrisons maintained by the Army in less populated areas in Hawaii, the Philippines, and Panama.

D The 8th Cavalry was organized just after the Civil War and played a major role in the Indian campaigns.

Rose had been looking forward to putting his education and experiences to good use in the field, so this staff assignment came as a personal disappointment. After serving as a line combat officer in the infantry and then commanding a cavalry troop, Rose had been delegated once again to the office-bound life of the adjutant. In some ways he had become pigeon holed because of his previous record and competence. He was stuck in the crushing boredom of the clerk's life. Handling transfers and discharges, furloughs and passes, and other personnel issues filled his hours; organizing and maintaining the Army's multiple forms and records were once again his daily routine.

Still, he was a professional and made the most of his situation, performing his duties in an exemplary manner. And, of course, Panama was a relatively comfortable duty assignment with a number of social and athletic diversions. The stables housing the base polo ponies provided one welcome break in the monotony of his work. Another, and far more pleasant distraction, was the presence of the young women who worked in the Canal Zone or on the base. One, in particular, caught his attention. Her name was Virginia Barringer. She was the daughter of Major James Lew Barringer (1892–1935), an officer in the Veterinary Corps then serving in the Canal Zone.

Born in Pittsburgh, Pennsylvania, on July 9, 1912, the vivacious and beautiful young secretary was twelve years his junior, and captured his heart immediately. The couple's family photo album of their time in Panama illustrates an active life together—picnics, riding, boating, golf, and dancing. But the relationship was not without some difficult moments, especially when the couple's thoughts turned to marriage. Virginia's family was not in favor of the union. Perhaps they did not want their daughter to experience the hardships and loneliness of a soldier's wife. It is not likely that Rose's religious origin was a factor, since he only revealed the religion of his birth to his bride on their wedding day.[7]

Whatever the objections of her family, however, the headstrong young woman was not dissuaded from making her own choice, and the couple was married on September 12, 1934, at Fort Davis, Canal Zone, on a cruise boat. **(E)** The marriage service was conducted by Frederick W. Hagan—a Protestant chaplain—and was witnessed by Ralph and Phyllis Schuyler, friends of the couple from the base. After the ceremony, the guests proceeded to the Officer's Club, where Rose's comrades formed a cordon of

---

E Marriage License No. 8728, U.S. District Court for the District of the Canal Zone, Cristobal Division, Registered Date September 15, 1934.

Family photos
(*Source:* Rose Family Album)

honor with raised swords to greet the handsome officer, immaculate in his dress whites, and his beautiful, young bride.

A rare glimpse into the soul of Maurice Rose immediately after his marriage can be found in his own words. In the only professional article that can be unquestionably ascribed to Rose, published in the *Cavalry Journal*, he described the extensive maneuvers held in Panama during late March of 1935. **(F)** Digressing into a description of the night before the onset of the action, he wrote:

> The night of March 24–25, was a perfect tropical night, especially designed for gay caballeros to whisper sweet nothings into the ears of coy senoritas to the accompaniment of the dulcet strains of strummed guitars instead of the typical phrases so familiar to the cavalry picket line.[8]

F There is controversy about the authorship of the only other article bearing Rose's name, a description of the Mons Operation of September 1944 and published in the June 1945 issue of the *Military Review*.

These are the words of a man whose romantic spirit has been more than just stirred.

His full analysis of the actual subject of the *Cavalry Journal* article—the early spring 1935 Panama Canal Department maneuvers—opens still another window into the mind, thoughts, and words of the young officer. The purpose of the corps-sized maneuver was to practice the defense of the Panama Canal Department, and especially its complex of vulnerable locks and supporting installations. Rose described the exercise as "the most strenuous, comprehensive, and instructive maneuvers that have ever been completed under peace-time conditions by any organization of the United States Army."[9] Whether the hyperbole of that claim is justified or not, certainly the scale of the field maneuver was impressive.

The exercise lasted more than three weeks, involved twenty-five-mile forced marches under wartime conditions, and engaged all the units stationed in the Canal Zone, including the 14th and 33rd Infantry Regiments, 2nd Field Artillery, and 11th Engineer Regiments, and the 1st Provisional Coast Artillery Brigade, along with supporting units. Also included was a Provisional Cavalry Troop under Rose's command, consisting of the post's polo ponies and manned and led by the other cavalry men stationed at the Corozol Depot.

There are a number of striking things about the article, not least the picture of Rose's emerging style in combat. After completing his initial reconnaissance, Rose was given the mission to "cover the outpost line and act according to your own judgment and training as a cavalryman."[10] His reaction was enthusiastic: "This is the sort of order we all love to receive. Being given a mission and allowed to work out the details is really a perfect 'setup' which we too seldom encounter." During the campaign in Europe, it was just such a command relationship between Rose and Lawton Collins, his VII Corps Commander, which enabled him to achieve such great success.[11]

Taking advantage of the wide latitude implicit is his orders, and displaying personal initiative and boldness, by the end of the maneuvers, Rose's outfit had distinguished itself and received very favorable mention and credits in the after action analyses. His troop had provided crucial intelligence, defended several vital positions, disrupted the "enemy's" attacks, captured numerous prisoners and equipment, and cut communications and supply lines. In an incident of unbelievable foreshadowing near the end of the maneuvers, on March 27, 1935, Rose led a raid deep behind the lines and captured the commander of the enemy's motor con-

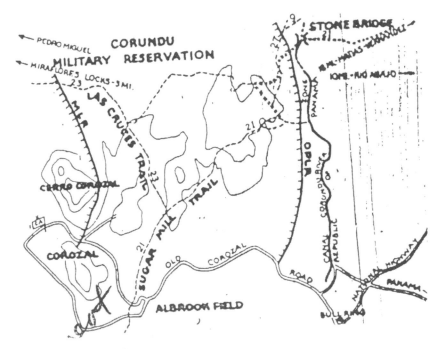

The Panama Canal Maneuver, 1935

voy and engineer pack trains. Almost exactly ten years later the same thing would happen to him, with much more devastating results.

At the end of the article, Rose argues for the permanent assignment of regular cavalry to Panama because of its special characteristics.

> Mechanization is splendid, but cannot operate in the jungles and trails, which exist throughout the isthmus, off the highway. If this small provisional group could have operated in a manner which merited the favorable comments of the Department and Sector Commanders, it is conclusive that a well-trained mounted organization would be highly beneficial to assist in the defense of the canal.

Rose's tone is politic throughout the article. While praising "mechanization" he also pays homage to school and branch: "Every tactical movement would have the approval of the faculty of the Cavalry School," and "The horse will always get through." The last thought is, of course, a clear example of "paying one's dues" by speaking the words expected of a loyal cavalry officer. He was also demonstrating his ability to think and write about the issues of the day. In fact, it later transpired that the only American mounted cavalry charge during World War II took place in terrain and under conditions described by Rose in his article. **(G)**

His career was undoubtedly helped by publication of his *Cavalry Journal* article. It appeared in the July–August 1935 edition, a year before his assignment to the very prestigious Command and General Staff School. Before that next crucial step, however, he would be given one more field assignment. After three years in Panama—a year longer than the typical overseas assignment—in August 1935, Rose was assigned as a troop commander in the 6th Cavalry Regiment, then stationed at Fort Oglethorpe, Georgia. **(H)**

Oglethorpe and its environs hold a special place in the military history of the United States. Numerous Civil War engagements were fought in its immediate vicinity, and it was selected as one of the first sites for the Army's "staff ride" technique of instructing young officers. Fort Oglethorpe was established in 1902 near the northern entrance to the Chickamauga National Battlefield Park just seven miles south of Chattanooga. **(I)** The post was greatly expanded during World War I, and its three separate camps were extended as far southward as the Civil War battlefield. The parade ground became the site of a detention camp for enemy aliens and prisoners of war.

For the newly married couple, Fort Oglethorpe was the ideal place to begin their life together. It was generally regarded as one of the most pleasant posts in the United States and the beauty and grace of its architecture

---

G During the Philippine Campaign of 1941–1942, the 26th Cavalry Regiment (Philippine Scouts), conducted the first and only American horse cavalry attacks during World War II against the Japanese on Luzon at Lingayen and Bataan. During the course of the campaign the regiment was virtually annihilated, and its men finally ate their horses and mules. For their heroic actions the 26th Cavalry was awarded three Presidential Unit Citations before surrendering to the Japanese 14th Army during April 1942.

H The 6th Cavalry was organized during the Civil War and carries on its flag thirty-six Campaign Streamers for actions in the Civil War, Indian Campaigns, Spanish American War, Boxer Rebellion, Philippine Insurrections, Mexican Border, and both World Wars.

I Chickamauga National Military Park was the first Civil War battlefield established by the federal government in 1890. Maurice Rose frequently rode around this field as well as Gettysburg.

lent an air of charm and gentility to the entire place. The 6th Cavalry had been the focus of the town's social life for almost two decades and the routines and practices of the cavalry were strictly honored. Adherence to protocol and tradition permeated the atmosphere. Rose's first obligation upon arrival was a social one. With his beautiful bride on his arm, he called on the post commander, the regimental commander, and all field grade officers and their ladies, presenting his embossed card, introducing his wife, and paying his respects.

Life on the post was very pleasant and there were athletic as well as social diversions. While Virginia sat in the stands, Rose played in the weekly Sunday afternoon polo matches—a passion he had developed and honed in Panama—which were famous throughout southeast Tennessee and northwest Georgia. Equally enjoyable for the young couple were the horse shows on the parade ground, as well as the performances of the drill team, mounted band, and the mounted guard.

And, it was increasingly evident that Maurice Rose was attracting attention in the right places. On New Year's Day 1936, Rose finally reached field grade level when his promotion to major was approved, more than fifteen years after he had joined the Regular Army. His next promotion, and those afterward, would not take nearly so long.

CHAPTER Six

Field Grade Officer
(1936–1940)

"Habits of thought were being trained."
George C. Marshall

As his one-year tour of duty at Fort Oglethorpe drew to a close in the fall of 1936, Major Maurice Rose had many good reasons to feel satisfied. Most importantly, his personal life was idyllic. After a failed marriage and years of loneliness, he had found in Virginia a true life partner. His career was satisfying, and he had within the preceding year achieved field grade rank and seen his work published in the cavalry's prestigious journal. Perhaps best of all professionally, he had been ordered to report to Fort Leavenworth, Kansas to attend the one-year course at the Command and General Staff School (CGSS). Unique in the Army's educational structure, it has been best described as one of the "sacred places of the army's emotional geography."[1] It was a peak moment in his career.

The school at Leavenworth has long been recognized as the apex of army education. It is located on the heights above the west bank of the Missouri River, close to the border between Kansas and Missouri. The "School of Application for Infantry and Cavalry" was established there on May 7, 1881, and should be viewed as the antecedent of almost all of the Army's "graduate" level professional schools.[2] It was originally set up to instruct newly commissioned lieutenants in the most basic field skills. Gradually, it evolved into an institution of education for higher ranks, more along the lines of traditional European academies like Sandhurst, St. Cyr, and the German *Kriegsakademie*. It is distinguished from West Point and other military colleges by the fact that its attendees were already commissioned officers.

As a result of reforms initiated by Secretary of War Elihu Root in 1902, the CGSS soon assumed a position at the top of the Army's educational hierarchy. From the turn of the century until the onset of World War I, the CGSS prepared officers for duties at division, corps, and general staff headquarters, or at levels higher than those already achieved by the vast majority of students. Leavenworth was a place where officers whose backgrounds and career paths had varied greatly came together and quickly learned to work cooperatively within a common system. This is in contrast to the more limited courses of instruction at the Special Service schools, which focused on the skills appropriate to company level officers in a specific branch.

To facilitate the cross-disciplinary approach and to stimulate thinking, both students and faculty were drawn from the full spectrum of the arms and services, creating a diverse mix of officers from the infantry, cavalry, engineers, air corps, and field and coast artillery. There were also foreign students from England, Norway, France, and China among the 237 men in Rose's class.

While somewhat similar on the surface to the German *Kriegsakademie*, the CGSS reflected the essentially democratic nature of the American spirit. It was certainly true that competition was intense for class rankings—especially the top twenty-five students who were named Honors Graduates—but enrollment criteria were not exclusionary. In contrast to the *Kriegsakademie*, a relatively high proportion of regular officers attended the school and virtually all those enrolled graduated. **(A)** But similar to the European schools, Leavenworth was viewed as a crucial career step, one that could "make" a career, or result in the opposite.

The result was the peacetime training of a fairly large body of competent officers all sharing a common vocabulary of doctrine and procedure, rather than a highly educated and exclusive elite, as in the German model. Leavenworth graduates first demonstrated their abilities on a large scale in World War I, most conspicuously as staff officers at American Expeditionary Forces (AEF) headquarters, and as combat commanders at

---

A The class size was typically about 250 officers. Thus, in the more than two decades between the wars, more than 5,000 mostly senior company and field grade officers, almost one third of the authorized total, passed through the school.

the brigade and regimental levels. Their performance further enhanced the school's reputation within the Army.[3]

The Leavenworth teaching methodology had remained fairly constant since the 1890s, when a technique known as the "applicatory method" was introduced. This "case method" system supplemented traditional lectures, memorization, and classroom recitation with exercises in the field that supported the development of analytic techniques of problem solving. The curriculum was rich in map exercises, simulated war games, and staff rides. By the time Maurice Rose enrolled at the school, such field problems and exercises accounted for about three-quarters of the total academic hours.

The purpose of the school was to inculcate in each student the habits and disciplines of critical analysis. Thus, its most important contribution was to help educate a class of "thinking" officers during the austere inter-war years. Many of its most illustrious graduates, including Maurice Rose, shared the reflection of George Marshall that Leavenworth was important, not because of what one learned there, but because it was there that one learned how to learn.[4]

> My habits of thought were being trained. Leavenworth was immensely instructive, not so much because the course was perfect—because it was not—but because (of) the association with the officers, the reading we did, and the discussion and the leadership.[5]

Maurice Rose appreciated very well that his assignment to the school was a major opportunity. His assignment was itself a signal of his growing stature, as he was one of a small number of officers who were assigned to the prestigious institution without having completed the advanced course in the Special Service school of his branch (in his case, two branches).[6] Both he and Virginia knew that assignment to Leavenworth was a major way station along the road to higher command, and that the contacts made there could very beneficial. He took the opportunity very seriously.

One of his classmates and closest friends, Capt. "Pete" Queseda, a bachelor at the time, recalled many years later that he shared a dormitory corridor with Rose and socialized with him during their off-duty time.[7] It is not clear whether Virginia accompanied him during his stay at the school. Perhaps the couple decided that the rigors of the curriculum could best be faced if Rose attended the program alone. For one thing, housing for married students was tight, and it was more than just a rumor that some students cracked under the pressure; divorce, depression, and even suicide were not unknown.[8]

In spite of the pressures, for Rose, who had received all his formal adult education in the U.S. Army school system, Leavenworth was a professional dream come true and a source of personal pride. As someone whose academic talents and interests were both practical and theoretical, the school would hopefully offer exposure to the Army's most fertile ground for the development of doctrine and strategy.

Rose was fully engaged in tracking the evolution of mechanized and armor forces in Europe, and the debates within the U.S. Army about the structure and employment of such forces. The newspapers of the day offered reminders, if any were needed, that these were not merely "academic" questions. Just before his attendance at the school, in March 1936, the German *Wehrmacht* had marched into the supposedly "demilitarized" Rhineland and basically "ripped up" the Treaty of Versailles. At the head of the fast moving columns were armored vehicles, under the command of *Panzer* General Heinz Guderian. **(B)**

Rose's hope that the reality in Europe would provoke "revolutionary" thinking about strategy, operations, and tactics was partly frustrated. The onset of truly innovative thinking and relevance in an organization like the Army are clear mostly in hindsight. During the 1930s, the CGSS was characterized by adherence to the traditional curriculum and methods. The school day was very long, partly designed to exhaust the students, and filled with hypothetical battlefield situations described in conferences, lectures, and field and map exercises. Students issued and executed orders while role-playing staff officers at division or corps level. Often the solutions were generated after many hours of off-duty study and discussion, which added to the fatigue. Much like the training of young doctors, the theory was to create great stress, then require the students to make rapid and decisive decisions and act on them even when completely exhausted.[9]

For most of the field problems there were accepted, or "school" solutions, and in the opinion of Rose and others, developments such as mechanization and close air support received scant attention. Still, there was more than enough material to appeal to Rose's academic interests and intellectual curiosity. Because the scope of the school went beyond just tactics, the program required courses in more traditional graduate education like languages, law, engineering, history, and economics.[10]

B Guderian had been an observer at the U.S. Army's 1927 summer "mechanization" maneuvers.

In some ways, the curriculum was focused on how to break the trench war stalemate of World War I and avoided dealing head on with such inter-service organizational (and political) issues as who should control air-power, and whether mechanized forces should be independent or controlled by the infantry or cavalry.[11] While the overall approach was not especially conducive to student creativity, it did not impede the development of personal initiative or boldness among the leaders who would rise to greatness during the coming struggle. The list of attendees (and instructors) during Rose's year of attendance is only one example of how many of the men who helped win World War II shared the common Leavenworth experience as young captains and majors. **(C)**

C Among the men in Rose's class (Source: 1937 student register) were a large number who held top staff and field commands during the war and afterwards. The partial list below cites the rank, branch at the time of enrollment, and some World War II and post-war achievements:

Cannon, John K., Major, Air Corps (CG, 12th Air Force)

Chidlaw, Benjamin W., Capt., Air Corps (CG, 12th Air Force)

Decker, George H., Capt., Infantry (Chief of Staff, 6th Army, later Army Chief of Staff)

Eaker, Ira, Major, Air Corps (CG, 8th Air Force)

Gruenther Alfred M., Capt., Field Artillery (Chief of Staff, 5th Army, later SACEUR)

Kepner, William, Lt. Col., Air Corps (CG, VIII Fighter Command)

Twining, Nathan Farragut, Major, Air Corps, (CG, 15th & 20th Air Forces)

Wolfe, Ken, Major, Air Corps (CG, 29th Bomb Group, PTO)

In this class there also were six men who commanded divisions in combat, including:

Maj. General Maurice Rose	3rd Armored	8/44–3/45
Maj. General Clarence Martin	31st Infantry	9/44–12/45
Maj. General Edwin F. Harding	32nd Infantry	3/42–2/43
Maj. General Willard Wyman	71st Infantry	11/44 8/45
Brig. General Tony McAuliffe	101st Airborne	12/44
	103rd Infantry	1/45–8/45
Brig. General Edmund B. Sebree	America l	1/43–5/43

Finally, there were many distinguished instructors at the school during 1937, including Major Louis Brereton, Air Corps (CG, 9th Air Force & CG, 1st Allied Airborne Army), Major Wade Haislip, Infantry (CG, XV Corps), & Captain Lucian Truscott, Cavalry (CG, 3rd Infantry, and VI Corps).

The roster of Rose's classmates also includes several officers with whom he would later serve, including Truman E. Boudinot, another cavalryman who served under Rose as commander of CCB, 3rd Armored. But probably his most important personal and professional association formed during his year at Leavenworth was with Elwood R. "Pete" Queseda, then a thirty-two-year old Captain in the Army Air Corps, and the man who would command the tactical air forces that supported his Armored division in Europe.

Like Rose, Queseda had worked his way up without benefit of either a West Point ring or a college degree. He had already received some publicity for his role in the flight of the *Question Mark*, which was piloted by Ira Eaker when, in 1929, it demonstrated air refueling.[12] "Pete" Queseda and Rose were a natural pair. Both "mustangs" and outsiders—one the son of a pious Jew, the other a Hispanic—they quickly gravitated to each other and spent some of their leisure time together, catching a movie or visiting the sights in Kansas City.[13] Rose also took advantage of the stables of the 10th Cavalry Regiment and spent time riding and playing polo as well as playing golf and tennis.

The two men also passed many hours discussing the pressing professional issues of the day, especially the necessity of close air support to successful mobile ground warfare. In fact, Queseda's biographer credits his relationship with Rose as a prime source for the earliest ideas of tactical air support "for which both men would later gain renown."[14] Each found the general approach employed by most instructors to be rigid and excessively fixated on the past.

As professional soldiers, they could appreciate the need for uniformity in a large-scale military education program, but they were concerned with the burning issues of the day. Armored warfare under skies dominated by modern aircraft seemed to the two young officers to be beyond the scope of the curriculum and the vision of most of the teachers. It was not until the very end of the academic year that the field problems started to emphasize "combined arms" operations, including the use of air power to "isolate" the battlefield, and to support armor "deployed far ahead of a main corps body."[15] During these exercises, especially, and in their off duty discussions, the fundamental groundwork was laid for their crucial working relationship during the war, and the basic tenets of close air support for armor were established. With remarkably prescient insight, the school text did note that airpower, while not organizationally a part of the mechanized forces, would be of such great use, in:

executing reconnaissance for the advance and flank security, for use in maintaining control of the columns . . . and for executing battle missions, that it should be considered an essential part of the mechanized combat team.[16]

Rose's experience at Leavenworth was unquestionably among the most important of his entire career. He had been marked for higher command, befriended men whose own careers would be vital to his own, and he had acquitted himself well in competition with the best of his colleagues. The exhilaration, however, did not last long. The routine cycle of assignment in the Regular Army also included dreary, crushingly dull, and personally unsatisfying assignments. After graduation in June of 1937, and a brief furlough, Rose picked up his wife and journeyed to Tyrone, Pennsylvania, for his next assignment as instructor to the 103rd Cavalry Regiment, Pennsylvania National Guard. The brick Armory on Logan Avenue was to be Maurice Rose's office for some of his most difficult years in the service. **(D)**

Tyrone was a dull, backwater, railroad town of about 10,000 people lying roughly midway between Altoona and State College. There were lumber mills, as well as iron and coalmines in the area, and Blair County was a highly industrialized area. For Major and Mrs. Rose, it was a far cry from the graceful charm of Panama, the quiet gentility of Fort Oglethorpe, or the lofty academic atmosphere of Leavenworth. There was a hard edge to service in the National Guard at this time, as it was frequently called in to quell labor unrest in the mines and mills, pitting soldiers against citizens against the background of economic depression and rage.

Times were hard in Tyrone. During Rose's stay in Tyrone in 1938, the rail trolley was closed and the automobile also reduced the importance of the Pennsylvania Railroad main line and short lines, and thus the importance of Tyrone. The Tyrone division of the Pennsylvania Railroad was merged into the Middle division, leading to the dismantling of the yard and shops in Tyrone, and the curtailing of company expenditures in the town. There was considerable unrest, which occasionally spilled over into disturbances.

After experiencing the pinnacle at Leavenworth, Rose felt he was in the wilderness. Only the presence of Virginia, and his deep sense of duty, made it bearable. He also felt a sense of nostalgia. He was back in the National

---

D The Armory was listed in the National Register of Historic Places in January 1993.

Guard where he started so many years before as a boy, and he was immersed in the sights, sounds, and smells of the cavalry. Of course, a great deal had changed since he joined up to chase Pancho Villa. **(E)** Officered and trained by men without Regular Army assignments, the Guard relieved the Regulars of any responsibility for curbing domestic disturbances, a highly unpopular role, as had been made most evident during the Bonus March disaster in 1927. Of course, the Guard's real purpose was to stand ready for immediate induction into the active army in an emergency.

The War Department, in addition to supplying Regular officers like Rose for instruction, also provided large quantities of surplus World War I equipment for training. Fully 10 percent of the department's budget went toward support of the Guard in the years between wars. Guardsmen were required to participate in nearly fifty armory drills and fifteen days of field training each year. While the units were not comparable to active army units in readiness for war, the Guard was better trained in 1939 than it had been when mobilized for Mexican border duty in 1916. On paper, at least, it was the largest component of the army of the United States at the outbreak of World War II.

As the world hurtled toward war, the army intensified its training and education efforts on all levels. While the top command started to build what would become the largest field army in our history, the professional training of field grade officers was not neglected. Those who would soon command the major units of our forces continued to draw assignment to the top strata of the army's educational system. Maurice Rose, already one of the most experienced staff officers in the cavalry, was ordered to Washington, D.C., in September of 1939 to attend the Army Industrial College. That same month the German armor-led *Blitzkrieg* struck Poland "like a planet," beginning World War II in Europe.

The Army Industrial College was the youngest of the General Service schools. It was established in 1924 by John W. Weeks, Secretary of War, to train officers in the skills necessary to manage procurement of military supplies, as well as the mobilization of men, material, and industry to wage modern warfare. The direct administration of the college was the responsibility of an Under Secretary of War.

E During World War I, the Army had absorbed the National Guard, and so the Armistice had required a reorganization. The National Defense Act of 1920 established a new National Guard with an authorized strength of 436,000 men, but the actual peacetime strength generally hovered at about 180,000.

Maurice Rose was enrolled in the last full year course before the school canceled its extended programs. His class numbered about eighty officers and was drawn from both Regular and Reserve ranks and included men from each of the branches of the service as well as a few foreign students. **(F)** While the majority of students had some experience with logistics and supply, there were others who, like Rose, had served in a range of line and staff functions.

Before World War II, the college's graduates had often been posted to offices of the chiefs of the branches, as well as procurement district offices, the War Department, General Staff, Army-Navy Munitions Board, and similar jobs. Rose attended the school during a period when it was obvious to many in the military that our involvement in the European war was fast approaching. Rose and his classmates were in fact the last to enjoy even a minimum of academic "distance." After several shorter courses of three and four months' duration, on December 24, 1941, the War Department discontinued further courses until after the war.

During Rose's year at the college, the pace of events in both Europe and Asia accelerated dramatically. Even during the period of the "Phony War" in the winter of 1940, there were spasms of violence. Denmark and Norway were invaded and conquered, and the naval war generated spectacular headlines. The Japanese continued their sweep through China, and relations with the West continued to erode. Finally, in belated response to these developments, the Americans were mobilizing their energies and resources to build the land, sea, and air forces for our inevitable entry into the world conflict.

As the course neared an end in June 1940, Rose was on the verge of another major career decision. This time he was driven to action in no small part by external events. The news from Europe was even more ominous than when he had first reached Washington. By the time June and graduation arrived, the *Panzer*-led forces of Nazi Germany had crushed their opponents on the Western Front. In a "lightning war," or *blitzkrieg*, thrust spearheaded by Irwin Rommel's *7th Panzer Division*, they had

---

F One of Rose's classmates was Brig. General James E. Wharton (1893–1944), who was mortally wounded by shellfire on August 12, 1944, several hours after he had assumed command of the 28th Infantry Division in the middle of the Falaise Pocket action. Just five days before, on August 6 , Maurice Rose had assumed command of 3rd Armored. Wharton was the only other ETO Division Commander lost in action during World War II.

defeated the numerically superior armies of Belgium, Holland, and France in less than one month and cut off and trapped the 400,000 man British Expeditionary Force at Dunkirk.

Tanks, armored infantry, and self-propelled artillery stood on the shores of the English Channel with only a pitifully few exhausted Hurricane and Spitfire pilots of the RAF blocking their way. It was clear to thinking professionals like Rose that the Germans had shown the way the war would be fought. He was convinced that the final outcome would be decided by strong, independent mechanized forces supported by air power.

He conferred with his friends about his next move. Roderick Allen, who had helped engineer his transfer to the cavalry a decade earlier, was a major sounding board and shared his feelings.[17] For years, the two men had followed the growing debates in this country and abroad about the use of independent armor units on the battlefield of the future. In addition to reading the works of their fellow officers, like Patton, Chafee, and others, they had read and discussed the work of the leading foreign armor theorists—men like J.F.C Fuller in England, Charles de Gaulle in France, and Heinz Guderian in Germany. Each of them had, like their American counterparts, struggled with the frustrations of interwar service, and agonized over how to align their careers with the emerging reality that they saw so clearly.

For the second time in his career, Rose requested transfer to another branch of service, the newly formed armored force. The request was approved, and Rose was assigned as commander of the 3rd Battalion of the 13th Armored Regiment, one of the first units formed in the newly organized branch. **(G)** Rose's Battalion was defined as "Light," or essentially equipped to perform the missions of the cavalry (i.e., reconnaissance, screening, and other fast moving assignments). Roderick Allen was appointed Operations Officer (S-3) of the 1st Armored Regiment, the other striking arm of the 1st Armored Brigade. The two friends were at the very center of the developments that would give rise to the creation of the American armored force and doctrine.

It was clear beyond any doubt that the men in charge had identified Rose as a natural leader of the new armor branch. He was ecstatic. His life was moving in the right direction. He was about to become one of the

---

G The 13th Armored Regiment was redesignated from the old 13th Cavalry Regiment at Fort Knox, Kentucky, on July 15, 1940, as the 13th Armored Regiment (Light), and assigned to the 1st Armored Brigade, the main striking force of the 1st Armored Division.

principal players in the recreation of America's tank forces, and was about to take command of one of its first combat units. Soon, if his perception of world events proved correct, his country would be at war and he would be in the middle of it. And, if that were not enough to make a warrior happy, as he boarded the train at Washington's Union Station bound for Louisville, Kentucky, his wife, Virginia, sitting next to him, was pregnant with their first child.

CHAPTER Seven

The Armor Officer Goes to War (1940–1943)

"An example which reflects the finest traditions of our armed forces."

Citation for award of the Silver Star to Col. Maurice Rose

On July 10, 1940, the U.S. Army created the Armored Force under the command of Brig. General Adna R. Chaffee, Jr., an early, though often frustrated, proponent of developing strong and separate armored divisions. The Armored Force was the direct descendant of the Tank Corps, established in 1917, and commanded by the charismatic thirty-three-year-old Colonel George Patton. As an aide to General Pershing, the dashing cavalry officer had made a name for himself in the Mexican Border campaign. He later commanded the first American tanks to see combat in the St. Mihiel Offensive, during which he was seriously wounded and also won the Distinguished Service Cross.

The end of World War I led to a radical downsizing of the army, and in the case of the infant Tank Corps, the result was even more dramatic. The National Defense Act of 1920 abolished the Tank Corps outright as an independent organization and subordinated tank development to the infantry. For the next twenty years there were only sporadic and relatively small scale attempts to build on the American experience with armor in the Great War, or to keep up with the fertile intellectual and practical developments abroad. These efforts were themselves largely captive to the internecine struggles between the Infantry and Cavalry branches. Outspoken advocates of armor often saw their careers sidetracked, or worse.

There were a number of half-hearted experiments in between the wars. In the fall of 1930, just as Maurice Rose reported for duty at the Cavalry School, the "Mechanized Force" was first assembled at Fort Eustis, Virginia. It was organized as a combined arms unit, including armored cars, truck-drawn artillery, engineers, anti-aircraft artillery, and infantry tanks. The tank company assigned to the force was from the 1st Battalion, 66th Armored Regiment. **(A)**

Chafee lost no time. On July 15, 1940, just five days after assuming command, he began to organize his outfit. His first step was the formation of the 1st Armored Brigade, built around two veteran cavalry formations, the 13th Armored Regiment and the 7th Cavalry (Mechanized) Brigade, both survivors of the mechanization experiments of the thirties. The 1st Armored Brigade became the combat nucleus of the 1st Armored Division, affectionately called "Old Ironsides." The Provisional Tank Brigade, an infantry-based tank unit organized at the same time at Fort Benning, became the nucleus of the 2nd Armored Division. These two units would be the first American armored divisions to see combat in World War II. Over the next several years Maurice Rose would hold important positions with each of them.

One of Chafee's most important tasks was finding the right men to lead and provide staff support for the units of the Armored Force. A number of field-grade officers from the infantry, cavalry, and field artillery had already requested transfer to the new branch, including many of the key commanders who would serve under Maurice Rose. These included cavalrymen, like champion balloonist and athlete Truman Boudinot and proud Texan Leander "Tubby" Doan, infantrymen Bobby Howze and Jack Welborn, the pipe-smoking lawyer Doyle Hickey, and West Pointer Fred Brown of the field artillery.

Now that the war in Europe was raging, the military attaché and other observers' reports started to flow into Armored Force Headquarters and changes followed rapidly. The emerging threat of Hitler's Germany in the late 1930s had already caused the army to re-evaluate the status of its mechanized warfare capability. The German army, backed by the powerful *Luftwaffe*, had overrun Poland in three weeks in September 1939 and forced

---

A During World War II, this Battalion (the oldest tank unit in the U.S. Army) was assigned to Combat Command A, 2nd Armored Division and was for a time under the command of Brigadier General Maurice Rose.

France's surrender in June 1940 after only a six-week campaign. In each case, the decisive factor was the independent *Panzer* divisions, consisting of a well-integrated mix of tanks, mechanized infantry, combat engineers, and artillery capable of mobile combined-arms operations on a large scale. The glue that held the elements together was communications, especially over secure radio and wire networks.

The success of these new formations shocked the War Department into a concentrated effort to create an American counterpart to the *Panzer* division.[1] One of the effects was a quickening of the pace of large-scale maneuvers on the corps and army levels to test various ideas. The newsreel coverage of the maneuvers focused on our lack of military preparedness—images of trucks labeled as "tanks" and men drilling with wooden "machine guns" predominate. The fact remains, however, that major changes in doctrine, tactics, logistics, command and control, and combined arms doctrine all emerged from these large scale and unprecedented field experiments. Many of the most important men who fought and won World War II—including Maurice Rose—were identified as "comers" during these maneuvers. A number of other high-ranking officers whose performance did not measure up were retired or otherwise bypassed for high command.

Less than one month after taking command of the 3rd Battalion, Rose's Regiment participated in the Louisiana Maneuvers of August 1940. The next major field exercise took place in Tennessee during June 1941, and those maneuvers became a major element in the preparation of the U.S. Army for World War II.[2] Rose, who had been just been promoted to Lt. Colonel, was at that time in transition to his first important high-level staff position, having been appointed as executive officer of the 1st Armored Brigade. His personal life was also happy. On January 30, 1941, Virginia gave birth to a healthy boy at the Fort Knox Post Hospital, whom they named Maurice Roderick Rose. His middle name honored his father's friendship with Roderick Allen.

There was no letup in the pace of activity after he assumed the new staff position. He participated in the VII Corps Maneuvers in Arkansas between August 18 and 28, 1941, and the Louisiana/Texas Maneuvers that immediately followed. On September 1, 1941, the 1st Armored Brigade moved to Camp Polk, Louisiana, to participate in the Second Army maneuvers. The brigade then moved to Ft. Jackson, South Carolina, to participate in the First Army Carolina Maneuvers in November 1941.

Rose performed very well in each of the field exercises. His personal initiative and thorough staff work impressed his superiors, who were eagerly looking for men who could command and provide staff support for major formations in the war that everyone now viewed as inevitable. Rose returned to Ft. Knox on December 7, 1941.

Even as the architects of the American Armored Force moved into high gear following Pearl Harbor, there was a bitter irony behind the unfolding events. For the real pioneers, in many ways, it was too late. Although some lived to see vindication, and some few like Adna Chafee and George Patton actually commanded the new formations, other visionaries, like Brigadier General Brad Chynoweth, had been sidetracked because of outspoken support for the revolutionary armored doctrines. **(B)** They could only glimpse the results of their efforts from a distance. Gone forever was the unchallenged notion during the twenties and thirties that joining the tanks would be bad for one's career.

Rose's identification with the Armored Force was now complete. After spending more than twenty years in military backwaters, partly hampered by his National Guard background and lack of a West Point or college education, Rose found himself at the very center of the rapidly growing U.S. Armored Force command organization. By the time of Pearl Harbor, the Armored Force had expanded to three divisions, had established a headquarters, armor school, and support infrastructure that would eventually lead to the formation of sixteen armored divisions by the end of World War II. **(C)**

In mid-January 1942, Maurice Rose was transferred to the 2nd Armored Division at Fort Benning, Georgia, as Chief of Staff. **(D)** Rose arrived during a period of leadership transition. The Commanding General, George Patton, had just received orders to take command of I Armored Corps. Rose's opportunity for extended service under the flamboyant leader would have to wait. Patton's deputy, Brig. General Willis D. Crittenberger, took over. The fact that he opted to retain Rose, rather than

---

B Brig. General Chynoweth was captured in the Philippines and spent the war years as a prisoner of the Japanese.

C Fourteen saw combat in World War II.

D Activated at Fort Benning, Georgia, on July 15, 1940, as part of the original Armored Force, the 2nd Armored Division spent its first two years developing and testing armored tactics and doctrines. It participated in the army's maneuvers during 1940–1941, and in August 1942, began training for amphibious warfare off the Carolina coast. The division gained valuable experience in assault landing techniques during its participation in the invasion of North Africa, which it put to good use in two more amphibious operations, Sicily and Normandy.

**Colonel Maurice Rose after assignment as chief of staff,
Second Armored Division**
(*Source:* Rose Family Album)

name his own chief of staff, speaks to Rose's growing reputation for efficiency and loyalty. Less than one month after arriving at Fort Benning
Maurice Rose was promoted to colonel. After having spent almost sixteen
years as a captain and four as a major, in less than a year and a half he had
jumped two ranks in grade. His boyhood dream of wearing the stars of a
general was no longer an impossible fantasy.

The next six months were consumed by intensive training, especially
field exercises at the platoon, company, and battalion level. Rose was

constantly in motion, at the office and in the field, essentially acting as the general manager of the division, monitoring and directing the General Staff officers, and offering the commanding general advice on every subject. General Crittenberger was a stickler for details—a real "spit and polish type," like Rose—and the discipline and personal appearance of the troops improved.

Another change in command during that spring brought tough talking Cavalryman Brig. General Ernest "Old Gravel Voice" Harmon to the division. Once again, the new commander retained the effective and efficient Rose. As Harmon later remarked, reflecting on his experience with Rose,

> The success of a general, I have had occasion to reflect, depends less on his talent in tactics than upon the choice of a brilliant and resilient chief of staff.[3]

Senator Harry Truman and
Colonel Maurice Rose review the troops, 1942
(*Source:* Rose Family Album)

There was little positive personal chemistry between the two men, however. The plainspoken, gruff, and sometimes profane Harmon, who occasionally liked to loosen up over drinks with his officers, found Rose to be

> ... a cool, able soldier, distant and removed in temperament, and no one could know him well.[4]

During late August of 1942 Harmon was summoned to the War Department under tight security. There he was ushered into the office of the Chief of Staff, General George C. Marshall. With George Patton and other high ranking officers present, Harmon learned that his division had been selected to participate in *Operation Torch*, the first American offensive against the Axis forces in the Mediterranean. That same evening General Harmon weighed down with charts, maps, intelligence reports, and other documents, returned to Fort Bragg.

Immediately after arriving, he took Colonel Rose and Lt. Colonel Lawrence R. Dewey, his Operations Officer, into a small room, swore them to secrecy, and told them of the invasion plans. They swelled with pride. The 2nd Armored Division would be among the first Army units to see action against the enemy. Until the troops were on the high seas, however, these three officers would be the only men in the division who knew where they were headed.

A tough schedule of nighttime exercises followed, including countless crossings of Mott Lake in rafts. There were also more high-level staff conferences. Shortly after dark on September 26, 1942, Generals Harmon and Lucian K. Truscott, Jr. returned together from Washington after one such meeting. Truscott was about to assume a major combat command in the invasion, but he was anxious to see old friends. Most of the officers at Harmon's HQ were old cavalrymen and Rose, whom Truscott knew from the Cavalry School, and the others "spent the evening reminiscing in the way of old troopers."[5]

By November 8, 1942, there was no further need for secrecy. Combat elements of the 2nd Armored landed near Casablanca, Morocco, as part of three assault groups assigned to the Western Task Force under MG George S. Patton. The fighting against the Vichy French, while intense in a few areas, was over very quickly. Limited shipping had kept most of the division back in the United States, and they would not join the advance force until late December 1942. Maurice Rose had remained behind to coordinate the shipment of the bulk of the division's men and equipment to Africa.[6]

Col. Maurice Rose and 2nd Armored officers in a light moment, 1942
(*Source:* Rose Family Album)

By the time he arrived in Africa on Christmas Eve, the fighting had been over for six weeks. At a cost of just over 1,000 casualties, including 337 dead, the 2nd Armored had completed its mission in Morocco on November 11, 1942. The focus soon shifted to Tunisia, where the Americans and British faced the vaunted Germans.

On February 14, 1943, the Germans struck hard. Two veteran *Panzer* divisions of von Arnim's *5th Panzer Army* attacked through the Faïd Pass, then split up to encircle the inexperienced Americans at Sidi-Bou-Zid. They pushed back the 1st Armored Division with very heavy losses, essentially destroying Combat Command A. The next day, a *Kampfgruppe* of Rommel's *Afrika Korps* struck further south at Gafsa. Finally, on February 19, the *10th Panzer Division* attacked through the Kasserine Pass driving the Americans before them.

During the battles, elements of the 1st Infantry and 1st Armored Divisions and other units were torn to pieces, and many formations were overrun and destroyed. American soldiers abandoned their positions, threw away their weapons, and ran in panic to the rear. After a week of very hard fighting and continued heavy losses, the Americans finally halted the

Germans, who then withdrew. The Americans, with British support, succeeded in recapturing the lost ground by February 26.

The Battle of Kasserine Pass was an unmitigated disaster that would continue to haunt the reputation of American arms for years to come. Six thousand men were casualties, including 300 killed, more than 2,500 wounded, and 3,000 captured. Nearly 200 tanks, a similar number of guns, and large numbers of other vehicles, as well as tons of supplies were destroyed or abandoned on the battlefield. In its first pitched battle against the Germans, the Americans were not only defeated but also humiliated. It was "among the worst and bloodiest thrashings the U.S. Army had ever suffered."[7]

One immediate result of the disaster at Kasserine was the "temporary" reassignment of Major General Ernest Harmon on February 20 as Deputy Commander of II Corps. His orders from Eisenhower were to evaluate American command performance, especially that of Major General Lloyd R. Fredendall, Commander of II Corps and Major General Orlando Ward, commander of 1st Armored Division. Harmon's assignment was somewhat delicate, as he was essentially a "spy" for Eisenhower, who was trying to fix responsibility for the debacle. It was not clear at Supreme Headquarters whether the blame lay with the senior officers or somewhere else entirely.

Maurice Rose was with Harmon every step of the way. He toured the battlefield, sat in on the briefings, read the reports, and interviewed the survivors. The evidence of a terrible rout was everywhere. It was a rude shock to men who could not imagine defeat. In this ambiguous and delicate situation, Harmon, with staff support from the taciturn and diplomatic Rose, performed very well. It was the first time that Generals Eisenhower and Omar Bradley were able to observe Rose directly in a sensitive position of responsibility. He helped write Harmon's After Action Report to Eisenhower, which recommended Fredendall's relief from command of II Corps, branding him a "moral and physical coward who was unfit for command."[8]

On March 20, nearly a month after Kasserine, the 1st Armored Division was still driving on Markassy, Tunisia, in an almost ponderous manner. The peculiar command situation was rapidly reaching a crisis. In early April, with the drive now bogged down, it was apparent that the 1st Armored was in very bad shape. The men and officers were tired, frustrated, depressed, and the outfit's reputation had hit bottom. By this time, Fredendall had already been relieved and George Patton, now commanding II Corps, had decided that Major General Orlando Ward also had to go. Major General Omar Bradley, II Corps Deputy Commander, and Ward's friend at West Point, was delegated to deliver the bad news.[9] **(E)**

When the fighting was over near Markassy, on April 5, 1943, Major General Harmon took command of the 1st Armored Division. Col. Rose, Lt. Colonel Dewey, Operations Officer (G-3), and Harmon's aide, Major Rooney all went with him to Tunisia. George Howe, an official army historian, assessed the period when the Tunisian Campaign came to an end as the time when the 1st Armored Division finally "came into its own."[10] On April 6, the division began an energetic pursuit of the retreating Germans, with Combat Command A attacking toward Mateur three weeks later. After the fall of Mateur, Rose was delegated to return for several days at a time to the 2nd Armored Headquarters, in order to share his combat experience with his fellow officers.

Rose was present, as the principal staff aide to Harmon and as observer for the 1st Armored's final drive on Bizerte, Tunisia. It was during the campaign to take Mateur that Rose won his first Silver Star of World War II. The citation is testimony to his style of leadership that became a constant throughout the remainder of his career.

> Colonel Rose proceeding on a mission as observer advanced to the reserve elements of a forward attacking battalion of the Combat Team. Upon inquiring as to the status of the reserve unit, he was informed that they could not advance to the support of the assault company because of heavy enemy fire. Colonel Rose voluntarily encouraged, reorganized, and led them forward and by his conduct inspired the men so that the entire outlook was changed and they followed him willingly and cheerfully to the front, where they were turned over to the proper commander.
>
> Colonel Rose then proceeded to the forward-most observation point and, rallying the men, encouraging them, and by complete disregard to enemy machine gun and shell fire, set an example which reflects the finest traditions of our armed forces. Colonel Rose's actions materially assisted in the reorganization and continuation of our attack. This was all the more noteworthy as Colonel Rose was not on the field of battle for this purpose.[11]

E In subsequent fighting Orlando Ward, as well as several of his key officers affected by the change in command, performed well.

By the end of the first week of May, the battle for Tunisia was essentially over. The Germans were ready to discuss surrender. On May 9 at 0900, Colonel Rose greeted three representatives of Major General Fritz Krause, Artillery Commander of the vaunted *Afrika Korps*, who had arrived in a vehicle draped with a white sheet to ask about the terms that would be granted to the German forces. The Americans had just taken Bizerte, and Harmon had ordered his tanks forward to crush the last German resistance in Tunisia. After he returned to his command post, Harmon phoned his boss, Omar Bradley, Commander of II Corps.

> A couple of Krauts just drove in under a white flag. They want to talk surrender. What d'ya want me to tell them? Or do you want to come up and handle this yourself?[12]

Bradley wanted to remain at his own HQ to monitor the situation on the whole front and to coordinate the approach of the other divisions so as to avoid any friendly fire accidents or unnecessary casualties. The three Germans had requested that an American officer accompany them to deliver the terms to the German commander. Harmon discussed his selection of Maurice Rose with Omar Bradley, who admired Harmon's "brilliant, young chief of staff."

> Fine, Ernie, but have Rose make certain they don't destroy their weapons. They are to collect their guns in ordnance piles and run their vehicles into pools. Tell them if we catch them trying to destroy their stuff the armistice is off. We'll shoot the hell out of them.[13]

Harmon gave the three officers his response. It was simple, direct, and dictated by political decisions already made at the highest level: "Unconditional surrender, with no effort to escape by sea or salvage equipment."[14] The second part of Harmon's response, however, was blunt and threatening.

> I said they could have until ten o'clock to make up their minds; if they hadn't surrendered by eleven, I added, I intended to move the attack forward and drive them into the sea.[15]

Harmon thought at the time that Rose didn't much appreciate his assignment, but the taciturn colonel boarded a command car, which was followed by a half-track carrying a powerful radio. With the three blindfolded

Germans aboard, Rose's vehicle headed toward enemy lines, as American tanks mopped up enemy positions all around him. He arrived at Krause's headquarters in a firestorm of explosives as American fighter-bombers continued to plaster the area.

By 1140 hours, the dour-faced and dejected General Krause was listening to Colonel Rose repeat the unconditional surrender demand. No doubt helped in his decision by the air strikes, Krause gave his grudging assent. At noon, just twenty minutes after arriving, Colonel Rose radioed Harmon that the Germans had agreed to unconditional surrender and wanted the firing to stop.[16]

Harmon's answer was typical: "How about that bastard up north— does he still want a fight?" The initial German request for terms had come from the enemy forces on the right flank. The Germans to the north of Bizerte were still fighting. Harmon later explained that his colorful terminology was "code" for General Willibald Borowiecz, the commander of the *15th Panzer Division*.[17] Still, the timing was a bit difficult for Rose, as at that moment he and the German commander "were in the midst of sealing the agreement over a bottle of champagne."[18]

Rose radioed back that General Borowiecz was also prepared to yield, and by the time Rose returned to the division CP, the general had already arrived to give up. The cease-fire was ordered and the battle ended. In the initial collection of prisoners, the tally was more than 40,000 German soldiers, as well as six generals, including Major General Gustav von Vaerst, Commander of the *5th Panzer Army* and General von Arnim, Rommel's successor as head of the *Afrika Korps*. Three days later, the prisoner of war cages in Tunisia held more than 250,000 Axis soldiers, almost half of them German.

Maurice Rose had been instrumental as the principal negotiator of the first application of the principle of unconditional surrender of Axis forces to Americans in World War II.[19] Rose had faced the arrogant, seemingly invincible enemy and seen the defeat in their eyes. He knew that they could be beaten and was the first senior American to face them in their humiliation. His secret satisfaction must have been boundless. Here he was—the son and grandson of rabbis—dictating terms to the Prussian professionals and hardened Nazis! He would know other great moments of victory, but the words of Omar Bradley, the senior American field commander, probably describe his feelings at that moment as well as any.

No other single incident of the war brought me the elation I experienced in viewing this procession of PWs. For until then we had counted ourselves fortunate in capturing dozens of them at a time.[20]

After the lessons of the campaign had been absorbed—a staff report to which Rose contributed, was written on the 2nd Armored Division's part in the campaign—Harmon returned briefly to 2nd Armored. He turned his attention to restructuring his outfit for its next assignment, the invasion of Sicily. He was also determined to promote to brigadier general rank several of his men who had performed well, including Maurice Rose. His first thought was to put Combat Command A under Colonel Lambert, and Combat Command B under Rose, but on May 27, 1943, when Rose returned to the 2nd Armored he was given Combat Command A. Ernest Harmon took command of 1st Armored Division and Major General Hugh Gaffey took command of 2nd Armored.

On June 3, shortly after Rose took over, Combat Command A moved to Bizerte. There it was attached to Lucian Truscott's 3rd Infantry Division (reinforced) to begin training for *Operation Husky*, the code name for the invasion of Sicily. Truscott's outfit was slated to become part of George Patton's Seventh Army. On June 25, Rose's command participated in *Operation Bookmark*, a full-scale rehearsal of the upcoming invasion, held close to Bizerte. Major General John P. Lucas, Eisenhower's deputy, was an observer of the exercise and took notice of the professionalism of both officers and men, especially the effectiveness of Maurice Rose.[21]

He had already been marked as a man on the move, an officer capable of higher command. On the invasion beach and in the hills of Sicily, he was about to enhance the reputation that he had been building for decades. Thousands of miles away, in Salt Lake City, Utah, another younger man was also on the move. On July 1, 1943, Maurice "Mike" Rose, the general's seventeen year-old first born son, volunteered for service in the U.S. Marine Corps and began a thirty-one-year career that ended on October 1, 1974, with the younger Rose retiring with the rank of colonel.

For *Operation Husky*, Rose's Combat Command A was a part of Truscott's unit, code-named "Joss Force." Commanding a corps-sized unit of nearly 45,000 men, and acting independently of Bradley's II Corps,

Truscott was responsible for the westernmost American invasion forces. Half his men would land at H-Hour on a front about twelve miles wide. His landing beach was near Licata, a city of about 30,000 people, and by dark of D-Day he was to capture the port and the airfield, three miles northwest of the town along the highway to Caltanissetta.[22] That town was situated near a 500-foot elevation rising above the Licata plain five miles away and lay at the foothills of a dome-shaped plateau.[23]

Rose's command would act as Truscott's reserve with four possible missions: 1) to advance northward towards Campobello, 2) move west to Palma di Montechiaro, 3) reinforce II Corps to the east, or 4) stop any enemy armored counterattack from any direction.[24] The immediate enemy threat consisted of 200,000 Italians, organized into four infantry divisions, and a host of other units, including 30,000 Germans. The latter were primarily organized into the mechanized *15th Panzer Grenadier Division* (Major General Eberhard Rodt) and the *Herman Göring Division* (Major General Paul Conrath). The Italians were considered of poor quality and ill prepared for a heavy assault. The Germans were, as usual, well trained, tough, and well equipped.[25]

By the evening of July 10, the initial invasion objectives had been taken, but aerial reconnaissance had spotted the *15th Panzer Grenadier Division* moving toward the beachhead from the west. General Truscott had earlier decided to land Rose's Combat Command A east of Licata with instructions to quickly move into the town. At midnight Rose went to Truscott's headquarters, where he was ordered to attack at 0600 the next morning and capture Naro, about fifteen miles northeast.

After returning to his CP, Rose issued orders that as soon as the remaining third of his Combat Command had debarked they should form up in company-size units and join up with the attacking forces.[26] After securing his objectives, Rose would dig in and prepare for a possible counterattack. With his tanks and troops holding Naro and the hills to the north, the enemy would effectively be blocked from approaching the American beachhead from the northwest.[27]

At 0330 hours on July 11, reconnaissance troops moved out towards Naro, followed at 0600 by the rest of CCA. There was resistance from snipers and small arms fire, and a strafing attack by two Focke Wolfe 190s, but the biggest headaches came from the terrible roads and rough terrain. It was during this attack that Rose used tanks as infantry carriers for the first time in battle. By late morning, Naro was in American hands, the first town in Sicily to be captured by the 2nd Armored Division.[28] Rose started to set up his defensive positions, but soon realized he didn't have enough men to secure the entire area against counterattack. He called in Captain Allen Jones, his senior combat engineer.

> On the first or second day ashore, as we were advancing with minimum resistance in the vicinity of Naro, General Rose called me in and instructed me to lay mines across a road to close a gap in the hilly terrain.[29]

After he finished securing the town and its environs, Rose was next ordered to send a strong reconnaissance force towards Canicatti where Highway #123 from Licata intersected Highway #122 from Agrigento.[30] That road then continued north, and except for the pass at Naro, was one of a few roads able to handle large mechanized forces. Just as the reconnaissance task force got

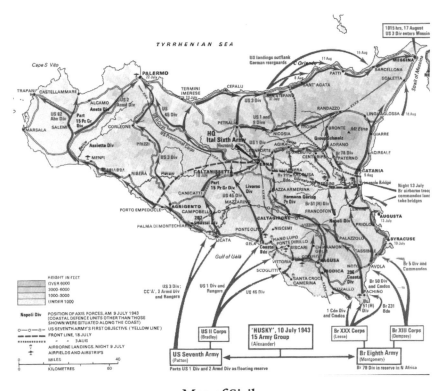

Map of Sicily
(*Source:* Atlas of World War II.)

moving, however, eighteen American medium B-26 bombers attacked Naro, partially destroying it. Luckily, CCA was already coiled in the woods outside of town, but it would not be the last time that friendly air would be more dangerous than the enemy.

The drive towards Canicatti got under way during the afternoon of July 11. Captain Norris Perkins, commanding H Company, 66th Armored, was leading his tanks forward when enemy anti-tank guns and artillery opened up, knocking out three of his Shermans moving along a ridge. He withdrew his company to the starting point.

> When I got back into town I found it packed with tanks and troops. This was not just a diversion or security move then; it was the big push! I found Pee Wee (Colonel Collier) there, and also the general in charge of the show (Brigadier General Maurice Rose). The general directed me to the forward observer's radio half-track just coming up, so I rode up on a hill with them and pointed out the guns I had seen, about a mile and a half away.[31]

Just then, both enemy and friendly airplanes strafed and bombed his column, causing casualties. Perkins noted that his men

> were several miles beyond the "bomb line," but were surprised that our own air did not recognize American tanks and our yellow smoke identification grenades.[32]

Not all the friendly fire from the air was the fault of the pilots, however. On at least one occasion, the men of CCA brought it upon themselves with potentially disastrous consequences. Captain Jones of the 17th Armored Engineers was in a column of vehicles when an anti-air gunner opened up with his quad mounted fifties.

> The CCA column of vehicles was strung out along a road at dusk. A gunner inadvertently fired on an American P-38 airplane. Seeing the tracers coming from an "enemy" force, the pilot wheeled around and strafed our column.
>
> One tank officer, trying to identify us as Americans, threw out what he thought was a smoke grenade, but was actually a concussion grenade; no shrapnel, but the loud bang gave us a pretty good scare.[33]

After this incident, during which the P-38 pilot was shot down (unhurt), Lt. Colonel Henry W. Allard, the S-3 (Operations Officer) of CCA noticed that friendly "air attacks against armor ceased for the duration of the campaign."[34] There was some improvement once the war shifted to France, but faulty air-to-ground liaison would continue to plague Allied ground operations during the entire war and well beyond World War II.

In spite of the stubborn resistance on the road to Canicatti, as darkness fell on July 11, Rose held the crucial mountain pass just four miles south of the town. Early on the morning of July 12, Truscott called Rose on his field telephone and ordered him to "get CCA moving on Canicatti."[35]

The attack got underway at 1330 hours, after a brief but intense artillery barrage. With men from the 41st Armored Infantry (Col. Sidney Hinds) riding on the tanks of the 66th Armored Regiment (Col. John Collier), CCA moved through the pass and approached the southern outskirts of the town. Rose, who was riding with the forward elements, saw a white flag flying over one of the buildings. Accompanied by Colonel Hinds, Rose got in his peep and drove in the open towards the town center to accept the surrender. Almost immediately, enemy artillery opened up from the hills to the north of Canicatti. As soon as the enemy fire began, Rose saw through his binoculars that the "white flag" was actually a Red Cross banner flying from the town hospital. Rose and Hinds barreled into a roadside ditch while American guns shelled the enemy positions for half an hour.

Captain Perkins geared up for the final push.

> We escaped damage and General Rose radioed me to move immediately into the city. We gave up leap frogging sections within platoons and charged down the last hill directly into the edge of the city, knocking down a few low rock walls and fences and tearing down housewives laundry on the clotheslines.[36]

The attack continued, and by 1500 hours Canicatti was secured.[37] Among the casualties was Captain Norris, who was badly injured when his Sherman was hit by an anti-tank shell.

After securing the high ground north of Canicatti by 1030 the next day, CCA was once again placed in reserve and moved into bivouac behind the 3rd Infantry Division. Most of the action afterwards consisted of aggressive reconnaissance patrols, during the course of which several more villages were captured. There were rumors of an imminent

German counterattack, but it never materialized. Instead, there was a brief interlude when the men could tend to routine maintenance and resupply activities.

There was also a bit of time for relaxation. At the headquarters of Company A, 17th Armored Engineer Battalion, the accommodations were downright luxurious. Under Captain Allen Jones' supervision, "the hot shower unit was set up—duckboards, canvas screening, and hot water—the men of the 2nd Armored bathed during this period of quiet."[38]

On July 17, as part of Patton's attack on Agrigento, Rose again pushed his reconnaissance units into the area around Serradifalco, which was captured by 2230 that evening. By the next morning, Rose's units had captured San Cataldo and Caltanisetta, thus securing the assigned area. At this point, General Patton detached CCA from 3rd Infantry and ordered it to rejoin the 2nd Armored in Seventh Army reserve. On July 19, CCA rejoined the division and, for the first time since the invasion, it was fully assembled.[39]

It was the time to count up the initial cost. During the first week of the campaign, Rose's outfit had lost 25 men killed, 154 wounded, and 30 missing. It had captured more than 3,900 enemy troops. More than 35 percent of the casualties, or about 75 men, and 14 vehicles had been lost to friendly air attack.[40]

On July 19, Seventh Army identified Palermo, Sicily's largest city and a major port, as its main objective. The 2nd Armored would stand ready to exploit the advance towards the city. In addition to the public relations benefits certain to follow the capture of such a prize—especially in the ongoing "war" for recognition between the British and the American High Commands—the maneuver offered a chance for the 2nd Armored to gain combat experience in a sweeping encirclement action. So far, except for Rose's CCA, the division had largely been held in reserve, where it had functioned partly as a decoy tying up enemy forces that could not be sure which way it would move.

As CCA prepared to march to a new assembly area near Agrigento, General Rose once again called in Captain Jones of the 17th Armored Engineers. He wanted to make sure that nothing would hold up his advance.

> Late one afternoon, I was called in by General Rose,
>
> "Move your company forty miles further up the coast and build a bridge across the stream near Sciaca for us to cross. It's not known whether that area is in American hands!"

> Arriving after dawn, we found the 82nd Airborne people were already fording what turned out to be nothing more than a creek. So we pulled off into a nearby field and got some shuteye.[41]

At 1600 hours on July 21, CCA began moving into position for the drive to Palermo, and by dark it was ready. The attack commenced at 0600 the next morning. The initial break-in was made by the 41st Armored Infantry Regiment, supported by a battalion of Shermans from the 66th Armored.[42] Resistance was generally light, as the Italian armor and Coastal Defense divisions had already been shifted east. After moving along the coastal road, CCA had turned 90 degrees to the north and, by the end of a long day's drive on July 22, was poised for the assault on Palermo.

As it turned out, a concentrated, full-blooded attack would not be necessary. Earlier that day a delegation of civilians tried to surrender the city to Brig. General William W. Eagles, Asst. Commander of the 3rd Infantry Division. He declined, under orders from General Truscott, who told him that General Keyes, Commander of the Provisional Corps, was to accept the surrender.

At 1830 hours, Rose sent a patrol into the city, but it withdrew pending corps orders that specified the order in which units would enter the city.[43] The patrol returned with Major General Guiseppe Molinero, Commander of Palermo's Port Defense "N." He surrendered all naval and military forces in the area to Generals Keyes and Gaffey. Both men then entered the city and at the Royal Palace, shortly after 1900 hours, formally accepted Palermo's surrender. General Patton reached the palace about one hour later.[44] Captain Jones and his men were close to General Rose, who entered the city right behind Patton's vehicle.

> The crowds in Palermo cheered us as conquering heroes, but some of my vehicles had been bunched up as we entered the capital (a 'no no' because of possible strafing) and also some of my vehicles were missing. General Rose called me into his headquarters after dark, chewed me out, then gave me a shot of liquor and told me to go round up my vehicles.[45]

It had been a stunning public relations triumph for the Americans, even if its strategic importance was limited. At a cost of just over 270 casualties (57 killed, 170 wounded, and 45 missing), the Americans had crossed the width of Sicily and taken Palermo and its port, cleared the western part of the island of the enemy, and captured more than 50,000 prisoners. The U.S.

Army, especially Lt. General George Patton, had also succeeded in "capturing" headlines, which helped restore some of the luster lost at Kasserine and persuade the British to take the Americans more seriously.[46]

Rose's Sicily combat role was over. Following the capture of Palermo, he established his HQ in a comfortable villa located near Mondala beach. With the battle over, his men settled into routine occupation duty, guarding installations against sabotage and organizing captured enemy matériel into dumps and storage facilities. Maintenance was also a major priority as the drive on Palermo had left almost all CCA's tanks unable to operate.[47]

Life at the villa was very pleasant. A morning swim was a part of the normal routine for General Rose and his officers. The image of American fighting men was also important to the General as Lt. Philip Reisler, one of the staff officers, observed directly.

> Captain John Ryan was our Medical Officer at CCA. He was from Ann Arbor, Michigan. John was a very good-looking fellow and General Rose thought that they complemented each other, both being such handsome "buggers." For instance, every time General Rose would walk to the Mondala Beach, he would insist that John walk with him because the two of them were so good looking that they would knock the socks off all the spectators.[48]

A few days after Rose moved into the villa, General George Patton paid a courtesy visit. Captain Jones of the 17th Armored Engineers happened to be there, as was Rose's executive officer, Major Benjamin Bailey, an old family friend of Patton. Jones remembered the occasion as quite convivial, essentially a reunion of old comrades. After a round of polite hand shaking, and congratulations, the officers chatted amiably. Patton offered Rose some advice about the snipers and saboteurs that had been annoying the occupying Americans.

> "If you're bothered by snipers in Palermo, set the timing devices on the shells of your tank cannons to zero." This would cause the shell to explode a few hundred yards down the street.[49]

While the role of CCA and the other elements of 2nd Armored had been limited, there were some important results from the Sicilian campaign. The tactical power and mobility of the American Army, especially Rose's CCA, had been dramatically demonstrated. Perhaps the most important

Brigadier General Maurice and the CCA staff, Sicily, October 1943
Staff includes (from left to right) 1LT Louis Bifano,
1LT James Jamison, Captain John Ryan, MD, Captain Shadrack Turner,
BG Maurice Rose, Major Henry Allard, Captain Dan Morton,
Major John Mettler, and 1LT Philip B. Reisler
(*Source.* Rose Family Album)

tactical innovation was the practice of having infantry ride on the tanks as
they approached the battlefield, which Maurice Rose introduced early in
the battle for Naro, and used successfully afterwards. Rose's aggressive use
of reconnaissance forces, and his drive on Palermo, displayed balance, control, and professionalism at a relatively tolerable cost.[50] Losses to 2nd
Armored in the second week of the campaign (18 to 25 July) were twenty-
five men—seven killed, fourteen wounded, and four missing.[51]

A number of problems surfaced in the after action analysis of the
operation, the most serious of which was the terrible state of air to ground
support and liaison, which had cost CCA significant losses. Maurice Rose
took steps to fix the problem at the Combat Command staff level. He

ordered Lt. Philip B. Reisler, an experienced and respected tank commander in the 66th Armored Regiment, transferred to HQ, CCA, as air-to-
ground liaison officer. In future operations, Reisler would be responsible
for tactical air support, controlling operations from a special Sherman
tank carrying Army Air Force radio equipment. It was a dangerous job;
Reisler's tank would ride at the head of CCA's spearhead column.[52]

In the aftermath of *Operation Husky*, Maurice Rose received professional recognition. For his role in the campaign, and especially the capture
of Palermo, he was awarded an Oak Leaf Cluster to his Silver Star.[53] Rose
had emerged from his first major wartime command assignment with battlefield success and valuable experience. He had won new admirers, including Lt. General George S. Patton, and justified the faith of those officers
who had championed his career and supported his promotion to general
officer. **(F)** In the growing pantheon of American heroes emerging from
the victories in Africa and Sicily, Rose was still on the periphery. He could,
however, claim at least some of the credit for the surrender of Bizerte, and
the well publicized capture of Palermo. More important, Rose and his
combat command were about to play a major role in the invasion of France.
Success in Normandy would win for Maurice Rose one of the most coveted
assignments in the United States Army.

F These officers were Maj. General Ernest N. Harmon, CG, 2nd Armored
Division and Lt. General Omar N. Bradley, CG, II Corps. Rose was appointed a
Brigadier General (Temporary) on June 2, 1943.

CHAPTER Eight

June 13, 1944:
Crisis at Carentan

"We are going on the attack and I mean right now!"
Brigadier General Maurice Rose

rig. General Maurice Rose and an advance party of Combat Command A arrived in England at the beginning of November 1943. The division had completed its combat role and three months of occupation duty in Sicily and had received a new assignment. Rose and a small group of his officers and men were responsible for preparing the way for the arrival of the entire division. That process would take more than a month.

As CCA completed its disembarkation and moved to its assigned quarters, it needed to get organized quickly. There was much to be done. First it would have to absorb new equipment and replacements.[1] Then it would begin a tough training program to prepare for the invasion everyone knew was coming. As the principal striking arm of one of only two combat-tested armored divisions in the U.S. Army—the 1st Armored was already engaged in Italy—it was certain to be earmarked for early commitment to *Operation Overlord*.

In order to expedite the transition, one of the units already established in England was designated to advise and assist in logistical and administrative matters. The choice was prophetic. Major William A. "Bill" Castille, a reserve intelligence officer from the 33rd Armored Regiment, 3rd Armored Division, got his first close look at his future commander. Any thought that the liaison assignment would be routine or easy duty soon vanished.

> Combat Command B/33rd Armored Regiment, then located at Warminster, England, was designated as the "host unit" to receive, accommodate, and get appropriately settled, the 2nd Armored Division's Combat Command A, commanded by Maurice Rose. Our entire staff spent three very difficult weeks trying to please a very demanding Brigadier General.[2] **(A)**

It was not a particularly pleasant experience for any of the welcoming officers. Castille thought Rose was a difficult officer to work for and described him as "tough, impatient, terse, and hard to satisfy." When Rose later took command of their division some of the officers of the 33rd Armored Regiment were downright nervous. In the end, however, a framework had been established for later relationships, since the men knew that a great deal would be expected of them and that sub par performance would not be tolerated.

Maurice Rose began final preparations for his second voyage to fight in France on June 1, 1944, at Tidworth Barracks, Wiltshire, England where his command had been training for more than nine months. Gathered at Tidworth were the main fighting elements assigned to his Combat Command A, including his Headquarters Company, the 66th Armored Regiment, the 3rd Battalion of the 41st Armored Infantry Regiment, and the 14th Armored Field Artillery Battalion. In addition, he had company-strength detachments from the 17th Armored Engineer Battalion, 48th Armored Medical Battalion, and 2nd Armored Maintenance. Several other units were temporarily attached to his outfit for the landing. **(B)**

A Then Colonel Truman Boudinot commanding 33rd Armored had been a classmate of Maurice Rose at the Command and General Staff School.

B The CCA Order of Battle for the Normandy Invasion was larger than typical since Rose, as senior officer present, was responsible for units, such as the 82nd Recon and the 92nd Field, that would later revert to CCB and division control.

Headquarters, CCA	BG Maurice Rose
Executive Officer	LTC Benjamin M. Bailey, Jr.
82nd Armored Recon.Bn. (+)	LTC Wheeler G. Merrian

While the other elements of CCA remained behind to complete their preparations, Rose left Tidworth at 0830 hours on June 1 with a small group of five officers and eight enlisted men that formed his advance Command Post (CP) and traveled to the marshaling yard at Barry, Wales. There, he joined the 9th Infantry Regiment, 2nd Infantry Division, for the passage to the continent. On June 2, Rose and his men boarded the Liberty Ship *SS Charles Sumner*. They remained at anchor during the foul weather on June 5, finally moving that evening toward the convoy rendezvous point off the Isle of Wight, via Lands End.

On D-Day, while the *SS Charles Sumner* was approaching Southampton, the other units of CCA began moving to the coastal marshaling areas. PFC Don R. Marsh, a twenty-one-year-old Signal Corps wireman from Racine, Wisconsin, had just been transferred from the 143rd Signal Company of the 3rd Armored Division, after making an "unfavorable impression" on his CO, Captain John L. Wilson. Initially, Wilson wanted to transfer the feisty young malcontent to the infantry, but luckily for Marsh a spot opened up in the 2nd Armored's 142nd Signal Company. Now, like thousands of others at Tidworth Barracks, Marsh wrote a "last letter" home before shipping out, instructing his brother Bob back in Racine to add some addresses of his friends to his papers, and

By the way, Bob, you have first pickins on anything of mine if I am unlucky enough to be planted on this side of the pond, not much, but you're welcome to whatever it is. This is it—so long chum—I'll

---

66th Armored Regt.	Col. John H. Collier
1st Bn.	LTC Carl O. Parker
2nd Bn.	LTC Lindsay C. Herkness
3rd Bn.	LTC Amzi R. Quillian
41st Armored Inf. Regt (1st Bn)	Col. Sidney R. Hinds
2nd Bn.	LTC Wilson D. Coleman
3rd Bn.	LTC Marshall L. Crawley, Jr.
14th Field Artillery Bn.	LTC Carl I. Hutton
92nd Field Artillery Bn	LTC William R. Buster
17th Armored Engineer Bn. (-)	LTC Louis W. Correll
CO. A, 2nd Armored Ordnance Maintenance Bn.	
Detachment, CO. A, 2nd Armored Division Supply Bn.	
CO. A, 48th Armored Medical Bn.	

(-) Elements of the unit detached or not present. (+) Reinforced.

write whenever I have time and when the spirit moves me. Best of everything to all. Your Bro. —Don[3]

The wire and radiomen from the 142nd Signal Company who were assigned to HQ, CCA boarded LST (Landing Ship, Tank) #1009.[4] **(C)** As he looked around the deck, packed with equipment and nervous men, Marsh wasn't sure he had been all that lucky in escaping from Wilson. His buddies in the 143rd Signal Company were still safe in their beds.

> The ramp was raised and the bow doors clanked shut as we then pre-pared to move away from the dock. We were now confined to the cargo area with strict orders to "stay below decks" until ordered otherwise. I grabbed a loose GI blanket and stretched out on the catwalk next to our peep. Now it was everyone to his own thoughts as we waited to assemble in our convoy. The very small Canadian corvettes circled us as we left the protected English coastline and headed across the Channel.
>
> Veno had carefully backed the peep— named "Sis" after his sister— into the LST where we were sandwiched between the Command Communications Radio M-3 half-track and an M-5 (Stuart) light tank. Our peep was in a combat ready condition: the engine was "waterproofed"; the top was down and strapped; the windshield was down, canvas covered, and lashed to the peep hood. We felt naked sit-ting among the armor plated machines in our landing force. All of them carried .30 and .50 caliber machine guns and cannons, whereas we were armed only with my .30 caliber carbine and Veno's .45 caliber Thompson submachine gun.[5]

There wasn't a lot of time to dwell on fears. There was too much to do. Marsh had earlier hooked up with another Wisconsin boy, Corporal William J. Veno of Ashland, to form a two-man wirecrew, which came to be

---

C A fairly large proportion of the Headquarters complement of CCA consisted of communications specialists. In addition to Marsh and Cpl. William Veno, the full roster included twelve signal corps soldiers assigned to "temporary duty" with HQ, CCA: *Wiremen*—Sgt. Earlie J. Jones, Andalusia, Ala.; Pvt. Fred J. Newland, Harlan County, Ky.; Pvt. Douglas J. Elfer, New Orleans, La.; Pfc. Clovis Waldroop, Salina, Ok.; and Pfc. Lawrence A. Hull, Brighton, Ma. *Radio Halftrack and Crew*—First Lt. Walter S. Moll, Indianapolis, In.; commanding, S/Sgt Tom Speirs, Picayune, Miss.; T/5 Hal Zappendorf, Chicago, Ill.; T/5 William Truitt, LaPorte, In.; and Pvt. Vern Evans, Jackson, Miss.

known as the "troubleshooters." It was an apt name, for they ran into plenty of trouble. Marsh felt lucky to be assigned to Veno, who was already a combat veteran of both the North Africa and Sicily campaigns and had emerged from both actions without a scratch. The corporal's luck would eventually run out months later when he was wounded in the head, but he survived and eventually returned to duty with only a nasty scar as a reminder of his very close call. That, however, was far in the future. Now, like tens of thousands of others, they were getting ready to land on a hostile shore full of apprehension and fear about what lay ahead.

> Apparently it was dark as the ship's Captain ran the bow on the bottom at the designated spot on Omaha Red Easy Beach. We would have to sit and wait out the receding tide before we would get the signal to open the bow doors and off load. Suddenly, without any warning, the deck anti-aircraft guns, comprised of quad .50s and 20mm Bofors started firing incessantly. The steady drone of heavy engines told us the Kraut bombers were attacking. The empty shell casings and constant plink of shrapnel hitting the deck continued off and on all night like a steady rain.[6]

During those early days, some of the bombs, shells, and other hazards got pretty close. On June 11, the landing craft carrying Major General Edward H. Brooks, Commander of 2nd Armored, and his senior staff was nearly overturned by the explosion of a German bomb that fell near their boat as it lay off the coast of Normandy preparing to land. On that same day, another LST struck a mine and went down with the loss of thirty-one medium and light tanks and an equivalent number of other vehicles.

The *SS Charles Sumner*, with Rose on board, anchored off the French coast on D+1 in the vicinity of the village of Ste. Honorine des Pertes. At 1830 on the evening of June 7, Maurice Rose walked on to Omaha Beach. He immediately established his forward command post just north of St. Laurent-Sur-Mer, very close to the headquarters of the provisional engineer brigade, which had covered itself in glory on D-Day. As the senior officer present from 2nd Armored, he immediately established contact with V Corps headquarters, to which 2nd Armored was assigned, along with the 1st Infantry and 29th Infantry Divisions that stormed "bloody" Omaha Beach just the day before.

The scene that greeted Rose as he stepped off the ship was grim testimony to the fierceness of that decisive day's combat. It was a tableau of the chaos and devastation of war and bore silent witness to what men had endured on that terrible stretch of sand. The stench of death and smoke clung to the landscape like a ground-hugging fog that would not dissipate.

Wrecked tanks, LCIs (Landing Craft, Infantry), and other mangled vehicles, in addition to barbed wire obstacles and I-beam anti-tank barriers, were scattered all over the beach. Hundreds of unused and useless waist tube life preservers littered the sand. Amidst the wreckage there was a great deal of activity. The beach crews were stockpiling crates of ammunition, high pyramids of gasoline Jerry cans, and pallets holding boxes of rations. Graves registration teams silently went about their grim duty, laying out the neat, tagged rows of dead GIs as well as the bodies of the enemy. The MPs had set up temporary barbed wire cages for the captured German POWs, who stood nervous and quiet, or sat waiting to be transported to England on the return trips of the LSTs.[7]

For the second time in World War II—and for the second time commanding the first major armor unit on a hostile shore—Maurice Rose had landed on a coastline in sight of the enemy. His mission was three-fold: First, to collect information on the progress of the landing operations for the division commander, who was still aboard his ship; second, to organize his command for early commitment to the battle; finally, to "receive, orient, and command" all the units of 2nd Armored that would land prior to the scheduled arrival of the division commander on June 11. In addition, he was to maintain close liaison with V Corps.[8] **(D)**

The *Overlord* plan called for the U.S. First Army, commanded by Lt. General Omar N. Bradley, to strike both sides of the Vire Estuary on the right flank of the invasion area. The V Corps (Maj. General Leonard Gerow) was to land on Omaha Beach with the mission of securing a beachhead between the village of Port-en-Bessin on the left and the Vire River on the right. The experienced 1st Infantry Division would lead the initial assault ("Force O"), spearheaded by reinforced elements of the 16th,

---

D V Corps was the first major headquarters assigned to the European Theater of Operations (ETO). It arrived in Belfast, No. Ireland in January 1942 with the mission of receiving and training U.S. forces, and assisting in the defense of Northern Ireland. Transferred to England that November, it began immediately to plan for the invasion. Maj. Gen. Leonard T. Gerow, a veteran of the War Plans Department, took command of V Corps in mid-July 1943.

18th, 115th, and 116th Infantry Regiments, as well as the 2nd and 5th Ranger Battalions.

Later on D-Day, the 29th Division, with elements of the 26th and 175th Infantry Regiments, would also go ashore, and the 2nd Division (with whom Rose hitched a ride) would land on D +1. Other V Corps units, including CCA, 2nd Armored, would continue the buildup process. The V Corps would then secure the beach exits and extend the beachhead toward the *bocage*, or hilly, wooded country to the south and, once reinforced with the fully assembled 2nd Armored, would advance south beyond the Cerisy Forest. **(E)**

While Rose was preparing the beach for arrival of his outfit, the major elements of CCA had begun loading onto LSTs and LCTs (Landing Craft, Tanks) for the Channel crossing. By noon of June 9, they started to land on Omaha Red Easy Beach. Don Marsh was relieved to be moving off the ship.

> As the bow doors opened, the CCA Wireteam in two vehicles descended the ramp into shallow water and followed the convoy up the exit draw, inland to an assigned wooded area to await the remainder of the command. Patrols were sent out to contact friendlies on the flanks. Defensive positions were set up around the perimeter. Immediately, all vehicles were de-waterproofed and combat-readied and put on standby. All vehicles were covered with camouflage nets day and night with movement kept to a minimum. Radio silence was also maintained and communications were handled by messenger and telephone wire.[9]

One of the first tasks was to shed the uncomfortable (and smelly) chemical impregnated clothing. Then, after preparing their vehicles, the men immediately began to move into the preassigned assembly areas. The men of

---

E *Bocage*, French for "copse, grove, or wooded region." In Normandy *bocage* consists of small fields or orchards bounded by thick, uncut, and double lines of hedges set on high banks. In the invasion area, these fields were intersected by rivers, streams, and narrow lanes and dotted with stone-built farms and villages. This created formidable obstacles dominated by hills and ridges. The *bocage* provided excellent cover and was ideal for blocking, ambush, and infiltration tactics. It thus offered greater advantages to Germans, inhibiting airborne operations, land movement, and the construction of airfields.

Rose's advance CP had already marked off the routes and boundaries of these locations. That night, Rose moved his headquarters to the village of Mosles, in order to be closer to the main CCA assembly areas.

By midday of June 10, CCA had entered the war in earnest. Gerow's V Corps was already feeling the early heavy losses in the assaulting infantry units. He ordered Rose to attach 3rd Battalion, 41st Armored Infantry to the 29th Division to help secure the bridgehead on the west bank of the Vire River, near Auville-Sur-Le-Vey. Later that day troops from both V and VII Corps made contact and linked up near the village.

Rose dispatched the reconnaissance company of the 66th Armored Regiment and units from the 82nd Reconnaissance Battalion south to establish contact with other friendly troops. For the remainder of the day he monitored the unloading and assembly of his men and equipment, and by 2200 hours that evening Rose had under his command more than 4,200 men and officers, and hundreds of combat-ready vehicles. That same day, CCA suffered its first losses on the European continent, as men from the 41st Armored Infantry engaged the enemy, losing two men killed in a skirmish outside Auville.[10]

A major risk of the *Overlord* invasion was that once ashore, the Allies would be unable to link and consolidate the five beachheads before the Germans mounted a major armored counterattack aimed at splitting their forces and driving them back into the sea. In the event, the landings during the first days were successful, although on Omaha Beach it was a very close run thing. Still, the threat of an enemy counterattack lingered for days after the invasion. The German talent for tenacious defense and the difficult terrain also raised the specter of stalemate.

Within one week of the invasion a threat to the linking of the beachheads did materialize. A number of factors combined to place Rose and his combat-tested unit at the site of the first major threat to the invasion at the critical moment. First, was the timely and tactical use of *Ultra* intelligence; second, Rose's reputation as an effective armor commander made his selection for the assignment logical; and finally, the fact that major elements of his command were already assembled and ready to move was propitious. As one semi-official history of the 2nd Armored noted,

> At this time, Carentan was perhaps the most vital point in the entire beachhead because of the narrowness of the American defenses there. The sector was at that time held by the 101st Airborne Division,

which had been virtually isolated in the region since D minus 1. Men of the 101st had been fighting off attacks continuously for more than a week and had suffered heavy losses, and were short on both ammunition and supplies.[11]

Carentan is a small town of about 5,000 inhabitants located in the Manche *département* of the Basse-Normandie region and lying slightly to the north of a flooded marshland at the base of the Cotentin peninsula. Situated on the left bank of the narrow Taute River, just above its confluence with the Douve River, it is about twenty miles north-northwest of Saint-Lô, and twenty-five miles west of Bayeau. It lies along Highway N13, a road linking most of the major towns of the region to the port of Cherbourg.

In the early planning for *Operation Overlord*, Carentan had been designated as a D-Day objective because it lay on the projected seam between the Omaha and Utah assault beaches. After further study, however, its early capture was deemed too ambitious, and it was decided that it would be taken later in the campaign, when the tactical situation was more favorable. The revised mission of the 101st Airborne was to take the river and canal crossings north and northeast of the city.[12] Still, General Bradley wanted to capture Carentan quickly, at one point unrealistically believing it could be taken on D+1.[13] If he could not take it, he was willing to destroy it, if necessary, noting in his memoirs:

> "We've got to join up with Gerow just as quickly as possible," I had told Collins, anticipating difficulty in those marshlands. "If it becomes necessary to save time, put 500 or even 1,000 tons of air on Carentan and take the city apart. Then rush in and you'll get it."[14]

In fact, the first bombs fell on the night of June 5 and the town was repeatedly bombed and shelled in the following days, reducing it to a blasted moonscape, with only a few medieval stone houses left standing. In addition to the severe casualties among the combatants, more than sixty citizens lost their lives in the fighting.

From the earliest moments of the invasion, the battle was bloody. Many American paratroopers were killed in the Carentan area during the night drop on June 5–6, victim to both the flooded marshland terrain and the stiff German resistance. While the Germans could call for artillery support, the Americans had lost most of their artillery before they even landed

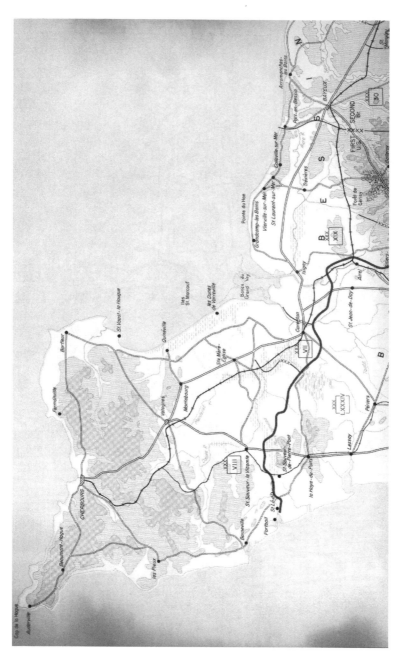

Normandy, July 1944

(*Source:* Center of Military History)

on the shore. The paratroops remained isolated and got little help from the units still fighting up from the beaches. After several days of fierce fighting they were low on supplies and were getting tired.

They had only one, albeit crucial, advantage: close air support from Pete Queseda's IXth Tactical Air Force fighters.[15] **(F)** The glider troops, some of whom came in over the beaches in LSTs, brought some antitank and other heavy weapons, but losses among those actually flying in on the gliders were heavy. Included among the dead was the assistant commander of the 101st Airborne, Brig. General Don F. Pratt, the only Allied general officer lost on D-Day.[16]

As early as June 7, during his first visit to the assault area—he was ferried by minelayer—General Dwight D. Eisenhower, the Supreme Allied Commander, was nervous about the linkage of the two American beachheads. He issued orders that altered the tactical plans immediately, directing that command attention should be refocused on the linkage as the top priority. He recognized that taking Carentan was the key and assigned the task of seizing and holding it to the 101st Airborne Division.

General Bradley, commanding U.S. First Army, changed his plans accordingly, and began to redirect his subordinates to address the new SHAEF priority. Lt. General Courtney H. Hodges, Bradley's Deputy Commander, was dispatched to Maj. General Maxwell Taylor's HQ to monitor and coordinate, while J. Lawton "Lightning Joe" Collins and the rest of VII Corps continued to concentrate on the drive to Cherbourg.[17]

The battle for Carentan would prove to be a protracted, difficult, and costly struggle, pitting two elite paratroop units against each other: the U.S. 101st "Screaming Eagles" Airborne Division, making its combat debut, and the veteran German *6th Fallschirmjägerregiment* (parachute regiment). The German paratroopers had already fought a desperate battle at Ste. Mère Église, losing all their vehicles in that first crucial action of the Normandy campaign. In spite of setbacks, however, which would have shattered the morale of any ordinary unit, the battle-hardened paratroopers were still highly motivated and fighting fiercely.[18]

F Queseda's forward headquarters of his IX Tactical Air Command was established on the European continent at 3:30 p.m. on June 10. During the battle for Carentan, the ground commanders called for close air support on numerous occasions—some of the requests coming at crucial moments—and there was considerable interdiction activity behind the front lines, preventing the movement of large formations towards the front.

During the night of June 11–12, Brig Gen. Anthony J. McAuliffe, artillery commander of the 101st Airborne, coordinated the final assault on Carentan. **(G)** Covered by massive artillery fire, including naval gunfire, the Americans struck at 0200, driving German paratroopers from the devastated town before dawn.[19] At about 0800 on June 12 the Americans captured Carentan, and in spite of continued sniper fire, a wild celebration greeted the men moving into the town. Flags, friendly mademoiselles, and fine wine long hidden from the hated occupiers suddenly appeared. The merry-making was short-lived, however, as probes and local counterattacks began almost immediately after the town was taken.[20]

With the capture of Carentan six days after D-Day, the 101st Airborne had established a linkup of the two American corps. While it was still tenuous, if it could be held and quickly consolidated, the Allies would control an unbroken stretch of coastline of sixty miles, across which men and supplies could be landed. It would also put to rest the fear that still lingered of isolation and piecemeal destruction of the American beachheads by powerful German armor counterattacks. The terrible memory of Kasserine still hung over the American—and British—Command.

Consolidation of the seam now depended on securing the approaches to the town by taking additional ground all around Carentan. The 101st Airborne planned a further advance early on the morning of June 13 in order to extend their control to the terrain west of the town.[21] The American attack never got underway. Early that morning, the *17th SS PanzerGrenadier* Division, supported by heavy guns, struck along the Carentan—Baupte and Carentan—Périers roads, the same routes the Americans had moved down the previous day.

The night before, in the very early hours of June 13, V Corps had alerted 2nd Armored that a German armored thrust was expected near the seam where the two American corps were vulnerably linked between the towns of Carentan and Isigny.[22] The warning originated from Omar Bradley's First Army and, as we now know, was based on *Ultra* radio intercepts and the code-breaking operations centered at Bletchley Park in England.

G Anthony "Tony" J. McCauliffe would later gain great fame while holding surrounded Bastogne during the Battle of the Bulge and because of his laconic answer to the German demand for his surrender: "Nuts." Earlier, McCauliffe, then a captain in the Field Artillery, had been a classmate of Maurice Rose in the 1937 class at the Command and General Staff School, Leavenworth, Kansas.

Bradley's first postwar memoir, published in 1951 (before the existence of *Ultra* had been revealed), attributed the warning to a late night visit of his G-2, Col. Benjamin A. "Monk" Dickson.[23] As the top intelligence officer of the U.S. First Army (intelligence based on *Ultra* intercepts was restricted to Army level and higher commands), Dickson was one of a very few authorized recipients of *Ultra* intelligence, which was conveyed very carefully via controlled teams called Special Liaison Units (SLU).

General Bradley's later autobiography (published in 1981 after the secret had been revealed) is more explicit about his appreciation of the codebreakers in connection with the Carentan Operation. In that memoir he describes it as one of a very few occasions where he unconditionally trusted *Ultra* as a basis for making tactical decisions.[24] Whatever the wisdom of that point of view, the field operations of Rose's Combat Command A in defense of Carentan was the first "real-time" tactical use of *Ultra* on the ground in the climactic European campaign.

In fact, the period between late evening of June 11 until the middle of the next day was the busiest time for the intelligence analysts in Hut #3 at Bletchley Park since D-Day, and arguably among its most profitable tactically during the whole war.[25] Several intercepts were quickly decoded that pointed to a counterattack near Carentan, which the 101st Airborne was then in process of capturing. One message on the morning of June 12 specifically mentioned the assembly of the *17th SS PanzerGrenadier Division* in the Saint-Lô-Bayeau area. Another message at midday requested *Luftwaffe* support, and suggested that the original time for the counterattack had been postponed, and further postponements were reflected in subsequent intercepts. Other messages gave the specific location of assembly areas—southwest of Carentan and west of Saint-Lô—and offered evidence that the Germans were intent on frustrating the Allied goal of cutting off and isolating the Cotentin peninsula.[26]

Bradley received the fully developed intelligence report warning of the German counterattack during the late evening of June 12. Later that night, he telephoned General Leonard Gerow, and without explanation, alerted him that it was likely that the enemy would attack the next morning between Carentan and Isigny.[27] Because of a foul-up in communications, Bradley followed up the phone call with a note instructing Gerow to assign a battalion each of tanks and infantry to help hold the thinly held corridor between the American corps.

Bradley specified that Maurice Rose's outfit should be committed, a dramatic statement of his confidence in him, writing in his note to Gerow,

"Sorry to have to bother you but consider this highly important."[28] Of course what he meant was that he was unable to share the full picture because of the stringent secrecy requirements of protecting the security of all *Ultra* intelligence; even corps commanders were not cleared to know the source of the information.

Gerow was initially hesitant to expose the flank of the 1st Infantry Division at Caumont by moving their armored support, but the British brought up armor to fill the gap created by Bradley's orders. Gerow then ordered Maj. General Edward Brooks to dispatch Rose's Combat Command towards the corps boundary.

At five minutes past midnight, Brooks ordered Rose to report in person to General Gerow's Headquarters to receive verbal instructions. By 0315 on the morning of June 13, elements of Rose's command were already on their way to the Montmartin-en-Graignes area to secure the bridgehead west of Isigny and to clean out the Germans dug in to the south. At Brooks' urging, Rose's force had been reinforced beyond Bradley's original instructions. Rose's force was now essentially the full CCA, including two tank battalions of the 66th AR commanded by Col. John H. Collier, Lt. Col. Marshall L. Crawley, Jr's Battalion of the 41st Armored Infantry, and the 14th Armored Field Artillery Battalion commanded by Lt. Col. Carl I. Hutton. The latter outfit was equipped with the very effective M-7 "Priest" self-propelled 105mm howitzer. In addition, reconnaissance, supply, maintenance, and medical units were also part of Rose's columns.

Three hours after moving out, Rose's force closed into an assembly area in the vicinity of the town of Les Veys, and patrols were immediately dispatched towards the railroad tracks near the village of Montmartin. Three American battleships—*Texas, Nevada*, and *Arkansas*—still off Utah Beach would provide heavy gunfire support for the patrols, if required.

The German counterattack had been hampered from the start by ammunition and fuel shortages. Allied aircraft, especially Queseda's rocket-firing P-47 Thunderbolts and British Typhoons, had badly battered the Germans, and in spite of repeated requests by the German commanders, the promised *Luftwaffe* support failed to materialize.[29] Ignoring these considerable difficulties, however, and under a covering barrage of artillery fire, the Germans pressed on, and the first attack struck the American airborne forces just after midnight, gaining momentum through the night.

It was now obvious that while *Ultra* had generally pinpointed the enemy objectives, their real target was Carentan. By daybreak the Germans had overrun the forward American positions and driven to within 500 yards of the edge of the city. Men of the 502nd Parachute Infantry Regiment helped to retake some of the lost ground, but the enemy attack continued, and at dawn, the junction of the beachheads was still in peril.[30]

At 0630 on June 13 just as Combat Command A was preparing to move south to Auville, Rose's mission was suddenly changed by direct order from General Bradley. The Germans had already struck Carentan, creating a threat from the southwest rather than southeast of Rose's position near Auville. The 101st Airborne Division had been hit hard by the *17th SS PanzerGrenadiers* and as Bradley feared, it was holding on to Carentan by its fingernails. The lightly armed paratroops had very little to counter the German armor.[31] Rose's outfit, still en route, was immediately attached to Maxwell Taylor's 101st Airborne for the duration of the struggle to hold the town.

By mid-morning, reacting to the rapidly changing situation, the remaining elements of CCA had joined the march to Carentan following the route scouted earlier by Rose's reconnaissance troops.[32] At 1030 hours the leading tanks commanded by Col. John "Pee Wee" Collier (Rose's future successor as commander of Combat Command A) had arrived at the outskirts of Carentan, where they were directed off the road, taking cover among the hedgerows.

The HQ section pulled off the road into a crab-apple orchard to wait for Rose, who was still enroute from V Corps HQ, where he had received Gerow's last minute instructions. It was at this moment that Pfc. Don Marsh saw his commanding general for the first time. The sudden appearance of General Rose, the first such officer Marsh had ever beheld, made an impression on the young private that has lasted more than fifty-five years. "Pyramid Six"—code name for the Commander of CCA—arrived without fanfare, except for a two-man motorcycle escort. The red metal flag plate with the large silver star was the only mark that distinguished his otherwise ordinary peep.

The small convoy stopped under a cluster of apple trees and the tall man dismounted. Key members of his staff, who were already at the orchard, quickly surrounded him. Rose's executive officer, West Pointer (class of 1939) Lt. Col. Benjamin M. Bailey, Jr., (KIA August 23, 1944) laid out the maps on the hood of the peep.

For an instant, it seemed to Don Marsh like a scene from a Hollywood movie, when sniper fire suddenly whizzed through the tree branches. General Rose never flinched as he snapped, "will somebody take care of that nuisance!" An aide quickly instructed the liaison officer from the 41st Armored Infantry to "get somebody on it" and within minutes the sound of a BAR raking the tree line was heard followed by a rain shower of leaves, birds flying in every direction, and then an eerie silence.

The Germans were already on the move, so the plan was simple enough: a frontal infantry attack supported by armor. One armored task force, consisting of the 2nd Battalion, 66th Armored Regiment and the 3rd Battalion, 41st Armored Infantry would move west along the Carentan—Baupte road at 1400 hours, along with the men of the 502nd Parachute Infantry. They would pass through the 506th Parachute Infantry still holding the forward positions. A second task force comprised of the 1st Battalion, 66th Armored Regiment and other elements of the 101st Airborne would attack along the Carentan–Périers highway.[33] The briefing ended and the men of CCA returned to the vehicles, ready to "mount up and move out."[34]

It was early afternoon, about 1330 when the staff liaison officers from the 101st who had attended the orders group got back to their units. A half-hour passed and there was no sign of movement. General Rose, alone, walked up the road and among the paratroopers who held fast to their foxholes dug along the roadside.

> Growing impatient by the apparent reluctance to begin the attack by the troopers, General Rose, alone, walked up the road ignoring any possible danger, past the stunned troopers who watched him in utter amazement as he strode by them as though he were on parade. He stood out like a sore thumb in his dove gray whipcord jodhpurs, highly polished cavalry boots, and tan tank jacket. His weapon, a standard issue .45 automatic, remained in his holster. Upon seeing a company-grade officer from the Screaming Eagles, in a firm voice loud and clear enough for all nearby to hear, he said,
>
> "Captain, let's get your men out of their holes and moving forward. We are going on the attack and I mean right now!"
>
> That was all it took. Reluctantly, the troops, led by the Captain, began to move forward to commence the attack to push back the Germans, assisted by all the power of Combat Command A.[35]

Fighting in the *bocage* was a nightmare, and the paratroopers had been among the first troops to experience its horror. It was CCA's first encounter with the centuries old hedgerows overgrown with thick tree branches. Many of the men had seen hedges before, but no one was prepared for the European version. Cultivated for dozens of generations to divide and contain farm plots, they were often as high as ten or twelve feet, and were intersected by sunken roads between the lines of hedges.

Each alleyway was a deathtrap, especially where they intersected the corners of fields. Machine gun fire was zeroed in on the natural avenues of approach, and any attempt to cross the fields was suicide. Hopping from field to field meant being caught out in the open without any cover, and being at the mercy of the rapid-fire and very accurate German MG34 and MG42 machine guns. Snipers were everywhere; some even tied themselves into the high branches of trees.

The tanks didn't have it much better. They were used to punching through obstacles, but where there were openings in the hedgerows; antitank weapons, including the fearsome 88mm anti-tank guns, often had them completely covered. Because of the thickness of the hedges, the tanks were unable to smash through and ended up trying to go over the top with their vulnerable underbellies exposed to the enemy's weapons. The ultimate solutions: bulldozer blades and other "cutting" tools welded to the front of the tanks were weeks away from being devised. What saved the men and tanks defending Carentan were luck and surprise, as well as the forward momentum of the attack.[36]

Unaware that Rose's armor was in the area, and expecting only light infantry opposition, the Germans were already out of their defensive positions and at the mercy of the Americans' direct and indirect fire. They were taken completely by surprise. Despite their determined assaults and heavy weapons support, they were repulsed several times. Both American columns received very heavy fire support from the 14th Armored Field Artillery Battalion, which fired furiously.

By 1730 hours, the remainder of Rose's command had arrived, and these reinforcements also joined the fight. At the height of the fighting, nearly sixty American tanks were in action, to the delight of the beleaguered paratroopers. By the end of the day, Rose's coordinated attack had pushed the Germans back and extended the American forward positions two miles southwest of the city. There Rose set up his forward CP.

The timely arrival of Combat Command A had insured that Carentan would be held.[37] The paratroopers were happy, to say the least. Lt. Richard Winters, who won the Distinguished Service Cross for his actions at Carentan, felt a palpable sense of relief.

> What a wonderful sight it was to see those tanks pouring it to the Germans with those heavy 50-caliber machine-guns and just plowing straight from our lines into the German hedgerows with all those fresh infantry soldiers marching along beside the tanks. Oh, what a mess they made.[38]

At least one paratrooper got the chance to thank a personal friend for helping to save his outfit. When Don Marsh of CCA got back to camp after the battle, he wrote his folks about the encounter.

> In the first few days over here I ran into Jim Magruder who is in a famous airborne outfit (101st Airborne Division) and we met twice—last week was the last time I saw him and he's still fit as a fiddle and rarin' to go. He said they (his outfit) were really glad to have us come up and lend them a hand.[39]

The artillery support proved crucial in breaking up the enemy counterattacks and penetrating the hedgerow lines. Captain Rae Guistwite, a recent replacement in the 14th Armored Field Artillery, who eventually served in CCA from Carentan to the end of the war, had been assigned to the 41st Armored Infantry as a forward artillery observer, a particularly dangerous job. He remembered that

> Rose demanded constant patrols into the enemy lines—and in the daylight. He wanted forward observers with them—and many of them were killed.[40]

It was for just such a patrol that Captain Guistwite was awarded the Bronze Star on the general's personal recommendation. Rose sent men into harm's way, but he didn't hesitate to reward them for their bravery and devotion to duty. In fact, in his photographs from the war, the only time he appears to be smiling is when decorating his men.

The terrain across which the German units advanced was marsh and swamp, covered with brush, and American weapons had every inch under observation. The coordinated efforts of tanks, infantry, and artillery—all working in what would later be described as "combined arms"—threw the enemy back several thousand yards, inflicting heavy losses, estimated at the time of the battle as exceeding 500 casualties. Rose's men suffered eight men KIA, forty-five wounded, and they lost four tanks.[41] After dark,

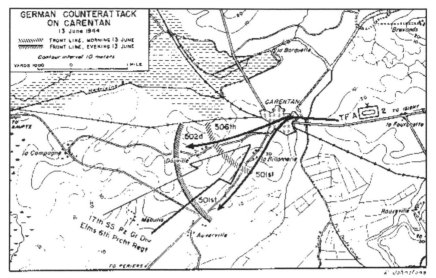

CCA, 2nd Armored defends Carentan, June 13, 1944
(*Source:* Harrison, *Cross-Channel Attack*)

the vehicles coiled off the road, but harassment fire continued all night, including well-directed mortar and artillery fire, which was answered by the 14th Field Artillery's counter-battery fire.

At dawn the battle resumed with similar results. After three-and-a-half hours of fighting, Rose's men pushed further down the two roads. For the rest of the day, they concentrated on rooting out snipers, and the tanks and infantry moved toward La Rayerie to drive out infiltrating enemy troops while the paratroops took over the front lines. The German dead littered the fields as the enemy retreated towards Périers, but it cost another man killed and four more wounded.

Generals Rose and Brooks visited the casualty clearing station set up by Company A of the 48th Armored Medical Battalion, which handled almost 80 percent of the wounded and injured during the month of June. It was an expensive victory. During the actions around Carentan, from June 11 to 15, 1944, Combat Command A lost nineteen men killed, seventy-one wounded, some of whom later died of wounds, and seven men were missing.

Carentan and the junction between VII Corps and V Corps were secure. For several more days, Rose's outfit was engaged in fierce skirmishes along the Carentan–Périers road. The fighting was hard but

German losses continued to far outnumber those of Combat Command A. Late on June 15, the 2nd Armored was placed in reserve and it executed local security missions around Balleroy, performing maintenance on its tanks and equipment.[42]

Maurice Rose had played a major role—perhaps the decisive role—in saving Carentan from recapture, preserving the still tenuous linkage of the American beachheads, and preventing the overrunning of the lightly equipped paratroopers. At the time, and ever since, the lion's share of the credit for the "Battle of Carentan" has gone to the heroic men of the 101st Airborne. The various official and popular histories and memoirs focus mainly on the initial capture of the town. Indeed, the paratroopers deserve most of the credit for that (along with air power), and the various sources describe their valor and tenacity during the first week's struggle in great detail. **(H)**

One possible explanation for the lack publicity of the subsequent action is that while the actions to secure Carentan were "considered by the high command to be of first importance," it was somewhat independent of larger events. Nor was Carentan initially viewed as a major objective of First Army, or even of V Corps.[43]

Yet it remains true that if Rose's force of tanks, infantry, and artillery had not arrived in the proverbial "nick of time," it is doubtful the exhausted and outgunned paratroopers could have held much longer. Quite simply, the official record does not give enough credit to Rose and his Combat Command's crucial role in the early beachhead battles.

Despite the difficulties of operating armor among the flooded marshes and the hedgerows, Rose had secured the seam between the V Corps and VII Corps beachheads. According to no less an authority than Omar Bradley,

---

H The publications of the Office of the Chief of Military History were prepared by professional historians—many of who had served in the field, or in headquarters assignments during the war. They are based on after action reports, interviews, and other primary sources, and should rightly be viewed as the "official" histories of the World War II. The studies most relevant to the actions around Carentan during the first ten days of the Normandy Campaign are the monographs in *The American Forces in Action Series*: *Utah Beach to Cherbourg* (#13), *Omaha Beachhead* (#7), and *Cross Channel Attack*, one of the books in the European Theater of Operations group of the multivolume *U.S. Army in World War II*. At least one memoir by a notable participant—VIIth Corps Commander J. Lawton Collins—does not even mention the role played by CCA, 2nd Armored in helping secure Carentan and ensure the linking of the beachheads.

the risk posed by the German counterattack at Carentan represented Rommel's best opportunity to split the beachheads early in the campaign. An enemy document captured on June 13 confirmed the gravity of the risk. The captured German field order outlined a plan that aimed at exploiting the gap between the forces with a thrust right to the beaches. The result of such an outcome would have proved serious, if not catastrophic.[44]

During the German counterattack, Rose's Combat Command encountered, and subsequently defeated, elements of the *37th* and *38th Panzer Grenadier Regiments, 14th Tank Battalion* (all from the *17th SS PanzerGrenadier Division*), *914th Infantry Regiment* (*352nd Infantry Division*), and the *6th Parachute Regiment*. In the entire encounter, only six German POWs were taken—testimony to the viciousness of the fighting.[45]

In his early actions on the Continent, General Rose, commanding a brigade-sized force, had played a significant role in protecting, and then expanding the American beachhead at one of its most vulnerable stages. Further, he was very possibly the first American battlefield commander in the decisive Western European campaign to exploit in "real time" the tactical advantage offered by *Ultra*. It would not be the last time he was entrusted with such an important mission. As the 2nd Armored's reputation spread, the nickname "Hell on Wheels," reportedly applied by George Patton was supplemented by another, more personal, sobriquet. **(I)** The political leaders of Germany and the men and officers of the *Wehrmacht* began referring to the division, and especially Rose's CCA, as "Roosevelt's Butchers."[46]

As he had done in North Africa and Sicily, Rose had forcibly pressed the attack forward, appearing personally at the farthest forward point to rally and inspire his men. Rose's reputation was growing. Bradley and Eisenhower—both of whom had approved his promotion to general officer rank—recognized in him the kind of soldier who got the job done with the resources at hand, without complaint, or concern for the cost.[47] In the Allies' next major battle—the breakout from Saint-Lô, in an operation called *Cobra*—his performance would earn the mustang officer one of the premier armor commands of World War II and his place in American military history.

I LTC Haynes W. Dugan, USAR, ret., wartime Asst. G-2 of the 3rd Armored Division, claims credit for the nickname "Hell on Wheels," conceived while serving as public relations officer for the 2nd.

CHAPTER Nine

July 1944: Rose Propels the *Cobra*'s Fangs

"I won't stop before I've taken the objective no matter
how dark it is, or how many men we lose."

Brigadier General Maurice Rose

After the successful landings and consolidation of the beachhead,
the Allies faced one more strategic imperative. They had to quickly
expand the lodgment area and break free of the murderous
hedgerow fighting. While it was now virtually impossible for the Germans
to drive the invaders back into the sea, stalemate and exhaustion were still
real possibilities. Unfortunately, SHAEF had no specific plans for the situation that had developed by the middle of July.

One man, however, was constantly thinking about the problem. Omar
Bradley's answer to these problems, *Operation Cobra*, shaped the next stage
of the European campaign. Its success would take the Allies to the borders
of the Third Reich in a breathtaking drive of just six weeks. He later
described it as "the most decisive battle of our war in Western Europe."[1]
The object of the operation was to achieve a penetration of the enemy's
defenses west of St. Lô and exploit the break with a strong armored and
motorized thrust deep into the enemy's rear.[2]

As Martin Blumenson, the official historian of the campaign, wrote:

Operation Cobra had immediate as well as long-range consequences. It smashed the German left-flank defenses, liberating the Americans from the bloody battle of the hedgerows, and it dissolved the specter of static, World War I–type trench warfare. It opened the prospect of exciting, mobile maneuver and projected the breakout that came close to encircling, and destroying, the two German armies in opposition. It propelled the Allies to their Overlord objective, the lodgment area on the Continent, and precipitated the allied pursuit of the German units across France.[3]

Bradley's plan did not—like the goddess of the ancient Greek myth—spring fully developed from the head of its creator. It was formed and shaped over time, conceived and modified over nearly a week in the solitude of a large wood-floored mess tent. There, Bradley had his aides set up a giant acetate map of Normandy, and he worked it over for days with colored pencils, marking roads and rivers, drawing division and corps boundaries, and searching for a way to break out.[4]

The idea that emerged was his response to the bloody reality that framed the Americans' main problem: how to neutralize the defensive advantages of terrain that hemmed in the beachhead and carried the threat of containment.[5] In the struggle around Carentan, the special bitterness of the fighting in the hedgerows and its terrible cost were never far from the GIs'—or their leaders'—minds. Maurice Rose also knew that before he could lead his tanks on a great drive, he would have to find a way to break free of the terrible thick bushes.

By the evening of June 14, Carentan had been secured and the commanders were looking toward their next major objective: expanding the lodgment. With an eye already fixed on St. Lô—the key to a breakout—Omar Bradley wanted a preliminary idea of the enemy's strength and dispositions along the Carentan-Périers road. Once again, Bradley picked Maurice Rose for the difficult assignment. Still attached to the 101st Airborne in support of the VII Corps mission of isolating the Cherbourg Peninsula, Combat Command A's work along the Vire River was not yet done.

Early on the morning of June 15, Rose organized a strong reconnaissance force, with fire support from the 14th Armored Field Artillery. He personally led it southwest down the road to St. Lô. He was stopped in his tracks almost immediately by heavy machine gun and small arms fire. Half an hour later, enemy anti-tank guns joined in, hitting the stalled column hard. Rose ordered up additional infantry and tanks to help press the reconnaissance forward, but that didn't help. After a day of inconclusive fighting and mounting losses and realizing that the enemy defenses were too strong to be breached without a major assault, he ordered a withdrawal.

That evening, the 101st Airborne took over the front line once again and dug in. Rose pulled back and counted the cost. While intelligence could not offer a conclusive count of enemy casualties, his losses were significant: nine men killed, thirty-one wounded, and seven men missing. Several armored vehicles had also been lost. Omar Bradley's peek at "the other side of the hill" had been expensive. Rose reported back that the Germans were not finished and still had plenty of fight left.

The role of CCA in holding the beachhead on the left bank of the Vire River was now complete. On June 17, Rose's force was detached from the 101st Airborne and returned to the 2nd Armored. He left behind one battalion of the 66th Armored to ensure that the Germans would not again threaten Carentan with armor. The Command then returned to its original staging area near Le Marais. There, along with the rest of 2nd Armored, the soldiers settled into the typical "between the battles" routine: servicing and cleaning weapons, maintenance of vehicles, and organizing personal equipment.

The 2nd Armored Division had been on the continent for just over a month, and while 3rd Armored had also landed, the 2nd was still the most experienced and battle tested American armored division in the European Theater. By the time *Operation Cobra* was launched at the end of July, Brigadier General Maurice Rose, commanding its cutting edge, was arguably the most experienced senior field armor officer in the U.S. Army.

Along with various routine chores and general maintenance, the tank units of Combat Command A were also re-equipped. Colonel John H. Collier's 66th Armored Regiment, Rose's main striking arm, received new M4A1 Sherman tanks, now equipped with the slightly more powerful high-velocity 76mm gun. **(A)** After "zeroing" the guns, the men painted the vehicles in the appropriate camouflage. The intensive training continued, especially in developing techniques aimed at defeating the hedges.

During the last two weeks of June, Rose's men conducted reconnaissance missions, patrolled the front lines looking for prisoners, and undertook operations to secure the Caumont sector. The men spent most of July in much the same way but saw little actual fighting. The routine was

---

A The early model Shermans were equipped with a short-barrel, low-velocity 75mm gun with limited penetration power.

broken suddenly when CCA was taken out of the front line in mid July and the 29th Infantry Division took over the positions facing St. Lô. The 2nd Armored men then had a few days to tend to their personal business, write V-Mails, and, depending on their ability to sleep through the visits of "Bed Check Charlie" (as they called the nightly harassment bomber), catch some rest.

Occasionally, the visits from the *Luftwaffe* were more than just annoying. On June 20, two large bombs fell on the 67th Armored Regiment assembly area, killing seven and wounding fifty-one. Shortly after that attack, the 195th Anti-Aircraft Artillery (Automatic Weapon) Battalion was attached to the division with Battery "D" assigned to CCA. **(B)** The men quickly discovered that as helpful as these half-track mounted guns were in driving off the enemy's airplanes, there was another, greater benefit to having them around. The volume of firepower provided by the quad-mounted .50 caliber machines guns on the M-15 and the 37mm cannon and two .50s on the M-16 was devastating against ground targets.

But the main concern was not control of the air, where the Allies' superiority was virtually unchallenged. The main problem remained the *bocage*, the peculiarly Norman terrain that was the major preoccupation of Maurice Rose, his staff, and the GIs of 2nd Armored. As a result of their combat experience at Carentan, the problems of fighting in the vine-encrusted, often twelve-foot high hedgerows was the highest priority for everyone. Rose concentrated all his efforts on preparing his men for the inevitable return to the hedgerow-lined fields where so many of their buddies had fallen.[6] **(C)**

The basic answer was fairly straightforward and had already been demonstrated at Carentan: combined arms, or close tank-infantry-artillery

---

B The 195th AAA (AW) Battalion (SP) remained attached to 2nd Armored for the remainder of the war.

C While Allied intelligence knew about the *bocage*, its defensive effects had been vastly underestimated. Training measures were consequently totally inadequate. Because direct observation was limited and the range of engagement was limited to a few hundred yards, tanks were ineffective, and infantry bore the brunt of the attack and suffered heavy casualties. The killing power of enemy artillery and mortar fire was multiplied, as it was frequently air burst among the trees. Tanks pushing slowly through the hedges and climbing the banks were vulnerable and picked off with relative ease by the well-concealed enemy. As June stretched into July, the tempo of operations slowed and casualties and gloom mounted.

coordination. Translating that concept into actual combat techniques, however, was neither obvious nor easy. Rose increased the training schedules and stressed extremely close cooperation and communication between the tanks and escorting infantry. The 17th Armored Engineers were also at work on the problem and practiced using their armored bulldozers to clear gaps and widen the pathways along the hedgerows. The logistics experts were also busy stockpiling large stores of ammunition since it had been discovered that expenditures were unexpectedly large in attacking the *bocage*. More technical solutions—like the welded "hedge cutters," also called the "Rhinoceros"—were still weeks away but would be ready for *Operation Cobra*. **(D)** At Carentan, Rose had also enjoyed the benefit of surprise; the Germans weren't expecting tanks. This time they would be dug in and waiting.

In addition to problems of terrain, it had now become painfully obvious to everyone, especially the tank crews, that the later models of German armor—especially the *Panther (Mk V)* and *Tiger (Mk VI)*—were greatly superior to the standard American medium tank, the M-4 Sherman. Neither the 75mm gun, nor the newer 76mm gun–equipped Shermans stood much of a chance in a direct encounter against the heavily armored German tanks.[7]

During the latter part of June, numerous tests were conducted against captured German equipment in an effort to discover ways of defeating them. These included the use of flame-throwers and explosives, as well as other anti-tank weapons like the bazooka and the self-propelled M-10 Wolverines of the 702nd Tank Destroyer Battalion, which had arrived on the Continent on June 11. But no alternative was truly effective. In the end, it was the quantitative edge and especially the bravery of the crews that made up for the qualitative deficiencies of our tanks. Thousands of men would pay the price for that inferiority, and the realization that they had been misled about the superiority of their weapons left many tankers bitter.

D The "Rhinoceros," or "Rhino," was a hedgerow-cutting device devised by Sgt. Curtis G. Culin of the 102nd Cavalry Reconnaissance Squadron. It consisted of welding elephant tusk-like prongs salvaged from German steel anti-landing obstacles on the Normandy beaches to the front of tanks. The "Rhino" tusks bored into the thick dirt base of the hedgerow, holding the front of the tank down and level while it crashed through the hedge.

Toward the end of July, Combat Command A was reinforced in several ways for the upcoming operation.[8] **(E)** One of the most important attachments was the 22nd Regimental Combat Team of the 4th Infantry Division commanded by Colonel Charles T. Lanham.[9] This veteran outfit had stormed ashore at Utah Beach on D-Day and had won a Presidential Unit Citation for the early fighting around Carentan.

The theorists and practitioners of American armored warfare had realized fairly early that the "one infantry-to-two armored" regimental structure of the heavy armored division was unbalanced. There simply were not enough foot soldiers to create or exploit breakthroughs, the principal task of armored formations. The expedient response was to attach infantry outfits from other units, but this created problems of integration.

The foot soldiers had little training with tanks, and coordination was often poor. Such a lack of knowledge could be dangerous; for example, standing too close to a tank firing its main gun could cause serious injury or death.[10] Maurice Rose, however, had served in both the infantry and cavalry, and understood well the importance of intensive training in coordinated warfare or "combined arms" doctrine. It was a lesson he learned early and honed during his studies at the Command and General Staff School, and he employed combined arms tactics throughout the war, especially making effective use of attached infantry in each of his major campaigns. Thus, the experienced 22nd Regiment, fresh from combat in Normandy, was a welcome addition. In the days before the commencement of *Cobra*, his command trained intensively with the infantrymen.

An equally important addition to Combat Command A was "Cutbreak." This Sherman tank was equipped with a powerful high-frequency SCR 610

E The original composition of CCA for the *Operation Cobra* campaign was:

Headquarters, CCA
22nd Regt Combat Team
66th Armored Regt.
41st Armored Infantry Regt (-1st Bn)
702nd Tank Destroyer Bn
14th Field Artillery Bn
17th Armored Eng. Bn. (-)
Battery D, 195th AAA (AW) Bn (SP)
CO A., 48th Armored Medical Bn (+)
Detachment, Maintenance Bn
24th Cavalry Squadron

radio and was responsible for air to ground liaison between CCA and IX Tactical Air Force.[11] In each major advance, a flight of four fighter-bombers was constantly maintained over the spearhead to provide close air support on an instantaneous basis. "Cutbreak" was the nerve center of the effort.

Lt. Philip B. Reisler was Cutbreak's commander and had served before with Maurice Rose in the Sicily Campaign. He knew his job well and was fully aware of its risks. The crew—which included Army Air Force personnel—had been issued "Cutbreak" just before the St. Lô operation; it was the third tank Lt. Reisler had commanded during the course of his dangerous assignment. Among his crew was the driver, Virgil ("Bill") Appleton, a colorful southerner from Tupelo, Mississippi who was nicknamed "Bazooka Boy." His buddy, Pvt. Doug, ("Joe") Elfer, who drove CCA's wire truck, described how he got the nickname in the fighting around Caumont.

> I remember one evening around 5:30 the Germans had us pinned down in a ditch. I don't know why. They were trying to kill us. I guess they were mad at us or something. Then this crazy guy comes up to me and says, "Hey man, where's a bazooka?" You see this big German tank was heading in our direction.
>
> I pointed out the bazooka man who was aiming at the tank but "shaking like a leaf on a tree." Appleton ran to the man, grabbed the bazooka, took a couple of steps, fired, and knocked off the track of the tank. Ever since then he was known as "Bazooka Boy."[12]

Finally, in mid-July, Bradley's staff had completed their preliminary work in developing his idea, and the basic outline of *Operation Cobra* was formulated. On July 12, Bradley held a meeting at his HQ near Omaha Beach. He was ready to share the plan with his full staff and his corps commanders. He was excited and told them,

> I've been waiting to do this . . . since we landed. When we pull it (off), I want it to be the biggest thing in the world. We want to smash right on through.[13]

On the next day, First Army published the first draft for *Operation Cobra*. The principal role was entrusted to Major General J. Lawton "Lightning Joe" Collins' VII Corps, now heavily reinforced and made up of six divisions and numerous attached units, especially artillery. In addition to "mobile" formations: 2nd Armored, 3rd Armored, and 1st Infantry, VII Corps also had three combat-hardened infantry divisions attached. Joe Collins enjoyed the full confidence of Bradley and Eisenhower and was admired by the British as well, a correspondence of opinion that was somewhat rare among the Allied leaders.[14]

The *Cobra* plan called for the infantry holding the front lines to pull back 1,200 yards to await the conclusion of a massive "carpet" bombing of a "rectangle" 6,000 yards wide and 2,500 yards deep, south of the St. Lô and Periér highway. Immediately after the bombardment was over, they would move forward and capture Marigny and St. Gilles. The road, National Highway N660, had been chosen partly because it was ruler straight across the front and would make an excellent landmark for the flyers.

The "penetration" phase would open a three-mile breach in the enemy front lines, and the infantry of VII Corps would hold open the flanks of the penetration while the two armored divisions and the mechanized 1st Infantry Division rolled forward. Their commitment would signal the "exploitation," or second phase of the operation. The plan—as revised later by Collins' staff at VII Corps—did not anticipate use of the "mobile" formations until the initial breakthrough phase had been completed. The aim of the exploitation phase was to seize Coutances, Brehal, and the crossings over the Sienne River, thereby outflanking and surrounding the Germans on the west coast of the Cotentin peninsula.

After the onset of the exploitation phase, blocking positions would be established to protect the perimeter of the breakthrough. After completion of the exploitation, the third, or "consolidation" phase would follow, whereby gains, including those made by the supporting VIII and XIX Corps, would be consolidated along the Coutances–Caumont line and any further German weakness, or even collapse, would be further exploited.[15]

The pace of preparations began to accelerate on July 17, when the British 50th Brigade relieved the 2nd Armored Division. On July 20, Rose traveled to division headquarters where he met with Generals Bradley and Brooks and was briefed on Field Order #4, which detailed the role of Combat Command A in *Operation Cobra*.[16] Rose returned to his HQ and held an orders group with his principal field commanders to give them their assignments. The plan called for CCA to move along two routes to seize the area around Le Mesnil Herman, including St. Sampson de bon Fosse and Hill 183, thus covering the flanks of 1st Infantry and 3rd Armored as they drove through the Marigny–St. Gilles gap.

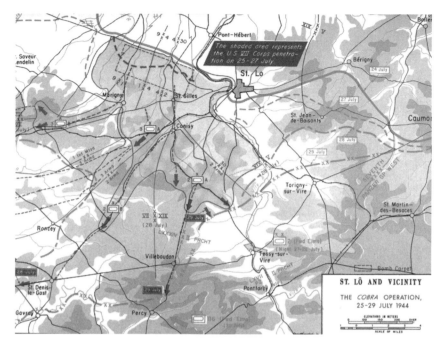

***Operation Cobra*, breakthrough July 25–29, 1944**
(*Source: West Point Military Atlas*)

The key imperative was to move fast, avoiding a pitched battle wherever possible. The plan called for the use of reconnaissance troops to screen the advance, bypass enemy resistance, and hold the final objectives until relieved by stronger forces. For this purpose, both the 82nd Armored Reconnaissance Battalion and the 24th Cavalry Squadron were attached to CCA. After taking the initial objectives, Rose was to be prepared to attack any enemy forces that might approach from the east or south on a line between the villages of Conde sur Vire and Hambye.[17] It was the perfect assignment for Rose, a classic cavalry action.

According to Allied intelligence the major enemy opposition would likely come from elements of the German *Seventh Army* commanded by Colonel General Paul Hauser, especially the *LXXXIV Corps* under Lt. General Dietrich von Choltitz, which was positioned on the left bank of the Vire River. Von Choltitz commanded three infantry divisions (*91st, 243rd,* and *352nd*) as well as the *17th SS PanzerGrenadier, 2nd SS "Das Reich" Panzer,* and the *Panzer Lehr* divisions.

Six weeks of hard fighting had reduced these formations considerably; for example, the vaunted *Panzer Lehr* entered the battle with less than 2,200 effective soldiers and only forty-five armored vehicles. Other formations were down to less than half-strength; altogether the Germans were estimated to have fewer than 200 tanks available to face the American VII Corps.[18]

On July 22, Rose was alerted to be ready to move on two hours notice. Everyone knew then that the fighting would resume very soon. The fear that comes just before a battle began to gnaw at the men, but at least they also had the confidence that comes from confronting the enemy and prevailing. Their morale was also much improved. During the delay the men received an issue of new clothing and a succession of hot meals. The temperature of the food was not the only improvement. Quality had also improved dramatically, as one regimental report noted, "it was amazing how many cows and chickens wandered into minefields . . . and ended up as sizzling platters."[19] The Special Services branch had arranged entertainment programs for the frontline troops, and even more importantly, the 17th Armored Engineers had set up portable showers just before the quick action alert, allowing many to bathe for the first time in weeks.[20]

After several delays, due mostly to bad weather and a costly bombing mistake on July 24, the attack got under way on July 25, a week later than planned. The front line troops pulled back 1,200 yards, after which more than 2,500 heavy, medium, and fighter-bombers unloaded more than 4,000 tons of bombs. Ernie Pyle, the much-admired war correspondent, had a front row seat with his buddies from the 4th Infantry Division when the bombs started falling at 0940 hours. Even a week later, the terror was still vivid as he recalled the sound and sights of what was, up to that time, the largest tactical ground support bombing operation in history.

> And then the bombs came. They began up ahead as the crackle of popcorn and almost instantly swelled into a monstrous fury of noise that seemed surely to destroy all the world ahead of us. From then on for an hour and a half that had in it the agonies of centuries, the bombs came down. A wall of smoke and dust erected by them grew high in the sky. It filtered along the ground back through our own orchards. It sifted around us and into our noses. The bright day grew slowly dark from it. By now everything was an indescribable cauldron of sounds. Individual noises did not exist. The thundering of the motors in the sky and the roar of bombs ahead filled all the space for

noise on earth. Our own heavy artillery was crashing all around us, yet we could hardly hear it.[21]

The men in CCA were hunkered down in their vehicles or still sheltering in their foxholes when the massive aerial spectacle began. The concussions were terrible, but the worst was seeing the planes hit by the sporadic ack-ack that the Germans sent up. The scene transfixed Private Don Marsh and his fellow wiremen.

> That B-17 coming down with all four engines dead is one sight I can never forget. He was losing altitude and the props were not turning. Then they popped out the red flares meaning they had wounded on board. The pilot was doing all he could to glide the plane in over our lines to crash land. We didn't see the exact spot he came down although they made it inside our lines. There was a helluva lot of air activity that day. We were watching all this from our foxholes and pulling for our guys to make it, knowing full well that some of those flyboys would not make the twenty-five-mission quota to return to the U.S.A.[22]

At 1100 hours the air attack was over and the infantry moved forward "under a pall of smoke up to 2,000 feet as far north as Carentan, where it was eight miles wide."[23]

The "short" bombing and heavy casualties, especially in the 9th and 30th Infantry Divisions, as well as the strong initial resistance of the Germans, quickly led to a feeling of disappointment. Reports poured into the various headquarters describing stiff resistance and only minor advances. The growing despair throughout the day was exacerbated at the highest levels by the news that among the "friendly fire" casualties was Lt. General Lesley J. McNair, the highest ranking general to be lost in the war, and a man liked and respected by the officers commanding *Cobra*. **(F)**

For a time, the view of just about everyone was that the "carpet-bombing" had resulted only in a minor variation on the previous exhausting—and costly—attempt to break through the hedgerows. The average advance was just 1,000 yards, far short of original expectations. As sunlight began

---

F In order to protect the *Overlord* deception operations, McNair's death was not announced, and he was buried in secret. His pallbearers included Patton, Hodges, and Bradley, all three-star Generals.

to fade on July 25, it looked as though the offensive had already petered out. *New Yorker* correspondent A.J. Liebling described the gloomy mood among the troops in a delayed dispatch.

> Discouraging rumors, such as frequently attend the opening of offensives, cropped up in the small, exclusive mess of the divisional artillery that night. One was that the Germans had not been shaken by the bombardment, another that they had been annihilated but that bomb craters had made all the roads impassable. The favorite explanation of the delay, I am afraid, was that the divisions ahead of us had snarled things up as usual. [24]

The necessary precondition for the beginning of the "exploitation" phase had earlier been defined as capture of the towns of Marigny (on the right) and St. Gilles (on the left), both road network centers considered essential to the commitment of the mobile forces.[25] The major risk of a premature commitment of armored and mechanized forces was congestion on a narrow front. As early as July 12, virtually coincident with when he first learned of the *Cobra* plan, Collins had expressed concern about how fast his armor would be able to move.[26]

> The only doubtful part of it (the original *Cobra* plan), to my mind is we shouldn't count too much on fast movement of armored divisions through this country; if we make a breakthrough it is OK but until then . . . (the armored divisions) can't move any faster than the infantry.[27]

If he were slowed down, his reinforced corps would be unable to exploit the very advantages inherent in its bulked up size and armored weight. The seemingly stiff German resistance after the hardest tactical aerial blow ever struck highlighted the risks of premature commitment of the armor. By late afternoon on July 25 it was clear to Collins that the moment of decision was at hand. In spite of the reports of strong enemy resistance, he thought he saw something else in the messages pouring into his headquarters.

> Noting a lack of coordination in the German reaction, particularly in their failure to launch prompt counterattacks, I sensed that their communications and command structure had been damaged more than our troops realized.[28]

His instincts proved correct, for the strength of the enemy's resistance was deceptive. The *Ultra* code-breakers and other sources had already discovered that the earlier (and successful) British attempt to capture Caen had "compelled Field Marshal von Kluge to commit all his reserves to Monty's front."[29] In fact, in spite of the internecine bickering and second-guessing at the time, Montgomery's July *Operation Goodwood* had led to a thinning out of the forces facing the Americans. The resistance was not as strong as it first appeared, and was far from continuous along the front. In fact, as Collins suspected, the aerial bombardment had been very effective.

> The enemy had taken a terrible pounding. Prisoners of war said our carpet-bombing was devastating. Heinies who were not casualties were stunned and dazed. Weapons not destroyed had to be dug out of the dirt and craters and cleaned before they could be used. Communications were almost completely smashed. Tactical control nearly ceased.[30]

According to Martin Blumenson, "For the Americans, the critical day was July 26, when General Collins had gambled."[31] Collins decided to commit his mobile forces before the road network was secured, that is, before the penetration phase was completed.

While the clear hindsight of history now reveals that Collins' gamble was not as risky as it then appeared, that changes nothing about the daring and bravery of Collins at that crucial moment. By the time darkness fell on that depressing first day, Collins had made one of the historic, decisive, and truly great battlefield decisions of World War II. It goes far to explain why virtually every senior Allied leader viewed him as the finest American corps commander during the war. And, as would be the case from that moment until the war was nearly over, Maurice Rose was Lawton Collins' major dealer in the high stakes card games to follow. Initially, however, Rose and CCA had not been given a major offensive role in the operation.

In the final version of the *Cobra* plan, MG Edward H. Brooks' 2nd Armored was given an important, but decidedly secondary and largely defensive role. While the decisive main thrust was to be made by the 3rd Armored Division, the 2nd Armored, positioned on the eastern end, or left flank of the offensive, was assigned a "protective" mission of guarding the flank of the *Cobra* attack. There it would defend against enemy counterattacks from the south and east from the line that ran through the villages of Tessy sur vire-Villebaudon-Percy-Gavray-Brehal.

General Brooks, however, either consciously or because of the way the circumstances unfolded, took a distinctly offensive posture. He moved his two Combat Commands aggressively forward, and then, dividing his forces yet again, mounted independent assaults that capitalized on the unfolding events.[32] While Rose exercised brilliant tactical control of the lead attack elements, it was Brooks' operational vision that changed 2nd Armored's role in the battle, and helped ensure the ultimate success of *Cobra*. It no doubt played a part in Brook's promotion to corps command and a third star. Of course, it was part of Brook's success that he fully appreciated that Rose was the perfect instrument to actualize his aggressive intentions.

Brooks respected Rose's battlefield style, and he also had the natural touch with his men. In general, most enlisted ranks had little affection or appreciation for officers, and generals were no exception. In fact, the longer the men were back in bivouac, the more they started to miss the rigors of front line duty.

> They're pretty chicken shit back here. The officers don't bother you much up there (the front) because they have their hands full all the time. But one day, the division commander (a two-star general) was up there and stopped near us on the road. He asked me if I had chow yet. I was so surprised by his question that I almost couldn't answer no. A few minutes later a guy in a peep brought up some hot rations (breaded pork chops) in containers![33]

At 2230 hours on the night of July 25, CCA moved west and south to an assembly area in the vicinity of Pont Hubert in preparation for its role in *Cobra*. With the attached 22nd Infantry riding on his tanks and other vehicles, Rose moved his command forward. As soon as he arrived at the assembly area at 0200 hours on July 26, he held a meeting with his unit commanders at his forward CP. There, he gave his men verbal orders. Based on the latest reconnaissance of the forward area, he was changing the plan of attack.

Instead of moving out in one column as originally planned, CCA would attack with two tank battalions moving abreast and astride the road. The 2nd Battalion, 66th Armored would move on the right, and the 3rd Battalion, 66th Armored would move on the left. Two infantry companies from the 22nd Infantry would ride with each battalion. The remaining six infantry companies would ride with 1st Battalion, 66th Armored Regiment in reserve. Six battalions of artillery would support the attack.[34] No matter

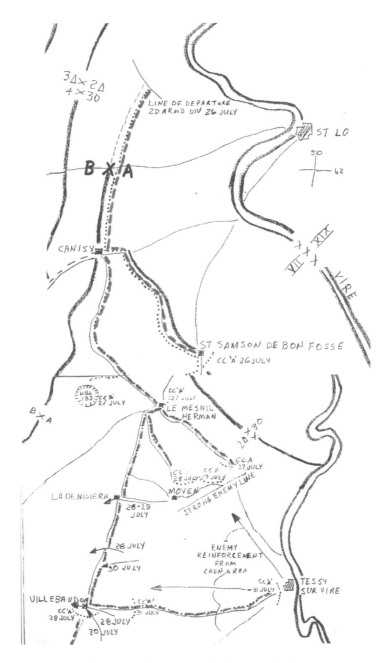

The route of CCA, 2nd Armored, July 26–30, 1944

(*Source:* Committee #14, Armor School)

what the enemy resistance, that morning CCA would pass through the 30th Infantry Division lines and move down the road to St. Gilles, bypassing strong points and securing the vital town as soon as possible.

Before he gave the order to move out, Maurice Rose walked openly amongst his men in the front of the column like Shakespeare's King Henry V before the Battle of Agincourt. Pfc. Doug Donahue of the CCA wire team was amazed to see General Rose walking so close to the front lines so boldly when there were still snipers all around.

> St. Lô was the first time I ever saw him in action. He was one that was out in front, walking around and almost daring something to happen to him. When the time for combat came, though, Rose was a tiger.[35]

Several war correspondents were riding with the lead elements of CCA and had made the night journey down from the assembly area far to the rear up to the jump-off point. Sgt. Walter Peters of *Yank Magazine* was in the command half-track of 3rd Battalion, 66th Armored Regiment commanded by Lt. Colonel Amzi R. Quillian. **(G)**

> The men's faces were brown with dust. Their eyes bloodshot from lack of sleep. Dirt clung heavily from their eyebrows and eyelashes.
>
> One of the men looked at his watch. "Ten-forty," he drawled. The drive had begun at 0900 hours. Our medium and light tanks, led by Col. Quillian, were far to the front and the men in the Combat Command half-track waited for word.
>
> Then the word came over the radio. The Colonel's voice was calm and serious. "We've made contact with the enemy and have taken a few prisoners," he reported.
>
> "You've waited a long time," another voice replied, "Get in there. Get punching. Get hitting." "That's the general, all right," said Pfc. Jack Giels, of Cleveland, "He's a bug on slogans."[36]

CCA moved out at 0900 and crossed the line of departure three quarters of an hour later. By 1030, the men had captured their first prisoners. The

---

G For its role in *Operation Cobra* the 3rd Battalion, 66th Armored Regiment, was awarded a Presidential Unit Citation with Streamer embroidered *Vire River* (WD GO 82, 1945). Colonel Quillian was killed in action on July 29, 1944, and many of his officers were also killed or wounded.

enemy soldiers confirmed that their comrades had suffered greatly in the aerial conflagration. Maurice Rose and his CCA were once again in the vanguard of a desperate attack, leading the division, the VII Corps, and First Army.

It was slow going. Almost as soon as they passed the American infantry positions, a well-concealed anti-tank gun knocked out the lead Sherman.[37] The Germans were not yet ready to quit; they set up road-blocks and defended the hedgerows with *Panther* tanks supported by infantry, artillery, and anti-tank guns all along the roads.[38] Even when they gave up ground, they extracted a continuing cost. During the initial phase of the attack, Sgt. Earlie J. Jones, the CCA, HQ wire team leader was making a routine wire repair in what he thought was "liberated" territory.

> Remember the time we spliced the telephone line—we pulled off the road—we had been sitting on a delayed fused mine. We were about twenty-five feet away and the thing went off leaving a hole we could drive the peep in.[39]

Booby traps weren't the only obstructions. As feared, even though the size of the bombs had been reduced, the craters from the aerial bombardment also slowed Rose's progress. He was forced to leave the main roads and that led to problems as well. As always, General Rose relied heavily on radio and wire to maintain very tight communications control with his columns and task forces, especially as they got spread out bypassing enemy strongpoints.

The strain on the Signal Corps personnel attached to his headquarters was great, and the dangers they faced were much the same as those experienced by the men "on the line." Before they entered the first town along the road, however, the German tried to stop them. The Signal Corps men found themselves sharing ditches and whatever other shelter they could find with the infantry, engineers, and gunners.

> I found out that Rose wanted wire with him at all times. That first day, we split the team up and you (*Marsh*), Hull, Veno, and Jones in the peep went up to Canisy while Joe Elfer, Fred Newland, Wally Waldroop, and myself stayed in the truck. As we approached St. Gilles, we got caught in a barrage of artillery. I'll never forget it.[40]

Pete Queseda's fighter-bombers weighed in at 0700 on the morning of July 26 just before the tanks moved forward. Five fighter groups, a force of nearly

200 aircraft, bombed and strafed St. Gilles, Rose's first objective.[41] Early that same afternoon Col. Harold Holt, commander of the 366th Fighter Group briefed his men for another mission. It was short and simple.

> All right, gentlemen—your attention please. Your mission today is Column Cover with Combat Command A of the 2nd Armored Division. Assist them in any way you can.[42]

The fighters took off in staggered formations so that a flight of four aircraft would always be over the lead tanks. When they were in position over the Shermans approaching St. Gilles that afternoon, Colonel Holt made contact with the IX Air Force liaison officer who was working with *Cutbreak*. "Hello Booty, this is Slipshod leader. Have you any targets for us?" Reisler did. There was a well-concealed 88mm gun and four Mark IV tanks blocking the road several miles north of St. Gilles. Holt blasted the gun while Rose engaged the tanks. As Holt flew over the column, he had the satisfaction of seeing the gun destroyed and the tanks moving toward the town.[43]

It was mid-afternoon before Combat Command A rolled into St. Gilles.[44] According to the original concept, the capture of St. Gilles would have triggered the exploitation phase of *Cobra*. As it happened, Collins' gamble of the early use of armor had paid off. Any lingering fears about the early commitment of armor or doubts about the decisiveness of the breakthrough soon evaporated. There was no let up as Rose maintained the pressure and the pace, continuing to drive his men forward. As at Carentan, he was once again at the tip of the attack directing his men personally. In fact, he was so far out in front, no one seemed to know where he was.

The four men of the CCA wire team that Sgt. Jones had assigned to the peep were ordered to track down General Rose during the fighting for Canisy. They never did find him. When they arrived at the edge of the village, it was in flames. Confusion reigned. Half the town was on fire; the rest was already a pile of rubble. The dead and dying lay all around in a terrible tangle of devastation. Marsh had not yet become inured to the sight of so much death and destruction.

> I will never forget that night. The St. Lô Breakthrough had just begun in earnest and we had already seen so much fighting that day. We had just passed through the carnage from the slaughter of both German and American losses of men and vehicles. What our tanks and

artillery didn't annihilate, our Army Air Corps fighter pilots in the P-47s did. The sight of burning, destroyed tanks with the men half draped out of the turret. Their fellow tank crewmembers' scorched bodies lay beside the tanks where they had fallen as they attempted to escape. No prisoners were taken that I can recall.[45]

It was after dusk on July 26 when the leading vehicles of CCA passed through Canisy, a burning tableau of hell on earth. One of Rose's officers remembered that the tanks "were silhouetted against a huge inferno that had been the village. The whole west side of the town was blazing fiercely from the successful work of the dive-bombers."[46] The wire team was in the middle of the column.

> Another incident that occurred during that push of ours was when we drove through "a city of fire" (caused by bombing and shelling in advance). Three of us (Hull, Veno, and Marsh) were in a peep and we tore through that wall of flame on both sides of us. All this was in the early hours of the morning, and we had been without sleep for over forty-eight hours at the time. After we had passed through and got up the road some distance, we had to double back and contact the rest of our column.
>
> We same three started back in the peep and a guard halted us inside the city saying there was a Kraut Tiger tank running loose in there. So instead of playing tag with that big baby, we moved up the road once more, found an empty house, and slept till dawn. Three of us walked in the house that night but there were four of us there in the morning. A Kraut had slept in the room next to us all night! He walked out in the morning and surrendered to one of our officers.[47]

As Rose's small command group moved south of the village in the darkness—it was near pitch black—some of his officers suggested that the men needed a breather. Rose wouldn't even consider it.

> The whole American Offensive depends on moving forward. I won't stop before I've taken the objective, no matter how dark it is, or how many men we lose.[48]

They kept moving, with the men of the 22nd Infantry riding atop the tanks. The training had really paid off. Whenever the tankers of the 66th

Armored encountered more than token resistance, the infantrymen, or "doughs" as they called themselves, "would dismount from their vehicles, fix the enemy positions, and lead the tanks in to finish them off."[49] Rose pushed on. Of course, bypassing the enemy often meant that they were in the rear with deadly weapons and still possessed of plenty of fight.

> When you're part of a Spearhead in a drive, you feel like the guy who put his head in the lion's mouth. You never know when the jaws will swing shut, and some of the pockets of resistance that we have to bypass enroute can sure cause some hellish nights for all concerned.
>
> We were moving up a road one night when one of the "small pockets of resistance" proved to be a little stronger than at first expected. There were ten Tiger tanks supported by Kraut infantry and they cut off our column. In general, everyone remained calm and we dug in on the spot.
>
> What made things tough was that darkness was about to fall and that's when the Kraut bombers came over. You can almost set your watch by them nightly. Just around 10:30 you can hear that heavy approaching drone that sounds like an overloaded truck crawling up a steep hill in low-low gear, cutting in and out. Anyhow they came over, dropped their flares, and began their run. Then they hung around to strafe us. The longer they stayed, the more inspiration they gave me for digging in.[50]

Many of the young men were unprepared for the horror of the St. Lô fighting. They were used to tough times, especially those shaped by the worst ordeals of the Depression, but nothing had prepared them for the terrible reality of combat. Most had never seen death before, or if they had, it had been the death of aged loved ones, passing away quietly without pain in the comfort and peace of their own beds. The carnage of a battlefield left even the toughest kids stunned.

> It was an unforgettable scene. In the aftermath, there was nothing alive on that stretch of road. A lot of the time you saw the dead and the dying, but not this time. Anything, man or beast, that had been alive once was now dead with bodies torn, dismembered, disemboweled, burnt, decapitated, flattened from tanks driving over bodies and mutilated beyond one's imagination. One tank stands out more than all others in my mind: the turret had been blown off, the charred remains

of what had been the driver was all that was left in the tank. I could see
a pair of burnt hands grasping the controls. Only the hands. The arms
and torso were gone. The man's head was missing. What was left of
his hips, pelvic area, and legs were burnt black and charred in his seat.
This was one of our tanks and one of our men. Unforgettable.[51]

The war was indifferent to the kind of victim it destroyed. Mixed among
the dead were animals unlucky enough to be caught in the maelstrom. For
many soldiers, especially the farm boys from the Midwest, the sight of
wounded and dying cattle was almost as disturbing as the heaps of human
corpses. The dead horses, still used in large numbers by the Germans, were
especially disturbing to some.

The nearby fields were littered with dead animals, more innocent vic-
tims who happened to be in the wrong place at the wrong time. I can
never forget the horse-drawn German gun carriages and wagons of
all descriptions that were shot to pieces on that one stretch of road.
The ghastly look on the face of the horses is still etched in my memory. Their eyes held that look of horror of war. I looked away from the
pitiful sight for fear I would see the same reflection of my eyes. The
beast in mankind killed the innocent beasts. Rigor mortis sets in
rapidly and soon their legs would be pointing to the road of death,
their bellies bloat from the gas in decomposition and contributes to
the aroma of death. That is the stench we remember all too well. The
odor of burnt flesh is the worst. You want to shower to get the smell
out of your clothing, hair, and mind, but showers are a luxury soldiers in war seldom get to experience.[52]

After halting for the night, CCA, with the 2nd Battalion, 66th Armored in
the lead, took the village of Le Mesnil Herman at 0200 the next morning.
The 22nd Infantry then captured Hill 183. Rose gathered his unit commanders for another impromptu meeting in the field. After being pressed
by his officers again for a brief halt, he finally allowed his men to rest, but
not for long and even the pauses were exhausting. There was really no such
thing as "stopping." The routine was always the same.

One day I dug three foxholes and each time we'd stop I'd dig in next
to a hedgerow the first thing. I'd no sooner get the damn hole dug
down and then back under when we'd get the order to move up

again. Most of the time the advance was only a couple of fields over, or a thousand yards or so.[53]

In spite of the pause, CCA needed to set up roadblocks to protect *Cobra*'s flank. Rose realized that the situation remained highly fluid and dangerous and that the time for boldness—gambling—had not yet passed. The speed of the advance left German soldiers and vehicles cut off and all around the Americans. There was still the real possibility of a German counterattack, and confusion was all around.

In the darkness it was nearly impossible to tell who was friend and who was the enemy. In one of his columns, a half-track with trailer was weaving between the vehicles until it reached the head of the column. The commander of the lead tank was pissed off as the half-track started to pass him, and muttered to his crew, "Hell, I'm supposed to be leading this column." In the next moment, he realized it was a German vehicle, probably unaware it was weaving through the enemy. He destroyed it at point blank range.[54] The darkness made every job more difficult. Then, there was the weather. July was hot, but the CCA wire crews had to go out at all hours in all kinds of weather conditions to locate and fix breaks in the wire—cut by bombs, shells, tank treads, tires, and the feet of marching men. Marsh thought fixing the wire in the dark was one of the scariest things he ever had to do.

> Broken phone wires . . . walking along the shoulder of the road in the pitch dark, seeing real and imagined corpses staring back at you while all the time holding the piece of broken wire running through your hand and being careful where you step is a real character builder. Up ahead a hundred yards or more, your partner in the peep has shut off the motor and is walking towards you to find the break. The rain and mud makes it all more of a challenge, but later in the snow and cold it was even more difficult. Using wire cutters and making a splice means taking off the gloves that were inadequate in the first place and that cold steel served to expedite the repairs. Then test the line and hope there is an answer on the other end. At the end of the ordeal . . . no glory, no medals, no heroics.[55]

The men in *Cutbreak* also had a close call with a German tank trying to return to its own lines. PFC Phil Geidel had been standing guard in the turret when he heard a German tank approach.

> The first night of St. Lô, a German Panther stopped beside "Cutbreak" parked on a lonely road. Men got out to discuss whether our tank was operational. They got back in again, pointing their 88 at us 'til out of sight. Stan (Figurski) and Robbie (Robinson) slept through this and didn't believe it when I told them. PBR (Reisler) and the Air Corps Liaison Officer were at CCA HQs. When leaving, the Panther ran over a peep.[56]

Geidel had ducked down and remained absolutely silent, while the other two crewmen, Stan Figurski and Don "Robbie" Robinson slept inside the Sherman. His self-control and their exhaustion spared them from almost certain destruction. Soon enough, however, the odds caught up with the crew of *Cutbreak*. Later in the war, both of the sleeping crewmen were wounded in action. *Cutbreak* was later renamed "Flypaper" after the Germans discovered the code name by monitoring radio frequencies in captured vehicles. But the battered Sherman made it all the way. When 2nd Armored entered Berlin after VE Day, it was there. It is still there.[57]

The speed of the advance had also left the American columns dispersed, and some of the men had been separated from their units. The wirecrew troubleshooters traveling in Veno's peep "Sis" were close to the HQ vehicles, but not all the Signal Company men were there.

> Donahue was hung up behind us at St. Gilles with Elfer, Newland, and Waldroop, and they were being shelled so bad they couldn't move, as they were pinned down. He lost his rifle that night in the confusion that followed and remembers that very well. He recalls our conversation afterwards, when Sgt. Earlie J. Jones was madder than hell at Bill Veno for almost leaving Jones in Canisy as we crawled over the burning rubble to escape the fighting in town. At one point, Jones threatened to smack Veno in the head with the stock of his Thompson submachine gun for starting to drive away, leaving him standing all alone among the burning buildings in the center of a city with German tanks running amok and shooting anything in sight.[58]

At 1600 on the afternoon of July 27, Rose held another meeting with his commanders in the field. He dispatched two columns of reconnaissance in force towards Villebaudon, his next objective. Once again, there was a strong enemy reaction from the men and guns just ahead.

> Rose pushed us so hard and fast that the Germans cut our column just to our rear. We coiled in the fields protected by the thick hedgerows and took a helluva pounding from the Nebelwerfers, 88s and small arms fire. Seemed like it was coming from every direction.
>
> That day I must have easily dug five foxholes with Larry Hull, as we would move up and then dig in, move up and dig in, move up and dig in. By nightfall we were damn weary of doing that, but had no choice as machine gun fire was raking the hedgerows surrounding us as we hugged the protection of the earthen banks.
>
> We could hear the burp guns firing all night in the field immediately in front of us where our guys from the infantry had a helluva fight on their hands.[59]

The battle for Villebaudon was rough going. German artillery was particularly effective, especially the air bursts which caused most of the casualties. The enemy wasn't the only thing to worry about. Your own men could easily kill you by accident. While the ground troops appreciated the P-47 Thunderbolts, the P-51 Mustangs, and the British rocket-firing Typhoons, the "love affair" had some rough moments.

> Although the pilots are eliminating a lot of obstacles in our path when they come down to bomb and strafe . . . well, they too sometimes pull boners—I know.
>
> One guy let go a 500-pound or more egg right above us. I was in my hole at the time and heard it coming. I rolled over and flattened out as much as possible in those cramped quarters. It seemed like a lifetime before it hit, and as its whine grew in volume I could have sworn it was coming straight for my hole. I felt the rabbit in me and I wanted to get up and run anywhere, do anything to get out of that hole. There was nowhere to go and it would have been my last run if I had, for it hit some twenty feet from where my buddy (*Larry Hull*) and I were lying.
>
> I felt a strong concussion and then as the dirt began to cover me I thought each clod was a piece of shrapnel and I was ready to die. It all happened in just a few seconds, and when the rumpus died down I shook the dirt off and got up. I was wringing wet with cold sweat.[60]

Even before they took Villebaudon, a major threshold of *Operation Cobra* had definitely been crossed. As the men of CCA continued to fight along the narrow roads and hedgerow-lined fields, the news of Rose's dramatic advance moved up the chain of command, all the way to his main sponsor, Omar Bradley. At the various headquarters—from division up to army—everyone realized what it meant: Rose's outfit cracked right through the German defenses; the front had been broken wide open.[61] The results were far beyond the original expectation.

> Nobody was thinking of a breakout when they launched *Cobra*. It was originally designed to have VII Corps sweep to Coutances (Southwestward) to cut off the Germans facing VIII Corps on the Cotentin West Coast. The operation succeeded so well that Collins' suggestion to Bradley that Collins stop short of Coutances to let VIII Corps advance alongside VII Corps to the south transformed the show. The results of *Cobra*, which lasted until noon of 27 July, as I recall, were so good, mainly because of Rose's advance, that Bradley exploited the *Cobra* operation into an immediate exploitation towards, and hopefully to, Avranches.
>
> Rose's drive to protect the other units heading to Coutance was so spectacular that Bradley and Collins were almost pushed into their—really Bradley's—decision to head south. One could, I am sure, say that Rose propelled the Cobra's fangs.[62]

In the end, the offensive would carry well past Coutances all the way to Avranches. It was a battlefield masterpiece. The annals of history record only a few such examples of the military art practiced with such drama and decisive effect.

On July 28, Combat Command A was detached from 2nd Armored, and along with the 13th Cavalry Group, was attached to XIX Corps under the command of Major General Charles Cortlett. For the remainder of the campaign, it was responsible for holding the extreme left flank and preventing the Germans from interfering with the advance that had now shifted to the western part of the battlefield. CCA attacked the town of Percy, the XIX Corps objective, on July 30 and fought off a strong enemy counterattack that threatened their rear. Bloody fighting also continued around the Villebaudon crossroads west of Tessy-sur-Vire, where a German assault spearheaded by forty tanks and supported by infantry was beaten back after a brutal thirteen-hour fight.

The fighting continued the next day as CCA countered strong attacks by the German *2nd Panzer* and *116th Panzer* divisions, before finally taking Tessy on August 1. CCA's major role in *Operation Cobra* was now over.[63] But the suffering and dying were not; neither was the bravery and gallantry. The text of the Presidential Unit Citation awarded to men of the 2nd Battalion, 66th Armored Regiment, is muted testimony to love of comrades that binds men together on a battlefield.

> In this murderous hour, as dead and wounded men littered the field or lay disabled across their burning tanks, the true gallantry of the officers and men in this battalion came to the fore. They worked feverishly to evacuate their fallen comrades as the enemy fire continued to pour in. The uninjured left the comparative safety of their vehicles to aid the less fortunate. Men gave up their seats in tanks and proceeded on foot to the designated assembly area so that wounded men could have the protection of armor as they were transported to the aid station. Tank men refused to leave the field until all the wounded infantry had been evacuated. No group has ever shown a greater display of gallantry in action than did these men.[64]

The cost of the victory had been very high. The 66th Armored Regiment—striking arm of Combat Command A—was hit hard. The regiment suffered 54 men killed, 202 wounded, and 53 missing in action, or total casualties of 309 men, including 22 officers.[65] In the 2nd Battalion alone, casualties were over 51 percent of its combat personnel killed or wounded and 70 percent of its tank strength destroyed or evacuated for repair.[66] During the battle, CCA took more than 1,200 prisoners, killed an estimated 230 German soldiers, and destroyed more than 40 enemy vehicles, including 6 *Panther* (Mk V) tanks.[67]

Once again the men were back in camp, cleaning their weapons and themselves, and once again writing home. It was only then that many realized just how exhausted they were. Don Marsh wrote his folks back home on August 5 that he was taking it easy. After what he and the others had been through, doing nothing seemed like a dream.

> Up until last night I've never had my shoes off for a little better than two weeks. I slept just as I was in my hole with just my raincoat on. There were quite a few nights I didn't get any sleep at all. The first three nights of our push I had only a few hours sleep all told. The third day I felt like I was out on my feet. By that time I had been bombed, strafed, shot at, and what not.
>
> I went into the push twenty-one years old and I feel like I'm now thirty-one instead. It was a bit on the rough side all the way.[68]

The war correspondents also got back to the rear where they could now file their stories about the battle, which had been delayed by the censors. Hal Boyle, an AP reporter who had been with the division since the landing at Fedala in North Africa, had a unique assignment. He was writing an article that would identify the presence in the European Theater of 2nd Armored—"Hell on Wheels"—to his readers. After describing the early history of the division including their earlier exploits—and Rose's role in them—in Africa, Sicily, and Carentan, he wrote about *Cobra*.

> Tanks of the division were fueled and ready on the morning of July 25, 1944. After the Nazi position west of St. Lô had been dealt one of the heaviest bombardments in history by American planes, the division cracked forward and breached the German Line.
>
> They surged into battle with doughboys astride tanks and with special equipment to break through the hedgerows. One column sliced through St. Gilles, seized and passed through flaming Canisy, went on to Le Mesnil Herman, and thrust down to Tessy-sur-Vire before pausing. I was with this Spearheading force and saw it erect its mobile wall of steel, to protect the American left flank. It pushed through regardless of casualties and met and rebuffed numerous trapped Nazi tanks as well as engaging the battered *2nd Panzer Division*, brought hurriedly over from the British front.
>
> Some of the men I talked to and joked with in the hedgerows below Point Herbert last Tuesday are dead now—one fine young Captain I knew was killed in a duel to the death with an enemy *Tiger* tank—but they live in the annals of their division and the glory of its achievement.[69]

For many of the men, now relaxing in the rear and mostly silent about their experiences, the terror of what they had just been through would never leave them. The fighting had been particularly gruesome; the scenes of death and destruction were beyond what anyone could have imagined. The horror of it was physically manifest; they literally reeked of death. The stench was in their clothes, their hair, and their skin.

> Sooner or later you get to wash your clothes, but how do you cleanse your mind of such horrible memories? You don't, you bring it home with you, among your souvenirs you can keep in a special place in a far corner of your mind. The door is never locked so you can visit the memory, if you are so inclined. Some do and some don't. Years go by

and you have never given it any thought, then out of the blue something clicks in your brain and the whole scene appears again in Technicolor. To me, the burning question is always "why?" If I ever figure out the answer, I'll write it down so others don't forget.[70]

For more than a half century, the image of Maurice Rose has burned in the consciousness of the men who saw him in battle leading CCA through St. Gilles and Canisy and Villebaudon. In war, it is the ordinary men who are our best witnesses and our best historians. The men that Rose led during those late July days and nights saw the things of combat with a clarity that often escaped them later in the routine life we all lead. In such a cauldron, however, the ordinary man becomes a poet. Your next door neighbor sees and expresses the unspeakable truth with blinding clarity, and summoned to the task of telling it, finds words that elude scholars.

Soldiers can still remember the smells, the sounds, and the full panoply of emotions that shook them to the core over an expanse of more than five decades. They describe what they experienced in a way that makes the story come to life for the rest of us. In this way they make real a hero whose deeds would otherwise remain colorless and lost in the dry descriptions of battles, and troops, and lines on a map. Doug Donahue remembered how Rose appeared the first time he saw him.

> I joined CCA around 15 June 1944. I remember seeing him around the area and what class he gave out. If ever you wanted a picture of what a pure professional soldier looked like it would have to be General Rose—the boots that shined, the riding britches he wore, the way he carried himself. He was indeed a perfect example of a soldier.[71]

This is the way that many veterans of CCA describe and remember Maurice Rose during *Cobra*. What they recall most is how he looked, how he stood, how he dressed. Such images echo the description of Caesar in the conquest of Gaul; dressed in a bright red cloak, in the front ranks so his men could see him amongst them, grappling with the enemy, fighting hand to hand. The boots, the britches, the erect posture are the things that men recall about General Rose. From this they took courage; from the presence of their leader sharing with them the perils of the battlefield, they drew the strength to face their own fear.

PFC Lawrence A. Hull, a Boston boy in the 142nd Armored Signal Company was attached to the wire team of HQ, CCA. He was in the wire peep at the front of the column and close to the commander as they awaited the order to move down the St. Lô road. It was the first and only time he would see the general.

> The only time I remember seeing Rose was at the breakthrough at St. Lô. Rose was standing tall by a half-track, dressed in his pink riding pants and high leather boots. As we were looking for cover, Rose never moved. He stood looking through his field glasses at what was happening to our infantry as our bombers dropped their bombs short . . . I believe Rose was the first general to use tanks to attack the Germans at night during the breakthrough.[72]

The men, of course, only saw the outward appearance. There was more to the man than colorful dress or a fearless demeanor in the face of the enemy. His superiors knew his mettle. For the second time in the Normandy Campaign, Rose had been chosen for a high stakes mission, one of the men upon whom Joe Collins' "gamble" had largely depended. From this point until the end of the war, the VII Corps commander would be the beneficiary of Rose's aggressiveness, his drive, and his willingness to risk everything for victory. Rose was a man who always seemed to be at the critical spot, at the critical moment, with the critical mission. It is there that audacity pays off the most, or leads to disaster. Rose would experience both during his long, bloody march across Europe. He was the consummate practitioner of armored warfare: maintaining very tight control of his columns, moving at night, never halting, bypassing enemy strong points, relying on strong reconnaissance elements to screen the advance and uncover the enemy's weakness.

The men running the war knew the value of such a warrior, and the opportunity to utilize his skills at a higher level soon appeared. In early August, when Joe Collins' patience with Maj. General Leroy Watson finally ran out, he insisted on Watson's immediate relief. Omar Bradley regretfully agreed and promised to send Collins an experienced armor officer. **(H)**

H Because Leroy Watson was a West Point classmate of Eisenhower and Bradley, Collins had been hesitant to suggest that he be relieved of command. When he finally did, it was Bradley who suggested a successor. Collins, who appreciated the sensitivity of his request, was happy to have Rose. Leroy Watson was transferred to the 29th Infantry Division as Asst. CO, where he performed well.

With his typical fine judgment of men he selected Maurice Rose. Then engaged in some tough fighting near Tessy-sur-Vire under the XIX Corps, Rose could not be released until August 7.[73]

On that early August day at 0922 hours, Maurice Rose was ordered to 2nd Armored HQ where he was relieved of command of CCA, and given command of his own armored division.[74] With the breakthrough complete and the full potential of American mobility now unleashed, First Army, now under the quiet and competent Courtney H. Hodges, was ready to move. The summary of First Army Operations described what happened next.

> Fend him off on the East!
> Hit him, hit him again!
> Close on him to the north,
> Swing on east for the Seine![75]

And that is where Maurice Rose would point his elite 3rd Armored Division. But first he would have to make it his own.

CHAPTER Ten

September 1944:
Collision at Mons

"Give my regards to Maurice Rose."
Lt. General George S. Patton

By the end of August 1944, in the words of Martin Blumenson's classic quotation, "The Allied armies were like knights of old who set out in quest of the Holy Grail but were not adverse to slaying dragons and rescuing damsels in distress along the way."[1] **(A)** Major Haynes W. Dugan, a senior intelligence officer of the 3rd Armored Division, remarked more than five decades later, "With Maurice Rose, we met lots of dragons, but no damsels in distress. Still, we executed one of the classiest and least appreciated maneuvers of the war at Mons."[2]

When Maurice Rose took command of 3rd Armored, it had been in existence for three-and-a-half years and had already passed through two distinct stages. The first phase could be called "Forging the Spearhead" and lasted from activation in April 1941 until deployment to France in late June 1944. The second, or "Baptism in Combat," was brief, and began with the fighting in the *bocage* on June 29 and lasted until the relief of Major General Leroy Watson, five weeks later on August 7, 1944.

A The "Holy Grail" was the Rhine River. The "dragons" were the enemy forces between the Seine River and Germany. The "damsels in distress" were the Channel ports, the Pas de Calais, and Northwest France, Belgium, and Holland.

The division's first experience of combat was a terrible shock, although the men recovered quickly. As Lt. Col. Nathaniel O. Whitlaw, commanding 2nd Battalion, 32nd Armored Regiment, and twice wounded during the Normandy campaign, observed of the action,

> We seemed to be stunned by the ferocity of the German small arms and mortar fire, but we collected our wits and advanced in the face of this fire just as we thought that we would do, and showed little self-concern during the remainder of the battle. We pushed on to our objective like veterans. I am sure that these men will give great accounts of themselves in future battles.[3]

Beginning with the first bloody engagements at Villiers-Fossard and Hill 91, through the St. Lô Breakout, the Mortain Counterattack, and the Falaise–Argentan fighting, the division had been painfully learning the hard business of armored warfare from the best practitioners in the business, the *Panzertruppen* of the *Wehrmacht*.

Losses in men and equipment had been heavy, with little ground gained. In just one month—from its initial commitment until *Operation Cobra*—more than 800 men had been killed or wounded and eighty tanks and sixty-five other vehicles had been lost.[4] While morale remained high, the results were modest considering the cost in blood and sacrifice. Of course, the reasons were simple: the hedgerow terrain, the very tenacious and highly motivated enemy, and the natural inexperience of the outfit. Still, the fact remained that so far, at least, the division had not yet lived up to the very high expectations that had accompanied its original formation and deployment to Europe.

At the highest command levels, there was some real disappointment about the division's performance in its first weeks of combat, and there were doubts about its top leadership. At VII Corps Headquarters, in particular, the evaluation was distinctly negative. Although 3rd Armored had been attached to his VII Corps for just a few weeks, Major General J. Lawton Collins rated Leroy Watson's performance as inadequate. Collins' patience with Watson reached the breaking point during the exploitation stage of *Operation Cobra*. During an administrative road march south from Coutances, which Collins witnessed, 3rd Armored and 4th Armored columns became hopelessly entangled in a giant traffic jam along the narrow roads.

In similar situations—this was a common problem as the Americans spread out after the St Lô Breakout—the senior officers (even top commanders) frequently went to the front and acted as "traffic cops"—but Collins found Watson back at his command post. After that episode, Collins had decided he had no choice but to ask for Watson's relief.[5] He softened his request by telling 12th Army Group commander Lt. General Omar Bradley that he believed Watson would probably make a good infantry commander, but emphasized that he was not suited for command of an armored division. **(B)** Bradley disagreed—he was a West Point classmate and friend of Leroy Watson and respected his proven ability as a trainer of men—but he complied with his subordinate's request.[6] Watson was already gone when Rose arrived, so that he would be spared the humiliating ritual of being publicly relieved by his young successor, already being acclaimed as a tough, professional armor officer.

Down in the ranks, there were differing opinions about the top leadership. Captain Robert W. Russell, an infantry officer attached as a liaison to Combat Command Reserve, was all in favor of the changes.

> General Rose made the 3rd Armored Division. We had a fine body of superbly trained men but we were very badly led until he took command. We were rushed into siege-like action in the hedgerow country in Normandy as the result of General Watson's desire to get us blooded. We were, and we lost many of our best men.[7]

Of course, there were others who felt that Watson and Brigadier General John J. Bohn, who had been relieved of command of Combat Command B a few weeks earlier, had gotten lousy deals, and that the leadership of the division had been unfairly disparaged. Many of the officers and men personally liked the amiable Leroy Watson. **(C)** Others felt that John Bohn had unfairly fallen victim to the legendary temper of Maj. General Leland S. Hobbs, commander of the 30th Infantry Division, to which Bohn's outfit had been attached during the early July fighting.

Whatever the feelings about the top command of the division, most men felt that the layer just below—the regimental and battalion commanders and their staffs—was superb. Major William A. "Bill" Castille, the S-2 (Intelligence) of Combat Command B was a reserve officer who had served with the

---

B In fact, Leroy Watson performed well as Asst. Commander of the 29th Infantry Division and in other postwar assignments.

C After the war, Watson became a politician and was elected Mayor of Beverly Hills, California.

division since 1942. As the commander of the advance HQ, code-named "Ontario Forward," he had a unique opportunity to observe many of the division's officers in action and admired them individually and as a group.

> General Rose inherited a superb combat machine. It was as if he was given a chauffeured Rolls Royce, with accompanying motorcade; and all he had to do was say, "Drive me to Berlin."
>
> My Bottom Line: The already great 3rd Armored Division carried its new commander, General Rose, to greater recognition.[8]

Bill Castille had a unique perspective on the change in command and felt some trepidation. He had met Rose before when the 33rd Armored Regiment hosted Combat Command A, 2nd Armored at Warminster, England, when it arrived from Sicily in the fall of 1943. He already knew from personal experience that the new commander would be tough as nails, impatient, hard to please, and very demanding.

When Rose arrived to take command—he was the fourth to lead the division since it was formed—the third or "Rose Phase" began. **(D)** This period lasted eight months, almost to the end of World War II, and dominates its combat history. From the time he arrived until his death, Maurice Rose wielded the 3rd Armored Division as his personal instrument of war. As in the lore and legend of many nations and many centuries, wherein the epic hero names his sword, Maurice Rose, after taking command, gave his division a name drawn from his own spirit and character: "Spearhead."[9] From August 7, 1944, until March 30, 1945, his story and that of the division are very nearly the same.

The titles of the "Green Books" describing the European Theater of Operations in the U.S. Army's Official History of World War II tell that story. The 3rd Armored Division spearheaded the First U.S. Army's *Breakout and Pursuit* (author, Martin Blumenson) across France and Belgium. It was first to engage the enemy in force in the *Siegfried Line Campaign* (author, Charles MacDonald) and fought decisively in the *Ardennes: Battle of the Bulge* (author, Hugh Cole). It was up front in *The Last Offensive* (author, Charles MacDonald) in the drive across the Rhine, encircling the Ruhr, and moving up to the Elbe.

D Brig. General Alvan C. Gillem was the commanding general at formation (April 1941). He was succeeded by Brig. General Walton W. Walker (January 1942) and then by Brig. General Leroy H. Watson (August 1942).

The 3rd Armored Division was activated on April 15, 1941, at Camp Beauregard, Louisiana. Among its first officers were a number of 2nd Armored personnel who were transferred as cadre to help set up the new division. By transferring experienced men in this manner, the army was able to activate the newly organized armored divisions quickly. **(E)** The 3rd Armored moved to Camp Polk, Louisiana, on June 11, 1941 where it remained for more than a year until it was sent to Camp Young, California, on July 26, 1942. There, at the Desert Training Center, it was the first armored division to receive training in desert warfare and participated in maneuvers with Patton's I Armored Corps. In January 1943, it crossed the country by rail and was stationed at Indiantown Gap, Pennsylvania, until it shipped out for England on September 5, 1943.

After crossing the Atlantic without incident, the division landed in England on September 18, 1943, and traveled by train to camps around Warminster, where for nine months it trained for its part in the invasion of Europe. The first elements of the division landed at Omaha White Beach below the village of Isigny on June 23, 1944. On June 29, Combat Command A, led by Brig. General Doyle O. Hickey, was attached to 30th Infantry and committed to battle to reduce a shallow salient at Villiers-Fossard. Combat Command B, under command of Brig. General John J. Bohn, first saw action on July 7, 1944, in a vicious seesaw battle to capture and hold Haute Vent, also known as Hill 91.

After these first bloody engagements, the division played a significant role in the *Operation Cobra* breakthrough as part of "Lightning Joe" Collins' VII Corps' mobile forces. When the change of division command took place on August 7, both of the Combat Commands were attached to other units, and engaged in the containment of the ferocious German counterattack at Mortain. **(F)** In fact, the men had barely learned of the relief of their well-liked leader when they were suddenly thrown again into bitter combat.

Maurice Rose, however, was determined to remake the division in his own image, no matter what anyone thought or whatever the external circumstances. In spite of the changes and disruptions—in the space of several

---

E Six hundred officers and 3,000 enlisted men of the 2nd Armored Division transferred from Fort Benning, Georgia, to the old National Guard station at Camp Beauregard, Lousiana. During the period 1940–1943 sixteen armored divisions were formed, fourteen of which saw combat during World War II.

F CCA was attached to 4th Infantry Division, and CCB was attached to 30th Infantry.

weeks the commanding generals of both the division and Combat Command B had been relieved—Rose acted quickly and decisively. At the beginning of the Mons Campaign—just three weeks after taking over—he relieved Col. Dorrance Roysden, the commanding officer of the 33rd Armored Regiment, and one of the division's "old timers." **(G)** Only a few days later, on September 2, while on the march to Mons, he relieved Col. Louis P. Leone, the CO of the 36th Armored Infantry Regiment (and Combat Command Reserve) for not being aggressive enough.

The relief of Col. Roysden, in particular, had a dramatic effect on the men. Lt. Col. Sam Hogan, one of the division's great Task Force commanders, saw it as an early signal of Rose's determination to put his own mark on the division.[10] Roysden had a reputation during training of being a sort of martinet, all spit and polish; what the men derisively called a "chicken shit" officer. That image changed sharply, however, when he took his men into combat. He made a name for himself in taking Hill 91—Haut Vent—and holding it against a fierce series of counterattacks by the elite *Panzer Lehr* division.

Later, during the drive across France, Col. Truman E. Boudinot, then commanding Combat Command B, complained that Roysden was not aggressive enough. His Task Force was facing an enemy dug in behind a raised railway embankment through which there was only one underpass, which was covered by concentrated German fire. Boudinot, to the rear, kept pressing Roysden to move forward, radioing him, "There is nothing in front of you but a thin line," to which Roysden, under heavy pressure and taking casualties, replied, "It may be thin, but it's damn tough."

Boudinot was not amused or impressed with Roysden's glibness. He ordered Roysden to report immediately to division HQ, where he appeared dressed immaculately in field uniform. He was kept waiting for quite some time when finally he was called before General Rose, who summarily and without explanation relieved him of command. He was the first field grade officer to feel the sting of Rose's impatience, but he was not the last.[11]

As Major Haynes W. Dugan, Asst. G-2, noted when it was suggested that relieving Roysden was Rose's way of showing that he was now totally in command, "it worked."[12] Everyone soon realized that there would be no tolerance for excuses, no second chance for men who didn't perform, no appeals, no matter what the circumstances or how difficult or dangerous the mission. Rose made his position clear from the very beginning. From this point forward, a visit by the commanding general in the field, or a

---

G Colonel Roysden was transferred to SHAEF as a staff officer.

summons to report to his HQ, always carried with it the threat of immediate relief or some other disciplinary action.

Maurice Rose took over 3rd Armored at a very busy time. The division, less Combat Command B, was besieged near Mayenne, approximately 150 miles west of Paris. CCB had just been released from its attachment to 1st Infantry Division and had been ordered to assemble at Reffuvielle (just eight miles west of Mortain) for rest, maintenance, and resupply pending reattachment to 3rd Armored in time for Rose's assumption of command. That same day, the German *Seventh Army*, with five elite *Panzer* divisions attached, spearheaded by the *116th Panzer* and *2nd SS Panzer*, launched its massive counterattack from positions just east of Mortain. **(H)**

Situated on a rocky ledge overlooking the small Cance River, and dominated by a beautiful thirteenth-century church, the small village of Mortain lies about twenty miles east of the Normandy coast and fifteen miles south of Vire. The German plan was to take Mortain and then advance to their ultimate objective: Avranches, twenty-two miles to the west, and a bottleneck along the crucial supply route for the Allies. Taking it would split First Army and Third Army, effectively cutting off the latter from its Normandy supply bases.

On the morning of the attack, Combat Command B and 30th Infantry Division lay directly in the path of the German juggernaut.[13] **(I)**

H The German *Seventh Army* was activated at Stuttgart on August 25, 1939, and played a relatively minor role during the early part of the war until the D-Day landing which took place opposite its *LXXXIV Corps*. It was quickly shifted to the left (western) flank of the invasion front, but when *HQ, Panzer Group West* was bombed on D+4, *Seventh Army* again assumed command of the entire front. Preoccupied with holding Caen against repeated British attacks, *Seventh Army* could prevent neither the isolation of the Cotentin Peninsula nor the fall of Cherbourg. It was more successful in the hedgerow country during the second half of June, but many of its units were destroyed in the fighting at Falaise and in the retreat across the Seine. After being mauled yet again at Mons, it was rebuilt during September 1944, fought during the Ardennes Offensive, and was still in the field on VE Day.

I Just east of Mortain is Hill 317 (designation of the hill, sometimes referred to as 314, is based on its height in meters) from whose summit one can see the countryside for more than twenty miles in every direction. It was from these heights that the surrounded 2nd Battalion, 120th Infantry Regiment, broke up the enemy attack, and at terrible cost fought one of the truly great, heroic small unit actions of World War II. During this engagement, the battalion lost 300 killed or wounded out of 700 men, or 43 percent casualties, and all four company commanders were awarded the Distinguished Service Cross. The Battalion was awarded a Presidential Unit Citation with a streamer embroidered *Mortain*.

The battle was very costly, especially to the armored infantry. The casualties amongst the 36th Armored Infantry leadership were ghastly—Colonel Cornog, the regimental commander was KIA, two battalion commanders, two acting battalion commanders, five company commanders, six platoon leaders, two first sergeants, and at least four platoon sergeants were also killed or wounded.[14]

After the Mortain battle, on August 12, the Combat Commands were once again returned to 3rd Armored Division control. Maurice Rose then led his reunited division for the first time in the battle to close the Falaise-Argentan gap. Before the Allies were able to close the thirteen-mile wide passage completely, the remnants of Germany's *Seventh Army* managed to escape encirclement and total annihilation by retreating towards the Seine River. The 3rd Armored finished its part in the battle when it linked up with the British on the Putange road on August 19. After several days of refitting, the 3rd Armored Division began its rapid advance across the width of France, reaching the Seine River on August 25.

That night the division began crossing in the vicinity of Tilly and by evening the next day was moving towards the storied battlefields of World War I. It "must have been the 26th of August" when Major Dugan saw a peep approaching the bridge where he was stationed. A man stood upright, with three stars on his shiny helmet, wearing an Eisenhower jacket with riding breeches, holding kid leather gloves, and sporting fancy revolvers at both hips. As he approached, Major Dugan stood to attention and snapped off a smart salute.[15]

> I was the bridgemaster, and during a lull in the traffic, a single peep came from across the river. Lt. General George S. Patton, accompanied by his driver, stopped and inquired: "Major, is everything under control?" When I answered affirmatively, he said, "Give my regards to Maurice Rose." Our General had briefly been his 2nd Armored Chief of Staff and then his subordinate in Sicily.[16]

On August 27, the men crossed the Marne River near Trilport, and the next day, General Collins, in an emotionally charged order, asked Rose to send a detachment to take Château Thierry in the name of VII Corps. **(J)** There were men on that battlefield who had fought there during World War I.

J The question still remains whether 3rd Armored or 7th Armored (XX Corps) arrived first.

The division then covered the forty miles to the Aisne River in just two days. Major Dugan, who was also the Public Relations Officer (PRO), had been keeping a daily diary. As they pushed on, he started to see reminders of the earlier world war,

> We're on the well-known road *Chemin des Dames*. German cemetery from the first part of this war on edge of bivouac. Many old stokes mortar duds and barbed wire entanglements around from last war.[17]

The men of the 23rd Armored Engineers were riding at the front of the columns to ensure that blown or damaged bridges would be repaired quickly. On August 28, Maurice Rose was, as usual, also riding at the head of a column. He pulled up just short of a damaged, but still standing, railroad-bridge over the Aisne River. The Germans were rallying on the opposite bank and had brought the bridge under artillery fire. It was obviously damaged and nobody was sure how sturdy it was, or if it could support heavy vehicle traffic. Of course, there was always the danger that it had been wired for demolition. The officers of the task force were discussing what to do and concluded that the safest alternative was to reconnoiter for another crossing point. Of course, that would allow the Germans more time to build up their defenses. It was at this moment that Rose suddenly appeared.

> "What's going on? Why are you stopping?" he demanded to know. He was told.
> "Has anyone checked the bridge?"
> "No," replied a frightened officer when he saw Rose's expression.
> "Then I'll do it myself.—"
> "General, sir . . . the bridge is mined . . ." officers shouted after him.
> Rose, crouching low, made his way carefully across the bridge, tested its strength, and probed for mines while machine gun bullets whizzed around him and mortar shells dropped close by into the river.[18]

Back in the peep and shaking with fear, T/4 Shaunce put the peep into low gear and inched ahead, expecting at any moment to be killed or wounded in a horrible explosion. There was none. He picked up the general. Satisfied that the bridge was in good condition for tanks, Rose returned to the stunned group of officers and ordered the tanks across. This time his luck held, but this would not be the last time Rose would take the risk of crossing a suspect bridge.

After expanding the Aisne River bridgehead and securing the deserted World War I concrete fortifications on the high ground north of Soissons, Rose attacked east towards Sedan. As they got ready to move, the men started to feel better. The rain of the past several days had finally stopped and the flights of four P-47 "Thunderbolts" were once again visible overhead, circling the spearheads like birds of prey.

By late morning on Thursday, August 31, the 3rd Armored was moving along five axes of advance towards Sedan, with units of Combat Command A already thirty miles beyond the Aisne River and in contact with the enemy's rear guard. General Collins was at his CP awaiting a routine visit from his boss, Lt. General Courtney Hodges, commander of the First U.S. Army. The field telephone rang. It was Hodges.

> "Joe, you've got to change direction at once toward Mons to help cut off the German *Seventh Army*."
>
> For the VII Corps, the right-flank unit of the First Army, that would require a change of direction of almost 90 degrees and would pull the corps away from the Third Army, with which I had been required to maintain contact.
>
> I asked: "But who will fill the gap that will develop between my right and the Third Army?"
>
> Courtney's reply was blunt, and to the point, as he hung up: "Joe, that's your problem!"[19]

Preoccupation with maintaining contact with adjacent formations was a key lesson from the setbacks of the early battles in North Africa. Collins gave this mission to the reinforced 4th Cavalry Group commanded by Col. Joseph M. Tully. Collins also instructed Tully to reconnoiter the ground to the east preparatory to another shift in direction should circumstances change once again. If Mons is a showcase for the skill and daring of Maurice Rose, it is also another dramatic display of Joe Collins' talents, justifying the opinion of many, including the senior British commanders, that he was one of the best corps commander in Europe.

In making the 90-degree turn towards Mons, 3rd Armored, in concert with other VII Corps units, was about to capture Maubeuge, Mons, Namur, Liege, and finally, reach Aachen. In this feat of arms, they would retrace, in reverse, the path laid out in the German General Staff modification of the classic von Schlieffen invasion plan for the conquest of Western Europe.[20]

Collins' plan was to deploy the battle-tested divisions of his VII Corps three abreast. The 1st Infantry with Combat Command B in support would be on the left. The 9th Infantry, riding behind Combat Command A, would be on the right and 3rd Armored's Combat Command Reserve would drive up the middle along the main Mauberge–Mons highway.

The eighteen-day drive of the U.S. First Army's VII Corps, "spearheaded" by Maurice Rose's 3rd Armored Division, across France and Belgium reached a climax at the giant armored ambush at Mons, Belgium, on September 3, 1944.[21] It was, by any measure, a brilliantly successful engagement. The semi-official 3rd Armored Division history, *Spearhead in the West*, citing the correspondents' excitement, describes it as "the decisive battle in the West" about which "thousands of words have already been written and will continue to be written."[22]

That judgment might seem overstated, even strange in hindsight, given that Mons was given only scant attention by the great post-war scholars. Although the newspapers did cover the story at the time, and the Official U.S. Army History and post-war memoirs treat it briefly, it remains essentially an "unknown victory." Even the correspondents who filed stories did not identify the units involved in the battle. In fact, the 3rd Armored Division was not taken off the "Secret" list for publicity until October 7, two months after Rose took command and more than a month after the victory at Mons.

Indeed, there was more scholarship on the First Battle of Mons, fought during late August 1914 and considered a watershed event in British military history. **(K)** Between the wars, cadets at West Point and

---

K Mons, a city of more than 90,000 inhabitants in southwestern Belgium, is capital of Hainaut Province. Located 30 miles southwest of Brussels, it sits on a hill between the Haine and Trouille Rivers, at the point where the Canal du Centre meets the Nimy-Blaton Canal. The latter canal was built by Napolean and is still the main commercial route to France. Mons lay at the junction of a number of important roads, including modern-day highways H5 and H15.

Mons has a long military history and has always been well-fortified. Originally a Roman outpost (called *Castrilocus*) in the third century A.D., it expanded around an abbey founded in 650 by St. Waudru, a daughter of the Count of Hainaut. Charlemagne made it provincial capital in 804, and it was surrounded by walls and ramparts. The brilliant French military engineer Sebastian Le Prestre du Vauban built its defenses during the seventeenth century. In the almost constant warfare that ravaged Europe between the sixteenth and eighteenth centuries, Mons was attacked and occupied many times by France, Holland, Spain, England, and

officers at the Infantry School, including then Captain Lawton Collins, studied that campaign in detail. Some, like Collins, had even visited the terrain while stationed in Germany after World War I.[23]

Perhaps one reason for the ultimately muted reporting of the Mons Operation at the time—indeed even after the war—might have been the requirement of tight security. While soldiers in the field are used to the phrase "orders are orders" as explanation, battlefield deployments based

---

Austria. Attacked during August 1914 by the Germans, it was bombed by the *Luftwaffe* at the beginning of World War II. While spared a direct assault, it was occupied from May 12, 1940 until 3rd Armored liberated the city. The headquarters of NATO's highest European Command—SHAPE (Supreme Headquarters Allied Powers Europe), the successor to Eisenhowers' SHAEF—is located on the Casteau Plateau, captured by Combat Command B late on September 2, 1944.

Mons holds a special place in British military lore. It was the first engagement of the BEF in the Great War. The first shots fired by English soldiers on the continent of Europe since Waterloo were fired at Mons, and the first soldier to die fell there. The first two Victoria Crosses were awarded to men of the 4th Royal Fusiliers, one of whom, Lt. Dickey, died defending a vital bridge. It was during the battle that the legend of the *Angels of Mons* began. At midnight of August 23, the sky was suddenly filled with a band of angels dressed as archers who terrified the Germans and "covered" the retreat of the 8th Brigade. In an example of astounding symmetry, Mons was also the scene of the last battle of the Great War, when on November 11, the Canadian 3rd Division liberated the city, losing some men who became the last Commonwealth soldiers to die in World War I.

The First Battle of Mons began on August 23, 1914. The German plan called for a breakthrough on the left flank by the heavily reinforced *First Army* of General Alexander Von Kluck followed by the isolation and rapid envelopment of the Allied armies in Belgium. The initial clash was along the banks of the Mons–Conde Canal, held for twenty miles by the British II Corps, with I Corps and a cavalry division in support.

The British regulars dug in among the heaps of slag where they covered all twenty-one bridges across the canal. Their rifle fire—the regulars were trained to get off fifteen aimed shots per minute—was so devastating and sustained that the Germans believed they were facing massed machine guns. But the German artillery fire was also effective, and under its cover, German infantry crossed the canal, and succeeded in enveloping and virtually destroying a British regiment. Finally, with the French Fifth Army in full retreat on their right, the British line was forced to withdraw several miles south and a general retreat began. By August 26, the Germans held Mons. The occupation lasted four years. Total British casualties reached 1,600, while German losses are thought to have been at least twice that many.

on enemy troop movements are the province of intelligence and sometimes hushed up by "security" demands. The most plausible explanation for the strict security about this particular operation was the *source* of the battle-field intelligence.

The key to the victory at Mons is the decoding operation at Bletchley Park, whose quasi "real-time" product, code-named *Ultra,* was delivered to a very small number of users by special means—via Special Liaison Unit couriers. Although not discussed at the time, those who were privy to the secret intelligence knew that Mons, like Carentan, was a dramatic demonstration that *Ultra* could prove decisive when used tactically on the battlefield.

It is not surprising, therefore, that given the high level of security accorded the activities at Bletchley Park, and the care employed in the dissemination of the *Ultra* product, that postwar interpretations of the significance of Mons are also understated. In Martin Blumenson's official history *Breakout and Pursuit,* the battle is described as a chance encounter or meeting engagement:

> The head-on encounter at Mons was, from a tactical point of view, a surprise for both sides. Neither Americans nor Germans had been aware of the approach of the other, and both had stumbled into an unforeseen meeting that resulted in a short, impromptu battle.[24]

That judgment was based mostly on First Army "After Action Reports" and intelligence summaries, and confirmed by Blumenson in postwar discussions with Collins and others. In fact, the First Army official report of the campaign offers the reason for the change of orders without describing the source of the information.

> During the last days of August as the army drove northeast through northern France it had become increasingly apparent that a large enemy force was operating west of the line Laon–Mons. A rapid change of direction in the attack of the VII Corps would serve to trap this force and deny it access to the roads leading east back into Germany.[25]

In one of the earliest studies of the operation, written by students in the Advanced Course of the Armor School in 1948–1949, the authors admit that they were unable—at that time—to determine the headquarters issuing the orders, or the actual reason for the order to change the direction of the attack.[26]

In fact, the order that ultimately led to Rose's order to turn the 3rd Armored was developed as a result of the intercepts.[27] The codebreakers of Bletchley Park, based on their careful analysis of the German order of battle intercepts, had detected a massive and disorderly withdrawal of elements of the German *Seventh Army*, along with units belonging to the *Fifteenth Army*. Among the thousands of troops streaming east were elements of the *II SS*, *LXVII Parachute*, and *XXX Corps*, as well as ten other identified divisions. After losing contact with higher headquarters, the German corps commanders organized themselves as a *Provisional Army* under General Lieutenant Straube, and they were streaming, broken, back towards Brussels by any means possible, on any roads leading east.[28]

As in other cases where direct reaction to "special intelligence" might have compromised the code-breaking operation, the intercepts were confirmed—and given "cover"—by increased aerial reconnaissance.[29] In a fortuitous stroke of luck, the weather, which had been generally cool, overcast, with occasional rain, had improved at the end of August.[30] As far as the men knew, it was aerial reconnaissance that discovered the German retreat.

> Here was the division widely spread out, as was the whole VII Corps, to the best of my knowledge, headed "balls out" for Germany. When an order came down saying it was based on Army Air Corps observation, that the German forces had pulled out of Normandy and Western France and were retreating generally along the Channel coast under bombardment from the air.[31]

Perhaps another reason for the relative obscurity of this great victory is just bad timing. The "Mons Pocket" operation happened during one of the most active and successful periods of the entire land war in Europe. The march of the 3rd Armored was just one more incredible advance in an avalanche of such events as Bradley's 12th Army Group and Montgomery's 21st Army Group broke out of Normandy and fanned out across France and Belgium. Within three weeks of the liberation of Paris, troops from Hodges First Army stood on the soil of five countries![32]

As Maurice Rose, driving with the lead column of Combat Command Reserve, moved east toward the borders of the Third Reich, the chorus of Allied victories and the deeds of great fighting units was at a crescendo.[33]

(L) Against that background, Omar Bradley described Mons as a "little known, but brilliantly conducted campaign."[34] Dwight Eisenhower, the Supreme Allied Commander, noted that because of the flood of victories, Mons barely got the notice that it had deserved and passed "almost unnoticed in the press."[35] Of course, he was preoccupied as well with his own command problems. On September 1, 1944, at the very beginning of the move towards Belgium, Eisenhower took control of the entire European land battle.

At 1000 hours on August 31, Combat Command Reserve—with Rose's peep just behind the lead tanks—moved out in the face of moderate resistance to secure the village of Nouvion. He continued the drive throughout the morning, eventually reaching Serraincourt at noon. By 1300 hours, the division's five task forces were all advancing eastward towards the original assigned VII Corps objectives of Sedan and Charleville, in the face of sporadic resistance. The lead elements were a scant sixty miles from the German border. The 83rd Reconnaissance Battalion was screening the advance of each column, reconnoitering the road with its M-8 armored cars and M-5 Stuart light tanks, and bypassing enemy resistance.

At 1315, a VII Corps Operations Officer arrived from Corps HQ at La Rue via liaison airplane and went immediately to Rose's forward echelon CP, located just south of Laon. There, the VII Corps officer was greeted by 3rd Armored's Chief of Staff, Col. John A. Smith and other senior staff of the 3rd Armored.[36] **(M)**

After being informed of the new movement orders, Smith immediately contacted General Rose on the command radio and, through the use of "coded conversation," Rose was informed that there had been a major change in the orders and that more information would follow. Rose immediately

---

L On September 1, the Canadian 2nd Infantry Division took Dieppe, where its men had met disaster on the beaches in the failed 1942 raid. The next day, the British 51st (Highland) Division liberated St. Valery-en-Caux, a village on the Channel coast, west of Dieppe, where in 1940, elements of the Division had been surrounded and captured by Rommel's *7th Panzer Division*. On that same day, the American 2nd Armored Division took Tournai after being the first Allied unit to cross the Belgian border, and by September 3, the British had captured Brussels, and the Canadians had a bridgehead across the Somme.

M Colonel John A. Smith was born in Texas and commissioned a reserve officer in the Field Artillery in 1917. He served as chief of staff to all five wartime commanders of the 3rd Armored Division. He was decorated with the Legion of Merit, Bronze Star, Croix de Guerre with Palm (France), Legion of Honor (France), and the Presidential Unit Citation for his role at Mons. He retired from the Army as a Colonel.

radioed a halt order over the division commander's radio net to his commanders with instructions to "coil" off the roads and await further orders. As one staff officer said, "You could hear the brakes squeal when we radioed the order to halt."[37]

The General Staff officers, especially Lt. Colonel Gene Orth, G-4 (Logistics), worked in conjunction with corps staff to quickly prepare the necessary orders. Soon, a liaison officer from HQ was dispatched and found General Rose at Seraincourt. He gave Rose the main outline verbally. Collins' orders were to break off the easterly advance, disengaging from enemy contact, and wheel 90 degrees to the left using routes of advance through Hirson and Vervins to secure Mons, the major road junction on the Belgian #9 and #11 highways.

Over the course of the next ninety minutes, through the use of voice and wireless messages and face-to-face battlefield meetings, Rose conferred with his combat commanders, task force leaders, and their staffs. On the hoods of peeps and armored cars, they mapped out the planned axes of advance and prepared for a major change in direction. It was a masterpiece of spontaneous battlefield reaction. It vindicated the highest expectations of American armored doctrine.

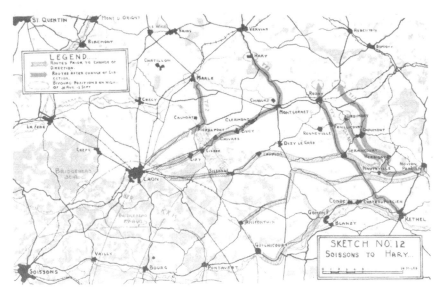

The 3rd Armored Division turn towards Mons, August 31, 1944

(*Source: Spearhead in the West*)

Rose and his commanders accomplished this change of plan while on the march and in contact with the enemy at several different points along the original route of advance. Division-wide orders were coordinated and issued at 1430, or less than an hour and a half after the first order to halt had been given. Much later that day the various units of the 3rd Armored received the written "Division Field Order No. 12," containing specific unit assignments and map overlays for the attack to begin at 0700, September 1 with Mons, Belgium as the final objective.[38]

The entire division halted as if in obedience to a sharp command on a drill field. It was a tribute to the discipline, training, and professionalism of the men, especially the NCOs and junior officers. It is all the more dramatic that the halt order, change of direction commands, and all the complicated details required for implementation were sent by radio. Of course, this placed great pressure on the voice and wireless sections of the 143rd Signal Company (and the code-clerks), especially the men assigned to the various field HQs, including those with General Rose's forward echelon. He had complete trust in the ability of his signals men, whose M-20 was always close behind.[39] In a very real sense, the success of armored operations can be laid directly at the feet of the attached signal company. Without them—the wiremen, radio and phone operators, code clerks, message center men and runners—the immense firepower of the combat arms would have been blind and unguided.

Even before he got Field Order #12 with overlays, Lt. Col. Edward S. Berry, commander of the reinforced 67th Field Artillery Battalion supporting Combat Command A, made sure that his forward observers had new maps as well as a new set of index and check-points. He wanted to be certain he could respond with concentrated artillery fire *when and where* required from the moment the attack commenced.[40]

After the initial turn and the reorientation of the columns, the division coiled once more and prepared for the attack. **(N)** Both Task Forces of CCA

N The term "coiled" was commonly used among armored units and is almost self-explanatory. After the fashion of pioneer wagon trains on the western plains, it is based on a 360-degree defensive circle. The medium tanks of the column form a 180-degree arc, presenting their front armor outward against the likely direction of an attacker. The remaining "soft" vehicles and the command group gather in the middle. The light tanks and tank destroyers take position to complete the circle. The infantry dig foxholes around the tanks and establish listening posts, roadblocks, and other positions. Patrols are then organized by the infantry and reconnaissance company to screen or "picket" the "coil."

were in contact with the enemy. Task Force X had to backtrack several kilometers to Hauteville before turning north towards Landouzy. Task Force Y was engaged in a rear guard action near Rethel, disengaged and then headed due north on the Rethel–Rozay road. Task Force 1 and Task Force 2 of Combat Command B had reached Perrepont and Notre Dame de Liesse by the time the halt order had been received, so they were in good position for the turn north. Combat Command Reserve had been halted in a wooded area west of Herbigny and headed north toward Chaumont and Wadimont. CCB was on the left, CCA was in the center, and CCR was on the right. The 9th Infantry Division was on the VII Corps' right, protecting the exposed flank and the 1st Infantry Division was on the left, charged with protecting that flank beyond the adjoining V Corps limit of advance.[41]

The 83rd Armored Reconnaissance Battalion, which had been leading each task force, now had the task of screening the right flank of the division as it turned north. Spreading out along the secondary road-net, leading and providing flank protection for every column, Lt. Col. Prentice

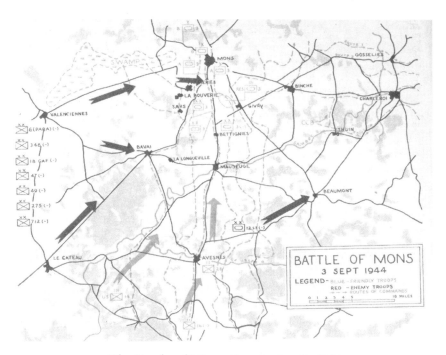

The Battle of Mons, September 3, 1944
(*Source: Spearhead in the West,* Emended by William Castille, S3, CCB)

Yeomans' men had no front or demarcation lines. They were out in the air at the extreme right flank of the division. This was armored warfare at its most terrifying; the only thing to be sure of was the enemy, likely to pop up at any moment, at any place.

At 0700 on September 1 the actual advance north began. Second Lt. Herbert E. Zimmerman was a section leader in 2nd Platoon, D Company, 83rd Reconnaissance Battalion fighting with Combat Command Reserve. When he reached the village of Hirson, the resistance was intense and lasted the better part of a day. Fifty years after first recording his impressions for the official First Army historians, he still had vivid images. The fighting was

> . . . a hairy situation. We entered the city and at the first house saw that the yard was dug up from tank treads. In the house water was still boiling on the stove. Several other soldiers and myself walked into the town. We had gone about a block when we saw a German tank pull out of a side street and go in the opposite direction. As we turned to go back where we had entered, a 2½-ton German truck and a motorcycle came out of the main crossroads. We of course shot it up and captured the survivors. We were then ordered to pull back. In the morning (September 2, 1944) we re-entered with additional troops.[42]

The men of the 703rd Tank Destroyer Battalion also had cause to remember the intensity of the battle. **(O)** With one line company—each supported by one reconnaissance platoon—attached to each combat command, elements of the battalion were busy setting road blocks, ambushes, engaging tanks, knocking out thin-skinned vehicles and horse-drawn wagons, and killing the enemy in very large numbers. On September 1, 1944, the men of B Company wounded and then captured a German general officer.

In spite of the speed of the march, the reality was grim from moment to moment. The passage of decades has not softened the sense of confusion and fear that accompanied every mile. Captain Henry Gosch was in the thick of the fighting.

O The 703rd Tank Destroyer Battalion was organizationally an independent unit under the Tank Destroyer Force Command. In reality it was an integral part of the fabric of the 3rd Armored and was permanently attached, except for a brief time during the Battle of the Bulge when it was attached to the 1st Infantry Division.

I commanded C Co., 703rd Tank Destroyer Battalion in the Mons engagement. Those were wild days of no sleep, intermittent fighting, and continuous day and night movement until we reached Mons. At one point, as we approached Mons, C Co. (and others) had to fall out of column and wait for diesel fuel since, if attacked, we had only enough left for a short fire fight. Supply was real short and could come forward only in tank protected columns. Our wounded, sent hopefully to the rear after initial treatment, were frequently denied passage by the bypassed Germans and were returned to us.[43]

Sgt. Jack Warden, a feisty Texas Irishman with a shock of red hair and a natural suspicion of officers (which persisted even after he won a battlefield commission) was leading his armored infantry platoon from his half-track.

We were mounted and moving forward until fired upon. Then we went after them on foot and destroyed everyone who didn't run away. About four in the afternoon, we were ordered to halt. I looked around and saw we were in a cabbage or beet field with the tops above knee high length. Suddenly, Pierre grabbed the driver's Tommy gun and fired across the field. I tore his ass up and asked why he did that. He said there was a German out there. I told him I wanted him to go out there and bring me that German. Nobody believed him. He bailed out and ran, yelling, "commin zee here, and hende hoch." Up popped a German. The thing I was upset about is you do not touch another man's weapon under any conditions. We all had a good laugh and forgot it.[44]

That night the men heard a strange sound overhead. For the first time during the war, they heard the drone of V-1 flying bombs. It would not be the last time.[45] Early on the third day of the drive north, September 2, it began to rain again, but that did not slow the advance. The German resistance was mostly limited to light infantry and artillery fire that was either pushed aside or bypassed.[46] At roughly 1600 hours, two tanks of Combat Command A approached the Belgian border. General Rose, who had been weaving between the Combat Commands all day, was in his peep just a few vehicles behind Hickey's lead tanks and was about to cross.

The race to the Belgian border had been followed closely by the correspondents and a real sense of history unfolding permeated the headquarters as the tanks pressed forward. At 1610 hours, those who were closest to

**Brigadier General Maurice Rose on the road to Mons
(September 2, 1944)**
(*Source:* Rose Family Album)

the radio heard it crackle as General Rose, now next to General Hickey's peep, sent this message over the commander's net, "Ottawa Six and I are now crossing the line." Among the first men of the division to cross the border were Wesley Ellison and Neil Fleischer, radio operators, and message center code clerk William Hatry, each of whom always accompanied General Rose.

As the lead vehicles rumbled across the border, Rose ordered Shaunce to pull the peep off to the side of the road so that General Hickey could be the first general across the border.[47] In spite of 3rd Armored lore, however, it was men of the 82nd Reconnaissance Battalion, 2nd Armored, who crossed the Belgian border first at 0930 on September 2, 1944, at a point northwest of Mons. The honor that Rose wanted for Hickey probably belongs to Brigadier General John "Pee Wee" Collier, successor to Rose as commanding general of CCA, 2nd Armored. Whatever the actual facts about the crossing, Maurice Rose was a man who understood the importance of such gestures; and stepping aside at the border was a tribute to, and acknowledgment of, the performance of a loyal and effective subordinate. **(P)** General Rose would have certainly agreed with Artilleryman Col. Ed Berry, who described Hickey as

> A tower of strength in tight situations and an inspiration to all who serve under his command. A man who clearly understands the advantage of being able to concentrate the fire of all his artillery and tank weapons against places likely to constitute enemy centers of resistance.[48]

As the various columns passed through the small border villages, the French and Belgian civilians, emerging from the four-year terror of German occupation, went wild. On September 2, Claude Ancelet was an eight-year-old boy living in the French village of Liesses, on the outskirts of the Trelon Forest in the Chimay border region. He was eating breakfast with his mother and sister when

> Gunfire erupted in all directions and we fled to a neighbor's house. The streets were deserted. All the civilians had taken shelter. About noon, the German trucks stopped moving and we decided to return home. Suddenly, about fifteen German soldiers armed with guns and grenades took position in front of our house near the intersection and told us to leave immediately.
>
> After the gunfire ceased we went to the intersection at Trelon and discovered that the Germans had departed. At 4:00 p.m. we heard a loud commotion and heavy tank traffic coming from the direction of the Château. When we went to see what the noise was

---

P Brigadier General Doyle O. Hickey (1891–1961) was born in Arkansas and educated at Hendrix College. Trained as lawyer he attended the First Officers Training Camp at Camp Stanley, Texas, and in November 1917 was commissioned a 2nd Lt. in the Field Artillery Reserve. He attended the Field Artillery School at Ft. Sill (1924) and the Command and General Staff School (1934–1936). After assignments with Army Ground Forces and the Armored Force, he became head of CCA, 3rd Armored Division in September 1943. He took command of 3rd Armored on March 30, 1945, and led it until August 1945. He received the Distinguished Service Medal, Silver Star (w/ 2 OLC), Bronze Star (w/1 OLC), Legion of Merit, Presidential Unit Citation for Mons, and several foreign decorations. He retired a Lieutenant General in 1953. General Hickey, universally admired and respected by his men, was one of the principal founders of the postwar 3rd Armored Division Association.

about, we saw across the field the arrival of U.S. tanks coming out of
the forest on the paths that lined the ponds. A multitude of
American flags appeared and everyone cheered our liberators.[49]

Dr. A. Eaton Roberts, a combat surgeon riding with the tankers, infantrymen, and other weary soldiers of Task Force Lovelady crossed the border
at 1610 on September 2 to the

> . . . frantic delight of the villagers who plied us with the best beer we
> had tasted since leaving the States, along with the usual gifts of fruits
> and flowers. A departure from French food, and one which followed
> us across Belgium, were little semi-sweet cakes made in the shape of
> waffles. Tobacco, too, was apparently more plentiful, because we were
> startled at being offered cigars and cigarettes instead of being asked
> for them.[50]

Along with the civilians, member of the Belgian resistance suddenly
appeared in public with their weapons. Caught up in the excitement, and
relieved that they could finally "join the battle" openly, they did not realize the Germans were literally all over the place and that they were still in
deadly peril. The Americans quickly came up with a solution. Major Bill
Castille, the Intelligence officer of Combat Command B

> Picked up and carried with "Ontario Forward" (HQ, CCB) two men
> that had been leaders of the Belgian Underground. With the rapid
> advance of our armor, pockets of the enemy would sometimes close in
> behind us and deal severely with members of the Underground that
> had emerged and identified themselves by donning their armbands.
> Therefore, one of the important tasks of my two Underground lead-
> ers was to warn their associates to "lay low."[51]

Later on September 2, advance elements of the division began to approach
the outskirts of Mons and reconnaissance patrols entered the city that
night. Rose's headquarter vehicles crossed Highway #9, a main supply
route into France, and bivouacked a few hundred yards off the road at the
Château de Warelles. The building was located on a small stream about
nine kilometers south of Mons and five kilometers north of the border
and was owned by the Warters de Besterfeld family. Major Dugan
described it as a "country club." That afternoon, Georgy Ewbank, the son-
in-law of the owners was at the house.

On Saturday, 2 September, the main Mauberge–Mons route was deserted. About 3 or 4 P.M., we heard a loud commotion coming from the sugar refinery and then saw the Americans go by. In the early evening, General Rose, commander of the division, installed his headquarters in a large ground floor room of our house. In no time, three or four officers filled the room with maps.

At noon on Sunday, my mother-in-law killed all the remaining poultry and prepared a luncheon for the U.S. Officers.[52]

Colonel Smith and the other senior staff officers were busy with their duties when the woman of the house entered the makeshift headquarters with a formal invitation. She announced

> . . . that the head of the house expected Monsieur General and his staff to join them at a rather formal luncheon. In spite of their generous hospitality and the quality of the food, I might state that at best it was a rather hasty meal and not infrequently we were glancing over our shoulders to make sure that some of the attacking Germans were not entering to share it with us.[53]

General Rose alone occupied the château while the staff worked out of their half-tracks. The men were livid when they heard that a captured German general was quartered inside the building (or an adjacent structure) but most accepted the explanation that it was important he be secure for intelligence reasons.[54]

The Château de Warelles was not the last elegant command post occupied by Maurice Rose, who occasionally took a personal hand in selecting his HQ.[55] He was a man who understood that "rank has its privileges" and it is not a bad thing for a general to enjoy them, within limits. Certainly the men who traveled—and fought—with him were appreciative. As Sgt. George Bailey, a linguist attached to the 503rd Military Intelligence Unit, put it

> When one does the grand tour of Europe as a member of the headquarters of an armored division one stays in the very best places—château's, castles, villas, and the like. Of course, there is some military sense in this: castles and château-forts are by definition strong points, fortified prominences of some sort. The best places also qualify by

their size for the honor of being commandeered as the command post of a general: the shelter must be large enough to accommodate the party. Even so, generals gravitate towards aristocrats because generals are themselves aristocrats in the most direct sense of the term. In wartime, at least, generals do not get to the top, and above all, they do not stay at the top, unless they belong there.[56]

There had been no time to establish the division CP within the defense perimeter of a combat unit, as was the normal custom.[57] Captain William Hemphill's Company G of the 36th Armored Infantry and the tanks of Company C, 32nd Armored, along with the men of the Headquarters Company, set up an all around defense as best they could, setting up listening posts and tank positions. A battery of 155mm guns was posted to the west of the command post.

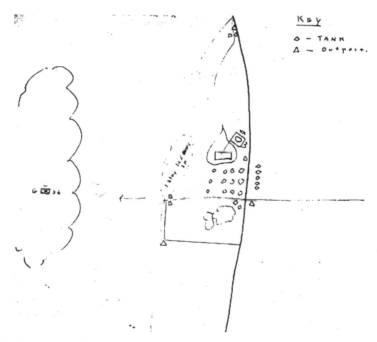

Defense of 3rd Armored Headquarters, September 2, 1944
(*Source:* The Battle of Mons Combat Interview)

Based on the information coming into the CP, Lt. Colonel Andrew Barr, G-2, and the Order of Battle Team #9, headed by Captain Milton Giffler and ramrodded by Master Sgt. Angelo Cali, were preparing their daily assessment for September 3. In addition to their current information, reports on the civilian radio suggested that the enemy, seemingly ignorant of the American presence in Mons, was likely to retreat by administrative march towards Highway #9. Barr had already identified elements of at least a dozen German divisions. He recommended that all units prepare road-blocks, but there was barely time to communicate the orders. By the time General Rose returned to the château late that afternoon, reports were already coming in of Germans trying to move through the lines at multiple locations.[58]

As Rose was reviewing the reports and studying the maps, he had an unexpected visitor. Joe Collins drove up to the CP to check on the progress of the 3rd Armored, which Collins felt had been "transformed into a great fighting machine."[59] Rose warned him that based on the G-2 reports, they were likely to be attacked at any moment and he should get moving. Collins went on ahead to Mons, which in the early evening was strangely quiet with no civilians on the streets—a definite danger signal. That night he returned to Rose's CP and ordered him to "hold tight." The corps commander then went off to Charleroi to prepare for the First Army advance east that had been anticipated at the very beginning of the Mons operation.[60]

The Germans probing the HQ perimeter were not Rose's only problem. Collins' order to prepare for an advance as early as September 3—the next day—presented a myriad of logistical problems and would push the division to the limit. Rose was already relying on supplies from depots as far away as 140 miles![61]

At his evening conference with the other General Staff officers, Lt. Col. Orth, the officer responsible for logistics, told Rose bluntly that he would not be able to support the kind of operation that General Collins had described earlier and also maintain a sound logistical base. The problem of fuel and lubricants was especially acute. In addition to the shortages, and the vast distances to the supply bases, it was getting more difficult to bring existing supplies forward because of the enemy. They were between the 3rd Armored and the supply columns. The division might possibly reach Charleroi, but that was about it. Even that would be dangerous, as it would delay resupply even further and be potentially catastrophic if the enemy mounted a serious counterattack. General Rose considered the G-4 report carefully and the other recommendations of his staff and announced that he would decide in the morning whether to push forward.[62] It was a decision he would not have to make. The enemy decided for him.

The advance had been so rapid that German soldiers and vehicles—individually and in small groups—were spread out all over the roads and fields. The reconnaissance troops were at the front and flanks of the American columns and were generally the first to encounter the enemy, usually without any warning and at very close range. On the night of September 2, 2nd Lt. Herb Zimmerman was riding point with his section of D Co. when he had a terrifying experience that could have been catastrophic.

> I was leading a column into Mons when we ran into fire from enemy tanks. The Task Force sent a unit to lead us in. As we followed in a peep, our lead tank suddenly and literally collided with a German tank. The Germans jumped out and ran into the fields.[63]

The terrified Americans were sure they were about to be killed and were amazed when they realized that the Germans were more scared than they were.

There were many other such encounters between opposing vehicles as they got mixed together in the darkness and confusion. Cpl. Clarence E. Smoyer, a Pennsylvanian of G Company, 32nd Armored, was a gunner in a Sherman commanded by Staff Sgt. Paul Faircloth. Late on September 2, his tank and a group of M-5 Stuarts, M-8 armored cars, and half-tracks had coiled in a field just off the road to Mons.

> On this first day, we had very little action; however, we could hear a lot of German equipment moving on the other side of a hill in the direction of Mons. Later that night, we heard a German tank moving in our direction and it kept getting closer and closer until it finally pulled into the same field with us. We knew about where it was, but could not see to fire on them. The Germans didn't know that we were there, so we all kept very quiet through the night.
>
> The next morning, as it started to break daylight, we got up very early. We could see the cross on the side of the German tank. They were only about 50 yards away, and had slept in the same field as us. As soon as it was light enough for me to see through the gunsight, we fired one armor piercing shell, which destroyed the tank.[64]

Before the battle was over, Sgt. Faircloth, who Clarence felt was "one of the bravest and nicest men I met during my time in the army," was dead, killed while trying to save the lives of some wounded soldiers.

While many of the SS troops resisted fiercely, other Germans surrendered without putting up much of a fight. Corporal Syd Johnson of A Company, 83rd Recon was riding in a half-track and after the endless march was feeling like he and his buddies were probably more tired than the retreating enemy.

> Some German groups tossed their weapons aside, and came into our bivouac area with their hands over their heads. We welcomed them with open arms and a closed, hastily built stockade. We captured them in droves, not knowing what to do with them. The problem was left with the MPs . . . it was about time that they earned their keep besides directing traffic.[65]

Not everyone felt that way about the MPs. Captain Gosch of the 703rd Tank Destroyers was amazed at the sheer flood of prisoners and the difficult job of guarding them.

> With close to 25,000 POWs on hand, the MPs (plus) had their hands full. German medical personnel were required to take care of their own, and German rations were collected—we certainly couldn't feed them. It was quite a sight watching company and battalion size groups of POWs marching back to internment. We wondered "would the war be over soon?"
>
> Strangely enough I can still remember clearly a small nine-year-old Belgian boy looking for food who entertained us with his impersonation of a Nazi officer. He would stiffly come to attention, click his heels, give the arms salute, and shout "Heil Hitler!" and smile in derision. He knew he was free. What a change was noticed when we met the real Hitler Jugend.[66]

The MPs, though, didn't have it easy dealing with the flood of prisoners, and it was getting downright dangerous. Provost Marshall Major Charles H. Kapes and his sixteen military policemen had been reinforced with several dozen men from the 1st Infantry Division. They were guarding as many as 4,000 enemy POWs in an old sugar factory within sight of the division command post.[67] **(Q)** After one fierce encounter at the factory they found themselves guarding another 300 newly captured prisoners!

By nightfall, Mons was in American hands. Combat Command B was located northwest and west of the city. Combat Command A was to the South and the division reserve was to the east. Each of the Combat Commands had established a large number or roadblocks covering all the major routes into and out of the city. Forward units began to spread out on the high ground west of town, with the artillery battalions deployed about five miles south and near the division HQ.

Elements of the division were strung out for twenty-five miles on the roads all the way back to Avennes. Lt. Colonel Sam Hogan's Task Force had taken ambush positions along the expected routes of the enemy's retreat.

> This resulted in the establishment of an area of blockades. The blocks, at least of my command, consisted of a few tanks and a platoon or so of infantry. One of our officer prisoners remarked that the "Americans didn't seem to have much but they had it everywhere." Quite a few Germans were able to escape on foot through the woods.[68]

Lt. Bryan Gruver, Jr.'s B Company of the 36th Armored Infantry was fighting with Task Force Doan in the eastern part of Mons. His men held several roadblocks, and after capturing a large number of prisoners deposited them in the Mons city jail. Sgt. Jack Warden's platoon was responsible for one of the more "spectacular actions that occurred" that night.[69]

> We set up roadblocks and prepared for the night. As we were on a main thoroughfare, I placed a rifle squad with a bazooka back in some trees between the houses and a street with a radio and took the rest of the men to the next intersection and set up shop. Civilians were all over us with food and drink.
>
> About 0600 the next morning, the outpost reported a truck towing something, and I told them to let it through and sit tight. The truck was really rolling and towing an 88mm gun with a man sitting on the seat of the gun. I alerted my men to hold fire until my command. We

---

Q The estimate of total prisoners is between 25,000 and 30,000, with the 3rd Armored credited with between 8,000 and 9,000. On September 3 alone, VII Corps captured 7,100 prisoners, 5,000 of which were taken by the 3rd Armored.

were screened by trees and could not be seen. As they got even with us we fired everything we had. Some ammo was hit and exploded, blowing everything sky-high. There were twenty-one soldiers in the truck. Their remains looked as if they had been BBQ'ed and none was left whole except the one riding the gun. Bodies were blown to bits and the bits blown through windows of houses along the street and into the trees. A real mess. We had a great K ration breakfast and pulled out for other exotic places.[70]

By the end of the day, B Company had destroyed two 88mm guns, their prime movers and other vehicles, and killed, wounded, or captured more than seventy-five men. [71]

That evening Corporal Johnson and his buddies in the 83rd Recon finally got a chance to rest and grab some rations.

As we sat around after supper having a typical GI bull session, a captured German officer who was being held for questioning tried to break away by making a dash into the nearby woods. Sgt. Apple pulled his .45 automatic from his shoulder holster and, without, interrupting the conversation, picked off the running Kraut at about a distance of 75 yards . . . a very long range for a pistol. He put his gun back into his holster, and the bull session continued as if this were a common occurrence.[72]

The pause didn't last long. Infiltration continued all-night and reached a crescendo even before sunrise. Then a melee began the likes of which few had seen before. No one was insulated from the wild confusion and the intense firefights. All along the front, and behind it, men found themselves suddenly fighting for their lives. The men in the trains, consisting mostly of supply, maintenance, and medical units, were supposedly in the rear, but fought pitched battles as the Germans tried to cross any road to get back to the Reich.[73] **(R)** Early in the morning of September 3, Sgt. Myrle W. Bostwick was in a peep leading a convoy of five trucks to gas up Task Force Y when he:

R This train consisted of about 200 vehicles including, the Maintenance Company, Service Company, Headquarters Company, Reconnaissance Company, and the B Trains of the 32nd Armored Regiment, as well as trains of the 54th Field Artillery Battalion and B Trains of the 3rd Battalion, 36th Armored Infantry Regiment. Also included was Co. A., 23rd Engineer Battalion.

... managed to capture the major general commanding the enemy *6th Parachute Infantry Division*. The general's aide, a German officer who spoke excellent English, informed the American soldiers that they should consider themselves very lucky and honored indeed in stumbling across such a prize captive. Replied Sgt. Bostwick: "You're the ones who are lucky, you son of a bitch, I had just as soon have shot you as not."[74]

At the division command post, General Rose, his staff officers, and their men, clerks, cooks, supply troops, and everyone else at headquarters all grabbed their personal weapons and went out to confront the enemy. Colonel John A. Smith, Jr. the chief of staff, led some men against a large group of enemy soldiers trying to infiltrate the Headquarters area. They became known as "Combat Command Smith."

All hell broke loose just before dawn! Our columns had gone directly before retreating Germans, who thought they had a fifteen-mile escape gap south of Mons. The *6th Parachute Division*, among others, was trying to get through us. General von Heyking, who commanded this division and had organized the assault on Crete, together with his G-2 and aide, captured. One German battalion surrendered intact. General von Aulock, slightly wounded was also taken. Was to have organized defense of Paris. During the night Signal Corps troops hit half-track passing division CP, went down the road burning and blew up. German planes overhead.[75] **(S)**

The 143rd Signal Company radio and wiremen, under intense pressure during the whole drive to make sure coordination was at a peak, had so far been pretty lucky, but their luck was about to run out.

CCA's wire crew were fired upon by a German tank that had been bypassed. A shell exploded in the trees, spraying the wire crew with shrapnel. T/5 Lowell P. Dillard and Pfc Robert Rosenberg, who were in a foxhole were killed instantly; T/5 Joseph Harris, Pvt. Edward Mickel,

---

S Four German generals were captured in the drive through Belgium, including Hubertus von Aulock, Rudiker von Heyking (CG, *6th Parachute Division*), Karl Wahle, and Bock von Wulfingen. A fifth, Konrad Heinrich, (CG, *89th Infantry Division*), was killed as he attempted to run a roadblock near Liege on September 7, 1944.

Pvt. William G. Emerson, Pvt. Maurice F. Hatfield, and Pvt. Julius V. Conn were wounded. The loss of these seven men presented a serious problem until they could be replaced with a makeshift crew.[76]

The whole CCA team had been put out of action. These men had been personal friends of Pfc. Don Marsh, now many miles to the north heading for Tournai with CCA, 2nd Armored (Rose's old command). Rosenberg and Dillard had sailed overseas with him on the same Liberty ship (*SS George Sherwood*) as replacements for the 3rd Armored. Fifty-five years later, Don remembered his buddies and the "brotherhood of war" that bound them together. Referring to the sometimes snobbism of the fighting elements, he said with a voice trembling with emotion, "maybe they weren't 'on the line,' but they got killed just the same."[77]

The correspondents traveling with General Rose had barely established themselves at the château when the battle began. Tom Henry, of the *Saturday Evening Post*, had what could only be described as a "front row seat."

> The Germans were completely unaware that anything stood in their way. They walked like sheep into a slaughter pen. I watched from the window of a Belgian château, where General Rose had set up his temporary headquarters, as groups of Germans emerged from patches of woods, where they had hidden all day, and tried to make their way across a pasture in bright moonlight. They were in the middle of the pasture, perfect marks, when the tanks opened fire. This was continued mercilessly unless the few survivors came slowly forward with hands over their head.
>
> Half-tracks carrying men came across the fields. A single shot would send one of them up in flames. In most cases, the occupants were cremated. Over the pasture would come a few nerve-tearing screams from the burning men, then silence, and ashes and twisted metal. In modern warfare there is probably nothing else quite so terrible as armored combat—for the losers.[78]

Even when it looked like the château was about to be overrun, General Rose remained unflappable. At one point he was observed calmly talking to one of the captured German generals, in an officially correct, but decidedly cold, manner. Sgt. George Bailey, a Midwesterner fluent in several languages, was responsible for interrogating the captured German generals. He was struck by the difference in appearance between the "sixtyish," short, heavy-set, almost jovial parachute general, Rüdiger von Heyking, and his own commander.

> Now Rose—he looked the very model of a Prussian Major General; thin-lipped, sharp features, closely cropped hair, a ramrod of a man whose legs drove him forward like twin pistons—Rose was the toughest looking officer I have ever seen. Appearances were not deceiving. Rose was a troubleshooter who had been brought in to take over the division in Normandy because the commanding general had been relieved of his command. There was not a man in division headquarters who did not fear Rose. I saw staff officers, full colonels, standing at attention before Rose, the sweat pouring off their faces, visibly shaking in their tankers' boots.[79]

By the time the battle around the division headquarters was over, the men had captured another 300 enemy troops to add to the thousands locked up in the sugar factory. Master Sgt. Phillip Zinner, commander of the Prisoner of War Interrogation Team #29, went from interrogating prisoners back to the firing line to help capture even more.[80] It was largely as a result of this and similar actions that the division headquarters was awarded a Presidential Unit Citation. The official text tells the story of virtually every unit in the battle.

> At Mons, Belgium, the Headquarters directly blocked the path of the retreating *Seventh German Army,* and for thirty-six hours, a battle between elements of German units attempting to extricate themselves and this headquarters raged unabated. Though surrounded and cut off from outside help, the entire group fought tenaciously against overwhelming enemy forces, and by its grim determination, repulsed the enemy and inflicted heavy casualties. During these actions, this division headquarters group killed or wounded 237 enemy soldiers, captured 2,432, and destroyed or captured 69 enemy vehicles. The heroic and gallant actions of all personnel of Headquarters, Forward Echelon, and Headquarters Company, 3rd Armored Division, exemplified the highest traditions of the military service.[81]

In addition to the Presidential Unit Citation awarded to the headquarters of the division another was awarded to the reconnaissance company of the 32nd Armored Regiment, which by the end of the battle had suffered more than 50 percent casualties.[82]

Among the men cut off at headquarters and fighting for their lives were the war correspondents, who usually traveled with the division. W.C. "Bill" Heinz, of the *New York Sun*, along with the others, was determined to get his copy out to the press wireless in spite of the distance and the enemy. In his postwar novel, *The Professional*, he remembered Mons through the voice of one of the characters, also a reporter.

> It reminds me of one day during the war. After the breakthrough at St. Lô, the Germans were trying to get back to the Rhine, and we were trying to cut them off. A half dozen of us were with the 3rd Armored, through the rest of France and into Belgium. We're just about to Mons and the press camp is back in Paris, so they're flying our copy out each afternoon in a Piper Cub.
>
> Late one afternoon, the PRO (Public Relations Office) calls us all over to his half-track. He was a nice young major out of the south, named Haynes Dugan, and the half-track was in this apple orchard behind this château, and he says, "Gentlemen, I have some bad news. The Piper Cub that takes the copy back was shot down."
>
> Well four or five of us said, in one voice, "Was he going or coming?" So Dugan says, "He was coming. The copy got through." We said, "Oh." I felt I'd just resigned from the human race. I still feel I did.[83]

Because of the breakdown in their communications, the enemy was unaware that the Americans had taken Mons, so they continued to retreat along the roads leading to the town in order to reach the Siegfried Line. Small units from each 3rd Armored Task Force had dropped off along the road to establish roadblocks and ambushes inside and around the city and were waiting for the Germans. Captain Robert W. Russell, a liaison officer, described the action as a "dogfight with mainly small unit encounters."[84] Captain Gosch's M-10 tank destroyers were manning a series of roadblocks in the eastern part of Mons.

> Streams of German units of all types from patrols to battalion size came in front of our guns. Some were fired upon directly; some were warned by machine gun bursts and voice. If they attempted to scatter or fight they were fired upon and destroyed or captured. All the gun companies plus "recon" of the 703rd took part directly in this action, which lasted several days. I believe at one point B Co. was credited with destroying a column of 40 vehicles in 15 to 20 minutes. German

horsedrawn artillery was particularly susceptible. Later it was not uncommon to hear Belgian farmers driving off the surviving horses down the road speaking to them in German.[85]

Actually, the tank destroyer platoon under Lt. Bill Smith destroyed twenty enemy vehicles during a six-hour battle![86] The roadblocks along the narrow roads also led to fantastic opportunities for both the artillery and the P-47 Thunderbolt fighter-bombers flying almost constantly overhead. The weather was great and there was no opposition from the *Luftwaffe*. On September 3, the IX Tactical Air Force Operations Officer, Colonel Ray Stecker, reported a "delicious traffic jam" of enemy trucks, half-tracks, staff cars, and wagons near Mons.

Over the next two days, three fighter-bomber groups mounted more than 1,000 sorties over the Mons area and claimed 1,200 enemy vehicles destroyed.[87] With the roads jammed with double and triple columns, the German retreat became a smoking ruin. Iris Carpenter, an English correspondent writing for the *Boston Globe*, observed that the fighter-bombers

> . . . hovered like buzzards over the forests, tight-packed with enemy supplies, and roads and fields so jammed with the debris of war that bulldozers had later to scrape a path for passage of Allied vehicles.[88]

The response of the 3rd Armored at every level was at peak. In the long march, Rose's forward echelon usually traveled with the most advanced elements of his division, accompanied in his peep by his aide and driver. Col. Sweat's Operations M-20 armored car, Col. Frederick Brown's division artillery peep, and several MP motorcycle riders also traveled with General Rose. He was now entering his fourth week of division command, and beginning to experience its awesome power in battle, now that it was cut loose from the hedgerows and static warfare of the first month.

Rose appeared to be everywhere, and there was no telling where and when he might show up. Lt. Zimmerman and the men of his reconnaissance platoon referred to the general as the "man with the 'boots,' but not with disrespect."

> I met General Rose only a few times and one of those was when he pinned a medal on me. He was, in my opinion, a General which every army wished they could have leading their troops. He was a front line soldier. He was always close to the action.

An incident which comes to mind was when I reported to Lt. Colonel Yeomans, the Battalion CO, that two of my men were killed by a bazooka in a small village (I cannot recall the name). Lt. Colonel Yeomans instructed me to meet him near the spot where this incident occurred. When I arrived, there was Lt. Col. Yeomans and with him was General Rose. He always seemed to be where the action was.[89]

General Rose's visits to the front were not always viewed positively. For one thing German artillery and mortar fire seemed to follow in his wake. For another, the field officers knew that Rose's tolerance for failure, or even a slower than demanded response to orders, was minimal. Lt. Colonel William B. Lovelady, a squat, tough, Georgia Tech grad who commanded 2nd Battalion, 33rd Armored Regiment, was developing a reputation as a great Task Force Commander. Still, a sudden appearance by the general was unnerving and not necessarily a good omen.

General Rose didn't mind coming up to the front line. He came up two or three times to relieve me, but when he saw I was doing a good job he didn't. Wesley Sweat would tell me about it later.[90]

General Rose decorating Bill Lovelady with the Silver Star
(*Source:* Linda Lovelady Sharp)

No doubt Colonel Lovelady, and every other battlefield commander, would have agreed with Captain Russell's assessment—stated half joking and half seriously—that "the reason we were so successful was that we were more afraid of the wrath of General Rose if we screwed up that we were of the Germans."[91]

Not every front line visit was a negative experience; there were a few light moments. Bill Lovelady recalled one episode during the Battle of Mons when "there was no front line." He had established a roadblock that was approached by a horse-drawn wagon holding two men wearing the blouses of railroad workers. They were stopped, patted down for weapons, and the wagon searched, all producing nothing unusual.

> Our men were on the point of letting them continue their trip toward Germany when General Rose arrived. Rose immediately ordered the two out of the wagon, ripped open their railway worker blouses, exposing the tunics of German Army officers. I felt like a fool.[92]

There were also some moments of intrigue and even a hint of "cloak and dagger." The young boy whose parents owned the headquarters château had a glimpse of the darker side of war just before the men occupying his house left to fight elsewhere.

> That morning the following incident occurred: General Rose asked our housekeeper to bring him some tea. When she arrived in the "map" room with the tea and noticed he was not there, she took advantage of his absence to take a peek at the maps. This act did not go unnoticed by a high-ranking staff officer. A bit later, General Rose called for my father-in-law and told him scornfully that if he and his division ran into trouble during their progression towards Charleroi, "severe measures" would be taken against him and his housekeeper. He left at the end of the day (September 4) with the accompanying tanks and was replaced by an infantry unit.[93]

The battle had been a numbing ordeal of rapid movement; now coiling off the road, resting a few hours, and back on the move, punctuated by periods of sharp combat and terror along the way.[94] **(T)** Diesel fuel was short, and had to be "fought forward" across roads that were frequently cut by

---

T In the fifty-hour drive from 1700 hours August 31 to 1900 hours September 2, the 3rd Armored Division traveled seventy-five miles through enemy-held territory.

retreating or already isolated enemy forces. Many units along the columns were frequently isolated or cut off from supply, and enemy tanks suddenly appeared at very short range. There were no clear unit demarcation lines, with combat, supply, and maintenance, as well as HQ units spread out along the road, subject to ambushes, roadblocks, and frequent sharp fire-fights; every man was "on the line" in the drive north.

Finally, suddenly, it was over. At 1400 hours on September 4, the 3rd Armored was ready to move east. Relieved by the 16th Infantry Regiment, 1st Infantry Division, its part in the Battle of Mons was over. During the first four days of September it had captured more than 8,500 prisoners, including three general officers, out of a total bag of 30,000. Estimates of enemy killed and wounded reached into the thousands.[95]

It was time to add up the losses. The division's casualties were between 150 and 175 men killed, wounded, and missing.[96] **(U)** Headquarters units had also suffered. In one engagement, the 703rd Tank Destroyer Battalion's Operations officer, Captain Self, was seriously wounded, and his driver Pvt. Villemure of the Recon Company, was killed by small arms fire. Major Charles E. Gravely, the division's Anti-Tank Officer was killed on September 3. He was a very popular officer and "it was said that a German soldier found with his field jacket never reached the prisoner of war cage."[97] There was hardly any time to absorb the sudden loss of friends before they were moving again.

The men remembered the exhaustion, the fear, and mostly that the nights were the worst. In the fierce engagements, hundred of vehicles were destroyed, and the dead Germans and their horses lay in piles all around. The carnage and the stench of rotting corpses sickened even hardened vet-erans. Many described it as a confused, terrifying mess with lots of by-passed but active German forces suddenly popping up, including tanks, frequent nighttime meeting engagements, ambushes, snipers, etc. One phrase heard often was, "there were no front lines."

Rose's performance as a commander was exemplary: up front, main-taining personal contact and coordinating the main columns, but allow-ing each unit leader tactical leeway on selection of routes of advance and coordination of movement along the secondary road-nets. The corre-spondents frequently observed him standing at the front of his columns.

> Leading the division and riding always at the front of his troops, was the 3rd's commanding general, a tough, daring soldier, winner of the

---

U These figures contain estimates for the 36th Armored Infantry, 83rd Reconnaissance Battalion, and 143rd Signal Company.

Silver Star three times, who rose from the enlisted ranks and became a Lieutenant in the last War at the age of seventeen.[98]

It (3rd Armored) is commanded now by an alert, modest, youngish general from Colorado, who pushes his men to the limit, though he goes himself wherever he sends his men. He is never ruffled no matter how tense the fight is.[99]

The forward echelon of the headquarters, radio call sign "Omaha Forward," rode in the van of the constantly moving division. There was little rest or food. The columns bypassed and engaged enemy units, were snagged by ambushes and roadblocks, and encountered resistance along the entire route to Mons.

It was at the Battle of Mons that the division first delivered the battlefield results that were originally envisioned in the formative period of the American Armored Force. The essential elements of the philosophy behind the American concept, all represented on the Armored Force shoulder patch, were brought together: combined arms, speed, maneuverability, firepower, concentration of force, indirect approach, bypassing enemy strength. All the tactical elements were focused on the main operational objective: to exploit the fluidity of the battlefield, to strike deep in the enemy's rear, and achieve envelopment and encirclement—the highest objectives taught by all the world's military academies, one way or another, since the battle of Cannae.

For the men in the field, it was the culmination of the stateside training, the hard early lessons in the *bocage*, and initial shuffling of command, but also a vindication of their abilities, bravery, and willingness to improvise with what were clearly inferior medium tanks. For Maurice Rose, however, it was something more, the fulfillment of his personal destiny.

In an article published in the June 1945 issue of *Military Review* bearing Maurice Rose's name, the events leading to the engagement at Mons are described. **(V)** While the article was almost certainly authored by Lt. Colonel Wesley Sweat, the narrative and description of the deployments

---

V The article was almost certainly written by the Division's wartime Operations Officer, or G-3, Lt. Col. Wesley A. Sweat. He composed it based on his G-3 Operations Journal and Periodic Reports, which he wrote while on the march through Belgium, in or near the G-3 vehicles, moving with the point of the forward echelon of the HQ. The text was probably written sometime after the penetration of the Siegfried Line in mid-September 1944, and before the Battle of the Bulge, which began on December 16, 1944.

reflect Rose at the pinnacle of his career as a battlefield commander. Regardless of its authorship, this article is one of a very few surviving documents reflecting Rose's operational view and tactical behavior on the battlefield. The genesis of the article can be traced to a request from First Army for material that could be published in the *Military Review*, the professional journal of the Command and General Staff School. The directive asked for descriptions of operations that were "out of the ordinary."

General Rose remembered that Lt. Colonel Sweat had attended the General Command and Staff School—he attended the fifth "special" class, graduating just before Pearl Harbor in December 1941. Rose asked if Sweat remembered any operations that went "contrary to general accepted principles." Colonel Sweat replied that Mons seemed to fit, as it went directly against the doctrine that once committed to action one should not alter the plan.[100] Rose, the ideal subordinate, the team player, the professional soldier who had spent almost thirty years adhering scrupulously to doctrine, surely saw the irony.

Even against the background of that extraordinary time of August and early September 1944, the victory at Mons had strategic implications. It demonstrated the mobility and maneuverability of the American Army. This potential was well appreciated by enemy intelligence. It was the enemy's realization of that potential that underlay their strategy of desperate defense in Normandy, where terrain largely negated the feared mobility potential. The Germans had already seen during *Cobra* that if given the chance the Americans had the resources and skill to capitalize on unanticipated opportunity and exploit all the advantages envisioned by the pioneers of armored warfare, including men like Maurice Rose.

Viewed from the perspective of Omar Bradley's Twelfth Army Group, the dramatic movement of VII Corps to Mons offered the opportunity of intercepting, and bagging a large part of the battered German *Seventh Army*. Although it had lost between thirty and fifty thousand men at Falaise-Argentan, *Seventh Army*'s headquarters infrastructure was still largely intact and it was still withdrawing northeast towards Brussels with some measure of discipline.[101]

In addition to further mauling a large number of disorganized German units, by rapid and effective action, Hodges' First Army would also limit the effectiveness of the Siegfried Line. These experienced soldiers of the *Wehrmacht*, had they reached the fortifications in strength, would have been an even more formidable foe, drawing strength from defending their own soil. Strategically, SHAEF's mission was to "undertake operations aimed at the heart of Germany." It was clear that as German forces retreated to that "heart," the advantages of the defense would be even more formidable than those encountered in Normandy. Anything that limited their power—like the destruction of the forces in the Mons Pocket—was a clear positive. The later painful attempts to pierce the Siegfried Line suggest how much worse it would have been had the *Seventh Army* passed unmolested through Mons.

The victory achieved there—the Unknown Victory—is written in the carefully prescribed language of heraldry describing the 33rd Armored Regiment—the heart of Combat Command B. In the visual imagery of this great fighting unit, Mons finds one of its simplest, yet most powerful expressions. The crest atop the shield tells the story:

> The shield is the green and white of the Armored Force. The thirty-three plates designate the number of the regiment. The white (silver) castle on a green mound is taken from the coat of arms of Mons, Belgium. Only two of the castle towers are shown, representing the two attacks on Mons in 1944 spearheaded by the unit. The capture of Mons from the German *Seventh Army* is alluded to by the meat hook (a charge found in German heraldry), the broken pieces of which simulate the numeral 7). The liberation of Mons is symbolized

Crest and Shield of the 33rd Armored Regiment

by the black lion taken from the coat of arms of Hainaut Province. The award of the French Croix de Guerre with Silver Gilt Star is symbolized by the green, red, and green shield with gold star. The five embattlements of the castle wall represent participation in five World War II campaigns.[102]

As a study in leadership, Mons displays Maurice Rose at his best. Even while maintaining tight central control, almost entirely by voice radio and wireless, Rose delegated to his battlefield commanders considerable tactical discretion. The battle teaches still meaningful lessons about the importance of real time responses to the full range of battlefield intelligence, the importance of logistics and flexible planning, and the catastrophic effect of strong armored forces operating deep in the enemy's rear.

Finally, Mons is a dramatic illustration of why sometimes doctrine can and must be set aside when circumstances dictate, and if the commander has the courage, confidence, and strength of will to "throw away the book" and take the professional risk of failure. Maurice Rose remains one of our best examples of a battlefield commander who knew just when to take that calculated risk.

CHAPTER Eleven

Autumn 1944: Movement Gives Way to Stalemate

"All right, Doc, now you can take care of me."
Major General Maurice Rose

W hen Maurice Rose left the Château de Warelles late on the afternoon of September 4, 1944, he was at the pinnacle of his career. Triumph had followed triumph and the men around him, especially the news correspondents, knew he was a man on the way up. As he left France behind and moved through southern Belgium he continued to generate excitement. There were headlines, of course, but neither he nor his division was actually identified by name. That blackout would last another month, finally lifted in early October.

The professional rewards that would flow from his victories would also be great. Honors, however, were not on his mind. He had but one thought: keep moving ahead, keep pressing the enemy right up to the borders of the Third Reich. After taking Charleroi without serious opposition the day before—in spite of his concern about the suspicious Mons housekeeper—on September 5, he reached Namur.

By late afternoon, Rose was comfortably ensconced in a stately mansion owned by a baroness. It was a stunning contrast to the decrepit quarters at Charleroi, which was surrounded by slagheaps and had been occupied the night before. After setting up the command post, Major

Dugan and several other officers and men went outside to the porch for a brief moment of relaxation and idle conversation and the war seemed to recede. The senior staff officers had become very close during the weeks of combat. For a brief moment, suspended in time, they were just gentlemen enjoying a pleasant aperitif on the veranda of a beautiful country estate.

> It was a delightful place, a beautiful home with sloping lawn towards the Meuse River, and we reached it during daylight hours. Fronting the structure was a veranda across the front of the house, with French windows opening thereon. It was a pleasant day, warm and sunny, made more pleasant by the granddaughter of the baroness, whom General Rose chatted up. She seemed to prefer George Bailey, who spoke her language.[1]

Just as daylight started to fade, Joe Collins drove up to headquarters for the second time in as many days. Rose and Collins went inside, but the door was left ajar. Collins was a spirited—some might say a tough—leader who inspired both respect and a healthy amount of fear. He was not averse to needling or even "dressing down" his subordinates in public. The field grade officers, gathered on the veranda smoking the last of their increasingly scarce American cigarettes, eating captured German rations, and sipping brandy, heard Collins' voice rising.

At first, they couldn't make out the subject of the conversation, but gradually it became apparent that Collins was unhappy about the location of the command post. While there was no heavy fire coming from the enemy at that time, earlier there had been casualties caused by snipers on the other side of the river. One of those hit, Colonel Barr thought, had been Rose's aide, struck while "he walked around among the vehicles parked in front of the mansion facing the river."[2]

Rose replied that the front was just beyond the lawn on the far bank of the Meuse River. Major Dugan described the next exchange as

> a classic example of an Army "chewing out," not unlike what one might expect from a first sergeant reprimanding a latrine orderly, ending with the words, "if you ever do that again I will relieve you!" During all of this General Rose said, "Yes, General" or, "No, General." For us it was most embarrassing. Bailey said that Rose was the toughest soldier he had ever seen, but on this day he was a very humble one.[3]

The men on the veranda did not hear the rest of the conversation. Later, however, when General Boudinot remarked about the snipers and casualties his men of Combat Command B had taken, suggesting that Collins had been correct, Rose replied sharply, "The corps commander can criticize me every day. You can't."[4]

As it happened there was another and more pleasant reason for Collins' visit to 3rd Armored headquarters. Collins wanted to personally inform Rose that he had been promoted to the temporary rank of Major General. The capture of Mons and the shredding of the German *Seventh Army* had earned Rose his second star. The stridency of Collins' initial words now gave way to congratulatory smiles and a round of hand shaking. Collins left shortly thereafter. Wine appeared and the General Staff officers drank a toast to the new major general.

The next day Rose, brimming over with satisfaction, was back at the head of his division, as usual riding with the most advanced elements of his command and personally directing the attack. The drive on Huy soon bogged down as the enemy mounted a desperate rear guard defense. Recognizing the importance of securing the crossing over the Meuse River, and learning from the Belgian Resistance that the bridge was still standing, Rose ordered General Boudinot to push a column to the bridge as fast as possible. Moving at nearly thirty-five miles per hour, the Task Force from Combat Command B secured the bridge intact. Once again, before allowing any of his troops or vehicles to cross, Rose conducted a personal reconnaissance, directing Shaunce to cross the bridge ahead of anyone else. They crossed the bridge without incident, but Shaunce was beginning to think that the general was using up both of their proverbial "nine lives" at a pretty rapid rate.

The 3rd Armored moved across southern Belgium so quickly that it soon outpaced the increasingly stretched supply line. When the men reached the large town of Liege, on the Meuse River, gasoline supplies were almost exhausted. General Rose ordered the fuel tanks of the headquarters vehicles, including those providing local security, to be drained. With this gas the division pushed a tank battalion five more miles that day.[5]

On September 9, as they neared the city of Verviers, General Rose again moved to the point of the most intense action, this time in full view of the enemy. In spite of extremely heavy mortar fire, he took the command group to a position on the forward slope of a hill. The shells followed his movement and one landed nearby, killing one officer and wounding four other men. After assisting in the evacuation of the wounded, he went back to the hill where he could best observe the action. For these, and other actions, Maurice Rose was awarded Distinguished Service Cross, the nation's second highest decoration for bravery.[6]

Only ten days after crossing into Belgium, 3rd Armored had reached the German border. The whole incredible advance, from the Seine to the Siegfried Line had taken only eighteen days! On September 12, Task Force Lovelady captured Rötgen, the first German town to be taken by Allied forces in World War II. Men from the 3rd Armored were the first Americans to cross the border to stay. **(A)** Shortly afterward, Maurice Rose became the first enemy division commander (and probably the first American general) to cross the German border from the west since the Napoleonic wars.

Preparations were quickly made to attack the Siegfried Line. The toll taken by the headlong pursuit had been considerable, however, and not just in blood. The vehicles, especially the tanks, had been pushed to the limit, and were in most cases beyond the remedy of simple field maintenance. Of the total 232 medium tanks authorized for the division, only seventy-five were in fighting condition. The ordnance men were falling asleep on their feet, struggling to keep up with combat and mechanical losses.

The supply situation had also become even more serious and the further the division moved east the worse it became. The main supply depots were by now more than 150 miles away. It was not only fuel and lubricants that were in short supply. The tankers and artillerymen soon realized that their ammo racks were never full and that resupply was slow and the number of shells being delivered was falling. By October the ammo shortage was a critical concern. Just as important were the shortages of every kind of spare part, antifreeze, and even cargo-carrying trucks. In fact all sorts of things were scarce, and the men were starting to grumble.

> In the fall, we had run out of all supplies. Winter was approaching fast and we didn't have any winter clothing. We were wearing everything we had on our backs. These were the same clothes we came ashore with back in Normandy! We did not even have overshoes. I was caught attempting to steal 1st Sergeant Koch's overshoes when we went back to the Signal Company to ask for winter gear and was told there wasn't any available. Of course all these rear echelon bas-

---

A Controversy still continues about who actually crossed the border first. Charles MacDonald, in the Army's Official History, *The Siegfried Line Campaign*, gives the credit to dismounted soldiers of the Reconnaissance Squadron of the 5th Armored Division. There is also controversy about where exactly the border was. What is clear is that men of the 3rd Armored were the first to *occupy* German territory and captured the first German town.

tards had theirs! Supply Sgt. Youngman told me to "try the Graves Registration check point" for a pair taken off a dead GI, which I finally had to do. I wound up with one rubber and one cloth covered "pair" of overshoes.[7]

In spite of the logistical difficulties, however, Joe Collins was in no mood to pause. Having advanced all the way to the Siegfreid Line, he was not about to let a lack of supplies hold him back. He persuaded General Hodges to allow VII Corps to conduct a "reconnaissance in force" towards Aachen, the first large German city across the border and one rich in significance for the German people. **(B)** This would be a prelude to a full penetration of the Siegfried Line. He planned to send 3rd Armored through the "Stolberg Corridor," while two battalions of foot soldiers from the 1st Infantry Division took the heights overlooking the medieval city.

Collins selected 3rd Armored to spearhead the attack into Germany because he had come to regard Rose as the "best divisional commander on the Allied side."[8] The later speculation that part of Collins' calculation in selecting Maurice Rose was his appreciation of the irony of assigning a Jewish officer to lead the first major attack into Germany is untrue. According to Collins' own autobiography, he had no idea of Rose's religious heritage until the middle of 1945.[9]

On September 13, the men of the 36th Armored Infantry Regiment had pulled up to the line facing the dragon's teeth and pillboxes in the Oberforstbach area, poised for an attack. The plan called for a frontal assault across open ground supported by tanks. The squad leaders mustered their men. Corporal Early Babineaux, a Cajun from Church Point, Louisiana, was already a combat veteran. Huddling with his buddies from B Company, the compact, wiry man turned to his right and saw the commanding general standing right next to him.

Realizing that his men would have no cover as they jumped off, and as easily as if he were talking to a foxhole buddy, he turned to the general and asked, "Sir, could we get some smoke?" General Rose turned to the artillery forward observer and issued the order. The shells fell, and Babineaux's men rushed forward, placing explosive charges through the pillbox slits, whereupon after the explosions the defenders surrendered in a daze. The Cajun was later badly wounded near Aachen in hand to hand combat, but not before he killed his opponent. He never forgot Rose's obvious regard for

---

B Aachen was Charlemagne's capital and the seat of the Holy Roman Emperor.

the front line soldier and his natural rapport with fellow warriors that Babineaux sensed that day.[10]

The attempt to exploit the initial penetration of the Siegfried Line failed for reasons that are not complicated or difficult to understand. Fatigue and shortages of men and equipment were the major factors. The attacking forces were simply not able to generate the aggressiveness typically engendered by their esprit de corps and Rose's relentless prodding. The terrible losses suffered by the tank crews were especially severe. The men now knew that going up against the German *Panther* or *Tiger* tank in the M-4 Sherman on even odds was suicidal. Attacking fixed positions where every avenue of approach was covered by the dreaded "88" was just as futile. This was becoming a serious morale and tactical problem.

There was also a growing feeling that the war could not last much longer and no one wanted to take excessive risks so close to the end. The long bloody pause at the border of Germany, and even more dramatically, the bloody Battle of the Bulge would change this perception. And of course, there were the Germans.

Although they had taken a beating, their morale remained high and they were not ready to quit. While VII Corps had prevented many retreating Germans from manning the Siegfried Line at Mons, those who were there already were still capable of fighting very hard. One such unit was the German *12th Infantry Division*, which had recently been re-equipped and was rushed to Stolberg just in time to blunt the drive of 3rd Armored, inflicting heavy losses, especially in tanks.

Another important factor was the terrain of the "Stolberg Corridor." This was the avenue of attack of VII Corps. Lying between the city of Aachen and the Hürtgen Forest, it was a twelve-mile wide stretch of land blocked by a double line of anti-tank dragon's teeth and other reinforced concrete fortifications. Pillboxes protected by mines, infantry armed with automatic weapons, and perfectly sited anti-tank guns blanketed the natural routes of advance. A plateau to the east of Stolberg offered the enemy unrestricted observation deep into the Americans' rear. The enemy had defilade, while the attackers frequently advanced over open visible ground. The flanks were deeply forested and ideal for defense. Shadows and thick tree cover created a kind of dark foreboding mood among the men, and contributed to their exhaustion, sapping their fighting spirit. Even after they got through the anti-tank obstacles, the fighting was a bloody nightmare.

Men of the 3rd Armored were actually the first to enter the Hürtgen Forest and immediately felt this enveloping gloom. Their experience, however, was mild compared to the reality to come for those who followed and were to bear the brunt of the sustained fighting during the fall and winter. The 3rd Armored was largely spared participation in that meatgrinder, described by one German veteran as a battle that "swallowed battalions whole."[11]

By September 21, Rose's men had reached Stolberg, southeast of Aachen. He was standing at the bottom of a hill just outside the town, when things started to heat up.

> Up ahead of him about fifty yards the first tank had been hit and was going up in orange flames. Around him mortars were dropping, and the small arms were rattling. Because he didn't duck, his junior officers didn't duck, and the GIs took the hill.[12]

The breathtaking drive across France and Belgium and into Germany was over. While the men had been able to punch through the first line of Siegfried Line fortifications, things changed immediately afterward. Lt. Col. Sam Hogan's Task Force made one of the early penetrations then hit a brick wall.

> Once through the line it got rugged. The Germans were fighting for the Fatherland, rushing troops up to the front of us and committing them piecemeal as they arrived, normally a bad way to fight but we were also in bad shape. We had been fighting and marching for weeks. Personnel and tank losses and breakdowns due to insufficient maintenance had cut our effective strength to about one half. As usual German intelligence was good so that he was able to put most of the troops he could get his hands on right across our path.[13]

In retrospect, some felt that if only they could have gone on, just a little further, they could have gone "all the way." Others looked around and realized that there was no way. Not even the iron will of Maurice Rose could push men and machines beyond what was possible. The correspondents who had been with the division since Normandy could tell that the limit had been reached.

> The tanks had been almost constantly on the move and in action for more than two months. The big steel machine was running on nerve and mechanical miracles. Tanks were tied together with baling wire.

The First Army was short of gasoline. The men had been pushed to the limit of human endurance.[14]

After capturing half of Stolberg, the division command post was established at Villa Walfriede, a property of the Prym family. It was a large, four-story mansion, located on a beautiful hillside overlooking the village. The "zipper" factory, source of the family's wealth, was just down the hill. There the division remained for almost three months, all during the battle to capture Aachen (which fell on October 21), the terrible battle in the Hürtgen Forest, and the bloody struggle to advance to the Roer River. It was the longest period of sustained occupation during the division's time in combat. It was also the period when many of the headquarters staff, both officers and enlisted men, were able to observe General Rose up close, and get rare glimpses into the personal side of Maurice Rose.

The general was well pleased with the selection of the Prym House and immediately took over the master bedroom suite. When the division was on the move, his living quarters were located in a custom built cabin installed on the back of a two-and-a-half ton truck. It had a built in bed, wash basin, cabinet, lights, mirror, map board, carpeted floor, and some other modest appointments.[15] When possible, however, Rose preferred to stay in more pleasant surroundings, even if for just one night. The mansion proved to be well suited to its wartime role as a division headquarters.

> There was a large drawing room, on the far side of which were two connecting smaller rooms, these were occupied respectively by the General and the chief of staff. Outside the chief of staff's room was located G-3 (operations) section, while diagonally across was the G-2 (intelligence) section facing a window which had been bombed out and replaced with boards, which did not entirely stop a considerable draft. Lt. Col. Jack A. Boulger and his G-1 (personnel) staff had found a quiet cubbyhole in another portion of the house, as had Lt. Col. Eugene C. Orth, G-4 (supply) and his group. Below us, but nearby, were the signals people and the message center.[16]

The Prym House was ideal, except for its location.[17] In spite of Collins' warning at Namur, this HQ was also within small arms range of the front line, which literally bisected the village. During the period of occupation, in fact, the HQ was shelled and bombed a number of times. It was in one such incident that T/4 Glenn Shaunce, Rose's driver, was wounded in the leg and evacuated to an English hospital. He had just been joking with some buddies in the Headquarters Company who were ribbing him about how "cushy" and safe his job was. Driving for a general, they were saying, was "easy duty." As they put him on the stretcher, he wondered if they would change their minds.

The push toward the Roer River continued, sometimes with bloody results. Each small village just beyond the front line seemed to be a fortress and was tenaciously defended. At a tiny hamlet called Dieppenlichen all hell broke loose and General Rose ordered Sam Hogan to pick up the pieces.

> Some men from a battalion of infantry got hit by a counterattack when they were too far from their supporting tanks and had lost most of their officers. Some of them threw down their M-1s and ran to the rear. This made General Rose very unhappy. He told me to go take the slag heap beyond the town and retrieve the rifles.
>
> Night fell and we still hadn't taken the slag pile. The General was still unhappy.[18]

By the next morning Hogan had taken the pile and retrieved the rifles, but the cost was high. Jake, a very popular platoon leader in Company C, lay dead, the victim of a sniper.

Not all the excitement took place on the front lines. On October 22, a brief, concentrated, but highly accurate ten-round artillery barrage struck the division headquarters enlisted mess during breakfast. Thirteen men were wounded, two seriously, including Pfc. John D. Pfeffer, Col. Sweat's driver. At the time, the shelling seemed like a random event, but it wasn't.

> What had actually happened was obvious enough. We had been holding the line desultorily in Stolberg for more than six weeks. During this time information—perhaps nothing more complicated than a telephone call across the front line—on the exact location of division headquarters had passed into the hands of the German army. Some German artillery officers had consulted their grid maps, plotted trajectories, and sighted their guns.[19]

Colonel Brown's artillery quickly silenced the enemy guns. The badly hurt were evacuated and those able to walk lined up outside the division surgeon's office to wait for treatment. General Rose, who had been outside during the shelling, walked up and down the line and chatted quietly with the men, until the last one had been treated. Then he stepped up to the medical officer and said, "All right, Doc, now you can take care of me." Without any other comment, he removed his blouse revealing minor shrapnel wounds in both shoulders. There was considerable discussion afterwards about Rose's motivation—whether it was done for effect, or whether he truly was the least seriously injured. Whatever the motivation, however, everyone agreed it had been an impressive performance.[20]

Life at headquarters soon had some unique rules. The occupation of enemy territory led to changes initiated by the newly activated office of the G-5, or Military Government staff. The rules were mandated by formal written orders and thus somewhat beyond Rose's control.[21] Once the division had established its headquarters at Stolberg, however, General Rose issued his own orders, including those that supported, under penalty of fines, the nonfraternization rules. Many men were fined for "personal" infractions, but even those with official duties sometimes found themselves in trouble. For some, the requirements of duty could conflict with the General's strict orders. One who felt the unpleasant effects of running afoul of the restrictions was Sgt. Bailey, the linguist attached to intelligence.

> I suppose it was inevitable, given my overriding interest in Germans, that I should be reprimanded for fraternizing with them. Rose had seen me talking on more than one occasion and suspected (rightly) that I was putting the broadest possible interpretation on my assignment. . . . Rose called me in and told me flatly not to talk to Germans unless I was specifically ordered to do so.[22]

Soon enough the war caught up to 3rd Armored. As the rest of First Army advanced to the border, the division and VII Corps began to mount attacks to exploit the initial break in the Siegfried Line and capture Aachen. The division, however, could not penetrate the heavily fortified defenses in front of the Roer River. The entire U.S. First Army's effort ground to a virtual halt. There was very bloody fighting in the Hürtgen forest, and sharp, costly assaults up and down the line, but exhaustion and the extended supply lines left little opportunity for even local successes. Rapid movement gave way to bloody stalemate. Losses during this time continued, and the division lost some of its most experienced soldiers and a number of popular veteran officers.

Life at the Prym House soon settled into army routine. It was the first pause in the action since Rose had taken command almost six weeks before. Even in bivouac Rose proved to be a tough boss. He was direct in his speech to his staff officers and other subordinates and expected immediate response to his requests for explanation or information. When questioned, he was taciturn, even stony faced and paused before responding to questions asked of him, frequently answering a question with a question. Of course, that was only when speaking with subordinates. When responding to his superiors, he was prompt, but also brief. No one could remember ever hearing him use profanity, nor could anyone cite an occasion where he overindulged either food or alcohol.[23]

As has often been noted, he was always carefully groomed and perfectly dressed. His personal code did not, however, spill over to excessive demands on his men. Sgt. Frank Woolner was attached to G-2, and apart from an occasional "rear echelon march-past review," couldn't recall any orders to "spruce up." This, in spite of the fact that "we wore no ties, were unpressed, often mud-smeared and probably smelled to high heaven; he (Rose) appeared to want results, not sartorial splendor."[24]

Maurice Rose also knew how to be a cordial and congenial host, without lapsing into the role of sycophant. Major Dugan, as Public Relations Officer, had an opportunity to observe him during visits of high-ranking officers, including Generals Eisenhower, Hodges, and Collins, as well as Admiral Richard E. Byrd, the latter a friend of Rose on a stopover on his way to a visit to Russia.[25]

On another occasion, General Rose hosted his old friend, Major General Terry de la Mesa Allen, then commanding the 104th "Timberwolf" Infantry Division, for dinner. The two men had known each other for more than twenty-five years and had crossed paths numerous times in both war and peace.[26] Allen was a tough, veteran soldier who had been relieved of command of the 1st Infantry Division after Sicily because of his men's lack of discipline in the rear—they were constantly brawling. Now he was back in action and had recently been attached to VII Corps. Throughout the evening, Allen needled Rose in front of his increasingly uncomfortable officers, reminding him of various embarrassing events in the past, most of which were not flattering to Rose. Still, while he was obviously miffed, Rose kept his cool and acted like a polite host.[27] Later, the two men would cooperate closely in the capture of Cologne.

The General's evening meal, called the "Gold Tooth Mess" was restricted to the division's General Staff officers. Other section heads (e.g., division surgeon, engineer, signals officer, etc.) were also invited. Field grade officers wore ties to dinner, as did the General. Often drinks would be served before the meal was served. Dinner, however, was not just about eating, and not always so pleasant. The talk at the table, at least that emanating

**Maj. General Maurice Rose and Gen. Dwight Eisenhower
at the Prym House, Stolberg, Germany**
(*Source:* Rose Family Album)

from the head of the table, could be rough. Everyone had to be ready for sharp questioning.

On one occasion, an officer referred in passing to an article he'd seen in the European edition of *Time Magazine* about tank destroyer tactics successfully employed in Italy. Rose exploded, "Why didn't I know about that?" It was as if the article had been hidden from him, rather than just one of a thousand bits of information encountered everyday by the staff that doesn't reach the commander. After that and other similar incidents, naturally those who had felt the sting of General Rose's short fuse, or observed its effect, were not inclined to speak up. The chief of staff, sensing the hesitancy and the quiet at the table, told the other G-Officers to speak up more at dinner; which generated considerable resentment.[28]

There were, however, some opportunities for relaxation. Maurice Rose liked movies and Jack Boulger was responsible for securing them from

Special Services for showings before the entire HQ staff. The general was especially fond of musical comedies and expected his men to like them also. Consequently, the showings were often crowded. Of course, there weren't too many separate titles or projectors, and these were passed around from unit to unit and back again countless times, in far from ideal conditions, so there were frequent "technical problems." When there was a breakdown of some sort, Rose's annoyed voice would rise over the darkened living room of the Prym house calling for Boulger to fix the machine or splice the tape, both of which were skills he lacked. After a while, Boulger found "official" excuses to skip the shows so that he would not be put on the spot.[29]

On November 26, 1944, the headquarters staff of 3rd Armored threw a surprise forty-fifth birthday party for their taciturn commander. Master Sgt. McGee, a resourceful man who had been a maitre d' Hotel before the war and was known as someone who could "organize" things, was in charge and managed to maintain secrecy. When the surprise was sprung, General Rose appeared genuinely moved, and during the celebration mentioned in passing to Jack Boulger that it was the first surprise birthday party that he had ever had.[30] Apparently, his celebrations with his wife Virginia had been private and did not include surprises.

The most pleasant event anybody could recall was the dinner party held at the Prym House in late November or early December. The officers invited nurses and Red Cross girls who were brought from Liege by truck. The men donned Class A uniforms, many searching desperately for irons to press their wrinkled blouses. Shoes replaced combat boots, much to the chagrin of the enlisted men who had to find the polish and shine the shoes. Decorations were affixed to jackets, and the men even took baths! When asked whether the lady guests had any trepidation about being so close to the front, they expressed relief at being out of Liege, which had been subjected to V-1 and V-2 rocket attacks on a regular basis.[31]

With music provided by one of the regimental bands, there was dancing, a lot of flirting, and even more intense interactions. It was no secret that some of the men at headquarters, including some high ranking married officers, were "womanizers." At one point, Jack Boulger heard one of the young women say in a loud voice to a senior staff officer, "you son of a bitch, you get your hand off my leg." Later, Boulger watched as a beautiful young Red Cross woman tried hard to attract the interest—and more—of General Rose. Boulger remembered thinking that it was an obvious seduction attempt, but while Rose was polite, it was clear to everyone that he wanted no part of an illicit encounter.[32]

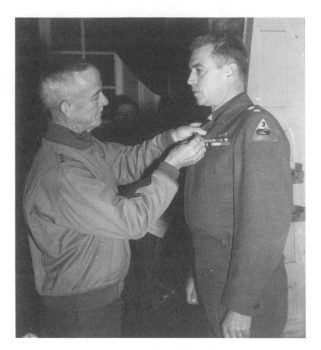

**Lt. General Courtney H. Hodges decorates Maurice Rose
with the Distinguished Service Cross**
(*Source:* Rose Family Album)

The war ground on. Progress was made toward the Roer River, but it seemed that the heavy action was over for some time. True, the war would not be "over by Christmas," but neither would fierce fighting resume any time soon, as winter would make any action very difficult. Now it was time to celebrate the victories. On December 10, T/4 Shaunce drove Maurice Rose to 1st U.S. Army Headquarters for a decoration ceremony. There, Lt. General Courtney Hodges pinned the Distinguished Service Cross to his jacket, already covered with decorations for bravery and long service.

A number of other generals were there, including Joe Collins and Ernie Harmon, Rose's boss in Africa. They were ebullient, shaking hands, and slapping each other on the back. These men, and others to the north and south, had brought the American Army from the disaster at Kasserine through the tangled *bocage* of Normandy up to the very edge of victory. Spirits soared; the champagne flowed. Even Maurice Rose was smiling. Within one week, their whole world would be turned upside down.

CHAPTER Twelve

December 1944: Bloody Ardennes

> "The policy of attacking, even with insufficient strength
> and against superior numbers, thus permitted the Division
> to hold when other methods would probably have failed."
>
> *Major General Maurice Rose*

During the exhilarating drive across France, Maurice Rose paused to give an impromptu battlefield interview to the correspondents riding with 3rd Armored. They were anxious to chronicle the achievements of the newly baptized "Spearhead" division and its brilliant, young, and handsome commander. Flush with his recent victories, and brimming over with confidence, Rose was anxious to oblige them. He was rising rapidly and appreciated the importance of favorable publicity to his career. He told Harold Denny of the *New York Times,*

> I cannot visualize a situation in which I would order a retreat. Anytime the high command gives us an order to seize an objective, that objective must be important to the big picture. So we go out and take it. If we get shoved off, we go out again. And we will keep on attacking with every trick we have learned until the objective is taken.[1]

Those words would come back to haunt Maurice Rose during the brutal Battle of the Bulge. During that bitter struggle, he would order both

Major General Maurice Rose, February 1945
(*Source:* U.S. Army Signal Corps)

retreats and hopeless assaults; his men would be driven out of their positions numerous times, suffering terrible losses and even defeats. There would be thrilling escapes as well as tragic errors, and Rose would feel the full impact of the ordeal. Its effects are visible in the photographs taken of him after the Bulge. They reveal a different man, tired, much older than his years and gray before his time.

Bitter cold, frostbite, and terrible confusion. Snow, frozen mud, fog, ice, and fear. Most descriptions of the Bulge include such words. What has often been described as the greatest land battle ever fought by the American Army was—at several junctures—a near disaster. If it had not been for the courage, skill, and endurance of the American soldier—and considerable luck—a much longer war or a major strategic setback could have been real possibilities at the end of 1944.

From the first moments, it was a battle of the ordinary GI. Many of the top commanders began the battle stunned, confused, and completely in the dark about what was happening. Several were not even on the battlefield. Some cracked. Several were relieved of command. One commander suffered a heart attack during the battle. **(A)** Others climbed to greatness after facing the terrifying specter of defeat. Maurice Rose was one. During the last weeks of 1944, he experienced some of the most difficult moments of his life, but he also displayed elements of exemplary leadership, even greatness. In the Ardennes, Maurice Rose, through daring, boldness, guile, and strength of will emerges as one of the greatest division commanders ever produced by our country.

When the surprise German counterattack in the Ardennes slammed into the American First Army early on the morning of December 16, Maurice Rose was, like his division, taking a breather from hard fighting. After the lightning advance to the borders of the Third Reich in September, the fighting had settled into a series of bloody frontal assaults towards the Roer River. This static warfare displayed nothing of the dash and brilliance of the drive through France and Belgium. The 3rd Armored was primarily occupied with building up supplies and strength for the renewal of the offensive, but the carnage continued. Just one month before the Bulge, on November 16, Rose's men had spearheaded another bloody attempt to break the stalemate and reach the Roer. When that attack ended unsuccessfully, it was clear that any further attempts to move forward would have to wait for better weather.

Three months of hard fighting and mounting casualties had left Rose's HQ exactly where it had been in mid-September, at the Prym House in Stolberg. The enemy was still within small arms range at the far end of the town. Probes and patrols were routine. Men continued to die.

The onset of the Battle of the Bulge did not affect the 3rd Armored immediately. For the first several days, Rose paced his headquarters and waited for orders. The division was put on a four-hour alert status after rumors circulated that the enemy had dropped paratroops near division HQ. Rose took security measures but still nothing happened.[2] After the initial shock of the German attack wore off, the senior Allied commanders began to regain their balance and redeploy their forces. The situation was engulfed in the "fog of war" and difficult to assess, but even worse, the

---

A Major General Alan W. Jones commanding the 106th Infantry Division was stricken in the early morning of December 23, 1944.

resources available to meet the new situation were limited. There were only a few strategic reserve units—essentially the Paratroops—so units already on or near the battlefield had to be moved from locations all along the front to plug the holes popping up all over the Ardennes.

For Rose, there was something painfully familiar about the situation. When he was alerted to begin planning to attach most of his forces to other units, he felt as if he was reliving his first few days of command of 3rd Armored. Just four months earlier, after a series of brilliant victories, and culminating in the breakout from St. Lô, he had been rewarded with command of his own division. Almost immediately, however, his new boss Major General J. Lawton Collins, informed him that his Combat Commands had been attached to other divisions because of the German counterattack at Mortain.

Now, once again in the midst of a major German attack, his division was about to be split up. Both of his Combat Commands were to be reassigned to other headquarters and dispersed geographically. Back in August, he had complained bitterly to Collins, but was assured that the attachments were merely a temporary expedient. This was different. After monitoring the first two days of sketchy reports, he could sense the scale of the confusion caused by the massive German attack—it must be credited as one of the greatest strategic surprises ever sprung on an American army in the field. He was not happy to be detached from VII Corps and Joe Collins, now his closest professional associate and strongest supporter, and a man with whom he had forged an excellent working relationship. In the present situation, he knew better than to complain.

On December 18, 3rd Armored got back into the war, albeit committed in piecemeal fashion. The first unit to move out was Combat Command A, led by the loyal and competent Brigadier General Doyle O. Hickey. It was attached to V Corps as a mobile reserve charged with the defense of Eupen, supposedly threatened by paratroopers led by Baron Colonel von der Heydte. That wily and dangerous adversary had survived his confrontation with Rose's CCA at Carentan and was back in action. Hickey was ordered to maintain a mobile defense on the assumption that von der Heydte's orders were to cut the Eupen–Malmedy road, a major supply route for the First Army.

In retrospect, it was a misuse of such a large armor unit, but it testifies to the confusion and reactive improvisation typical in the first few days of the German offensive. Clearly, a force stronger in infantry would have been more appropriate, and the general lack of organic infantry in the heavy armored division structure was about to be painfully demonstrated. Similarly, the difficulty of employing armor in the weather and terrain conditions of the Ardennes was also about to revealed with devastating results.[3]

Combat Command A remained detached until the afternoon of December 21 and reached the division assembly areas early in the morning hours of December 22. Even then, it was held in reserve except for Task Force Richardson, which would later play a crucial role in the struggle to hold the village of Manhay, a crucial road junction located right on the boundary line of several important units.

Combat Command B under command of Brigadier General Truman E. Boudinot moved out next. It was attached to V Corps briefly on December 19 and initially charged with defense of the vital supply installations located in the Belgian towns of Verviers and Theux, both close to First Army Headquarters. When Boudinot's columns reached their assembly areas on December 20, however, they were immediately reassigned to XVIII Airborne Corps and committed to the recapture of several villages already lost to the enemy, including La Gleize.

On that same day, Task Force Lovelady was split off from Combat Command B and attached to 30th Infantry Division. Lt. Col. Bill Lovelady was ordered to recapture the village of Stavelot on the Ambleve River and stop the advance of the enemy's spearhead, a *Kampfgrupppe* of the *1st SS Panzer Division* commanded by the infamous SS Lt. Colonel Joachim Peiper.

It was during this engagement in the tiny hamlet of Parfondruy that members of Task Force Lovelady saw with their own eyes the atrocities committed by the *1st SS Panzer Division* against innocent Belgium civilians. In the midst of combat, men of the Task Force came upon the remains of men, women, children, and even infants, shot and hacked to death.[4] After these atrocities were reported to the 30th Infantry Division, the men returned to the fighting with a renewed appreciation for why they were fighting. They took fewer prisoners, especially among the SS. Combat Command B remained detached from 3rd Armored until Christmas Day.

Just before noon on December 19, what was left of Rose's division was attached to XVIII Airborne Corps, SHAEF's last strategic reserve, and alerted for a night march to Hotton, Belgium. The XVIII Corps was under the command of paratroop veteran Major General Matthew Ridgeway.

(B) Rose was not particularly comfortable with his stern, patrician commander, or the detachments, but he instinctively grasped how dangerous the American position was. As a professional he realized that the initial phase of the German attack was likely to be a highly fluid and dangerous situation, and he would have to make the best of the command relationships and the forces at hand.

His first major problem was how little he actually had left. The detachments of his main striking power had left him with precious few soldiers or heavy weapons. Essentially, he had one very small makeshift Combat Command built around the headquarters of Lt. Col. Prentice "Mike" E. Yeomans' 83rd Armored Reconnaissance Battalion and Colonel Bobby Howze's 36th Armored Infantry Regiment. The reconnaissance battalion was equipped with M-5 Stuart light tanks and M-8 armored cars. He did have a few remaining medium and light tank and infantry battalions, but his forces were no match for the *Panzer* units flooding into the Ardennes. His men were experienced and his units were led by seasoned veterans, but even massed they couldn't hope to make much of an impact against a determined enemy advance. His situation worsened when the 703rd Tank Destroyer Battalion, his last remaining anti-tank asset, was sent to VII Corps and split up among several of its units.

Just after sunset, at 1640 hours on Tuesday, December 19, the division left Stolberg with the reconnaissance troopers riding point, and Rose just behind them at the tip of the column. **(C)** The journey itself was another poignant moment, as it largely retraced (in reverse) the drive to the Siegfried Line in September, starting at Stolberg and passing through Aachen, Verviers, Liege, and back through the once again threatened Belgian villages along the Meuse River valley. Lt. Colonel Sam Hogan was leading his Task Force into the unknown.

B Matthew Bunker Ridgway (1895–1993) was born at Fort Monroe, Virginia and attended West Point (1917). He served in China, the Philippines, and Nicaragua, graduating from the Command and General Staff School and Army War College. In June 1942 he took command of the 82nd Infantry Division, which became the 82nd Airborne. In July 1943 the division jumped into Sicily, the first large airborne assault in U.S. Army history. The 82nd (and Ridgeway) also jumped into Italy and Normandy. In August 1944 Ridgway took command of the XVIII Airborne Corps.

C At that time of year sunrise was approximately 0800 and sunset was about 1600.

The battalion started moving a little before dark. The roads were icy and there was fog in spots. The only light was the eerie flicker of buzz bomb exhausts as they roared through the night to Liege and other supply points. Beyond Aywaille the route was a bit vague since probably even the German high command did not know where their leading elements were. Certainly we didn't. Already we were getting rumors of Germans in American MP uniforms directing our columns astray. It was a wild, nervous, and sleepless night. We were all relieved and felt the worst was behind when we closed into the vicinity of Hotton in the early morning of 20 December.[5]

The march was a horror of frozen mud and black ice roads. The fog reduced visibility to a few feet. Each of the columns moved slowly in blacked out conditions without any headlights, guided by men with flashlights. Vehicles frequently drove off the edge of the road or bogged down on it. The men, under the most extreme conditions, displayed an understandable lack of march discipline, and it was impossible to maintain the usual interval between vehicles. The columns halted often as winches were brought up to move the stalled and wrecked tanks, half-tracks, trucks, and peeps to the roadside where the harried ordnance teams tried to fix what they could.

Officers and enlisted men peered into the ink black night as V-1 "buzz" bombs periodically exploded close by. Major Dugan and the other officers who had been at the HQ dance only a few nights before, remembered what the nurses from Liege had said about the gnawing fear of robot bombs. They quickly understood why the ladies were so happy to be out from under them.

One buzz bomb exploded very close to General Rose's peep as he approached Liege. It was a very close call.

Driving past a chateau with his aide, the General heard a robot bomb go into a sickening dive, and the next instant, he saw the bomb crash a few hundred yards away, but knew in a split second there was nothing he could do. The blast sent the aide, Captain Robert M. Bellinger of White Plains, New York, sailing through the air to the roadway, but he was not badly injured. The concussion gave General Rose a headache for three days. Bellinger commented that anyone who travels with "Front-line Rose" must be prepared to be pot-shotted almost daily.[6]

While the columns continued their tortuous march towards Hotton, General Rose detoured to Chaudfontaine, site of the hastily relocated U.S. First Army headquarters. General Hodges and his staff had been forced to move out of their comfortable digs in Spa by the approach of the Germans, and the confusion was palpable. Radio and telephone communications were in a shambles and no one knew what was going on. There was no hard intelligence about the enemy, only rumors.

Rose greeted General Hodges and the two men, accompanied by their operations officers, went inside. Less than a week before, on December 11, they had met amidst celebration when Hodges had decorated Rose with the DSC. Now, the mood was somber, the shock of a terrible surprise and even a hint of panic was evident. After exchanging pleasantries, they got down to business. Rose was given very general instructions, guidance more than orders.

He was instructed to take his division to Hotton, where he was to prepare to attack "either east, southeast, or south" in order to plug the gap developing between Malmedy and Bastogne. This very general guideline is itself evidence of the confusion and uncertainty plaguing the higher command even four days after the start of the German offensive.[7] Hodges informed Rose that more detailed orders would be waiting for him at XVIII Airborne Corps headquarters and would be issued to him by General Ridgeway personally.

T/4 Shaunce waited at the entrance to the large house, watching the hectic activity around him. He knew that things were screwed up. He gassed up his peep and got some coffee and a quick bite to eat. There was no telling when he would be able to get a square meal. After just a few minutes, the general emerged, stony faced and looking worried. Shaunce could not remember a time when his commander looked more nervous or preoccupied. He got into the peep without a word, took out a cigarette, and began looking at his maps. Shaunce headed down the road and followed the signs and MPs' directions to XVIII Corps headquarters.

Captain Bellinger, his head in his chest, was still stunned from his encounter with the buzz bomb and said nothing during the drive. Shaunce headed for Werbomont, site of General Ridgeway's XVIII Corps headquarters. Upon arrival, Rose greeted his new commander formally with a curt salute and went inside, where he received his mission. In Rose's words, he was ordered to

> Initiate intensive reconnaissance in the Hotton–Grandmenil Sector, to locate the enemy, and to secure a line running east from La Roche

to Crossroads (CR) 576853, and to tie in with the 82nd Airborne Division on the left and the 84th Infantry Division on the right.[8]

In fact, the mission was impossible to accomplish given the disparity between his own forces and the strength of the enemy, but he didn't know that on December 19. He was actually encouraged because the orders were better than he had expected. For one thing, the plan of maneuver was left to his discretion. Further, the line to be held was only thirteen miles wide and didn't extend to Malmedy as Hodges had suggested. The line he was to defend sat astride a well-paved highway that ran between Liege on the Meuse River and the crossroads town of Bastogne. The road also passed through the village of Manhay (and its vital crossroads south of town) and then west through Soy to the village of Hotton on the Ourthe River. To the east, 3rd Armored would establish contact with the 82nd Airborne and on the west with the 84th Infantry. Rose would be holding the extreme right flank of XVIII Airborne Corps.

The fighting in and around the two towns—Hotton and Manhay—would become the focal point of the crucial struggle waged by 3rd Armored during the last ten days of 1944. Upon its outcome the defense of the crucial Meuse River line would be decided. In spite of the initial setbacks and reversals, by ultimately holding that important line along the "northern shoulder" of the Bulge, and preventing a German breakout towards Liege and across the Meuse River, Maurice Rose contributed significantly to the ultimate victory.

There was a certain irony in both the mission and in the remaining forces under his direct command. At one of the critical moments of the entire European campaign, Maurice Rose was called back to his days in the cavalry. He was charged with a critical reconnaissance aimed at determining the enemy's strength, dispositions, and intentions coupled with flank security for a higher headquarters, both of which are classic missions for men on horses. Perhaps it was fate that his only remaining fully constituted unit was the 83rd Armored Reconnaissance Battalion, the closest surviving vestige of the horse cavalry in the modern armored division.

He collected what meager intelligence was available, arranged for liaison between his division and XVIII Corps, and then headed south. Quickly rejoining the main column, he took his customary position at its head. After several nerve-wracking hours, Shaunce approached the northern approaches to Hotton. He was scared. He could hear artillery and small arms firing all around and intermittent flares punctuated the bleak night.

Men from 3rd Battalion, 325th Glider Infantry and a tank destroyer platoon had set up a roadblock north of the town. Positioned at the very edge of XVIII Airborne Corps' right wing, they had been warned to expect the lead elements of 3rd Armored around midnight. A few hours before, however, one of their patrols ran into the "point" vehicle of the armored column, a peep. They were unnerved when they discovered it held the commanding general of 3rd Armored. Rose answered their challenge correctly, saluted smartly, and sped off toward Hotton.[9]

It took Shaunce a few hours more to complete the journey, and it was past midnight when they finally arrived. Rose's staff, which had arrived earlier, had already commandeered the *Hôtel de la Paix* on Valee Street as a forward command post. The occupation of the town was accomplished so smoothly and quietly that the locals had no idea of what was happening, even the proprietor of the hotel!

> When Charles Grandjean, proprietor of the *Hôtel de La Paix* (now the *Hôtel d'Ourthe*) on Valee Street rose from sleep early in the morning, as was his custom, he saw with amazement that during the night, the Americans had broken into his establishment and were occupying the ground floor.
>
> On the tables, which had been moved to the center of the room, a large number of maps had been laid out; some officers were examining them with fountain pens and ruler. All of the soldiers were closed mouthed; it was obvious that that some VIP had chosen this for his headquarters.[10]

As Rose entered the dining room shortly after midnight, his staff greeted him with silent salutes and he took his customary place at the head of the map table. Soon he was making his plans and issuing orders.

Rose had been thinking about the mission throughout the long, difficult night. He realized that a lot was at stake in the initial holding action. If he could just hang on, he would achieve several major objectives. First, his mission already anticipated an American counterattack, and it looked like he was being positioned to screen the gathering of Collins' VII Corps, which he guessed had been earmarked as the major counterattacking force. It was assembling on the Condroz plateau behind the Ourthe River.

Second, it didn't much matter where the Germans were headed, as long as he held the line. If they were headed for Liege, then the Bastogne–Liege highway would be an important enemy axis of advance, and blocking it would prevent them from crossing the Meuse River. If the enemy were headed further west—in the direction of Antwerp—then the highway would still be important. The enemy would need to secure the crossroads located at Baraque de Fraiture and at Manhay in order to secure their lines of communication from flank attacks.

Even in retrospect Rose believed that holding the crossroads at Baraque de Fraiture was the key to the mission and vital to his own survival. In the immediate aftermath of the battle, he told the official historians that

> The defense of Crossroads 576853 (Baraque de Fraiture) from 20 December to 23 December was very important for the Division, since it gave time to organize our position. Without the action of the unit at the crossroads, the Division most likely would have been overrun.[11]

He probably should have added that holding Hotton was equally important, for had the Germans captured its crucial Ourthe River bridge, then holding the Baraque de Fraiture crossroads would have ultimately proven irrelevant as it would have been outflanked.

As he settled in the Hotel de la Paix, Rose was in a foul mood. Although he did not show it, his head ached from the explosion caused by the buzz bomb. The discomfort was no doubt aggravated by the precariousness of his position.[12] Stripped of his main combat power at the outset of a battle for survival, he had no reliable intelligence on the strength or dispositions of the enemy in his vicinity, and only the vaguest idea of what friendly forces were in the area. With fuel and ammunition at dangerously low levels, he was facing a major enemy attack with less than a third of his division and little prospect of reinforcement any time soon.

It was at this desperate moment that Maurice Rose made one of the crucial battlefield decisions of the entire Ardennes campaign, and perhaps the greatest of his entire military career. Fully cognizant of his precarious position, and with the full realization that he was exposing his command—and himself—to total destruction, he organized his weak force for aggressive reconnaissance and a general advance across his entire front. As he later told the historians of the First Army, he knew full well the chance he was taking. As Rose saw it,

> The operation was a bluff, because on occasion the enemy had enough strength to overrun the Division. During the ten days of the

first phase, the Division succeeded in its mission essentially because it adopted a policy of attacking, instead of initiating a passive defense. The policy of attacking, even with insufficient strength and against superior numbers, thus permitted the Division to hold when other methods would probably have failed.[13]

In the annals of American military history, there are few examples of such an audacious, almost reckless, and potentially disastrous strategy. The desperate and seemingly hopeless bayonet charge of Colonel Joshua Lawrence Chamberlain's 20th Maine down the slopes of Little Round Top immediately comes to mind. There, too, a desperate commander on the extreme flank of an Army with weakened forces and facing repeated attacks by a strong and determined enemy, ordered an advance against all logic and prevailed. **(D)**

Those early morning hours marked the beginning of what Maurice Rose considered the most critical five days of his entire military career.[14] His plan was both simple and dangerous. He created three small Task Forces; each built around one of his experienced commanders, and each consisting of about 400 men, a company of M-4 Sherman medium tanks, a platoon of Stuart M-5 light tanks, a reconnaissance troop, as well as battery of M-7 Self Propelled 105mm howitzers. These Task Forces would move south along three parallel routes to seek out the enemy, secure the line he was ordered to defend, and establish contact with the friendly forces on his flanks.

In addition, he maintained a small division reserve under the control of Col. Robert L. Howze, and consisting of Lt. Colonel William Orr's 1st Battalion of the 36th Armored Infantry, three companies of tanks, as well as a company of combat engineers. This reserve would line up behind the middle Task Force, ready to exploit the situation or salvage it.

D On the second day of the Battle of Gettysburg, July 2, 1863, during the attack of Confederate General John Bell Hood's division, the 20th Maine Volunteer Infantry Regiment was battered, with ammunition nearly exhausted. Holding the extreme left flank of the whole Union Army on Little Round Top and with no hope of resupply or reinforcement, Colonel Joshua Lawrence Chamberlain ordered the survivors of the regiment to fix bayonets and charge down the hill, which routed the battered veterans of Colonel William Oates' 15th Alabama Volunteer Infantry. Because of his men's efforts—and those of the other regiments supporting his position—the Union V Corps held the crucial ground that day.

In forming his strategy General Rose had quickly weighed his situation. He knew that the amount of frontage for which he was responsible was too great for the forces under his command. If any of his thin columns encountered a superior enemy force, it would be impossible to reinforce and the likelihood of encirclement would be great. In such circumstances the best that he could hope to achieve would be delay of the enemy.

The terrain—because of the thick woods, marsh land, hills—and the weather were "among the most difficult imaginable" for armored warfare, but would equally hinder the Germans, whose main task was to maintain the momentum of the forward drive.[15] A major terrain feature was the jumble of small roads and trails that crossed the area and would naturally channel any advance to the few larger and paved routes that could be covered by superior American artillery. Given his lack of knowledge of the enemy, the width of his front, and the defensive advantages of his ground, General Rose decided to walk the fine line between reconnaissance and attack. The situation demanded boldness, guile, and the skills of a poker player. Going out to seek the enemy was a bluff of almost unbelievable audacity.

Rose alerted his senior field commanders to report to him personally to receive their orders. It would be a long night. At 0300 on December 20, he briefed Lt. Col. Prentice Yeomans, his reconnaissance chief, about the overall scheme of maneuver. Yeomans would be the tactical field commander of the operation, maintaining direct contact and coordination, while Colonel Howze would exercise general and administrative control. After briefing Yeomans, Rose grabbed a few hours of sleep.

At 0800 the next morning, Col. Frederick Brown, commander of Division Artillery arrived, followed by Col. Howze about an hour later. Howze joined his men and headed off to Soy, finally arriving at the *Hôtel Bon Sejour* (the Deville House) in the middle of town, where he set up his HQ at 1445 hours. The last to arrive at Rose's HQ were the three Task Force commanders. Rose didn't have much to tell them beyond their orders. As Sam Hogan put it,

> The information of the enemy given to us was zero. This was only a little less than usual. However, the information of friendly troops given to us was also zero and this was quite a bit less than usual.[16]

The officers and men of the division's G-3 (Operations) staff had been working all night to prepare the written orders, map overlays, and other paperwork that would set the bold plan in motion. Major James Alexander,

Jr. assistant operations officer had been dispatched to gain Ridgeway's approval of the general outline of the plan and arrived at XVIII Airborne Corps headquarters at Werbomont at 1030 hours. He remained at Corps as a liaison throughout the battle. At 1135, Alexander radioed back to General Rose; "Your plan is approved." General Rose then sent back a message in code, "The attack will begin at fifteen minutes past noon."[17]

By 0900 on December 20 most of the elements of the forward and rear division HQs had reached Hotton and begun to set up operations in the buildings on the east bank of the river. The 200 men of Captain William Rodman's Headquarters Company, elements of the 143rd Signal Company, and Company E of the 23rd Armored Engineer Battalion, got settled, and started to prepare a defense of the town. They were soon joined by a platoon of the 51st Engineer Combat Battalion commanded by Capt. Preston C. Hodges, which deployed on the western bank of the river. Another small group of engineers dug in at a footbridge 2,000 yards south of the town.

During the remainder of the day small groups of men, tanks, and guns from various units continued to arrive and were incorporated in the impromptu defense. Lt. Jack Warden of B Company, 36th Armored Infantry, had just received a battlefield commission. When he brought his men into town, he witnessed the confusion. He wasn't sure who was there, or where anybody was actually stationed. It was a mess, especially around the bridge.

After receiving the word from Alexander, Rose set his forces in motion just after noon on the afternoon of December 20. He remained at headquarters to monitor the first movements and then Shaunce drove him to the front so he could observe the attack for himself. The owners of the hotel had front row seats.

> The American command post continued to operate at the *Hôtel de la Paix*. Every time a messenger arrived by peep or by motorcycle there was activity. In the kitchen a duplicating machine operated at full speed. Orders were typed, sketches and additions were drawn in multiple copies, signed, and placed in sealed envelopes. In the afternoon motorcyclists stopped in front of the hotel, where each was given an envelope. They left in all directions.
>
> Two hours later the officer in charge left the establishment. In the street, peeps waited for the officers. At that moment, as quick as the wink of an eye, grabbing the elbow of Marcel Grandjean, the son

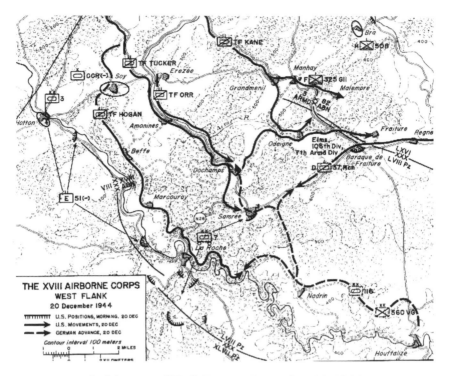

3rd Armored Task Forces, December 20, 1944

(*Source: The Ardennes: Battle of the Bulge*)

of the hotel owner, a GI softly whispered in his ear: "General Rose." The doors slammed shut, the caravan moved out and vanished on the road to Soy.[18]

Lt. Col. Samuel M. Hogan's Task Force was on the right and set off at 1220 hours with sixty vehicles in the direction of the village of La Roche, which was on the right flank boundary of the XVIII Airborne Corps. His advance was screened by the Ourthe River, and initially was unopposed. When he reached his objective, he found that supply train units from the battered 7th Armored Division had already set up roadblocks in defense of the town. He then sent out scouts that probed three miles further before encountering the enemy. As darkness descended, and with his flanks blocked, Hogan dug in.

Major John Tucker's Task Force of the 83rd Recon Battalion was in the center and proceeded south along the Aisne River valley towards the village of Dochamps. There the road climbed up from the valley to the ridge above Samrée. Tucker proceeded east onto the La Roche–Salmchâteau road, which ran along a narrow ridge where it intersected the main Liège–Bastogne highway near Manhay. This crossroads was at a place called Baraque de Fraiture, which was to become a major focus of 3rd Armored's battle in the Bulge.

At first, Tucker's column was unopposed, but at Dochamps it came under heavy fire. Trying to bypass the resistance, Tucker divided his forces, sending one column southwest to Samrée, where units from 7th Armored were fighting desperately and unsuccessfully to hold the town. After General Rose was informed that the town had been lost, he ordered the 83rd Reconnaissance Battalion to recapture Samrée, since its location on the high ground and along the highway to the division objective made it a crucial piece of real estate. Colonel William R. Orr, commanding 1st Battalion, 36th Armored Infantry, picked up additional forces and joined Tucker and took command. His force arrived outside of Dochamps just before midnight and immediately set up a roadblock. A second group turned east towards the vital crossroads and finally made contact with Task Force Kane.

Lt. Col. Matthew W. Kane's reinforced battalion had been moving on the left flank and initially found the going pretty easy. Acting as the pivot for the swing south and east, Kane's column had orders to occupy the village of Malempré, about 3,000 yards southeast of the vital Manhay crossroads. The hills to the east and west provided good observation, and there were thick woods to the southeast that offered cover from which fire could be directed on the crossroads. Kane's men reached Manhay and then pushed all the way to Malempré before meeting any enemy troops.[19]

By the time darkness fell on December 20, General Rose had set up his advanced command post in the *Hôtel de la Clairiere*, a hunting lodge at Pont d'Erezee. The rear division HQ remained at Hotton. While information was still sketchy, he was starting to think that his risky strategy was working. His three Task Forces, thin and spread out over the entire sector, were indeed isolated, but each had achieved at least part of the mission. They had discovered the general direction of the German attack—northwest from Houffalize—and two of the columns had established contact with the enemy. They were still largely intact, and while vulnerable, each was well dug in and holding its ground. He made plans to reinforce the attempt to retake Samrée, the vital communications and supply center, which had been captured the previous afternoon. He contacted General Ridgeway to ask if he could delay further movements until he retook the town and the situation stabilized a little.[20]

By the next day, the picture became much clearer. Some prisoners had been taken, and Lt. Col. Andrew Barr, the division intelligence officer (G-2), had identified the major opposition; it was considerable. Facing Rose's depleted division of about 4,000 men and less than 100 tanks, was General Walther Krüger's *LVIII Panzer Corps*, with the crack *116th Panzer Division* on the right and the *560th Volksgrenadier Division* on the left, and in support. These units were part of General Hasso von Manteuffel's *5th Panzer Army*. To the left of Krüger's *Corps* was the *II SS Panzer Corps*, a part of *SS* Colonel General Sepp Dietrich's *6th SS Panzer Army*, with the *2nd SS Panzer Division* deployed near Highway N15 and the Baraque de Fraiture crossroads.[21] **(E)** Barr's G-2 section estimated that these forces probably outnumbered Rose by more than 10 to 1 in men and at least three times in tanks.[22]

Rose did not realize it, but his hardest days were still ahead. The enemy was headed for both Hotton and Manhay, and the loss of either would threaten a breakthrough to the Meuse and beyond. In fact, that was the strategic objective of the whole German campaign: a breakthrough to Antwerp, which would cut the Allied armies in two and possibly lead to a negotiated settlement to the war in the West.

Hotton is a small village that sits astride the main channel of the Ourthe River at a point where the valley widens. In the middle of the town, a network of roads converge, crossing the river at a two-way wooden bridge able to hold heavy armored vehicles. A number of roads also converged at the important junction center at Marche, less than a mile to the northwest. It was at Marche that Collins' VII Corps was supposed to assemble in preparation for a counterattack. Part of Rose's mission, and that of XVIII Airborne Corps, was to provide a "screen" for these forces as they gathered.

At 0815, Rose contacted Ridgeway's XVIII Corps HQ to report that 3rd Armored was once again preparing to move south. Less than a half-hour

---

E The *2nd SS Panzer Division*, *"Das Reich"* fought in the 1940 campaigns against the Low Countries and France and participated in the invasion of the Balkans. During the Russian Campaign it fought at Smolensk, Moscow, Kharkov, and Kursk. It later fought in Normandy at Caen, St. Lo, and spearheaded the drive on Mortain, and held open the Falaise Gap. It fought as part of *II SS Panzer Corps* during the Ardennes Campaign, and at the end of the war took part in the final attack near Budapest and surrendered to the Americans.

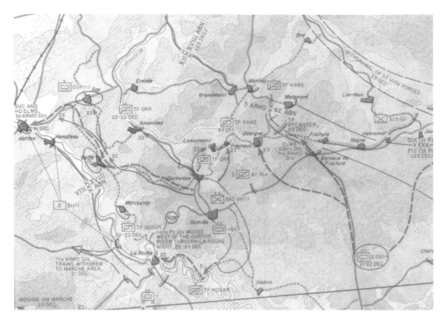

3rd Armored Sector between Hotton & Manhay, Belgium
December 21–23, 1944
(*Source: The Ardennes: Battle of the Bulge*)

later, however, German tanks were spotted moving toward Hotton. They were from the advance guard of Krüger's *LVIII Panzer Corps*, and were driving northwest at top speed towards Hotton, where they hoped to cross the Ourthe River and concentrate on the far bank before the Americans could stop them. General Krüger had received confirmation from *OB WEST* that a combat command of the U.S. 3rd Armored Division had moved to the Werbomont area on December 19. That was reassuring, as his men had so far encountered relatively weak units of the 3rd Armored Division and thus had little reason to expect tougher resistance.

Colonel Johannes Bayer led the spearhead task force from the *116th Panzer Division*, along with elements of the *60th Panzergrenadiers* and the *16th Panzer Regiment*, was sent to cut the Soy-Hotton road and take the Hotton bridge in a pincer movement. During the night of December 20, *Kampfgruppe Bayer* moved northwest on a road parallel to and in between those on which Task Force Hogan and Task Force Orr had advanced that day. The Americans didn't spot his force. At 0850, Rose received word from

Colonel Howze that "many enemy tanks" were astride the Soy–Hotton road and were heading west toward Hotton. Rose canceled the dispatch of reinforcements for Samrée and ordered every available man and machine to defend Hotton.

The men at Hotton were in the middle of breakfast when small arms fire and a brief mortar barrage signaled the enemy attack. Maj. Jack W. Fickesson, the executive officer of the 23rd Armored Engineer Battalion, took command of the defense, assisted by Captains Rodman and Wilson.[23] **(F)** Fickesson dispatched the engineers' trucks to the roadblocks and distributed the available bazookas and machine guns. Leading the enemy attack were four or five tanks using the woods on the eastern edge of Hotton for cover. Two American tanks were knocked out immediately, but an M-36 tank destroyer equipped with a lethal 90mm gun appeared from nowhere and knocked out two *Panthers*. The enemy infantry took most of the buildings on the near bank, but were blocked short of the bridge by a hailstorm of fire from the Americans on both sides of the river. After heavy fighting, the engineers at the footbridge were overrun, but it was a hollow victory as the bridge was not able to hold armored vehicles.

By mid morning, the defenders, now over the initial shock, were holding their own. They were able to evacuate some ambulances, along with most of the wounded and medical personnel. Bazookas and a 37mm anti-tank gun knocked out several more enemy tanks at close range. At 1400 hours the German tanks still in town withdrew to the hill east of Hotton and turned to face Colonel Howze's counterattack along the Soy road.

Although Rose had ordered Howze to put his entire command into the effort to break through the German roadblock, it was soon apparent that it was not enough to force the road. The main problem was the terrain between Hotton and Soy. In addition to the stream bordering the road on the south, cuts ran through the road, and the Germans were dug in on the hill between the two towns, allowing them to command the entire route.

Howze did succeed in getting a small force of tanks and infantrymen into Hotton after bypassing the attackers to the north. This gave the defenders much needed reinforcements, but it was still impossible to call in friendly artillery fire and Hotton remained isolated and vulnerable.

During the day, Task Force Orr had been forced to withdraw to Amonines, three miles southeast of Soy. There, on a slight rise overlooking the Aisne

---

F For his role in the defense of Hotton, Captain Rodman was awarded the Silver Star.

Valley Road, Orr's column formed an all around defense and dug in for the night. Task Force Hogan, which had been stopped the day before near La Roche, was also pushed back towards Amonines, fighting all along the way, and was eventually forced on December 22 to bivouac on a hill near the village of Marcouray. Although he didn't yet know it, Hogan and his 400 men—nearly out of food, ammo, and gas—were surrounded and cut off. Facing him were elements of three German divisions, and he was outgunned and outnumbered many times over. He remained there until Christmas Day.

Task Force Kane passed another quiet morning and sent a detachment to the crossroads at Baraque de Fraiture, reinforcing a scratch force of troops already there. Arriving by mid afternoon, they joined the fighting already in progress. The remainder of the Task Force went to Grandménil before halting for the night.

As darkness fell on December 21, General Rose had reason to feel somewhat relieved. His luck had held for another day and the first critical moment in the battle had passed without disaster. The enemy had made the same mistake that his own commanders had made: piecemeal commitment of their armor. It was clear to him even then that had they pushed all their tanks forward in one massive effort, he would have been overrun. The Germans would later credit "the bravery of the American engineers" at Hotton for their own failure to take the town. Credit must also be given to the men of Headquarters Company and the 143rd Signal Company, as well as the unidentified gun and tank crews and infantrymen who made the desperate stand. Finally, the remaining forces of the stripped down 3rd Armored—the division reserve at Soy and the three thin Task Forces in the field—deserve credit for threatening the German's flanks, thereby dissipating the attack of the *116th Panzer* and *560th Volksgrenadier* divisions and preventing a concentrated advance on Hotton.

True, Rose had failed to retake Samrée (this task would later become the assignment of his former command, CCA, 2nd Armored Division). He had been forced to use his last reserves in the fight to hold Hotton, and his western and center Task Forces had been pushed back. But there was reason to believe the worst was behind him. The bridge at Hotton was still in his hands and the 84th Infantry Division was reportedly moving to relieve him there. A battalion of the independent 517th Parachute Infantry Regiment was on its way to Soy to reinforce Howze. The crossroads at Baraque de Fraiture was still under heavy pressure, but the small band of defenders was hanging on by its fingernails. Rose's command situation was improving, as he had been notified that he was soon to revert to

Collin's VII Corps, where he felt most comfortable. The best news of all was that Combat Command A, which had already been scheduled to rejoin the division on December 22, had closed into assembly areas north of Manhay.

Of course, the enemy was still in the field, and there was little information about their actual strength or intentions. Had Rose been able to take a peek at "the other side of the hill," he might have been even more upbeat. The situation maps at *Wehrmacht* headquarters that night placed the *116th Panzer Division* in Hotton, and also showed that *LVIII Panzer Corps* was the most advanced unit of all the German forces driving west. But, the German maps were wrong.

The stubborn American defense of the Hotton bridge had persuaded the cautious General Krüger that his strategy of shifting his attack northwest to Hotton to find a quick and painless way across the Ourthe had failed. His men had suffered heavy casualties during the fighting that day, troop morale was poor and getting worse, supplies were running low, and his men were tired. The tough American stand convinced him he would have to move even further west to reach the Meuse. While Rose still faced a difficult, even critical situation, the Germans also faced serious problems. For the first time since the offensive had begun, their drive was starting to bog down. These command developments were not, however, having much of an effect on those who were fighting for their lives.

On December 22, all three 3rd Armored Task Forces again encountered very strong resistance and their attacks south failed with heavy losses. Hotton continued to come under attack and was partially occupied by enemy infantry. Howze's persistent attempts to clear the Soy–Hotton road were also largely unsuccessful. But while the situation to the west remained precarious—particularly that of Task Force Hogan, now surrounded at Marcouray—the focus of the action had shifted east to Manhay and the vital crossroads to the south of the village. It was in this struggle that the small reserve still available would be consumed, and where he would face his worst crisis of the war, staring defeat full in the face. On the morning of December 23, Maurice Rose— a man not easily rattled or inclined to give expression to his worst fears—contacted his Reserve commander, Col. Howze, with a blunt admonition.

> Impress on every individual that we must stay right here or there will
> be a war to be fought all over again and we won't be here to fight it.[24]

Baraque de Fraiture has changed little since late December of 1944. While several of the farmhouses are now commercial establishments, it remains a small collection of buildings grouped around a crossroads. Taking its name from the tiny village of Fraiture to the south, it is located at an elevation of just over 650 meters and is one of the highest points in the Ardennes. The ground around the crossroads is clear, with woods to the north, west, and southeast. Running through the crossroads is a major north–south paved highway (#N15) that passes through Bastogne and Liege and is perfect for tanks. The east–west highway (#N28) is a secondary road that runs along the northern bank of the Ourthe River and is the most direct route connecting the towns between St. Vith and La Roche.

Terrain and the road net were only a few of the elements giving this position its importance. The unfolding battle, and especially the XVIII Airborne Corps and 3rd Armored movements, dictated its crucial role in the struggle to hold the "northern shoulder" of the Bulge. Rose's original orders to the three Task Force commanders were to move up to highway N15 and take the crossroads, but only Kane was able to reach it. Now it would be random, unplanned actions, uncoordinated movements, and the bravery and personal initiative of individual soldiers and officers that would determine the outcome of the battle.

The day before General Rose sent his three task forces towards Baraque de Fraiture, Maj. Arthur C. Parker III, an officer of the 589th Field Artillery arrived at the crossroads with three salvaged 105-mm howitzers. His orders were to set up a roadblock behind the 106th Infantry Division, which was still fighting desperately to hold St. Vith. Over the next twenty-four hours other small groups of men and equipment arrived and joined Parker's makeshift command. Among these was a small group of tanks from Task Force Kane. Parker's men fought off several probing attacks during the day, killed a number of the enemy, and took several prisoners. From this time forward, the crossroads at Baraque de Fraiture would be known as "Parker's Crossroads."[25]

On December 21, General Gavin went to Rose's Command Post at Manhay to express his growing concern about the threat to his flank developing at Baraque de Fraiture. The crossroads stood on the highway that formed the boundary between the 3rd Armored and 82nd Airborne Divisions and between XVIII Airborne and VII Corps. Rose, who was in the VII Corps sector but still attached to XVIII Corps, assured him that holding it was his major priority, but the potential for confusion with such divided command responsibility was great and was about to be played out with tragic results.[26] In spite of Rose's reassurance, Gavin sent more paratroopers to help defend the crossroads and surrounding villages.

Neither man knew that the highway was also the route along which the veteran *2nd SS Panzer Division* was planning to advance. It was also the boundary between the German *Fifth Panzer Army* and the *Sixth SS Panzer Army*. The fulcrum of the whole war was, for a moment in time, firmly hinged on that single road and the crucial crossroads. The next day passed with only sporadic fighting, but the *2nd SS Panzer Division* was moving in position to reduce the crossroads and drive up Highway #N15 to Manhay and beyond. Fuel remained a major problem, but by evening of December 22, the Germans had been able to move the *4th SS PanzerGrenadier Regiment*, some tanks, and an artillery battalion forward.

During that night the *4th PanzerGrenadiers* moved to cut off Parker's Crossroads from the west and north. Before dawn on the December 23, the Germans attacked the tiny village of Fraiture, but were driven back by Gavin's paratroopers. Fighting continued throughout the day, but time was running out for the men at the crossroads. By 1800, it was over. Three tanks and a handful of men managed to escape. The rest were killed, wounded, or captured. Major Parker, however, was not there. He had been badly wounded and evacuated on the day before.[27] **(G)**

Just before the fall of Parker's Crossroads, Rose realized how serious the situation had become. His HQ was sitting on the next major intersection, only four miles north of Parker's Crossroads. If the Germans took that, they would be astride the road between Trois Ponts and Hotton, sitting on the flank and in the rear of both the 3rd Armored and 82nd Airborne. He ordered Combat Command A to recapture the crossroads. Lt. Col. Richardson drew the assignment.

> General Hickey came in to see me and reaffirmed that I was in command of everything at the Manhay road junction over to the west and that I was "not going to let anything come up that road." That was a pretty tall order.[28]

Richardson quickly formed a Battle Group under the command of his executive officer, Major Olin F. Brewster. **(H)** His orders to "Brew" were simple: "retake the crossroads."[29]

G Losses were heavy. For example, of the 116 men of Company F, 325th Glider Infantry at the crossroads, only forty-four returned.

H Olin Finley Brewster (1915–1999) was born in Texas and graduated from Texas A&M in 1941. Commissioned as a Reserve Officer in the cavalry, he served

By the time Brewster led his quickly assembled force south from Manhay, the Germans already held Parker's Crossroads in great strength. As we now know, and as must have also been apparent even then, Richardson's order was clearly impossible to obey. Had Brewster been ordered to hold the Germans from advancing further, the whole story might have been different.

After doing a reconnaissance under fire with Maj. Elliott Goldstein, Parker's second in command, Brewster set out with a half dozen Shermans from H Company, 32nd Armored, and about 150 men of A Company, 509th Parachute Battalion. Other stragglers, both tanks and infantry, joined him from the south and a platoon of tank destroyers from 9th Armored also appeared. With this force he set out to battle the full might of the veteran *2nd SS Panzer*. Even before he was able to deploy his meager forces, tanks and *Panzergrenadiers* were already moving north up the Manhay road and through the forests on each flank.

As darkness fell, Brewster set up a roadblock on the north edge of some woods about 3,000 yards north of Parker's Crossroads in a hamlet called Belle Haie. All night, the Germans tried to infiltrate past his positions to reach Manhay, managing to capture Odeigne, less than a mile to the west, but Brewster held fast. At about noon on Christmas Eve, Brewster received C Company, 290th Infantry Regiment, from the green 75th Infantry Division. He wasn't overly grateful. The division had arrived on the line on December 13 and everyone knew the problems of units in their first combat—usually a disaster.

By that time, in spite of some artillery and air support, the several attacks he had already mounted to retake the crossroads had all failed. With great trepidation, he ordered C Company to attack, supported by direct tank fire, but that was also unsuccessful with heavy loss, probably due—at least partly, Brewster believed—to the inexperience of the company commander. Of course, the men of the 290th thought they had been poorly led and used as cannon fodder.

The Germans stepped up their pressure, but still did not mount a major attack. They had their own problems. For one thing, the Americans had good cover. The main highway was only about twenty-two feet wide

---

as a company commander and battalion exec of 1/32 Armored Regiment in the 3rd Armored Division. He was wounded on January 5, 1945, during the Battle of the Bulge. He received the Bronze Star, Purple Heart, and Presidential Unit Citation and retired from active service with the rank of Lt. Colonel.

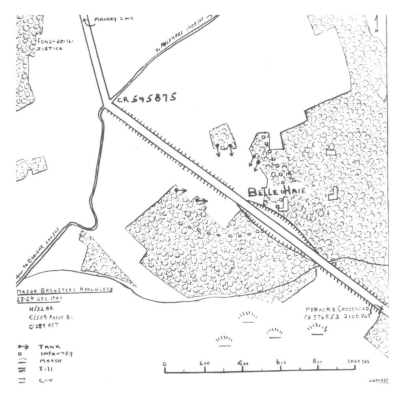

Major Olin F. Brewtser's roadblock at Belle Haie, Belgium
December 23–25, 1944

(*Source: The Armored Division in the Defense*)

at the point of attack, channeling the German tanks into a thin column, and the surrounding ground was poor for armor. Also, the weather had cleared a bit and the American fighter bombers were hovering up above in their usual four plane relays. General Hans Lammerding decided to wait until his infantry cleared the area on either side of the highway before making his move.

Back at Combat Command A headquarters, General Hickey was trying to coordinate a retreat with his counterpart in 7th Armored to "straighten the line." This withdrawal order was issued by General Montgomery who had earlier been put in command of the "northern shoulder" of the Bulge by the Supreme Allied Command. Because of the peculiar command relationships—the 7th Armored had just been inserted between 3rd Armored and 82nd Airborne—Hickey wanted to make sure of his orders. Col. Richardson was waiting for instructions about what to tell Brewster, who now found himself in limbo between the VII Corps and XVIII Airborne Corps boundary lines. He had no idea who was in charge—or who was watching out for him. Richardson was starting to get worried about his men.

> General Hickey found Rose—fortunately ran into him very quickly—and he came back with some bad news for me. He said, "I am to personally to deliver to you the order that you will hold at all costs." I said, "do you mean, all costs, regardless?" General Hickey said, "Yes. That is an order from General Collins, General Rose, to me and now to you." So I called Brewster on the radio and told him he was going to have to hold at all costs.[30]

Brewster prepared for the worst. There were some bright moments though. Rumors of relief accompanied the medics still able to evacuate the wounded. That evening Col. Richardson alerted Brewster to be ready to pull back at a moment's notice. That was good news, but the word did not come. Even after he heard the sound of enemy tanks to his rear, Brewster held, but by that time Manhay was in critical danger. The full implications of the changes in unit boundaries, back and forth detachments and reattachments, the withdrawal of 7th Armored, and the interference of Bernard Law Montgomery with his mania for "line straightening," had all combined to cause its loss. Hickey did not know what was happening. Orders were not communicated between the two CCA headquarters and, in fact, the *2nd SS Panzer* hit Manhay just as 7th Armored was withdrawing. It was a nightmare.

Originally Brewster was supposed to withdraw with the onset of darkness, but the plans and circumstances had changed, although he didn't know anything about it. Task Force Kane had been isolated and forced to move back. The 504th Parachute Regiment was driven out of Malampre, but still Richardson told Brewster to hold on. Finally, early on Christmas Day, the order came from Richardson over the radio: "Get out now if you can, but don't use the road you went up on, try east." By that time, Brewster had been bypassed on both flanks and enemy armor was maneuvering in his rear. He didn't know that Malampre had been lost, so he took his men out on that road.

Shortly afterwards, his lead tank and two in the rear were knocked out and heavy machine gun fire raked the column from the right flank. There was no choice but to get out on foot, so they destroyed the remaining vehicles and took off. At about three in the morning on Christmas Day, Brewster contacted Richardson by radio for the last time, indicating he was heading towards Bra. The sky was clear, there was snow on the ground, and the moon was bright. By dawn most of group were safe.

Brewster got back to division HQ at Barvaux and ran into Lt. Col. Wesley A. Sweat, division G-3, and a good friend. He greeted Brewster with surprise, "My God, Brew, we thought you were dead." He answered, "Not quite." Next he reported to Col. John Smith, Chief of Staff, and recounted his experience since his last radio message. Then, before he could even wash, change his filthy clothes, or eat, he went with Col. Smith to division HQ. At that point, Brewster recalled, he had been fighting for forty-eight hours with no sleep, was unshaven, filthy, and looked like "Sad Sack." He went into the General's office.

> General Rose was sitting behind his desk looking like he had just stepped out of a band box and said, "Brewster, what happened?" I explained the situation and he asked if I had any ammunition and fuel left. My answer was yes. He said, "And you quit fighting?" My explanation was that I had very few vehicles left that could be replaced and I had some good soldiers that would be hard to replace and I chose to bring them out on foot to fight another day rather than stay surrounded and sacrifice them. Without hesitation, the General said, "Brewster, you are under arrest for misbehavior before the enemy. Give the chief your gun!"

Brewster walked out stunned and headed to the mess tent, where he got his long awaited Christmas Dinner: canned spam. The next day, Brewster gave a sworn statement to Lt. Col. Sylvester, the Division Inspector General. Then, the two officers visited Lt. Colonel Richardson, who told them about his midnight meeting with General Rose.

> I went into the room and there was the Chief of Staff and General Rose, looking "just whipped," exhausted. He told me to sit down and said, "the reason I have you here is that I have just heard that Brewster lost all his equipment and that you too lost a lot of equipment." I told General Rose that the equipment that the staff officers were talking about was from the 7th Armored, and that at daylight they could look at the markings. I said that Brewster had followed my

orders and I was the one who had ordered him to get out when he could. I did not want to lose all those men, but the General said, "I hear differently."

We had a little discussion and I repeated, "It was my order. Brewster did exactly as I ordered him to. He was no coward, he held as long as he could and destroyed the equipment on my orders." Finally, he said he wanted me to prefer charges against Brewster. I replied, "No way, Sir, will I do that." Of course, I was tactful about it, believe me. Then he said he would look further into the case and kicked me out of HQ.[31]

Brewster and Major John "Bunny" Tucker, exec of the 83rd Reconnaissance (who had also been relieved by Rose) then cooled their heels for about a week. On January 2 at about 1230 hours, and once more accompanied by Colonel Smith, Brewster saw Rose for the last time. The General looked at the major intensely and then spoke dispassionately,

Major Olin Brewster after Being Wounded
(*Source:* Brewster Family)

Brewster, I want you to know that I never change my mind. But in your case, I am. Colonel Richardson says he needs you and right now. However, I am going to keep an eye on you and if you ever screw up again, I will throw the book at you.[32]

Brewster returned to duty and the American offensive began the next day. On January 8 he was wounded in the leg and evacuated; his war was over.

What happened? General Rose could not prefer charges by himself. Both Richardson and General Hickey would have to agree, and both of them, to their credit, resisted Rose's pressure and refused to countenance a court martial. General Richardson corroborated this fact in subsequent interviews and personal conversations.[33] Forty-five years later, General Richardson repeated what he believed all along, "Brewster was one hell of a soldier and one of the finest men I have ever known."[34]

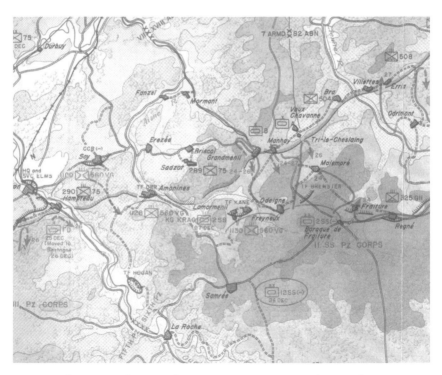

**3rd Armored Sector between Hotton & Manhay, Belgium
December 24–27, 1944**

(*Source: The Ardennes: Battle of the Bulge*)

At the other end of the battlefield, Colonel Sam Hogan's ordeal had ended on quite a different note. He had been surrounded since 22 December on a hilltop at Marcouray and cut off from all aid. The Germans had formally asked for his surrender. His colorful response—"If you want this village then come and take it"—never got the publicity of General McCauliffe's reply to the same demand at surrounded Bastogne: "Nuts!" but it was just as defiant and heroic.

Several resupply efforts had already failed but General Rose ordered another airdrop of plasma and gasoline on Christmas Eve. Colonel Hogan and his men looked skyward with growing optimism that soon turned into despair.

> Late in the afternoon seven C-47s circled by very low with their drop doors open. We saw the drop made near La Roche and then a terrific amount of AA opened up on them. Four of them went down almost at once and two more a little later. We saw several bodies falling but the chutes opened so close to the treetops that we thought they were all killed. That night two of them came into our perimeter. The evergreens had broken their fall. They had taken off from England with only a vague idea of where we were.[35]

Another drop was scheduled, but Hogan had seen enough. That night he sent out a patrol led by Lt. Harold W. Randall to scout out a route of withdrawal. It would be impossible to take the vehicles, as the road north was jammed with German traffic. Before long he got the orders he was waiting for.

> Christmas Day was clear and freezing with about an inch of crisp snow and ice on the ground. About noon a message signed by General Rose directed us to destroy our equipment and make our way out the best way we could. In closing it he wished us good luck. I thought we would need it.[36]

The men blackened their faces with burnt cork, soot, or axle grease and threw away their helmets (to lower their silhouettes). Then, they ran the motors of their vehicles with sugar in the gas tanks and without oil. Captain Spigelman, the battalion dentist, and three medics heroically volunteered to stay behind with twelve wounded men who couldn't be moved. "Hogan's 400" moved out at 1600 hours and headed north through the woods. One of the wounded men covered their seventeen German prisoners with a Thompson submachine gun until the others made their escape. Captain Spigelman, the medics, and the wounded men made their way to the German rear in ambulances and remained POWs for the remainder of the war.[37]

After several close calls, Hogan reached American lines by early morning, December 26. One soldier had been lost, killed by friendly fire.[38] **(I)** There was only one more thing left for Sam Hogan to do.

> I reported to General Rose after I came out of Marcouray. The only thing I remember is his question why I was the last one out and answering that "my feet hurt." I am sure the other part of our conversation was routine, such as his assurance that I would be speedily re-equipped and back into action. The order to destroy my equipment came directly from him and I think indicates the seriousness with which he considered such action.[39]

The higher ups were pleased and the press covered the escape as a thrilling victory. **(J)** Sam Hogan walked, limped really, out of disaster into the glow of celebrity, while Olin Brewster sat under house arrest for doing essentially the same thing as his fellow Texan.

Much hard fighting remained, but the danger to the existence of 3rd Armored and Maurice Rose had passed. On January 3, the First U.S. Army began its counteroffensive to erase the Bulge. The VII Corps attacked southeast toward Houffalize with 2nd Armored followed by 84th Division on the right, and 3rd Armored followed by 83rd Division on the left. Units from Patton's Third U.S. Army were driving for the same goal from the south. The race was on between Harmon's 2nd Armored, Rose's 3rd Armored, and Bolling's 84th Infantry.

I The story of the Christmas Day escape of Task Force Hogan has been retold many times. The successful retreat of TF Kane from Lamorenil and Freyneus the next day has received almost no attention.

J On January 1, 1945, Collins wrote to Hogan: "Your indominable courage and leadership not only assisted in checking the German advance to the north, but resulted in saving some 400 men. Equipment can always be replaced but not such men; men proven and true who soon will be ready again to lead the way to victory." Maurice Rose transmitted this commendation "with a feeling of great pride that I know is reflected in each member of the division."

**Maurice Rose (left) and BG Doyle O. Hickey at the start
of the Bulge counterattack, January 1, 1945**
(*Source:* Rose Family Album)

When the 3rd Armored finally got down to take the crossroads just outside the town, they found that the 2nd Armored had already beaten them to it. This followed a magnificent 1,500-yard dash into the village of Samree to put artillery into an observation position to close the gap, which was credited mistakenly *by Stars and Stripes* to 3rd Armored. General Rose's reaction to that was to lift his phone and suavely acquaint the infuriated Ernie with the fact that, "The 3rd Armored, of course, did not need credit for what they didn't do."[40]

This time, the prize went to CCA, 2nd Armored, which met elements of the 11th Armored Division on January 16, 1945. The link-up chopped off a large piece of the Bulge. "The next day, January 17, the First Army went back to the open arms of Omar Bradley."[41] By January 19, the 3rd Armored gained its final objectives, clearing an area south to the Ourthe River.

It was over, but the cost was enormous, for thousands incalculable. There were the tangible losses that could be counted. The division lost almost 1,475 soldiers, including 187 men killed in action. This figure represents one tenth of the authorized strength of the division. The equipment losses were also considerable, and totaled 325 vehicles, including 165 tanks, or almost two-thirds of the authorized total. In each combat unit the story was the same. Task Force Richardson had left the Stolberg area on December 18 with sixty-five tanks. At the end of the battle they had only eight that were in operating condition and had lost a battery of self-propelled 105mm guns as well.[42] Task Force Hogan had lost all its equipment. The Germans also suffered heavily. Lt. Colonel Barr's G-2 section estimated that more 1,700 enemy soldiers had been killed and more than 2,500 captured. German tank losses were estimated at about 100 *Panthers* and *Tigers*.

But there were other costs. For some men, the payment would last the rest of their lives. The 3rd Armored Division and its proud, confident commander had been shaken and bruised to the very core. Maurice Rose had faced defeat and annihilation in the face, and had escaped both only by the thinnest of margins. The truth was that luck had been as important as professional skill.

The loss of Manhay, even though it was soon recaptured, took the luster of invincibility off Rose, at least for a time. It caused immediate recrimination among the American commanders. Ridgeway was livid and ordered an immediate IG investigation even as the battle raged. Five years after the war, professional armor officers were still studying what had happened and the special problems and risks when operating on corps boundaries. **(K)**

Even though the VII Corps (and 3rd Armored) boundary was west of Manhay and split Manhay from Grandmenil, Rose could not escape the taint of failure. It turned out that some part of the confusion leading to the humiliating loss of Manhay was due to his own CCA's failure to coordinate its movements with 7th Armored's CCA.[43] **(L)** It was Major Olin Brewster who paid the ultimate price.

K Olin Brewster may be one of the most written about majors in the U.S. Army. Nearly every serious book about the Battle of the Bulge describes the battles at Parker's Crossroads and Belle Haie and cites Brewster by name. See especially footnote 29 and the U.S. Army Armor School Committee Reports.

L The failure of CCA, 3rd Armored, to coordinate its withdrawal was described in the *XVIII Airborne Corps Inspector General Report of Investigation, CCA, 7th Armored, Manhay, 24–25 December 1944, 6 January 1945*, cited in the Official History.

While General Rose relieved many officers, in this case, his reaction was out of character and obviously inconsistent with his treatment of Lt. Colonel Hogan. The Brewster incident reveals Rose to be like other men—likely to weaken under constant pressure and physical exhaustion, capable of terrible errors, misjudgment of character, and foolish stubbornness. But like other great commanders, he returned to the inevitable struggle and prevailed, even over himself. His mistakes were soon dwarfed by his victories, but for some there was no return to glory.

Let there be no confusion or equivocation. Olin Finley Brewster did what honor and courage demanded; he did what was possible. He retreated only when he was surrounded and ordered by his commander to do so, saving his men from certain death or capture in the process, but his Army career was effectively over. His serious leg wound early in the January counterattack erased any possibility for him to do something spectacular to regain an opportunity for advancement and erase the stigma of Rose's charges. Maybe if Rose had lived, perhaps he would have cleared the record. Certainly Richardson and Hickey felt that a great injustice had been done, but neither man could reverse what had happened. There was no just end to Brewster's ordeal. For the remainder of his life, he felt that Rose had treated him wrongfully. Only the men who walked out of Belle Haie won.

In the story there is the powerful echo of another tragic moment in American history that cascades over deserted and forgotten battlefields. During the Battle of Kernstown on March 23, 1862, Brigadier General Richard B. Garnett ordered the withdrawal of the Stonewall Brigade when it was on the verge of being overrun. For this "unauthorized" retreat, Garnett was relieved of command and charged with cowardice by General Thomas "Stonewall" Jackson. Although hearings were held, an actual court martial was never convened. In May 1863, at the Battle of Chancellorsville, Jackson was killed accidentally by his own troops.

> While paying his respects, Garnett turned to Jackson's aides, and said, "You know of the unfortunate breach between General Jackson and myself. I can never forget it, nor cease to regret it. But I wish here to assure you that no one can lament his death more sincerely than I do. I believe that he did me a great injustice, but I believe also that he acted from the purest motives. He is dead. Who can fill his place?"[44]

Garnett later led a brigade in George Pickett's division, and on July 3, 1863, at Gettysburg, he took a position in the front rank of that immortal charge. Some say he went into the attack on horseback to dispel once and for all Jackson's charges that hung over his name. He disappeared twenty yards in front of the Union battle line.

In conversation with the authors near the end of his life, Olin Finley Brewster repeated words similar to those uttered by General Garnett. The years had somewhat softened the bitterness and resentment. He knew that there were men who believed that he had been falsely charged and would try to vindicate him. Then, with a look in his eyes that were already gazing over to "the other side," he expressed envy of Garnett's end.

CHAPTER Thirteen

Winter 1945: The Rhine, the Cemetery, and the Letters

"General, there is only one way I know to lead
this division, and that's at the head of it."

Major General Maurice Rose

After the Battle of the Bulge, Rose returned to the Prym House. He was happy to get back. The battle had taken a heavy toll and he was completely exhausted. For a while the only reminders of the war were the droning of V-1 buzz bombs on the way to Liege, or an occasional overflight by the new German ME-262 jet fighters.[1] For the men and their leaders, it was a time to rest, catch up on mail, see a movie, or pay a much-appreciated visit to the showers set up by the 23rd Engineers.

It was during this period that the division received several new, and long-awaited, pieces of equipment. The first was the M-24 "Chaffee" light tank, armed with a 75mm gun, a big improvement over the undergunned 37mm M-5 Stuarts and M-8 armored cars. Concluding that there was "no place in an armored division for a light tank whose principal weapon is a 37mm gun," Rose considered the M-24 an "excellent vehicle for the reconnaissance battalion and the reconnaissance companies with the armored regiments."[2]

More important, however, was the arrival of the T26 "General Pershing" tanks, with their thick frontal armor and 90mm main gun armament.

(A) A surge of optimism quickly spread through the ranks of the tank crews and commanders. The preliminary combat results were good and Rose felt that the T26 was fully capable of confronting the Germans "on equal terms."[3] The enthusiasm was tempered by the fact that so few of the new tanks had actually arrived, but at least the Spearheads would be better off. No longer would the first unexpected encounters with German tanks mean suicide for the men in Shermans.

During the lull before the drive to the Rhine, some men took the opportunity to seek out old comrades and catch up on the news. PFC Don R. Marsh and the other 2nd Armored "exiles" from the 143rd Signal Company heard their old outfit was close to Hagelstein, Belgium.

> We drove into their bivouac area and asked for the location of the Wire Section. Some of the guys spotted us and hollered, "Look what the cat dragged in!" (or worse). We had not seen each other since the previous May when Captain Wilson shipped us off to the 2AD as a package. It was then that we got the sad news of those killed and wounded in the 143rd, starting with one of my friends, Bob Rosenberg from NYC.
>
> Bob was killed on 2 September 1944 at Mons. We shipped overseas and joined the 3AD together. He was a quiet, likable guy with a passive demeanor and a great sense of humor. Lowell Dillard was also KIA that same day. My old sidekick, Harry Tuttle, from Long Island, brought me up to date on the past eight months, including the action at Hotton during the Bulge, where Ken Speers got wounded retrieving a desperately needed .50 caliber machine gun that somebody abandoned in a firefight.
>
> When the conversation got around to talking about their Commanding General, Major General Maurice Rose, and our former CCA commander, they all agreed that he was "a hard charger and hell

---

A The T26 (also referred to as the M26) "General Pershing" was a forty-one-ton, five-man crew, tank mounting a powerful 90mm gun and thick armor. It was equipped with a gyrostabilizer, which enabled it to fire accurately while moving. The T26 was the only American tank able to engage the later model German tanks on equal terms. The Pershing had arrived in small numbers late in the war—only 200 were delivered before VE Day—and they were assigned to a very few select Task Forces. Less than twenty actually saw combat, with half assigned to the 3rd Armored Division. It was standard practice to position a Pershing at the tip of an advancing column just in case a German Panther (Mark V) or Tiger (Mk VI) suddenly appeared.

bent on always being up front." They learned, as we did, that where he went they went, as he insisted upon having his wire, no matter the conditions or situations. The danger was always shared. Late in the day, we wished each other good luck and returned to our unit. We would never see each other again.[4]

The wiremen were not the only ones to take a road trip in search of a little relaxation. General Hodges could see the visible strain in one of his best men and ordered Maurice Rose to take some time off. He told him to go to Brussels, gently suggesting that he see the sights and get some rest. All six "bird" colonels—Smith, Brown, Doan, Welborn, Howze, and Rohsenberger—went as well. The other men at headquarters were glad to see the top brass leave, figuring that they would be able to let loose a little also, but the excitement was short-lived. The general returned the next day, complaining about the rich food, the billets, and especially, the quiet.[5]

The quiet did not last long. At dawn on February 26, radio silence was broken and at 0600 the fighting began again. Now refitted, rested, and brought back to full strength, the 3rd Armored was once again committed to combat. Moving alongside Terry Allen's 104th "Timberwolf" Division, Rose's men—with the advance CP right behind the lead elements as usual—quickly crossed the Roer River, where so many of their friends had given their lives and their blood the previous autumn.

Just two days later, Rose stood on the West Bank of the Erft Canal. It was the last barrier before the Rhine River and Cologne, the fourth largest city in Germany, now only nine miles away. American self-propelled 155-mm guns of the oft-attached 991st Armored Field Artillery Battalion had already brought the western suburbs of Cologne under fire. Rose ordered Colonel Howze to move Task Force Hogan and Task Force Richardson into position. The General had a unique incentive in mind to drive his commanders forward, and Sam Hogan eagerly moved up to the line.

> An early objective was to secure crossings of the Erft Canal. Dating back to our early training in the United States there had been a great deal of friendly rivalry between my battalion and the 3rd Battalion of the 32nd Armored Regiment commanded by my friend and fellow Texan Walt Richardson. I suppose General Rose had heard of this rivalry. A Division Liaison Officer told us the General would give a case of Scotch to the first unit to secure a crossing over the canal. I got men across on foot over a partially destroyed bridge but Rich was able to get the first

tanks over and I later had to move my tanks over his bridge. However, the General sent me the Scotch, which I split 50-50 with Rich.[6]

For the next several days, Rose built up his forces in the Erft Canal bridgehead for the assault on Cologne. On March 3, as he had so many times before, General Rose established his forward CP close to the action.

> At Niederaussem, war correspondents had merely to look out of the window at division forward echelon headquarters and they could see the battle progressing less than 1,000 yards away. They agreed that General Rose preferred the front line to a more healthy place somewhere in the rear.[7]

The division was now only four miles from the Rhine. Shortly after setting up the HQ, the whole area came under heavy artillery fire. One shell exploded in the back yard near the main building, sending a shower of metal fragments through an open window right into Rose's office. Haynes Dugan was one of the first men to enter the map room after the barrage stopped.

> When Lt. Colonel Wesley A. Sweat and his G-3 section examined the damage they found that one tiny piece of red hot metal had pierced the exact center of the division's new objective on the operations map![8]

The war was drawing near to General Rose.

Later that day, General Collins was making one of his customary tours of his unit headquarters and drove up to General Rose's CP. He noticed right away that the small house was at the very edge of the town and under direct observation of the enemy positions. Small arms fire crackled nearby. General Rose, oblivious to the sound of the gunfire, came to the front of the house and warmly greeted his commander. This time, Collins' tone was not threatening, but the message was by now familiar.

> "Maurice, do you always have to have your CP in the last house in town?" He drew himself up as he replied: "General, there is only one way I know to lead this division, and that's at the head of it!"[9]

The two men went into the parlor, where the punctured situation map was located, to confer. As they walked inside, observers could hear them joke about the coincidence, if that was what it was. Neither man saw it as an

**Major General Maurice Rose checks the
advance toward Cologne, March 6, 1945**
(*Source:* Rose Family Album)

omen or a signal but afterwards, as Collins was leaving he ordered Rose to
move the HQ back towards the center of the town.[10]

During the meeting, Collins briefed Rose on his role in the upcoming
VII Corps attack on Cologne. The plan called for the 8th and 104th
Infantry Divisions to cover the flanks of the 3rd Armored, and was

> . . . one of the most complicated attacks it (the division) had ever
> attempted and one of the most successful. The maneuvers, feints,
> and timing had many of the aspects of an often rehearsed "touch-
> down play" as executed by exponents of the "Razzle Dazzle" game
> of football.[11]

The final assault on Cologne began on March 5 at 0400 hours. Resistance
from remnants of six *Panzer* and *Volksgrenadier* divisions was relatively light,

and Task Force Doan crossed the city limits from the north at 0710 hours. House to house fighting quickly developed, but the men were not deterred from marking their achievement for all to see. As Iris Carpenter and the other war correspondents drove past the city line the next day they saw a large "Welcome" sign. It featured a

> . . . pine tree on yellow ground, which is the division sign, and the slogan, "You are entering Cologne by courtesy of the Spearhead Division." Men had stayed up all night painting it, and their handiwork was almost more than the "Timberwolves," fighting side by side and only just behind, could bear.[12]

To the delight of the sign painters, General Rose had his picture taken at the sign with his aide, Major Bellinger as soon as the snipers were silenced.

The main objective of the attack was the Hohenzollern Bridge, which spanned the Rhine and joined the two parts of the city. The latest intelligence reports suggested that it had either been mined or already blown up by the retreating Germans. Rose, however, wasn't so sure, or maybe he just wanted the thrill of trying to risk crossing it himself, just as he had done on several previous occasions in France and Belgium.[13] He told the correspondents that he was sending a Task Force to take a look.

> "We're going up around two o'clock and it should be quite a good fight. If you're scouting around the city, meanwhile, keep away from the area around the cathedral, because, even if the Germans *have* pulled back across the river, they've got observation on everything that moves around the bank on this side."[14]

Located close to the bridge was the Cologne Cathedral, or *Dom*, which dominated the city even during the hell of combat. It remained in extraordinary good condition considering the pounding the surrounding area had taken from tens of thousands of shells and bombs. The air intelligence officers estimated that after 167 air raids and countless artillery bombardments, more than 50,000 tons of explosives had hit the jewel of the Rhineland.[15] Many considered it a miracle that the 512-foot tower of the thirteenth century church still stood. General Rose issued strict orders to exercise extreme fire discipline near the church, but death and destruction came right up to the steps of the entrance nonetheless.

**Major General Maurice Rose and Major Robert Bellinger
entering Cologne, March 1945**
(*Source:* Rose Family Album)

Cpl. Clarence E. Smoyer, the young Pennsylvanian veteran, had served
as a gunner with E Company, 32nd Armored Regiment since the beginning of the war. Now he was in one of CCA's new T26 Pershings driving
towards the Rhine. On March 6, 1945, in one of the most celebrated (and
oft-photographed) tank-to-tank encounters of the European campaign, he
demonstrated the lethality of the new tank in the most vivid way imaginable. As Task Force Doan closed in on the Cathedral and the Hohenzollern
Bridge, a German Mark V Panther, which appeared to have been knocked
out, suddenly went into action, destroying a Sherman and killing three of
its five-man crew. Smoyer's Pershing was ordered to move down an adjacent street and knock out the enemy tank. **(B)**

B The T26 crew included: Robert Early (tank commander), Clarence Smoyer
(gunner), John Deriggi (asst. gunner), Willliam McVey (driver), and Homer Davis
(asst. driver).

> As we entered the intersection, our driver had his periscope turned
> toward the German and saw his gun turning to meet us. When I
> turned our turret, I was looking into the Mark V gun tube; so instead
> of stopping to fire, our driver drove into the middle of the intersec-
> tion so we wouldn't be a sitting duck. As we were moving I fired once.
> Then we stopped and I fired two more shells to make sure they
> wouldn't fire at our side. All three of our shells penetrated, one under
> the gun shield and two on the side. The two side hits went completely
> through and out the other side.[16]

The still photo of the knocked out German tank at the very threshold of
the Cathedral became famous. T/3 Leon Rosenman and T/4 James Bates—
a decorated First Army movie man now attached to 3rd Armored—also
shot a live action 9mm film of the encounter. But the soldiers did not see
the pictures right away. For decades, Clarence wondered what had happened to the German crew, until he finally saw the film. It clearly shows
three of the German crewmen barely escaping from the burning tank, only
to die moments later. A letter from another soldier who was there that day
said he had looked through one of the shell holes and saw one other man
burned to death inside. Apparently, none of the Germans survived the
engagement. They joined the three American tankers as the last soldiers
killed in the battle of Cologne. As Clarence remarked, in a moment of
thankfulness for his own survival, "That T26 tank was the best we had during the whole war."[17]

By March 7 the fighting was over. Master Sgt. Angelo Cali of intelligence thought it looked like "someone had taken an egg-beater through
the city."[18] Another GI described the town center as "wrecked masonry surrounded by city limits."[19] The rubble-filled streets were quiet and the men
set up defensive positions and waited to be relieved by the men in the
infantry divisions. It was time to savor the victory. The G-2 headquarters
staff arrived in the city just after the fighting had ceased. The first place
Sgt. Cali visited was the world famous wine cellar in the Dom Hotel, right
next to the Cathedral. He was too late.

> There was almost nothing left in the cellar. The men were looking for
> whisky and threw away everything else. They smashed the bottles and
> the cement floor was covered with broken glass and about two inches
> of sweet brandy. We salvaged a couple of cases of overlooked
> Vermouth and took them back to the mess. To celebrate the victory,

there was a steak dinner and the slabs were piled 18 inches high on the long table. We smoked the light brown cigars we had captured at Huy, Belgium, and had a great time.[20]

A camera team from *Life Magazine* photographed Generals Rose, Hickey, and Boudinot standing on the steps of the Cathedral for their story on the capture of Cologne.[21] On March 11, General Collins held a formal flag-raising ceremony in the Sports Arena, gave a stirring speech, and saluted the commanders and units who had participated in the victory. The stadium, which had until recently rung with the celebrations of Nazi victories, now echoed with the *Star Spangled Banner*. The symbolism was not lost on the defeated Germans.

On the next day, General Rose traveled to First Army Headquarters at Duren, Germany, where he received the French *Croix de Guerre* with Palm

Rose on the steps of Cologne Cathedral, March 7, 1945
(*Source:* Rose Family Album)

and the Legion of Honor for his actions the previous summer in France. With great ceremony and to the accompaniment of La Marseillaise and the National Anthem, French General Koeltz pinned the medals on his jacket, embraced him, and bestowed the ceremonial kiss on both cheeks. Shaunce was sure that the stony faced Rose hated that part of the ceremony. He remembered with a grin how uncomfortable Rose had been with the kisses showered on him as Shaunce drove him through the liberated villages of Belgium the previous summer.[22]

Once again Maurice Rose was at a peak moment in his career. The horrible days of the Bulge were finally behind him. He had captured a major enemy city and was being saluted, decorated, and praised by his superiors, men whom he both respected and admired. His own men considered him the greatest fighting general of the war . . . of any war. Newspapermen were hailing him as the "Captor of Cologne."

That night he sat down in his office to write a letter to his four-year old son, the first he had ever directly addressed to the boy, whom he called

Maurice Rose receives the *Croix de Guerre*, March 12, 1945
(*Source:* Rose Family Album)

"Reece."[23] The letter is extraordinary. Apparently, it is the only family correspondence to survive. **(C)** In addition to its rarity, the tone is very personal, so much so that the general's wartime personal secretary, T/4 Nathaniel Peavy, found it hard to believe it was authentic.[24] For one thing, no one could recall ever seeing the general use a typewriter, and in fact there are numerous corrections made in ink on the document. The general's son, who has in his possession a copy of the original letter as well as the typewriter upon which it was written, was assured by his mother that the letter is authentic.[25] **(D)**

The letter is one of the very few portals we have into the soul of Maurice Rose. It reveals his affection for his young son, his deep love and longing for his wife, his warm feelings for his parents and brother, his pride in himself, and hints of an endearing, self-deprecating humor, and even modesty. It mixes optimism and resignation in poignant counterpoint and foreshadows events of the final weeks. While we can not be certain it was Rose's actual last letter home—the proverbial "last letter" from the battlefield—it is the last *known* letter sent to his wife and son.

He begins by speaking about that day's decoration ceremony and the medals he received, which he sent home for his son, writing "accept them with my love." That is one of only two uses of the word "love" in the letter. The other comes at the end when he writes, "All my love to all the Roses." He never expresses his love directly to his wife or his son. In connection with the medals, he describes later in the letter having been scolded by General Hodges for not wearing his ribbons, observing that he is probably the only one overseas that does not wear them, implying a kind of modest reserve. That is echoed when describing the decoration ceremony, suggesting that he did not really know why they gave him the medals, unless "they just had some extra" and needed "to get rid of them." He also adds, however, that of course, he was pleased to have them. It is soldier talk, as much for his wife,

---

C Mrs. Virginia B. Rose, the general's widow, reported that all the general's papers, letters, memorabilia, decorations, and other objects had been "lost in a flood" in Kansas. In 1996, her son also suggested that no other letters survive.

D The original letter and envelope are in Sam Rose's personal family album. It is typed on official stationery bearing the insignia of the division. It is two pages long, single-spaced, and dated March 12, 1945. It was sent from Germany, APO (Army Post Office) #253, and the envelope is post marked at the receiving APO on March 15, 1945. General Rose signed as his own censor in the lower left hand corner of the envelope and his signature appears authentic. The letter was stamped and sent via air mail.

herself an army brat, as for his son, who clearly did not understand much of what his father was saying, at least not at that moment in time.

He talks at some length about his mostly German pistol collection, citing his preference for his personal standard army issued weapons, " . . . for service I still wear my .45 with my eight-inch knife attached, as I have for the past more than two years. Maybe it is sentiment or maybe it is just that I have confidence in those two weapons. . . ." His close family, who surely read the letter, must have thought back to the police revolver story that pointed to the young Maurice Rose's destiny.[26] There is no mention of wearing a shoulder holster, which became an issue later. He compares his collection to that of "Georgie," clearly a reference to Patton, establishing that he had a personal relationship with the flamboyant general and his former commander in Sicily.

In a very strange passage he says that he recently sent his "Pop" (Sam Rose), his Mom, and "Arn" (his brother, Arnold) an Easter cable, one of six references to Easter, but doesn't mention Passover, a more likely subject for greeting his parents at that time of year. Clearly, it is not the moment to attempt to explain the difference to his son, who was being raised as an Episcopalian.

In a poignant passage that offers a rare example of Rose's personal side and gracious nature, he describes a brief conversation with Major Bellinger right after the capture of Cologne and its humorous outcome. He is generous in his praise of his loyal aides.

> A couple of days ago, I mentioned to my aide that if I had a couple of onions and some vinegar (no lemons here) I would prepare that jar of Christmas caviar that my sweetie sent me. He apparently found some because there is a bag of onions on my desk that has just about smelled me out of the room. I am sitting here with my eyes watering and do not know what to do with the onions, because the only other room that I can put them in is where I have my cot. I am afraid the room would not be fit for sleeping if I left the onions there for a couple of hours. My aides are certainly on the job and I do not suggest anything but that it is acted upon very promptly.

Towards the end of the letter, he refers to wife and son as "you two youngsters," a playful reference to the dozen-year difference in his and Virginia's ages, clearly something they had joked about before. But he is also sensitive to the strain of their separation, suggesting that she looks "droopy and wet nosed" in Reece's birthday photos, saying to his son, "it is up to you, young fellow, to keep her cheered up and happy. I know you can do it." At the end, he speaks directly to her, sharing his own weariness and loneliness.

> I know that she gets mighty lonesome at times, and so do I and that is a hard thing to overcome. But this thing can't last forever . . . I hope.

The last paragraph explains his reason for writing. "Well son this is the long visit that I wanted to have with you for a long time just to let you know that I am thinking of you and all of you all of the time." Finally, he closes by signing "Your Devoted Pop," the same term of endearment he used with his own father. Like Nat Peavy, his men would no doubt have been surprised—and moved—to know that the general, the seemingly iron man, could have such ordinary, common, and wonderful feeling for those he loved.

During the next ten days there was almost no combat action, as the First Army prepared for the final offensive towards Berlin. The men once again had a breather and dealt with routine matters. For the first time since leaving England, the rear echelon headquarters moved to within a few blocks of the forward echelon. This facilitated equipment maintenance efforts, especially among the radio teams and wiremen, whose performance in the Cologne operation had elicited generous words of commendation from General Rose.[27] The commanders were also attending to their duties.

On March 18, 1945, the Supreme Allied Commander, General Dwight D. Eisenhower sent identical letters to the commanding generals of his two "heavy" armored divisions the 2nd and 3rd—asking about the performance of their equipment, especially tanks. The complaints about the inferiority of the medium M-4 Sherman tank were finally starting to register at the highest headquarters.[28] On March 21, Rose replied to Eisenhower's request.

Before doing so, he called in his commanders, including several battalion commanders, as well as enlisted men and interviewed them personally about their combat experiences. Among those he summoned was the veteran (and lucky!) Staff Sgt. Robert Early of Company E, 32nd Armored Regiment, Clarence Smoyer's tank commander and the man whose T26 Pershing had knocked out the German Panther in front of the Cologne Cathedral. Sergeant Early was blunt.

> I am a tank commander and have had nine months' combat experience. I have had a 76 tank for five months and a 75 tank for three months. I have had a 90 tank for about one month. I haven't any

confidence in an M-4. Jerry armament will knock out an M-4 as far as they can see it. If the T26 was armed in weak spots by putting assault armor on it, we'd have a tank superior to Jerry. The 90mm gun is far superior to what we have had. I believe the T26 will make us more equal to the Jerry tanks.[29] **(E)**

The other soldiers' comments were consistent with Early's report. The tone of Lt. Colonel Matthew Kane, a successful Task Force Commander, and survivor of six months of hard fighting, paints a terrible picture of the cost of victory. "This battalion has lost eighty-four tanks through enemy action in nine months." He states what everyone knows: "success on the battlefield is attributable to our superiority in numbers of tanks and resolve to sustain heavy casualties in men and tanks in order to gain objectives."[30]

General Rose's personal observations are remarkably honest in his critique of the shortcomings of American weapons, but also balanced in evaluating their advantages. For instance, he has high praise for the half-tracks, trucks, and other general purpose vehicles, and artillery. He is critical of the light tank 37mm armament and the ineffectiveness of American bazookas, but it is his highly critical opinion of American tanks that is most striking.

It is clear from Eisenhower's tone that the higher-ups believed that the criticisms of American tanks were exaggerated, the result of "the human tendency to make startling statements," or the result of newsmen giving their own views and "quoting only those statements that support such views." Rose does not forget that he is addressing the Supreme Commander, but neither is he a sycophant or apologist. "It is my personal conviction that the present M-4 and M4A3 tank is inferior to the German Mark V." The proof is simple. His position "is borne out by the excessive number of losses we took while fighting in Belgium in December and January."[31]

During that time, the weather limited both air and artillery support, which had helped close the qualitative gap, and the Americans did not enjoy quantitative superiority. During the Battle of the Bulge, the fighting was tank to tank and the outcome was bloody: 3rd Armored tank losses totaled more than 160 vehicles, while the Germans lost less than 100. It was only the willingness of the men to take great risks and their courage that led to the very costly victory.

E The numbers 75, 76, 90 refer to the main gun armament of the American tanks as measured in millimeters of shell diameter.

In closing, Maurice Rose considers the "matter of clothing" and makes several suggestions about combat shoes and other parts of the tanker's uniform. He also offers a flamboyant suggestion, partly for practical reasons but mostly to enhance the esprit de corps of the armor branch.

> May I further suggest that a uniform headgear, such as a beret of distinctive color—green is suggested as it is the Armored Force color—be issued to all Armored Force personnel.[32]

It was not the armor branch, but rather the Army's post war commandos that took Maurice Rose's suggestion, donning the famous green beret.

Before the final drive began there was one more formal decoration ceremony. On March 24, Maurice Rose traveled to the Maurer Estate close to Remagen. The headquarters of 3rd Armored Division was to be honored for

**Maj. General J. Lawton Collins decorates Maurice Rose
for his victory at Mons, March 24, 1945**
(*Source:* U.S. Army Signal Corps)

its action at Mons and awarded the Presidential Unit Citation. In addition, many of the senior line and staff officers were decorated as well, and the VII Corps Commander, MG J. Lawton Collins, awarded Maurice Rose the Bronze Star for Valor. He had also just been informed that he had been awarded the Distinguished Service Medal for his leadership of the 3rd Armored Division in the march across Europe. His next package of medals for Reece would be even more impressive that the last one. The time when he would be able to play with the boy was drawing near. There was just one more battle to fight.

After the crossing of the Rhine, and the securing of the several bridge-heads on the far bank, the Allies prepared for what would prove to be the final campaign of the European war. Lt. General Courtney Hodges' First Army, with its three experienced corps, was aimed directly into the heart of the Ruhr. Collins' VII Corps, long since established as the premier Allied attack unit, with 3rd Armored as its "Spearhead," was ordered to seize the road network at Altenkirchen, then to proceed east to a crossing of the Dill River between Dillenberg and Herborn.

The attack commenced on March 25 at 0400 hours, as Rose's division, reinforced by the 414th Infantry Regiment passed through the other divisions of VII Corps to drive on the initial objective. Rose deployed his units in the time-tested formation that had worked so well in the past. Combat Command A was on the right with Combat Command B on the left, each was divided into two Task Force columns. Combat Command Reserve followed the two center routes, ready to intervene wherever the battle dictated. The left flank was protected by the 83rd Reconnaissance Battalion, which followed the northern route. The 4th Cavalry Group protected the right flank.

By the end of the first day of the advance, the division had covered six to nine miles. German resistance varied in intensity, but some units encountered heavy fighting, and by nightfall several bridgeheads were secured across the Mehr River. On Monday, March 26, the division HQ was located on a dairy farm in Maulsbach, where several correspondents finally caught up, anxious to be in on the final drive into Germany.

General Rose's mobile living quarters had pulled up near the main building. That evening, Brig. General Truman E. Boudinot of Combat Command B arrived at HQ and got permission to catch some sleep in General Rose's quarters until the staff conference. Shortly after the meeting began, the Germans hit the HQ area with a massive artillery barrage. One shell hit an ammunition truck, setting off a fantastic series of explosions. Then another shell struck close to the main HQ building. Shrapnel riddled General Rose's mobile quarters, rendering it unusable for several hours. Fortunately, there were no casualties, but Boudinot was shook up. It was another reminder that armored warfare made no distinction between "front" and "rear." As it happened, just a few weeks after the map incident, it might have been recognized as yet another signal to Rose that the war was getting close to him personally, but the men at headquarters saw no change in his behavior.[33]

The next day, Tuesday, March 27, the division, led by Combat Command A, made a spectacular thirty-mile dash to the Dill River at Herborn. General Rose was at the river's edge supervising the crossing of his advance elements. Once he saw that they had crossed the river on a secure bridge and had taken the high ground on the far bank, he headed back to his headquarters.[34] His forward echelon consisted of his peep, a second peep carrying artillery chief colonel Fred Brown and driver Pfc. A.C. Braziel, and the Operations M-20 armored car with Lt. Colonel Wesley Sweat and four enlisted men aboard. The two regular motorcyclists, Pfc. James Omand and Pfc. Aaron Nichols, who usually accompanied General Rose, were also part of the small caravan. That made a twelve-man "combat squad" of four field grade officers (including a Major General, Colonel, Lt. Colonel, and a Major) and eight enlisted men.

On the way back to the command post that evening Shaunce was driving along a narrow, back road near the village of Rehe when General Rose spotted a group of fifteen to eighteen Germans, probably stragglers cut off by the rapid American advance, crossing the road ahead of his peep. **(F)** They ducked into a roadside cemetery and took cover behind the surrounding wall and headstones. Major Bellinger described to AP correspondent Jack Thompson what happened next,

> Suddenly, the General, who rides in the front seat of the peep, said, "Look what's out there, Jerries!" A bunch were running from a woods.[35]

Before Shaunce could bring the ¼-ton peep to a complete stop, General Rose ordered, "Stop!" and leaped out, yelling to the others to follow him. He

---

F Accounts differ about some details of the encounter. Jack Thompson's version cites about thirty enemy soldiers, *Spearhead in the West* mentions fifteen. Thomas Henry counts twenty, claiming that ten were killed, and the rest captured and transported on General Rose's peep. Most reports count the number of POWs at twelve.

grabbed the Thompson submachine gun strapped to the passenger side and charged toward the cemetery. He was already well ahead of the rest of his party when the enemy opened up with small arms, firing from behind the wall around the cemetery. Just as he got to a point where he had defilade and could see the enemy soldiers around a corner, he tried to fire. Nothing happened. He thought the submachine gun had jammed, but actually, like any excited soldier experiencing "buck fever" he forgot to flip off the safety. He threw the Thompson to the ground in frustration and without a pause, drew his .45 automatic and started firing.

Shaunce and Bellinger had followed right on his heels. Shaunce, also carrying a Thompson, experienced the same mental lapse of not taking off the safety. Like his leader, he also figured that the submachine gun had jammed, so he threw it down as well, drew his .45 pistol, and began firing back at the Germans. Colonel Brown and Pfc. A.C Braziel soon joined them and opened fire as well. One German ran out from his position and aimed his Mauser rifle directly at Rose. The General shot him where he stood. **(G)** Several of the enemy fled and the remaining dozen Germans surrendered.

The men in the M-20, which had by now driven up, joined the others just as the fire-fight ended. They watched in amazement as General Rose personally herded the prisoners out of the cemetery at the point of his pistol. Motorcyclist Pfc. James Omand said that the image of General Rose leading the enemy soldiers at the point of his gun, "was a sight to behold." Rose kept the prisoners covered from his peep until they reached the POW compound.[36]

It was the kind of action for which men are awarded the highest decorations for bravery. It might even be argued it was "action above and beyond the call of duty." It might also be described as foolhardy, since overwhelming friendly forces were close by and could have easily handled the incident with no risk to so many important officers. However it is characterized, it points to the warrior spirit that animated Maurice Rose, shaped his behavior, and determined his fate.

Rose got back late to his CP and there was much work to be done. That night he got only two hours sleep.[37] Men were busy at the higher headquarters, as well. By the morning of March 28, the high command had made the final decisions that would end the war in Europe and establish the postwar boundaries for more than fifty years. The military objectives had essentially been ambiguous, dating back to the invasion of Europe.

G Heinz's version reports that Rose's pistol shot killed the enemy soldier.

The directive guiding SHAEF was intentionally vague: "to undertake operations aimed at the heart of Germany." What exactly is the heart of an enemy nation in the twentieth century? Indeed, was it any different then than it had been for Alexander, Caesar, or Napoleon?

With the Red Army advancing rapidly toward Berlin, surely a leading candidate for the "heart" of the Third Reich, General Eisenhower changed the direction and plan of the final American and British drive away from Berlin and towards Leipzig. Bradley's 12th Army Group would make the main effort rather than Montgomery's 21st Army Group, which was positioned to the north and still included the U.S. Ninth Army and the 2nd Armored Division. In turning away from Berlin, Eisenhower described the decision as a military, as opposed to a political, calculation. Down at the division, no one really cared. The idea was to make it home alive.

By midday on March 28, Combat Command B had driven almost due east, practically unopposed, with Task Force Lovelady reaching the Lahn River and capturing Marburg, and Task Force Welborn halting at Runzhausen. Howze's Reserve advanced to the Dill River, seizing Dillenburg by late morning. That afternoon, Generals Collins and Pete Queseda met with Rose at the latter's headquarters southwest of Marburg. During their conference, they worked out the operational details for another rapid change of direction. Instead of moving east from Marburg, the VII Corps, with Rose's 3rd Armored in the lead, would swing north toward Paderborn, to complete the encirclement of the industrialized Ruhr (also a "heart" of Germany) in conjunction with Simpson's Ninth Army moving from the north. Lt. Colonel Prentice Yeomans' 83rd Reconnaissance Battalion would pass through the division reserve at Dillenburg in order to secure the "turning line."

Shortly after the senior commanders had left the headquarters, Public Relations Officer Major Haynes Dugan invited several correspondents into the division headquarters. The Major had a good reputation among the newspapermen, augmented no doubt by the fact that he was a graduate of Columbia School of Journalism and had worked at their trade before the war and knew what they wanted. Sgt. Andy Rooney, covering the war for *Stars and Stripes,* described the best PROs as those who could "tell a reporter where to get some action without getting killed."[38] Haynes Dugan was definitely one of the best. Also present at the late night press briefing that night were the tough, bearded, John "Jack" Thompson (*Chicago Tribune*), W.C. "Bill" Heinz (*New York Sun*), and the attractive British reporter Iris Carpenter (*Boston Globe*).

General Rose's office was set up in a comfortable house in the cross-roads village of Schönbach. As usual, he had set up his office in the downstairs parlor, with his desk facing the door in the middle of the room. A table was covered with documents, telegrams, maps, and phones, and the large division situation map was mounted on a wall on the far wall behind the desk. The newsmen entered the room and saw that Rose's "face was pillowed in his arms on the mahogany parlor table."[39] As they entered, he quickly stood up

> As straight as the sketched soldiers in the field manuals. At forty-five he looked eight years younger, and he was a handsome man. He stood six feet two in his high-topped, Texas-style, flat heeled boots. He weighed about 185 pounds. His face under his close cropped, gray hair was flushed with color and, while he smiled, he seemed to hold his lips as though they were puckered.[40]

The general was gracious and seemed uncharacteristically anxious to talk to the reporters. He invited them to sit down, and he did the same, as erect as he had been while standing after he realized they had entered the room. The visitors were naturally curious about the "top brass" conference that had just ended. They knew from experience that such meetings were often followed by dramatic combat action and asked if any changes of plan had emerged.

> Rising wearily, he pointed to a map on the wall. From this village where we had halted earlier that day, the projected line of advance turned north almost at a right angle. There was something vaguely familiar about the picture. "Did you ever see anything like that before?" General Rose asked. The reporters looked puzzled. "Of course you have," he went on. "It's precisely Mons all over again—the same movement and the same object."[41]

General Rose showed the men where his units were and how the campaign would likely progress. He could not suppress a bit a battlefield humor.

> Yeomans will probably be the first man on the objective the way things look now. He'll get there and then radio me some caustic note like, "The first team is here, when is the division coming?" I sent Yeomans a message today. It was sent in the clear so the Germans

must have picked it up. I told him I'd give him a case of Scotch if he captured von Rundstedt, Kesselring, or Guderian and one bottle for Hitler, dead or alive. The message was garbled and someone put Goering for Guderian. Now I suppose if he brings Goering in here, I'll have to give him a case of Scotch.[42]

The correspondents stared at the objective circled on the map—120-road miles to the north. Someone followed up without actually using the name of the circled town, "When do you hope to reach your objective, General?" They were shocked by his answer. "I have just told General Collins that I would be in Paderborn at midnight tomorrow." The newsmen probed further. They asked him about his relationship with "Lightning Joe" Collins, already a legend in Europe. It was no secret that Rose and Collins were close collaborators and that they had won many great victories together.

I like working with the Corps Commander. He just tells me where he wants the 3rd Armored to go. He doesn't tell us how to get there![43]

One of the correspondents looked closely at the map again and did a quick calculation. With a voice betraying a bit of skepticism, he asked again about the objective, "You think you'll be there tomorrow—that's better than 100 miles!" General Rose answered wryly, with a hint of a smile, "You said hope. I can hope can't I?"[44]

That seemed more than a little boastful. The Westphalian countryside into which they were headed was unexplored. Reconnaissance scouts had not yet penetrated the area, nor was there any hard intelligence about the defenses waiting in the dark forests and rolling hills. The longest one-day American advance so far had been on the order of fifty or so road miles. Even so, the tough correspondents were not about to press the challenge with a man who had done the impossible several times before. The general continued:

2nd Armored of Ninth Army is driving down to Paderborn. I'm gonna drive up. Inside, there's the Ruhr, the whole damned hunk of it. His dark, eagle-like face looked thoughtful for a second, and then he grinned, and queried, be nice to zip it off, wouldn't it? . . . Coming along with us to try?[45]

The conversation soon turned to other, more personal matters. As the time passed, it seemed to those present that the general welcomed their company, as if he didn't want to be left alone, and they stayed until well past midnight. They asked him what he wanted to do when the war was over. His voice lapsed into a kind of sentimental reverie as he imagined himself after the war reverting to his permanent Regular Army rank of lieutenant colonel and commanding a cavalry squadron at some obscure post from his past like Fort Bliss, Texas. There was a hint of fatalism in his voice, however, that belied the believability of his words. Then he spoke about his family, "I have a son. He's four years old, and I don't know him. We're going to get acquainted and that's going to take a long time."[46] The whole "press conference" had an air of unreality about it. When it broke up, the participants felt they had seen a far different side of the tough, professional, and taciturn battlefield commander that had filled their dispatches with colorful copy filled with victories.

Early the next morning, Thursday, March 29, Rose's men led the VII Corps drive towards Paderborn. There was scattered resistance all along the route and they halted around midnight. Maurice Rose was not actually in Paderborn, but his lead task force had dug in just south of it and 3rd Armored had entered the record books. The "Spearhead" division had completed the longest, opposed armored advance in the history of warfare, more than 100 road miles, a record that still stands. Maurice Rose was on the threshold of a great victory, one of the greatest in our history, but in only twelve hours, his triumph would turn into tragedy.

CHAPTER Fourteen

March 30, 1945 (II)

"Let's go. We're sitting ducks here."
Major General Maurice Rose

The general had made the most important decision of his life. When Maurice Rose gave the order to move out, no one thought of questioning his judgment. He inspired confidence and instant obedience. He was not some rear-echelon, bunker-bound headquarters leader; he was a combat commander. Every man with him that night had been under fire with the general. Some had fought the enemy hand-to-hand under his direct leadership only three days before!

He had brought them through every deadly danger: small arms, mortar, artillery and tank fire, V-2 rocket explosions, as well as air strikes. They trusted him completely. The men who were with him most—his driver and his aide—felt secure in his company, even though they had known moments of incredible terror riding the battlefields of France, Belgium, and Germany with him. This day, though, was unusual by any measure. Major Bellinger sensed it early. They were in the grip of a strange bond—the kind that only exists among men at war, and even then only rarely. It bound the three men in the peep tightly to a common fate.

We hear the crunch of the rubber tires of the armored car following.

Three men in a jeep—a General, a Major, and a T/4—having covered combat mile after combat mile together in this same small car. I never felt more exposed, more hopeless, more kinship.

I felt strength from the General as he hunched forward, straining to see the road. It was almost as if we had shaken hands.[1]

Maurice Rose was not the kind of man who inspired feelings of an emotional connection, so it was all the stranger. For Bellinger, events had taken a turn into the surreal. Shaunce had felt the same way earlier that day, when Rose, totally out of character, had begun speaking openly of his deep feelings for his four year-old son. He spoke to Shaunce like a foxhole buddy. In fact, during that night Shaunce "spoke to him as often as he spoke to me."[2]

On the most personal level, the driver and the aide, silent in the peep, both realized that this day was different, different that is except for the war; the immediacy of that remained close by. The sounds of battle were a reminder—not that any was needed after the horror of the past few hours—that the reality all around them held the possibility of sudden, violent death or, maybe worse, terrible wounds and searing, endless pain.

It was about 1930 hours, when, crouching in the ditch, Shaunce heard a tank approaching them from the rear and closing fast. The moment had come. Under fire they mounted the three vulnerable vehicles. Rose, his aide, the two artillery officers and their drivers piled into the two jeeps parked near the ditch. The others ran to Lt. Colonel Sweat's undamaged M-20, still parked on the side of the road. They got under way quickly with a full "bird" colonel riding point. The small caravan turned right off the road and headed north across country in a mad dash for survival. Machine gun fire and flares followed them all the way.[3]

> We turned at right angles to the road and went across open country until we had defilade from the tanks in the vicinity of Point C. We then followed the route shown on the sketch, proceeded in defilade west, until we got on Route #3 between Points C and D, in rear of the tanks at C. We proceeded down the road to Point D, turned right and proceeded to Point E. At Point E we found a knocked out T26 with a peep in front of it.[4] **(A)**

Colonels Brown, Garton, and their drivers got out of the peep to take a closer look at the knocked out T26 Pershing. Even without the aid of

---

A The designations T26 and M26 are used interchangeably.

flashlights, they could see that its suspension system had been badly damaged. The tank lay dead and useless in the middle of the road. It was common practice to put a Pershing at the head of the lead column. Poking around in the growing darkness around the tank, the men could not find any tracks leading north on or near the road. General Rose quite logically concluded that the Pershing had been the lead tank in Welborn's column since there were precious few of them—even this late in the war only six were actually engaged in the battle for Paderborn. It seemed likely that when it was hit, Welborn had changed direction to bypass the main road north to Paderborn. With communications cut, Rose had no idea that Welborn himself was less than a quarter mile ahead and to the north, taking refuge in the Hamborn Castle.

All three men sitting in the general's peep waited nervously while the others examined the terrain. Shaunce was tense, but took encouragement from Brown's report. He was happy to have left the ambushed column and felt more comfortable the darker it became.

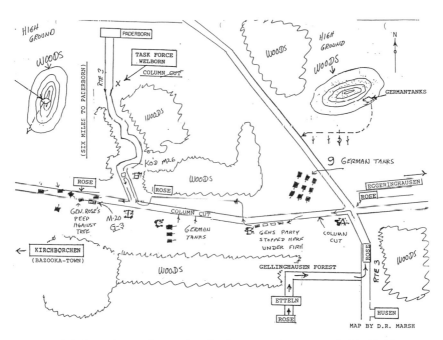

Vicinity of Hamborn Castle, late evening, March 30, 1945
(*Source:* Don R. Marsh)

> We got down there and found one of our own tanks knocked out.
> Colonel Welborn went straight ahead so we turned around and got
> back up to the road we had been on and turned right straight on
> down the road. We had the two peeps, the armored car and had
> thrown the motorcycles away.[5] **(B)**

It was about 1945 hours when the small convoy—now heading south along
Route #3—reached the Hamborn intersection of the Eggeringhausen road.
Brown stopped again, just before making the right turn referred to by
Shaunce. For the second time in less than fifteen minutes, the passengers
in the artillery commander's peep dismounted to examine the terrain. In
the rapidly fading half-light of late dusk, Colonel Brown and the others
got down on their hands and knees to search the ground for any evidence
that would help them figure out what to do.

> We could see and feel tank tracks leading west out of the crossroads
> at point D, so we decided that Welborn had proceeded west on that
> route and that the tanks shooting up the column east of point C
> were the tanks which had been on the high ground to the northeast.[6]

Bellinger, still wedged in the back of the peep, was straining to see into the
darkness, which was faintly pierced by the flares intermittently fired by the

---

B There is some confusion about when the motorcycles were abandoned and
who was riding them. Bellinger states that the two motorcycles were left behind
when the forward command group left the ditch and made a run for it cross-country. Colonel Brown suggests that the cycles were with them right up to the last
moment before he escaped. James Omand describes how he was left behind at the
ditch after losing his mount. According to Shaunce, Aaron Nichols was the other
regular motorcycle driver but he is not mentioned by any of the witnesses as being
with the group after the column was first cut. An MP attached to HQ Company,
Leonard Goff, claims that he was picked up by Col. Sweat's peep, after losing his
bike, but Sweat was in the crowded M-20, and none of those passengers mention
Goff as being aboard the M-20. Further, there were only three peeps in the group,
those belonging to Brown and Rose, and a third peep (Colonel Garton's) which
was destroyed in the ambush that cut Rose off from TF Welborn. There is no mention of a fourth peep. Goff may have been close by, as he frequently was, and was
quite likely a part of TF Welborn, but he was not a part of the forward echelon
command group, and was not an eyewitness to the later events.

Germans. He could barely make out the outline of Colonel Brown's peep just ahead.

> The jeep ahead has halted. Enemy mines? No! Colonel Brown is walking back.
> "Fork in the road, General, which way?"
> We dismount, and see vehicle tracks that look fresh. This could be our force that slipped through before the cut-off.
> "Let's go. We're sitting ducks here," the General commands.
> We are moving rapidly down the dark road—the tracers are well to our rear now—each second counts. The breakout will be a success![7]

For the first time in hours, Bellinger was starting to feel a sense of relief, even hope. He was glad to get out of the cramped back seat and stretch his legs, even if just for a few moments. Maybe it would work out OK, after all. The sounds of battle, now to their rear, were getting farther away. In fact, things could not have been worse. The tracks they had found were from earlier German movements and the enemy was in motion again to the front of the small group.

American intelligence on the German movements and situation was fragmentary. The truth was they really had no idea what was going on out there. Earlier in the day, reconnaissance units—either elements of Lt. Col. Prentice Yeomans' 83rd Armored Reconnaissance Battalion or units that were part of Task Force Welborn—had reached Hamborn, but had returned along these same roads without encountering any enemy resistance or spotting any German positions.[8] The advance had been so rapid that the results of prisoner interrogations had not reached the men in the field and the order of battle information was sketchy, at best.

The Army Air Force, which had provided close support several times during the day, hadn't spotted the full buildup of enemy armor and had overestimated the amount of damage they had inflicted on the tanks they had seen and bombed. Not only had enemy tanks not been destroyed—they had been hit by napalm, not tank-busting 500-pounders—they were still fully operational and had started to deploy. Based on the high ground all around, but no longer visible to Colonel Brown, the armor that had savaged Welborn was now moving along the same road as Rose's forward echelon HQ group.

Machine gun fire suddenly barked at Rose's small party from the wooded area to the rear and the source was close by. *Hauptmann* Wolf

Koltermann's *3rd Company, 507th Heavy Panzer Tank Battalion*, was getting closer. Koltermann had begun the battle with the *1st* and *3rd Platoons* (or, *"Zugs"*) forward, and the *2nd Platoon* in reserve to cover Kirchborchen. There, it had lent support to the *SS* infantrymen and cadets who were battling Task Force Richardson. At the same time that Rose's party was trapped in the roadside ditch further east, *Hauptmann* Koltermann's men, with infantry support, had begun the final stage of their awful work: the complete annihilation of Welborn's column still trapped on the road to Paderborn. They had been interrupted by Colonel Brown's artillery fire, but were still keen to finish the job.

At about 1930 hours, Koltermann concluded that he could contribute nothing further to the battle with Richardson at Kirchborchen, and ordered all three of his platoons to concentrate and move east toward *Battalion HQ*. By 1945 hours, the four *King Tigers* of the *3rd Platoon*, with several large-caliber self-propelled tank destroyers (*Jagdpanzers*) accompanying them, had started to move east on the road towards the village of Eggeringhausen.[9]

At the same time, Rose's tiny three-vehicle column had turned right at the Hamborn intersection, heading west toward Kirchborchen. After proceeding about a hundred yards, they started to climb a small hill. After going over the top, Colonel Brown spotted a large tank coming downhill towards them. At first he thought it was one of the new T26 Pershings. As the massive outline in the darkness drew closer, he cried out exultantly, "that's one of Jack's new tanks."[10]

> I proceeded up the main road west from the crossroads at Point D. After going about 75 yards, I saw a tank coming towards us. Someone made the remark that it looked like an M-4 (*Sherman*) all right, so we proceeded as fast as the vehicle would travel. As I cut to the left of the tank I saw it was a German 75 assault gun, and realized then that we had run into the German tanks which had been on the high ground.[11]

Just as his peep passed the first tank, Garton screamed, "Holy shit! It's a *Tiger*. Get off the road."[12] **(C)** Brown quickly scanned the terrain and made his move.

C It was probably Col. Garton who noticed that the tank had dual exhaust pipes (e.g., *Tiger II*), as opposed to the single exhaust pipe system of the American M26 Pershing.

I decided that the only course was to run the gauntlet before the Germans recovered from their surprise. On the high ground above us to the left I noticed a self-propelled 88mm, apparently covering the road. About 50 yards beyond the 75mm assault gun, I saw a large tank coming toward us in the center of the road, leaving very little room to pass. I decided to take a chance and try to make it.[13]

Brown had successfully evaded the first armored vehicle and two more that were following close behind, and he was looking desperately for a place where he could turn off the road. The fourth tank slewed across his path just as it crested the small hill. Brown tried to squeeze his peep between the *Tiger* and a tree along the side of the road, but he didn't quite make it.

We hit the side of the *Panther* (actually a *Tiger*), and bounced off, but the vehicle did not overturn, went down into the ditch and came out behind the tank. Thinking that this was the last of them, we started to slow up, and debated which direction to go next. We saw another tank at the top of the hill, about twenty-five yards in front of us, moving towards us, blocking the road, so I pulled the vehicle sharply to the right and cut out across country in front of the tank.[14]

In the process of evading the last tank, the spare gas can strapped to the left side of the peep was ripped loose.[15] For many years after the event, in the recounting of the story of the wild, desperate ride in the dark, Fred Brown remembered the loss of that gasoline can with words of self-deprecation about his skill as a driver. His son, Lt. General Fred Brown, III (ret.), heard the story often. "He used to chuckle about his quick reflexes— he scraped the side of the peep along the tank, crossed the ditch, bailed out, etc."[16]

Glenn Shaunce and Bob Bellinger spotted the first of the German tanks just moments after the men in Brown's peep. In the fading light, Shaunce was straining to keep the peep on the road.

After we turned right down the road we ran into a "Heinie" tank. We met it and went on past it. Then we met a second one and went by it, but in trying to pass this one there was a tree alongside it, so both peeps scraped the tank. We met a third one and Colonel Brown swung to the right and got off to the field and then the tanks swung a little bit sideways. I couldn't get to the right, so I swung to the left where I thought I could get through, but couldn't make it because there was a tree alongside it. We got stuck between the tank and the tree.[17]

It was the tank that Brown had slammed into. Shaunce also noticed two more armored vehicles along the sides of the road, in addition to the tanks he had already encountered.[18] They were the four tanks of the *3rd Platoon* of Koltermann's *3rd Company*, and a self-propelled gun from one of the other units in the field, most likely a 128mm *Jagdpanzer* (Tank Destroyer) from the *500th Heavy Panzer Battalion*.

At first, Major Bellinger was elated when he spotted the dark outlines directly ahead coming towards them. He fully expected to see the high, squat, and unmistakable outlines of Sherman tanks from Task Force Welborn emerge from the indistinct shadows rapidly approaching.

> "Good—tanks on the road, Sir," I report.
>
> Giant tanks loom up forward in the darkness, stalking and sputtering like monsters—a welcome sight from our tiny jeeps.
>
> Buttoned up in full combat procedure, it will be difficult for them to recognize us. We can only hope that they will hold their fire until we can make our identity known.
>
> The monster in the lead pulls sharply on his left track, giving Col. Brown's jeep room to squeeze through. We dart past him. Col. Brown ahead is scurrying past tank number two. Suddenly, I turn my head, wiping the dust from my eyes and lips.
>
> "My God, General, we've had it—Those are German *Tigers*."
>
> My heart has stopped. Tank number three is swerving into us. There is a crunch of metal, and we are wedged against the belching *Tiger* tank, and staring into the muzzle of an 88mm.[19]

Just behind General Rose's peep, PFC James Stevenson was trying to keep Colonel Sweat's M-20 armored car as close to the general's vehicle as possible. John T. Jones, the headquarters G-3 stenographer, who thought he was along to record the details of a great victory, was still rattled from the constant gunfire. It seemed to converge from all directions on the small group of vehicles as they crossed the field and the roads. After the two short stops to figure out which way to go, they were moving once again.

> We came to a dirt road and scraped against a huge tank. Col. Sweat yelled, "What outfit are you with?" A head popped out of the turret and the Colonel said, "My God, it's a German tank."

Somehow our driver backed around the tank and as we did, we saw the General's peep start back across the field in the direction we had just come. Evidently Colonel Brown's peep had somehow managed to get around the tank. We followed the General's peep without any action from the German tank. They must have known we would not go far. I recall yelling to Col. Sweat,

"Why don't we head for the forest to our left and try to join our forces there?"

But he yelled,

"No, no, we must stay with the General."

Back across the open area we went amid thousands of bullets, and again we were not hit.

As we came to the hard road, our scout car had trouble mounting a three-foot ditch and we fell behind the General's peep. As we got on the road finally, we did not go far when we stopped, confronted by four German tanks blocking our way.[20]

PFC William T. Hatry, the tough twenty-two-year old New York City kid, and one of Rose's code clerks from the 143rd Signal Company, was also aboard Col. Sweat's M-20 scout car. Hatry had no doubt from the first moment he saw them that the tanks they encountered were German.

After leaving the highway and going on a back dirt road we ran smack into one Royal (*Tiger tank*) which the peeps had already passed. Because of our size we couldn't possibly do the same so "Steve" (Pvt. James Stevenson of HQ. Co., driver of the armored car) ran the car right under the gun, which under those circumstances looked like the entrance to the Holland Tunnel. The tank commander yelled something and they moved the big thing over. We took advantage of that and then passed him.

About 200 yards from there we ran into two more that were sitting in the Y in the road and another in the corner of the field. They did open up with small arms on us but luckily no one was hurt at that time. They threw a white flare over our heads and we must have looked like a bunch of clay pigeons.[21] **(D)**

D PFC William T. Hatry wrote a letter to his friends describing his experiences on March 30, 1945, which was included in the unofficial company history.

Up ahead, and now out of view of the men in the M-20, the general's peep was trapped by the front right tread guard of the *King Tiger* tank and one of the mature plum trees that lined the road. The peep had recoiled several feet after the collision but there was not enough room to squeeze by. As Shaunce described it more than forty years later, the tank and the tree "left me about a four-foot hole to get about a five-foot jeep through."[22] He tried to move but it was impossible.

It was now about 2000 hours. The hatch on the top of the giant Porsche-made turret opened quickly, and the upper body of the tank commander appeared. He was pointing at what looked like a Schmeisser MP-38/40, or small submachine gun, aimed directly at them. Standing more than a dozen feet away from him atop the giant tank, the man appeared as a shadowy silhouette to Shaunce. He could not see his face at all.[23] There was, however, no doubt that there was a weapon in the crewman's hands. Shaunce could see that clearly.

The German immediately began screaming at the three men who quickly got out of the peep with their hands in the air in the act of surrender. Shaunce thought that the Jerry tank commander was hollering, "Hands up." He was also screaming something else, but Shaunce could not make it out.[24]

General Rose got out on the right side of the peep as did Bellinger, and both men stepped slowly to a point about three feet in front and to the right of their trapped vehicle.[25] They were less than two yards in front of the German tank. The aide stood to the right of his commander. Shaunce, also with his hands held high above his head, got out on the driver's side, walked in front of the peep and joined the others, standing to the left of the general. It was only at this point that he realized that he had broken his leg in the collision with the German tank.

The three Americans stood in front of *King Tiger #3* of Koltermann's *3rd Platoon* with their hands in the air shoulder-to-shoulder a few feet apart, almost touching.[26] It was dark—dark enough so that men and vehicles appeared as mere shadows—but it was not yet pitch black. There was some intermittent moonlight, and flares in the distance also offered some partial illumination. There was noise. In addition to the motors of the tanks all around them, in the distance vehicles from Task Force Welborn trapped on Route #3 were exploding, the conflagration fed by gasoline and ammunition. Small arms fire barked from all sides, as the opposing infantry continued to fight each other in small, desperate, intense life and death encounters.

A high pitch of excitement, and the total confusion and fog of battle blanketed the scene, but there could be no question that the three men had surrendered. The German was screaming, but he had not shot. Right up to the moment they raised their hands he could have killed them with impunity, but his screams at least suggest that that the German understood that the men in front of him were his prisoners. There was no resistance. He could not see their faces, or their ranks, but he knew that they had their hands in the air.

Bellinger was in a state of shock. He was fixated on the man in the turret.

> I can't believe it. We are prisoners—our hands above our heads. T/4 Shaunce and I flank the General as he stands facing these incredible odds. For the first time in his life, he has no alternative but to surrender. I know of no man who detested surrender more. Our last hope of rescue is gone, as we hear our armored car overtaken to the rear.[27]

The M-20 armored car had been slowed by the rough terrain as it tried to keep up with the general's peep in the cross-country ride. By the time it came up, German tanks and infantry were visible on both sides of the road. But at that very moment, the scene in front of the huge *King Tiger* tank, just fifty feet ahead, was reaching its awful climax.

Only a few moments had passed since the three Americans had dismounted from their peep with their hands in the air in a clear acceptance of surrender. The screamed commands of the German tank commander, over the roar of the *Tiger*'s engine, were suddenly cut short by several blasts of the *Schmeisser* that sent bursts of red-hot lead directly into the body of Major General Maurice Rose. He fell to the ground, lifeless.

At this moment the life and death of Maurice Rose passed over the boundary line from history into legend. In spite of everything that would follow, and all the stories that would be told, only three men actually saw what happened: the aide, the driver, and the enemy tank commander. **(E)** For an instant, each was frozen in time, transfixed by what had happened in front of their eyes. It is only by unraveling the threads of their stories— woven from that very moment until now—and critically measuring their

---

E All attempts to identify the tank commander of *Tiger #3, 3rd Platoon, 3rd Company, 507th Panzer Battalion*, including extensive correspondence with survivors, were unsuccessful. The survivors, while acknowledging that they knew his identity, were unwilling to identify him. It was impossible, therefore, to get his version of events.

recollections against other evidence—especially the crucial autopsy report—that we can determine what actually happened to Maurice Rose. At this point in the story, no one except the three men really knew, and like all witnesses to the same event, each saw something completely different.

The men in the M-20 quickly realized that they did not stand a chance of escaping. PFC William T. Hatry, General Rose's code clerk, knew that the game was up when the *King Tigers* started to turn their main guns in his direction.

> When they started to swing the 88s around we all figured we had had it so we lost no time in getting the hell out of the car. I did remember to toss my Luger overboard first though. With a gun in my back I was "escorted" to another *Royal* and put on the back of it with the rest.[28]

The G-3 stenographer, John T. "Africa" Jones saw the infantry on both sides of the road surrounding the M-20 and knew that escape was impossible.

> Much yelling followed—we were taken from our scout car—I threw away my .45 pistol and machine gun and the Germans herded about seven of us together. I was sure they were going to shoot us—instead they made us mount the rear of a *King Tiger* tank. I happened to be the first to climb on the rear and was pushed to the far end; Col. Sweat was next to me, and the others followed.[29]

Colonel Sweat, in command of the M-20, got out of the armored car after it stopped just short of the now empty command peep. It was dark, and he proceeded, cautiously and under guard, to another German tank that had stopped at the edge of the ditch just to the left side of the road.

Just as Sweat turned to mount the German tank, he heard the sound of gunfire behind him.[30] At virtually the same instant, he turned back toward the sound and saw a helmet spinning in the air, but he was facing away from the shooting, and did not actually see General Rose being shot. He asked one of his men, Jones (he thought), if the general had been hit, and thinks he said yes, but Jones never claimed that he had actually seen the shooting.[31] PFC Stevenson, the M-20 driver, also reacted to the sound of the gun firing.

> I had just turned my head away when I heard the shooting of a German machine pistol. As I turned around I saw the general's helmet fly off his head.[32]

The enemy infantry rounded up the rest of the men who were still in the M-20, and they began the long and difficult journey that led to German POW camps and more than two weeks of captivity. They were not liberated until mid April 1945 and most were not interviewed until later that summer. But, the fact remains that none of the men in the M-20 actually saw the German tank commander shoot General Rose.

As the fatal shots were fired, Shaunce reacted instantly. With his heart pounding, and the adrenaline flowing, he forgot about the pain in his leg and ran. In fact, he remembered moving even before Rose's body had hit the ground.

> I hollered at the Major to beat it, we were going to get shot, so I run up right against the tank and to the rear of it and jumped into a big ditch, where I sprained my ankle. I crawled across a good-sized field out there and they kept throwing flares trying to locate me for about a half-hour. I kept crawling until I finally got out of range.[33]

Shaunce has repeated the story of his escape numerous times with remarkable consistency. **(F)** More than forty-two years later, and without having access to, or even remembering, his original sworn statement, he described in a letter what happened immediately after General Rose was shot.

> The General started to fall, and I yelled to the Major (Bellinger), "Run!" and we did. I jumped up against the tank and got around to the back and started crawling, as I got a busted leg when we collided with the tank. And to make a long story short, I crawled around all night.
>
> But I will tell you one thing. We were all plenty scared, as we had just went through a hell of a mess.[34]

In his first taped interview in 1987, he gave virtually the same account.

F From October 5, 1987, to January 15, 1998, Glenn H. Shaunce exchanged cassette tapes in eleven separate sessions with the authors, discussing the events of March 30, 1945. This series includes one face-to-face interview conducted and taped at Shaunce's home in Albert Lea, Minnesota, on August 18, 1996. These taped interviews are numbered 1 through 11, and will be cited by tape number and date.

> Then I hollered "run"; it was the only thing I knew to do. I reached up
> to the corner of the tank and grabbed it—I was only a few feet away
> from it—and went right along the side of the tank by the track, close
> as I could get, around the back, and right down into a ditch. Then I
> crawled into a big field.[35]

Almost as soon as he hit the ditch, the Germans started firing tracers and
flares in an attempt to find him and finish him off. The first thing he did
was bury his trophy Walther P-38 pistol, convinced that if he were recaptured the souvenir would be his death warrant and probably the instrument of his execution.[36] Next, he dug a hole and buried the papers in his
pocket, figuring they would give him away as the general's driver. In the
same hole he buried his helmet because it created too large a silhouette.
Then, he started crawling. Soon, though, the pain in his leg and exhaustion caught up with him, and Shaunce passed out cold.

About three-quarters of an hour after the shooting, or about 2045
hours, he met up with several other Americans who had escaped the
destruction of TF Welborn. They helped him get to a small wooded area,
about 400 meters away, where they took cover for the night. They saw other
troops, but did not know who they were, and did not risk making contact.
One of the soldiers hiding out that night was L.D. McQuade, an infantryman from F Company, 36th Armored Infantry, who had seen General Rose
earlier that evening and escaped the annihilation of TF Welborn.

> Later on that night I came upon a man that was having trouble get-
> ting along. I helped him for a while and when we stopped to rest one
> of the men from F Company located me and said I was wanted up the
> line. I informed him I was helping this man and did not want to leave
> him. He assured me he would take over. The man I helped told me he
> was General Rose's driver and that they had been ambushed and the
> General was shot after they had given up. I noted he had either a bro-
> ken or badly sprained ankle as the ankle was wrapped with a web belt.
> That is the last I saw of him after the other man took over.[37]

Sgt. McQuade went with another man to search for Colonel Welborn. The
others stayed with Shaunce until morning (March 31), when they decided
to try to find a town. Shaunce realized he would not be able to keep up
because of his busted leg, and they promised to send help, but nobody
came back.

Back at division HQ on the morning of March 31, Colonel Smith, the chief of staff, prepared to tell the world that his general had been killed. After Rose's death had been confirmed, Smith ordered the briefing officer to assemble the war correspondents just after breakfast.[38] **(G)** Major Bellinger and T/4 Shaunce were still missing in action and Smith had only just heard that Col. Brown had made contact with elements of TF Richardson near Kirchborchen. Still lacking any concrete details, his formal remarks were terse:

> General Rose was killed in action last night by a German tanker. No details are available at this time. His vehicle, apparently partially crushed by the tank, was found nearby his body which had numerous bullet marks which caused his death.[39]

Until additional information became available and more descriptive—and fanciful—newspaper articles began to appear, the press carried only the simple one line wire release: "Major General Maurice Rose, commander of the 3rd Armored Division, has been killed in action in Germany, the War Department announced today."[40]

When the press briefing concluded, there was a mad dash to get the story to the rear where it could be put on the press wireless for inclusion in the morning dailies. First, the correspondents had to hitch rides in the convoy heading to the rear for supplies. The convoy included armed vehicles because the speed of the advance had left many Germans behind the forward lines. As one sign read, "Jerries cleared to the edge of the road."[41]

By the time that Smith had briefed the newsmen, Rose's body had been retrieved. That task had fallen to Staff Sgt. Arthur N. Hauschild and Sgt. Bryant Owen, both from the HQ Reconnaissance Platoon, 1st Battalion, 33rd Armored Regiment. Hauschild had been with TF Welborn during the terrible action of the previous day and had spent a frightful night in the woods before reaching Welborn's command post at the Schloss Hamborn. At 0800 hours on March 31, Captain McCann, the CO of Headquarters Company, ordered him to take a patrol to find and retrieve the general's body. It turned out that his destination was pretty close to where he was located.

G A number of journalists had joined 3rd Armored at Maulsbach, Germany for the drive to Paderborn. They included: Tom Henry (*Washington Star*), "Bunny" Austin (*Sydney Times*), Jack Thompson (*Chicago Tribune*), Martha Gellhorn (*Collier's Magazine*), and Iris Carpenter (*Boston Globe, London Herald*).

> Having received instructions, I took Sgt. Owen and four others and proceeded under cover as best we could to a point approximately 400 yards, which later proved to be the scene of the incident. The route from that point was across open ground, so I took Sgt. Owen with me and left the other four men to cover us and proceed forward.[42]

The two sergeants found the road between Hamborn and Kirchborchen and soon after saw the deserted vehicles of the general's party ahead on the crest of the hill along which the patrol had been walking. The general's peep looked as if it had been partially crushed, but the M-20 armored car was undamaged. They looked around a bit and found what they were after.

> We found the General's body on the right hand side of the leading peep, lying face up near the front wheel. There were no other bodies there. The General was lying in a full-length position. About two feet from his left hand lay a pistol and pistol belt, which we assumed to be his. Upon examination of the body we found bullet wounds in the chest and also in the head.
>
> His helmet was on the opposite side of the vehicle (left side). There were two bullet holes in it, which had gone through the rear and come out the front of it. In the process of carrying the General's body from where it was found to Col. Welborn's CP, the helmet was lost. **(H)**
>
> Upon examination of the .45 cal pistol found by the General's body, the pistol was in the holster on a pistol belt, with a round in the chamber, cocked and on safety, with an apparent full clip in the gun and two full magazines in the magazine pouch.[43]

They wrapped the general's body in a GI blanket they found in his peep and dragged the body over the open ground. The two men soon encountered 2nd Lt. Tom Waldrop of B Company, 36th Armored Infantry, who reproached them for the disgraceful way they were treating the body of their fallen leader.[44] The two men were exhausted from handling the body and the combat of the previous day, and were in no mood to listen to a lecture on respect for the dead from some shavetail, ninety-day wonder. Owen told him in colorful and graphic curses where to get off, and they headed on their way. In spite of some heated threats of a court martial by the

---

H The helmet was later recovered and is now displayed at the Armor Museum at Fort Knox, Kentucky.

Rose's helmet at Fort Knox Museum
(*Source:* David J. Fleischer)

angry young officer, nothing further came of the incident. The two sergeants soon reached Welborn's CP, delivered the body, gave their report to Capt. McCann, and went back to the war.

Sgt. Owen "borrowed" Rose's .45 automatic pistol, still in the holster with the flap buttoned down, and used it for the next several days, firing several clips in combat.[45] The pistol was never returned to Rose's family. Lt. Walter May, a Liaison Officer attached to TF Welborn, was at the *Schloss Hamborn* when the body was brought in.

> Colonel Welborn had the General's body laid out on the dining room table in the CP, and here I saw him for the last time. For me it was another grim experience. I was mildly surprised that the plain raincoat had been removed revealing his Patton-like attire. I now suspect that he was so dressed in order to make a grand appearance in Paderborn.[46]

Colonel Welborn made the first formal identification. Later, on the afternoon of March 31, General Rose's body was placed aboard an ambulance and taken to a small house about one-and-a-half miles northeast of Etteln. The ambulance retraced the journey of the previous day back along Route #3, arriving late afternoon at the location of B Company, 45th Armored Medical Battalion treatment station.[47] Things there had been hectic all day as Don Mahr and the other men of his section were flooded with nearly eighty casualties from another round of hard fighting around Paderborn.

> Soon we heard the sound of an approaching ambulance. We had grown used to the sound of those ambulance motors. As it came to a stop between the barn drive and the surgical truck, we waited anxiously as the ambulance door was opened. I could see a litter with a body covered with medical blankets. The person was very tall, as his feet, covered with beautifully shined leather boots, extended from the end of the litter. Along side the body sat two division MPs. It was the dead body of General Rose. It had been brought to the surgical section of Co. B, 45th Medical Bn., to be held overnight.[48]

The body was placed in a grain bin with the MPs taking turns watching over it as an honor guard throughout the night. With Germans wandering all around the countryside, the medics felt a whole lot safer with the MPs on duty.

At mid-afternoon of March 31, Shaunce stirred and began to crawl again. He went another 100 meters to the top of a little hill and lay there for the rest of the day. Looking down, he saw men moving around the area where he had been captured, but could not make out who they were, so he stayed put. It was twenty-four hours since he had last eaten and as evening fell, he started to get really hungry. Hoping he might find something to eat or drink, he crawled most of the night, pausing once to light up a cigarette, then quickly snuffing it out when he realized it might give away his position. He was in pretty bad pain and felt faint a few times, but tried to keep moving.

The next morning, April 1, Easter Sunday, he reached a stand of trees near a road, where he heard a large number of tanks and men, finally recognizing them as Americans. He had a piece of parachute silk around his neck that he wore as a scarf, so he took it off and started waving it. The Americans saw him and picked him up. A few recognized him as General Rose's driver, and he told them what had happened. They took him to a headquarters, where he thinks he talked to some men, then put him in an ambulance. The next thing he remembers was being on his way to a hospital in England and then to the States.[49]

Actually, he had been taken first to the Headquarters of CCA's Task Force Doan (Col. Leander A. Doan), where he was given first aid for his leg injury and a shot of morphine. Next, he was taken to HQ, CCA (BG Doyle O. Hickey) and finally to division HQ. He did not remember moving between the various headquarters, or that on April 1, 1945, he had given a sworn statement to the Summary Court investigating the death of Maurice Rose.[50] It was only after giving the statement that he was sent on the journey that would take him back, finally, to Minnesota and the family farm. In that April 1 statement, Glenn Shaunce gave his version of how General Rose was killed, a version that he maintained from that moment until the present.

When the shots were fired and Shaunce yelled and ran, Major Bellinger was also moving. He realized immediately that the German was not going to take prisoners, and that the two survivors did not stand a chance.

> The driver, Shaunce, dashed to the rear and to the right ditch in back of the tank. I dashed to the left ditch. I started to crawl across a plowed field. I was fired upon frequently while flares were sent up from the tank.[51]

The Germans continued to fire at both men, with bullets coming ever closer as they scampered through the parallel ditches on opposite sides of the Eggeringhausen road. Bellinger heard the tank commander's *Schmeisser* firing directly at him as if he was determined to finish the job.

> The hellish staccato burp pierces the night again. His fire follows me into the ditch. Damn him! The "plop-plop" of the bullets rake up and down my trench. The tank following, probably not knowing what he is firing at picks up the game. Thank the good Lord for the cover of darkness.
>
> I leave my helmet as decoy, and crawl on my stomach along the ditch. My only chance is to leave this hellhole, and inch along across the ploughed field to my left. Before I do this, I must discard my insignia designating me as a general's aide. The pressure for information would be rough if I were captured. Better they think I'm a line officer.
>
> I am over the hump, and in the ploughed field, moving with the greatest caution. The moon slides out from behind a cloud. I must wait for the next cloud. Then—go, man, go![52]

For one incredible moment, Bellinger felt the exultation experienced by those who have just barely escaped death, but it passed quickly. His ordeal was just beginning. Hearing shouts to the rear, he decided to head for the high wooded area visible to the north of the field even in the dark. There he might be able to find cover. He barely got started, however, before he stopped in terror.

> I hear marching infantry. This is all I need; I see them coming down the road, parallel to the tanks and just to the front of my path.
> I freeze and pray.
> They file past—some so close I could almost reach out to them.[53]

After regaining his strength and resolve, he started to move again, crawling towards the woods. He heard voices just inside the tree line, and decided that it was not safe there. So, timing his movements with the moon's passage through the clouds, he crawled along the edge of the woods, listening carefully for any sound. His muscles ached from the crawling, but finally he made it into the woods. He rested for a while, feeling safe for the moment. He took inventory.

> There is no weapon available—no food, no water, no helmet, no maps—and I am still behind the German lines.
> I resolve that I must get to the other column of our troops somewhere in the direction I am moving. It is important to get to high ground for observation and direction. Before dawn I am moving through the woods, seeking an observation point. By first light, it is easy to relax because I am sure I am in the clear. Those forces must have moved on.[54]

Once again, his feeling of relief was short-lived. Walking upright through the forest, he came to a clearing, where he spotted several German trucks parked under camouflage netting, with two soldiers lounging nearby. He retreats. It is clear that moving during the day is dangerous. Hunger and thirst are gnawing at him constantly, so he waited for dark and moved towards the high ground. Hopefully, there, he thinks, he will be able to spot a place where he can find food and water. It is the evening of March 31.

> The still of the night is broken. The sound of a galloping horse probably means that a messenger is bent on delivering his orders to a C.P.

The sound fades into the night. I continue in the difficult underbrush. Our forces cannot be too far away—they can't be. This thought crowds my mind.[55]

On the next morning, April 1, Easter Sunday, he spotted a group of houses with white sheets fluttering from the windows and moved toward them. Almost there, he saw Germans coming out of a barn nearby with mess kits in hand. He crawled back to the hill to sweat out another day. At this point, he started chewing the grass to alleviate his hunger and thirst.

When night came, he crawled to a fence line, eventually finding a stream running through a grazing pasture. Elated, he feels like running, but knows better. He kneels down to drink for the first time in days.

Damn, damn, damn! MUD! It is the filthiest water I have ever tasted. Dysentery will result—it is not worth it. Move on and forget it. I wade across the stream, getting soaked to the armpits. This night I shall lie in the thickets, hungry, thirsty, and wet to the skin.

I am so miserable as dawn breaks (April 2) that I decide to move on, despite the risk. I have now come to a dirt road, with vehicle tracks. A jeep with two American GIs is cruising towards me.

I step out—after three days and four nights—into the path of freedom![56]

On April 2, suffering from dehydration, hunger, and exposure, Bellinger returned to division HQ. There he talked with some division officers informally, and then gave his statement to the Summary Court collecting evidence in the death of General Rose. He had actually been gone three nights and two full days—a lifetime of fear and terror—and was able to give only a very brief statement to the officer taking the sworn affidavits of the witnesses. Before being taken to the hospital, and still suffering the effects of his ordeal, he also talked with several of the newsmen still gathered at division HQ. As we shall see, the picture of the events of March 30, 1945 that emerged from this impromptu press exposure played a large part in the misstatement of facts and exaggerations that formed the fabric of the story of the death of General Rose for more than five decades.

By this time, all the men who had escaped that night, including the men in Colonel Brown's peep, had finally gotten back. They had a narrow escape and a terrifying night as well. As General Rose and his companions stood with their hands in the air, Colonel Brown was trying to escape. He had gotten past the last German tank and turned right off the road. Because he had personally adjusted the artillery fire earlier, Brown knew where the neutralized areas were. He headed north and found defilade in the field as quickly as possible.

> I asked where the other vehicles were, and someone said they were not behind us. I could not look back myself to check on it, but in the light of the flares, as I was driving north across country, I looked for vehicles driving north across country parallel to us, as I expected they would do, but saw no one.
>
> I realized at that time that the general's vehicle, and probably those behind it, had been caught by the tanks, but I could not see that far in the flare light to determine what was happening back there.[57]

While still at the wheel, he heard the bursts of machine gun and *Schmeisser* fire that followed Shaunce and Bellinger as they crawled through the roadside ditches. He also saw the flares loosed by the tanks of Koltermann's *3rd Platoon*, desperately trying to find the escaped prisoners in the darkness.

After spending the night in a ravine, Brown and his companions made contact with TF Richardson on Route #2 and returned to the division CP on March 31 and made his report. The next day, he took some men back to the scene of the shooting and went over the whole route, retrieving his vehicle in the process. He saw the general's peep and from its position,

> I surmised that the tank had pulled south across the road, and blocked it, as the general's vehicle had its bumper against a tree and was half in the ditch, and from the tank tracks judged that the right side of the vehicle had hit the track of the tank on that side, thus blocking it completely. I found my tracks on the far side of the tree in the ditch.[58]

Among the group of soldiers Brown took back to the scene of the shooting was T/5 James Omand, the motorcycle driver from the division service company who had been stranded in the ditch the night of March 30. After hiding in the forest that night, he had made it back to the CP the next day. He searched the G-3 armored car and retrieved the SOI decoder, which he returned to the division CP. This was great news for the 143rd Armored Signal Company, where there was considerable unease at the prospect that the Germans had taken it when the men in the M-20 had been captured.[59]

Colonel Brown studied the terrain, made notes, and then went back to division HQ where, later that day, he gave his very detailed sworn statement. He made it very clear, however, during the interview—and afterwards—that neither he, nor any of his passengers, were actually eyewitnesses to the shooting of General Rose.

On that same day, Colonel James L. Salmon, MC, the division surgeon, took charge of the medical investigation.

> About midmorning, a command car arrived with Col. Salmon, the division surgeon. He had come to make an official investigation of the death of General Rose. He remembered me from his having been our CO at Camp Polk, and asked me how long the body had been with us. He checked the body for the death wound and replaced the blanket over the dead body. The shiny boots were still so significant.[60]

On April 1, 1945, at 0930 hours, Dr. Salmon performed an autopsy in the surgical section of B Company. Then he arranged to have the general's body taken by ambulance back to the division trains area, where it was prepared before temporary interment at the VII Corps cemetery at Ittenbach, Germany, on April 2, 1945. As the ambulance departed, bearing the body of their fallen leader, the men of B Company, "stood speechless, our hearts heavy with sorrow."[61]

The whole spectacle seemed unbelievable to the men involved. No one could recall ever seeing a real autopsy performed in the whole time they had been in combat. But the death of a division commander was not a routine event. Even before the two surviving eyewitnesses had returned, the pressure for a formal investigation had begun to build. Up and down the chain of command, from Joe Collins' VII Corps, up through Hodges' First Army to Bradley's Twelfth Army Group, the demand for answers and the suspicion that there had been foul play had started to intensify. Eisenhower's SHAEF opened a formal investigation, and officers from both 3rd Armored Division and VII Corps were assigned to assist. Shortly after, two files were opened in the War Crimes Offices of the Judge Advocate General Divisions of the War Department in both Washington and the European Theater of Operations. The pressure to find out what happened—and whether Maurice Rose had been murdered—would gain even more momentum when the politicians got involved.

CHAPTER Fifteen

The Investigation

"I recommend no further action."
Lt. Col. Leon Jaworski

Almost immediately after the general's body had been recovered, the pressure for an investigation into the shooting started to build. The battle to close the Ruhr Pocket was still raging, men by the thousands were being killed and wounded, but the demands of the top brass could not be ignored. At 3rd Armored Division headquarters the administrative wheels were turning at full speed to gather the facts.

The Division's Inspector General (IG), Lt. Col. Ellis P. Sylvester, was in charge. His staff took the sworn statements of the various witnesses who had returned from the incident and prepared the first response to the higher command to find out what had happened to Maurice Rose. The purpose of the Division's IG report was to determine whether "prima facie evidence of a War Crime" existed. The specific offense suspected was "Refusal of Quarter."[1] **(A)**

After the three-day investigation was completed, on April 3, 1945, it was forwarded through channels to Major General Collins' VII Corps HQ for review and endorsement. Then, it was sent through General Hodges'

A "Under the modern laws of war, any individual or body of troops is entitled to demand and receive 'quarter'—that is, if they lay down their arms, surrender, and do not resist capture, the enemy must do nothing further to injure or kill them, and they are from that moment entitled to the rights of prisoners of war."

First U.S. Army to General Bradley's Twelfth Army Group Headquarters, and finally to the headquarters requesting the investigation, Supreme Headquarters, Allied Expeditionary Force.[2]

The core of the report is the sworn testimony of six witnesses, especially the eyewitnesses to the shooting, Major Bellinger and T/4 Glenn Shaunce. Equally important was the affidavit of the 3rd Armored Division Surgeon, Col. James P. Salmon, who performed an autopsy in the field about thirty-six hours after General Rose's death. **(B)** In his summary, Lt. Col. Sylvester presents the simple outline of events that eventually became the factual basis of the "official" version of the death of Maurice Rose:

> Thinking that the tanker wanted their weapons, as stated by Major Bellinger, he (Bellinger) proceeded to take his holster completely off his shoulder. He does not remember if General Rose removed his pistol or not, as at this time the tank commander opened fire with a light weapon and General Rose fell forward. T/4 Shaunce's testimony varies at this point as he states that the General had his hands raised when the tanker fired upon him.

When General Rose's body was found at the scene of the incident his .45 cal pistol, fully loaded, cocked and on safety, in its holster, and slung to a web belt was found nearby.[3]

The report highlights the key discrepancy between Bellinger and Shaunce's versions—namely, the position of General Rose's hands when shot—without an assessment. In the subsequent reviews, and in the final disposition of the case, this discrepancy is ignored. Further, while Sylvester's report includes Dr. Salmon's autopsy summary, it makes no reference to its results. Finally, the IG report does offer some preliminary information about who might have been responsible for the shooting. Based on the excellent and speedy work of Intelligence Chief Lt. Col. Andrew Barr's Order of Battle and Prisoner Interrogation teams, the

---

B The full list of witnesses (and their assignments at the time) includes: T/4 Glenn H. Shaunce (Fwd Ech), Major Robert M. Bellinger (Hq, Fwd Ech), Colonel Frederick J. Brown (Hq, Fwd Ech), Colonel James L. Salmon (Hq, Rear Ech), S/Sgt. Arthur N. Hauschild (1st Bn, 33rd Armd Regt), and Lt. Col. Andrew Barr (Hq, Fwd Ech). Brown's statement also includes a map and Salmon's autopsy report includes a sketch.

report named the veteran *507th Heavy Tiger Battalion* as one of the units known to be in the immediate vicinity.

Clearly, the most important evidence was that given by Shaunce and Bellinger. Shaunce—who returned first—told the investigators a very simple, essentially undramatic story—a story that has not varied materially in almost fifty-six years. In his sworn affidavit, Shaunce described the events leading up to the moment when the three men are standing in front of the *King Tiger*. Then with the tank commander screaming unintelligibly at them from the turret,

> I told the general he may want our pistol(s), I don't know. That didn't seem to be it. He hollered again for something. He seemed to be pretty mad. The general told him (in German) "I don't understand." Then he opened up with his burp gun and started spraying the general from the left, swinging around to the right. I saw the general had his hands up when he was shot.[4]

Over the years, Shaunce made some corrections to his original statement and added a few details. His later letters and tape-recorded recollections assert that after they got out of the peep, no one spoke except General Rose, whose only words were *"no versteh, no versteh"* (or, "don't understand" in truncated German). In his later accounts he makes no mention of anyone saying that the German wanted their pistols, or anything else.[5] He is adamant that "Bellinger never said a cotton picking word; the General never said a thing, except 'no versteh,' maybe twice. I don't know where the stories come from."[6] Shaunce never strayed from his original story that none of the three prisoners ever dropped their hands, or unbuckled their pistol belts, or made any movements to cause the shooting. To this day, he strongly believes that General Rose "was murdered in cold blood."[7]

The evolution of Major Bellinger's story over time is more problematic and ambiguous. His first account, given in his April 2, 1945, sworn statement, was recorded right after returning from his extraordinary sixty-hour ordeal of hunger, thirst, and fear. The strain of his experience is still evident in the brevity, sparseness of description, and lack of explanatory detail, especially compared to his later memoir, which is colorful, literary in style, and at parts, emotional. The crucial part of his testimony concerns the moment when the German tank commander popped out of the turret and immediately started yelling excitedly at the three men.

General Rose tried to understand what the tank commander was saying in his excited German. The general told him we could not speak
German, but he kept calling out some garbled phrase which none of
us could understand. The general said he thought they wanted our
pistols. I know that I got mine completely off my shoulder, as I was
wearing a shoulder holster, but due to the excitement of the moment,
I am not sure whether General Rose dropped his hands to unbuckle
his pistol or not. But just as I got my pistol off, the tank commander,
still in his turret, fired a light weapon, either a Tommy gun or burp
gun, and General Rose fell forward.[8]

Twenty years later—in response to a request for information about the
death of Maurice Rose—Bellinger once again journeyed through his memories of that night, this time including more detail and literary color as
well as his opinion about what happened.[9]

Unhurt, we leap to the road, as guttural commands are shouted from
the turret.
"I think he wants our guns!" General Rose is saying.
We disarm. Shaunce throws off his shoulder holster. I likewise
hurl mine to the ground.
The fortunes of war now go against the general. He drops his
hands to release his pistol belt from his waist. In the dark, unable to
recognize rank or purpose, the nervous tank commander misunder-
stands the general's actions as hostile.
There is a staccato burst. A machine pistol is fired from the protection of the turret. A groan—as the general falls forward.
They have killed him.[10]

The later recollection differs from the original in three main respects. In
both accounts, Bellinger claims that General Rose said the German wanted
them to hand over their sidearms, but in the second account he drops the
assertion that first General Rose said that he didn't understand the shouting. In the first version, he is not sure whether the general lowered his
hands to unbuckle his pistol belt; in the second, he says that Maurice Rose
did just that. Finally, in the second version, he offers *his opinion* that the
"nervous" German misunderstood General Rose's actions as "hostile."
This latter statement is consistent with a letter Bellinger wrote nearly a year
after the incident in response to Arnold Rose's request for more details

about his brother's death. "As to why they fired, no one will ever know, but it may be that they felt he was reaching for his gun to resist capture."[11]

There is no question that in the Army's various investigations, the testimony of Major Bellinger, a field grade officer, was rated as more reliable than that of the general's enlisted driver.[12] **(C)** In fact, in several of the reviewing officers' memoranda all reference to Shaunce's version, especially the crucial discrepancy, is dropped completely. But, the fact remains that Bellinger's written accounts give rise to serious questions. The problems are compounded further—and perhaps explained partially—when we turn to the very first newspaper accounts of the death of Maurice Rose, apparently based on impromptu interviews with Bellinger at division headquarters. These conversations took place before the major was shipped out to the hospital, but at a time when he was still suffering from his ordeal.

The demands for a War Crimes investigation in Washington were stimulated, at least in part, by the news reports that appeared under the bylines of respected war correspondents beginning April 3, 1945. They rose to a fever pitch when German propaganda broadcasts and foreign press reports claimed that General Rose had been murdered after surrendering by the "werewolves, guerrillas planning to resist the Allies no matter what the outcome of the war."[13] Just one week later, Colonel Melvin Purvis, Acting Director of the War Crimes Office, sent a request to the Headquarters, European Theater, for additional information to supplement the newspaper clippings in the Pentagon's already opened "War Crimes File No. 12-407 (Rose)."

These articles reported "the shooting of Major General Maurice Rose under circumstances indicating the commission of a war crime."[14] The articles forwarded to European Headquarters, Paris included those written by Don Whitehead (*AP*), John Thompson (*Chicago Tribune Press Service*), Andy Rooney (*Stars & Stripes*), as well as UPI and other wire service reporters.

While the first articles vary somewhat in the specific details, they all claim to be based on information received from Major Bellinger. While a few mention the presence of the general's driver, none of the Washington papers name him or refer to his testimony or version of what happened. The composite picture of the death of General Rose that emerges from the newspapers is the following:

C Henry Stimson, Secretary of War, does not even refer to Shaunce's testimony in his April 17, 1945, response to the request of Senators Milliken and Johnson request for an investigation into the death of Maurice Rose (Congressional Record—Senate, pg. 3660).

General Rose, his aide, and driver dismounted their peep with their hands in the air after colliding with a *King Tiger* tank. In response to the screams of the German tank commander, General Rose replied repeatedly—in English—"I don't understand." Next, all three captured men lowered their shoulder holsters over their heads, at which moment, the inexperienced, "pink-faced young German," shot the general in the head. Everybody else, including the men in the Operations M-20 escaped and returned to the division within hours. Major Bellinger thought that the reason General Rose was shot was that the German thought he was going for his gun.[15]

The articles appearing in the Washington press were dramatic enough, but the hometown papers, especially the *Denver Post, Rocky Mountain News,* and *Intermountain Jewish News,* carried even more fantastic tales. **(D)** The stories—especially under the charged headlines—were enough to stimulate political activity. As early as April 5, four Senators, including Democrat Edwin C. Johnson and Republican Eugene D. Milliken, both of Colorado, sent a letter to Secretary of War Henry Stimson requesting a formal investigation by the War Department. As it happened, parallel investigations were already under way at Army Headquarters in both Washington and Paris.

Even with the war in Europe still raging, the top American officers—men like Eisenhower, Bradley, Hodges, and Collins, all sponsors and admirers of Maurice Rose—were stepping up the pressure. The order was simple and grew in intensity as it moved from the top down the chain of command: Find out what happened! That proved to be more difficult than anyone might imagine. What is even more ironic is that some of these men ended up distorting the very truth that they sincerely wanted uncovered.

Legends and myths about the deeds of great warriors grow best in the soil of confusion. They come to full maturity when eyewitnesses mingle their factual accounts of their observations with opinions about what they saw or did not see. The distortion of fact and exaggeration of the truth gain momentum and fervor when "those who should know" and other highly placed and respected individuals add their voices to those of the "ordinary" witnesses.

There was no more fervent admirer and supporter of Maurice Rose than J. Lawton Collins, his wartime corps commander. Citing Major

---

D The texts of the unsigned *Denver Post* articles vary considerably in the April 3, 1945 morning and evening editions. For instance, the date of the shooting is first given as Saturday, March 31, and Bellinger is described as a passenger in the M-20 "half-track." In the evening edition, Bellinger is back in the peep with driver "Chantz" and they escape together and drive back to Division HQ.

Bellinger as the source of his "detailed account of what happened," then four-star General Collins wrote in his 1979 autobiography the story that he got right after Rose's death.

> The German commander motioned with a "burp" gun to the occupants to dismount with their arms up. They had no alternative. Then he shouted something about "pistolen." Major Bellinger and the peep driver, Tech 5 Glen H. Shounce (*infra*), who like most officers carried their weapons in shoulder holsters, dropped their holsters without lowering their arms. Rose, who habitually wore a pistol belt, dropped his arms, presumably to remove his belt. But the tank commander, evidently thinking Maurice was reaching for his revolver (*infra*), fired a stream of bullets at point-blank range. Rose, killed instantly, pitched forward in the dusty road.[16]

It is again striking that the other eyewitness—enlisted man Shaunce—is not cited as a source. This is yet another version provided by Bellinger, with new details added. Neither Bellinger (nor Shaunce) reported hearing the word "*pistolen*" in the torrent of screams coming from the turret (even though it is likely that is what the German was shouting). Shaunce has consistently denied that he ever removed his weapon, and Bellinger's convoluted method of taking off his holster without dropping his arms varies from other accounts of actions related to his sidearm.

General Rose was found lying on his back, with his face up, so every account, including those of both eyewitnesses, appears wrong when it claims he "pitched forward." There is no evidence that the body was moved. A .45 automatic is *not* a revolver (as General Collins, or more likely his "ghost" writer, should have known) and the road between Hamborn and Kirchborchen was more than likely damp, rather than dusty, based on the weather conditions immediately preceeding March 30, 1945. Finally, repeating an opinion, even one offered by an eyewitness—such as, Rose was reaching for a weapon to resist capture—does not make it true, no matter how illustrious, or otherwise respected, the speaker may be. While Collins mentions that the pistol was found in its holster near Rose's body, he does not cite that as evidence to challenge Bellinger's conclusion. General Collins, who more than any other senior officer was motivated by a sincere affection for Maurice Rose, perpetuated myths about his death.

At the 3rd Armored Division, the final conclusions were no less misleading. Its final report was issued under the sponsorship of Brigadier

General Doyle O. Hickey, Rose's successor at 3rd Armored Division. **(E)** The statement—undoubtedly written by an aide—claims to be based on the witness' statements, but the details about General Rose's death are taken mostly from Bellinger's various accounts.[17] There are, however, a number of discrepancies in the document compared to the previous witness statements, including that of Major Bellinger.

First, on the question of who spoke after the surrender, the Hickey statement claims that 1) Rose responded, in English, that he didn't understand the German's shouts, 2) Bellinger was the first to suggest that the screams were demanding the surrender of side-arms, and 3) Rose then responded to Bellinger. Secondly, it also claims that Bellinger took off his shoulder holster and placed it on the deck of the *King Tiger* tank that captured them (a detail that appears in no other account).

There are a number of other misquoted or incorrectly reported details: Lt. Col. Garton was riding with Colonel Brown during their escape; it was the third tank that stopped Rose, not the second; Bellinger returned to the division after sixty hours, not forty-eight; more than three bullets hit Rose's head, etc. But, the most striking part of the statement is that General Hickey offers his own opinion of what happened.

> It is my personal opinion, after a thorough examination, as is also the unanimous opinion of those present and those who investigated with me, that the occurrences in this case do not constitute an act of atrocity nor was his an intentional killing of a helpless man. It was an incident that in the excitement and tension of combat is most likely to occur.[18]

The claim of unanimity is absurd. Glenn Shaunce has never accepted Hickey's opinion. The final disposition of the War Crimes Investigation, however, would bear remarkable similarity to Hickey's opinion.

By the middle of June 1945, the actual investigation by the Army investigators had been completed. In addition to the evidence collected right

---

E This statement (incl. diagram) is entitled Statement from Brigadier General Doyle O. Hickey, Combat Commander of 3rd Armored Division, n.d., 3 pg. (photocopy, original in Rose Family Album). Capt. C. Craig Cannon, Aide to General Eisenhower, forwarded it to Arnold Rose, on March 12, 1946, in response to Rose's letter of January 21, 1946, to Eisenhower. It was most likely written after the middle of April 1945, since it makes reference to the liberation by the British of the POWs from Col. Sweat's M-20.

after the death of Maurice Rose, sworn statements had been recorded from the released POWs who had been riding in the M-20, including enlisted men Stevenson, Hatry, Ellison, and Lt. Colonel Sweat. The "Official Position" eventually emerged in the exchange of several memoranda, the most important of which is that of Lt. Col. Leon Jaworski, written on June 11, 1945. **(F)** It is based on the reports and summaries prepared by lower ranking JAG and other investigating officers and included in the European Theater of Operations War Crimes Office File #12-352A (Rose). It concludes that no war crime was committed because a

> . . . fair interpretation of the facts impels the conclusion that the shooting occurred as a result of a combination of unfortunate circumstances including, (a) the fact that the general and his party had made desperate efforts to escape when they were blocked in by the tank, (b) the failure of General Rose to understand the commands, apparently several times repeated, of the tank commander and (c) the unfortunate movement in unison of General Rose, his aide, and the driver toward their guns for the purpose of unstrapping them.
>
> The contention that the tank commander intended to murder General Rose and his men in cold blood is inconsistent with the undisputed fact that the tank commander did not fire upon them when they first raised their hands but tried to make them understand some orders he was giving. It must be remembered that this all happened in darkness. The lowering of the their hands to the direction of their guns was an unfortunate and ill-timed movement and but for such action it is not believed that the tank commander would have fired.[19]

Finally, Colonel Jaworski gives his recommendation. "I do not believe that further investigation is warranted. I recommend that no further

---

F Leon Jaworski (1905–1982). After graduating from high school at age fifteen, he attended Baylor University on scholarship, and was awarded a law degree in 1925, the same year he became the youngest person ever to be admitted to the Texas bar. He served in the U.S. Army Judge Advocate General's Office during World War II, rising to the rank of colonel, and was a prosecutor in the 1945–1946 Nürenberg trials of Nazi war criminals. He was the officer responsible for the final disposition of the ETO War Crimes investigation (File # 12-352A) into the murder of Major General Maurice Rose. He later rose to national prominence on November 5, 1973, when he was sworn in as Watergate special prosecutor.

action be taken." It was November 20, 1945, before the recommendation actually became official and the case was administratively closed and filed. In the interim, other officers added their lower-ranking voices to Jaworski's conclusion.

The "Official Version" was now in place. No war crime had been committed. It was understandable, if not actually reasonable, that the German had shot General Rose, because he and the others had lowered their hands towards their sidearms. Maybe if they had not done that, they would have been taken prisoner and Rose would have survived. Besides, it was dark and the German may not have seen that the men were removing their holsters, and assumed they were reaching for their weapons to resist capture. There had been a lot of combat that evening. It was a case of action taking place "in the heat of battle," unexplainable in the confusion and "fog of war."

What really happened?

After the men dismounted from their peep, hands in the air, it seems clear that General Rose was the only one who spoke. Shaunce's recollection, repeated many times, that he said *"no versteh, no versteh"* several times seems logical. The claim that none of the three prisoners understood German is not correct. Maurice Rose grew up in an Orthodox Jewish home and spoke and understood Yiddish, a language closely related to German, even before he spoke English. In his close association with General Rose, Lt. Col. Wesley Sweat, his principal operations officer, often observed General Rose reading and speaking German.[20] When he responded to the German with the phrase *"no versteh,"* (or, that he didn't understand), he was either playing for time, or he wanted the German to know he could not understand the excited shouting. By answering in German, he was signaling that the rapid-fire commands were not being understood, but that he wanted to comply.

The German continued shouting rapid fire orders, as both witnesses testified. One of the words that Rose must have heard was *"pistolen."* Every GI knew what that meant. Both Shaunce and Bellinger, at different times, stated that they thought that the German wanted their guns, so they both must have heard something that at least suggested that was what was being demanded. While Bellinger gave several accounts on what was being demanded, and Shaunce says no one ever said anything, it seems clear that Rose did say something like "I think he wants our pistols." General Rose was still the man in charge, the man who always spoke first, and in this crisis situation it is hard to imagine that either of the other men—frozen with fear and shock at being captured—would speak before the general did.

When Bellinger heard Rose speak, he started to take off his shoulder holster by lifting it over his head. He did not attempt to unsnap the holster rig, but lifted it with his right thumb and open palm, keeping his left arm high above his head. He was too focused to watch either Rose or Shaunce at the time, making sure he did not lose eye contact with his captor. That is why his first statement said he could not be sure if General Rose lowered his hands or not. By the same logic, he could not see what Shaunce was doing, especially as General Rose was between Shaunce and himself. Finally, he dropped the holster onto the front deck of the tank. Hauschild did not find it the next morning, nor was there any mention of a second weapon near Rose, as they would have picked that up too.

After speaking, General Rose, wearing his standard GI web waist pistol belt with combat knife attached, immediately dropped his hands to unbuckle the belt. There can be no doubt that this is what he understood the German wanted. It is inconceivable that after having already surrendered, and with his hands already in the air, he would have risked any movement to provoke his captor. Had he been trying to reach for a weapon, as some believed at the time and still believe, he would have done so when the peep first collided with the tank, before the German had them covered with a weapon, and not after he had already raised his arms.

He either heard the work "*pistolen,*" as Bellinger told General Collins several days after the event, or may have actually heard a more specific demand. With his right hand, he twisted the frog keeper on the belt and released it from the mate on the left side. Grabbing the gun belt with his left hand, he dropped it to the ground near his left foot.

Then, having obeyed the lawful command of the man who had captured him, still his prisoner and under his power, Rose started to raise both hands once more over his head to assume a position of total submission. He brought both hands from his waist up in an outward motion, elbows bent, with the back of his hands facing the German. He was careful not to make any sudden, unexpected moves so as not to rile the German who was pointing a gun at him. When his hands reached eye level and just as he started to turn his wrists, thus presenting both palms to his captor, the guttural commands ceased, and without any warning the Schmeisser machine pistol cut loose with the first burst of ripping sound.

The autopsy and accompanying diagram provide vivid testimony to the sequence of events that ended Maurice Rose's life. His two hands were close to the level of his helmet rim when the first burst hit him. Two slugs (#1 and #2) hit his right hand, the first cutting into his right thumb and

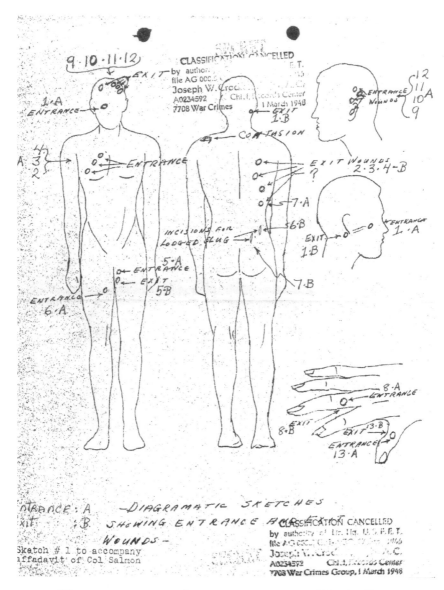

Diagram accompanying autopsy report on Mauice Rose
(*Source:* War Crimes Office File #12-352A)

the second his middle finger, where it smashed the small bones in the second phalanges, both bullets exiting past his head. Simultaneously, the third (#3) slug slammed into his right cheek, exiting along the jaw line. This wound, while no doubt painful was not fatal, but it resulted in the general's helmet being knocked back off his head into the air.

Two more rounds from the first burst struck the airborne helmet, passing through the rear, and exiting the front of the helmet near the two general's stars, one slug clipping off the point of one of the silver stars. It was at this moment that Colonel Sweat and PFC Stevenson both turned and looked in the direction of the shooting, claiming to see the helmet spinning in the air. The force of the bullets' impact sent the helmet flying ten feet to the left. That is where Sergeants Hauschild and Owen found it the next day, on the ground to the left of the peep and in the ditch.

The next burst of four bullets from the *Schmeisser* (#4, #5, #6, and #7) caught the general in the upper right chest region in a tight group with all the slugs exiting his back. While these were very serious wounds, and potentially fatal, especially if left untreated for any length of time, they did not kill him outright. The four slugs impacting his body jerked it violently to the right, however, causing his head to turn in the same direction, thus exposing the left side of his face to the man in the turret.

The third burst (#8, #9, #10, and #11) struck Maurice Rose in the head, entering the left temporal area above and below the left ear in another very tight pattern. The bullets caused massive brain and tissue damage and all four exited the frontal region and scalp. It was this burst of gunfire that ended the life of Maurice Rose, who died instantaneously.

Rose's body after being jerked violently to the right at this point started to sag in death, but before he hit the ground a final short burst of three more shots entered his body. One hit him in the left groin area (#12) and one penetrated his right thigh (#13). Another slug, probably a ricochet off the frontal armor of the tank, struck him in the lower right back (#14) possibly as his body was twisting in the final plunge to the earth. Two slugs from this last burst lodged in his lower back and were extracted during the autopsy and retained as evidence. Maurice Rose finally fell to the earth, his feet still only a yard or two away from the front of the *King Tiger*, and on his back. He did not fall forward.

It is impossible to ascertain the total number of shots fired at General Rose, but the stick magazine of the *Schmeisser* holds thirty-two rounds. Half that number hit his body or the spinning helmet.

The official investigation had ignored the key fact—repeated countless times by Shaunce, but discounted by the investigating officers—that the general's hands were in the air when he was killed. The autopsy offers very powerful support for that theory. Had he been shot with his hands at his waist, there would have been multiple abdominal wounds present. The orientation of Rose's right hand and angles of entry of the hand wounds are strong evidence.

Another major point in the Official Version points to the degree of darkness at the moment of the shooting and questions implicitly whether the German was able to see clearly what his prisoners were doing. This interpretation suggests that even if he had been ordering the Americans to surrender their weapons, perhaps it was so dark that it appeared to him they were *reaching for their weapons rather than surrendering them*. On this issue, the testimony and recollections of many of the men present at the time—the occupants of both peeps and M-20—point to a period of twilight, or rapidly fading daylight, after the sun set that day, but not pitch blackness.

In addition, there was some artificial and natural light. While the actual pattern or sequence is impossible to reconstruct, numerous flares were being fired intermittently in the area of operations of the *507th Heavy Panzer Battalion* during the whole period. In addition, Major Bellinger referred to the moon passing through clouds. While there was not enough light to discriminate detail, outlines were clearly visible, at least in open ground. When Colonel Brown and his men paused in front of the knocked-out T26 on the Hamborn road looking for tracks, and bemoaned the lack of a flashlight, they were on a narrow road, surrounded by heavy woods. The stretch of road where Rose was killed, however, was lined at intervals by mature plum trees, but ran through open fields. The German must have been able to see that Rose's hands were back in the air.

The shooting was unprovoked, deliberate, and not in the "heat of battle." This is clear from the passage of time between the initial surrender, the disarming by two of the prisoners in response to a direct command, and the raising of Rose's hands a second time. If there had been any question in the German's mind about whether the men in the peep were resisting, he could have shot them with impunity at any time before they raised their hands. Finally, the firing of four separate bursts, the total number of rounds (fourteen) striking Rose, and the tight patterns of the bursts all indicate a determination to ensure that the victim was killed and not merely wounded.

It is impossible to determine the German's true intent, crucial in any formal legal charge of murder. Anger, possibly sparked by the frustration of his orders not being carried out as quickly as directed, is one explanation.

Perhaps there was something about Rose's demeanor that singled him out. Maybe the German did not want to get out of the turret to take charge of the prisoners and did not see any of his infantry support close by. Maybe he had received orders to move out quickly. Also, the men of the *507th* were veterans of the brutal Eastern Front, where the routine killing of prisoners was a common, and accepted, practice.

But, whatever the motives of the German tank commander, what happened to Maurice Rose cannot be described as resulting from "the heat of battle," or, "the fog of war." The *Schmeisser* spoke in some kind of rage and was a denial of quarter. Under the rules of war, when a man has raised his hands in surrender, after that act he may not be harmed.

Up until the moment the general was shot, Shaunce and Bellinger had been frozen in fear with their hands high above their heads. As Shaunce stood to Rose's left, his right shoulder and uplifted arm obscured his peripheral vision, and he didn't notice Rose's first swift action of dropping his hands to unbuckle his web waist belt. In the brief interval of time that this occurred, Shaunce was transfixed, with his gaze forward; he never took his eyes off the German with his deadly weapon clearly visible and pointed at all three men. This explains why he always claimed that Rose was shot with his hands raised. He never saw him drop his hands, and when he saw him shot, his hands were in the air.

Nor did he hear him say, "I think they want our guns." All he heard was "*no versteh, no versteh*" as the men left the peep. Perhaps, the noise of the tanks and other background sounds distracted him. When he heard the *Schmeisser* fire, however, he was jerked back to reality and out of a kind of semi-trance that was caused by his intense focus on the German screaming at him, a natural fear, and the searing pain of a broken leg. In spite of Bellinger's claim, he never made any move to take off his shoulder holster. He still had his captured *Walther P-38* in the field where he escaped.

Shaunce saw Rose's hands in the air and assumed they had always been there. He then reacted instinctively, as the fire-red bullets came cascading directly down and into the body of the general. Automatically, he started to move and shouted "*Run!*" ostensibly to Bellinger, but also as an instinctive response rather than to anyone in particular. At this point the instinct of self-preservation gained ascendancy over fear. He ran, as did Major Bellinger, and the German tried to finish the job by spraying the rest of the clip in the direction of the escaped prisoners.

This, then, is our best reconstruction of the events surrounding the death of Major General Maurice Rose. But the official investigation never got this far. In spite of the contradictions in the key testimony, and many other questions, the men charged with uncovering the truth stopped considerably short of a thorough effort to uncover the facts. What had gone wrong with the investigation?

After the field work in Europe had been completed by the IG staff of 3rd Armored Division, 1st Lt. Myron N. Lane, War Crimes Branch, Judge Advocate General Division, was charged with the responsibility of evaluating the reports concerning the investigation into the death of Major General Maurice Rose. His first action was to send a sixteen-line, handwritten summary of the case—File No. 12-352A Rose, {V}—to then Lt. Col. Leon Jaworski, Chief of Trial Section, JAG. This interoffice memo, dated May 27, 1945, was like all documents associated with the case marked "SECRET."

1. This file relates to evidence by Major Bellinger, Aide to Maj. Gen. Maurice Rose and T/4 Glenn Shaunce, driver of peep the General was riding in when he met his death. On 30 March 1945 the above three were in a peep near Paderborn, Germany, when they were forced to surrender to tank of either 507th Heavy Tiger Bn. or 500 Heavy Panzer Training Bn. They had their hands over their heads and that a commander of German tank was yelling excitedly at them. There is confusion as to whether Gen. Rose attempted to remove pistol and belt thinking that was the German's command or not. The tank opened up and the General was shot several times being killed instantly. There is no evidence as to the accused's identity except as above stated.

2. No action is necessary, as it is questionable whether any war crime was committed.

3. It is recommended that this case be closed and filed under "Index and File."

Lt. Lane had access to the original 3rd Armored IG Report summary authored by Col. Sylvester, which clearly stated, "Tech/4 Shaunce's testimony varies at this point as he states the general had his hands raised when the tanker fired upon him." This should have sent up a red flag and required a follow up interview in the field immediately. What is striking is that Lt. Lane refers to confusion about what happened, but doesn't recommend additional efforts to clear up the confusion. The failure to do so indicates a clear lack of interest in pursuing the implication of Shaunce's testimony, namely that General Rose was murdered with his hands in the air after surrendering.

Instead, Lt. Lane took the same position as BG Doyle O. Hickey to disregard the testimony of T/4 Glenn H. Shaunce, one of only two eye-witnesses, that the general had both hands in the air in clear evidence of surrender when he was killed. Both men accepted the testimony of the general's aide, Major Robert Bellinger, who in his sworn testimony, was uncertain about the position of the general's hands when he was shot.

T/4 Glenn Shaunce was still serving in the army and was an outpatient in a stateside hospital. He was not discharged until October 1945 and was obviously available. It would have been relatively easy to conduct a follow-up interview by an army field agent. Several such interviews were conducted between June and September 1945 with former crewmembers of the M-20 armored car, some of whom had already been discharged and were civilians.

Several weeks after Lt. Lane wrote his summary, Lt. Col. Jaworski authored his memo essentially mirroring the earlier finding by Lane and Hickey. The decision on how to proceed was delayed for more than five months. Finally, on November 8, 1945, Captain Francis W. McGuigan recommended to Lt. Colonel Griffin, Chief of Prosecution Subsection, that the case be closed, because "all the testimony shows that this encounter with the Germans was made *in the heat of battle*" and "the tank commander was very excited when General Rose was killed." But the captain's closing comment probably sums up best what many on the investigation staff must have thought, even if they were loathe to say it aloud, "If the victim here had been a private, probably no newspaper notoriety or investigation would be germane." True enough, but not a good reason for closing an official investigation.[21]

On November 19, 1945, Major T.S. Sealy, next up the chain of command, reviewed McGuigan's recommendation. He wrote that he "emphatically agrees with the conclusion reached by the officer who wrote the review, but I believe page two thereof should be rewritten so as to delete therefrom the Note to Reviewing Officer." The note offered his observation, of how the conclusion might be received by the top brass and politicians.

This opinion may rankle higher authority because of the prominence of the victim and the circumstances which were erroneously reported in various newspaper articles which are contained in the file. It is, however, believed by the undersigned that no war crime has been committed.[22]

The same day, Colonel Jaworski endorsed the memo with his handwritten notation, "Delete note and close administratively." The offending "Note to Reviewing Officer" was then deleted, the memo was redone (as we now have it) and forwarded to Lt. Col. Griffin by J.W. Bruton who agreed with the opinions rendered. On November 20, 1945, Col. Leon Jaworski, now Chief of Trial Section of the War Crimes Branch, sent a brief memo to the Chief, Record Subsection, to close the file per Capt. McGuigan's memo. That was it, Case Closed. With the most important questions still unanswered, with key eyewitness testimony in direct conflict but unexamined, the investigation ended.

Everyone, especially the newly promoted Colonel Jaworski, had more notorious murderers to prosecute. While the victim in the Rose case was important, and the political pressure was intense, the perpetrator, even if he could be found, indeed even if he were alive, was not important enough to merit further pursuit. What object lesson was there in convicting a single tank commander of murdering a single prisoner, even a high profile prisoner, in the middle of a battle? The world had buried tens of millions, and millions more had been turned into smoke. The whole concept of a "war crime" had been expanded beyond the individual; it was finding the murderers of thousands, millions, now imperative.

On November 20, 1945, the same day the clerks in Record Subsection put Case File #12-352A, Rose (V) in a cabinet drawer—where it remained unseen for more than fifty years—the Nürenberg War Crimes Trial opened its first session. By the end of the trials, only several hundred murderers had faced judges.

CHAPTER Sixteen

Summer 1945

"He was a man to the last and a great soldier—
just as he always wanted to be."

Rabbi Samuel Rose

Dressed formally in black coat with striped trousers, the old man sat rigidly upright, obviously distraught but struggling to maintain his dignity. The old woman was prostrated with grief, weeping uncontrollably. General Quade and several other army officers were calling on Rabbi and Mrs. Sam Rose to provide additional details about the death of their son. Sam received the story, based mostly on Major Bellinger's account, with the kind of stoicism displayed by soldiers who hear of the death of men they have known. He was not surprised when General Quade told him how Maurice had died.

I expected it! I expected it! When I read how he was personally leading his men in such danger, I knew he would never come back to us.[1]

With the fortitude and strength of a biblical patriarch, and in obedience to the ancient laws of his people, he tore his garment and that of his wife and surviving son. As the reporters and officers sat respectfully in the upstairs parlor of the rabbi's modest home, the phone rang. It was Virginia Rose saying that she would come by with her son to try to console her in-laws in any way she could. She knew it was what her husband would have wanted, and perhaps it would help soothe her own pain as well.[2]

But Sam Rose was distant. He was thinking back to that day many years before when Maurice first went off to war in the trenches of France. He warned the headstrong boy that death waited patiently for every soldier. He remembered the telegram announcing that Maurice had fallen, and the relief when it turned out to be untrue. This time, however, there was no such dawn at the end of a dark night, and despair descended on his spirit without relief. In the pain, however, there was also pride. In an instant, the father saw before him the child, the scout, the honors student, and the tall, uniformed man all drawn up in one image, and Sam was proud.

He was a man to the last and a great soldier—just as he always wanted to be.[3]

He also felt pride in his people. John Stephenson, a reporter for Denver's *Rocky Mountain News*, was present in the rabbi's parlor. He was taken aback when the old man, after closing his eyes briefly with his lips moving silently in prayer, began to speak. His eyes were fixed on a distant place visible only to him. Gesturing with his cane, his voice was that of a prophet, a Jeremiah or Isaiah, now rising and then falling.

It is well that since this had to be, it happened in the week of Passover. As Jehovah said, "When I see the blood, I will pass over you." He spoke not only to the Jews but to the Gentiles, to Americans, to Germans, to all peoples. When I see the sacrifice, the blood, I will pass over you.

And so, may Jehovah accept this sacrifice, and see the blood and pass over all peoples for their sins, at this Passover time. For my son's sake.

The Jewish people have demonstrated their love of liberty and freedom for all peoples since the days of Abraham, Isaac, and Joseph, and I am proud that they are still demonstrating it in the wars of the world, this Passover time—in the deeds and the death of my son.[4]

The message—patriotic, generous, and tolerant—was picked up by the wire services and carried by newspapers all over America. The eighty-nine-year-old rabbi became a national figure overnight.[5] Just one month later, on V-E Day, May 8, 1945, Rabbi Samuel Rose, ill and speaking from his bedroom through a special connection to Denver's KOA-NBC radio studio, spoke to a national audience of millions, expressing gratitude for the end of the war in Europe.

On this day of victory, we bow in prayer to our Almighty Father, Thou Living God and Everlasting King, that this V-Day serve for all mankind as a lesson always to be remembered—that the Lord of Peace and Goodwill will not permit the haters of humanity to continue their evil actions. May this day of victory, by thy loving kindness, O God, bind all peoples together in good faith and brotherly love.[6]

The pain and anguish of his loss intensified the natural infirmities of old age. Increasingly bedridden, Sam found it difficult to pursue his hobbies of painting and poetry, but two days after celebrating his ninetieth birthday, on May 15, his last poem was published in a newspaper with an ink-drawn border of flowers and leaves surrounding the text.[7]

SAD HEARTS

Thy fate is the common fate of all
Into each life some rain must fall.
For Life is like a mighty river
Rolling on from day to day
And passes like a dream;
While we in our daily life
Are struggling and pulling
Against the stream.
And everything we love and cherish
Like a dream goes past.
While the hearts forget and perish
And the eyes are closed at last.

Only two months after the V E Day broadcast, Samuel Rose died on July 10, passing away quietly in his sleep

Mrs. Maurice Rose was attending Easter Services with her four-year-old son at Denver's Episcopal Cathedral when the Army officers from Lowry Field found her. Jo Berry, wife of Lt. Col. Ed Berry, CO of the 67th Armored Artillery Battalion, was friendly with Mrs. Rose, the two women often exchanging information contained in letters from their husbands. They attended church services regularly and occasionally would have lunch together.

That terrible Sunday, Jo was late to church and noticed Virginia sitting a few rows in front of her. It was then Mrs. Rose saw the officers approaching her. She knew immediately why they were there and broke down completely. The men had to support her physically as she was taken from the church in tears. The officers escorted her to her apartment before going on to the home of General Rose's parents. At this time they knew only that the general had been killed in action.

After the service, Jo went immediately to Mrs. Rose's apartment and there the terrible news, which she already suspected, was confirmed. She remained the rest of the day placing herself between the distraught widow and the besieging press and other callers. Mrs. Rose's grief was intense. The depth of her relationship with her husband was now clearly apparent to Jo Berry in all its raw emotion and the pain of a never-ending loss.[8]

The next morning at 10:15 a.m., Denver time, a telegram was delivered to Mrs. Rose from the Supreme Allied Headquarters in Europe.

My Dear Mrs. Rose,

Although I have not been privileged to meet you personally, my admiration, respect, and affection for your late husband were so profound that I feel impelled to send you some word of sympathy in your tragic loss. He was not only one of our bravest and best, but was a leader who inspired his men to speedy accomplishment of tasks that to a lesser man would have appeared almost impossible. He was out in front of his Division, leading it in one of its many famous actions, when he met his death.

I hope that your realization of the extraordinary worth of his services to his country will help you in some small way to bear the burden of your grief. The thoughts and prayers of his legion of warm friends in the Theater are with you.

Most Sincerely,
Dwight D. Eisenhower.[9]

Later that week on Thursday, April 5, Mrs. Berry helped to arrange a Memorial Service in the chapel of the cathedral that was attended by many of Mrs. Rose's friends.[10] That same day, the last day of Passover, a Memorial Service was also held for General Rose in the synagogue in which he had become a *Bar Mitzvah*.[11]

The Denver Jewish community had been struggling for months with a major communal goal: building a new $1 million, 150-bed, fully equipped, nonsectarian hospital. It would be the first, privately sponsored, postwar hospital in the country. The Jews of Denver had a long tradition of building hospitals that served every citizen. The first such institutions, aimed primarily at helping those suffering from tuberculosis, had established Denver as a national leader in providing quality health care to all its citizens. Sam Rose had benefited from this largesse when he first moved to Denver at the turn of the century.

Almost immediately after news of the death of General Maurice Rose reached Denver, the Jewish community leaders realized that a hospital named in his honor could catalyze and broaden the effort. What better memorial to the top Colorado combat commander and "highest ranking Jewish General" of the war? By April 8, 1945, a committee had been formed, leaders chosen, and initial plans put in place to establish the General Rose Memorial Hospital.[12] It became apparent quickly that a broad-based effort to honor the fallen hero would ease the local fundraising burden and engage the attention of the whole country.

A major and early boost to the effort was the backing of W.C. Shepherd, the influential publisher of the *Denver Post*. This early media sponsorship was soon followed by an overwhelming response from Jewish and Christian philanthropies all over the country. Telegrams of encouragement and promises of support flowed in from Colorado's senators and other political leaders, and within days more than $200,000 had been pledged.[13] Just two weeks after Maurice Rose's death, the Hospital Association had set up a temporary office in New York to solicit funds and help mobilize the backing of the national and Jewish press.[14]

As the leaders of the drive began their active fundraising campaign, they got a tremendous psychological gift. Mrs. Maurice Rose, still reeling from her loss, but genuinely moved by the depth and intensity of feelings for her late husband, added her voice to the philanthropic effort. On April 20, 1945, she sent a letter to the hospital association expressing her support for their plans. The organizers could now rightly claim that the program had the support of all of the general's survivors.

Dear Friends,

I have been greatly touched at the organization of the "General Rose Memorial Hospital" to found and endow a hospital for Americans of all creeds. Such a move should be an inspiration to everyone, in these days of world hysteria.

> On behalf of myself and son, I desire to thank you for the high
> esteem you hold for General Rose and for your intentions of dedicat-
> ing this Memorial in his honor.[15]
>
> Sincerely,
>
> Virginia B. Rose

Mrs. Rose's letter gave a large impetus to the "big gifts" effort, culminating in the first annual General Rose Memorial Hospital Association $1,000
a plate dinner on Sunday, May 27, 1945. Governor John C. Vivian introduced the keynote speaker, famed entertainer Eddie Cantor. His address
was broadcast nationwide by NBC's Denver radio affiliate, KOA.[16] **(A)**
Renowned bandleader Paul Whiteman, famous journalists Walter Winchell,
Damon Runyon, and Max Lerner, and national political leader Fiorello La
Guardia, to name a few, lent their voices in support of the campaign and
issued outright appeals for funds.[17] Telegrams of praise from Rose's mili-
tary superiors Generals George C. Marshall, Dwight D. Eisenhower, and
Courtney H. Hodges were read at the first dinner. Colorado Senator Edwin
C. Johnson, a member of the Military Affairs Committee, read General
Hodges' message. The dinner was a phenomenal success, generating pledges
totaling more than $450,000!

Rose's 3rd Armored Division also responded with great generosity,
generating additional favorable publicity. Welcomed to both New York
City and Denver by the Hospital Association, the division's chief of staff
Colonel John A. Smith, Jr.—accompanied by Colorado native Master
Sgt. J.O. Atherton—presented a check for $30,000. Donated by 10,000 of
the general's soldiers in honor of their fallen commander, the formal
presentation of the check was carried live over NBC radio to a national
audience.[18]

By the middle of June, more than half of the required $1 million had
been raised.[19] Just three months later, the architectural plans had been
unveiled, construction was ready to begin, and three quarters of the money
required had been collected.[20] The stunning momentum of the fundraising campaign and its nationwide profile had been a remarkable achievement and an incredible testament to the memory of a great hero. It was no

---

A Cantor later became enamored of the idea of capturing the life of General
Rose on film. He wrote Colonel John A. Smith, Jr. (March 14, 1946) about the idea,
advising that Mrs. Rose engage a Hollywood agent, suggesting John Weber of the
William Morris Agency.

less a reflection of the energy, skill and dedication of the men who had contributed their efforts, and money, to a selfless expression of compassion and commitment. **(B)**

As a local fund-raising campaign, especially given the competing claims of wartime, it was perhaps unprecedented. It could not have worked out better. But events were about to take an unexpected and potentially tragic turn. As the enthusiasm grew, and the excitement reached a crescendo, a decision made long ago by the teenage Maurice Rose was about to threaten the whole effort. While everyone's intentions were good and honorable—indeed motivated by the highest values—the result would be painful for those who were closest to the fallen hero, especially his widow.

Months before, a chance visit by a chaplain started a chain of events that threatened both the fundraising campaign and the peace of Rose's survivors. Rabbi Abraham J. Elefant had only been in Germany for a few days when he heard from another chaplain, that Major General Rose, "the Jewish General who was killed," was buried just twenty miles away under a Christian cross. He went with Chaplain Arthur Brody to the cemetery at Ittenbach and without any formal authorization removed the Cross and replaced it with a Star of David. The two men said the *Kaddish*, or prayer for the dead, over the grave of Maurice Rose, and those of the other Jews buried there, and returned to their base.

The next day Rabbi Elefant wrote his parents back in Ohio about the episode.[21] The elder Rabbi Elefant then wrote Sam Rose about what had happened. The general fund solicitation campaign for the hospital was about to open, and whispers about the cross, intermarriage, conversion, etc. had begun to surface. Sam, counseled by Arnold and others close to the Rose Hospital campaign, released Rabbi Elefant's letter for publication in order to "silence idle tongues and malicious rumor mongers."[22]

The rumors and the heated words did not abate. Soon after the fundraising campaign gained national recognition, editorials started to appear in several Jewish publications that were critical of using Maurice Rose as a "Jewish" symbol. On the opposing side were others who decried the "nefarious libel against General Rose," namely, that he had converted to

---

B The men who led the General Rose Memorial Hospital Association were prominent leaders of the Denver Jewish Community. Maurice Schwayder and Max Goldberg, in particular, were largely responsible for the fundraising, advertising, and the administration of the hospital in the early years. They did this voluntarily, at great personal cost, spending considerable time traveling and in other activities.

Star of David placed over Rose's grave by Rabbi Elefant, April 1945
(*Source:* Rose Family Album)

Christianity.[23] Concern mounted that the emerging controversy might hurt the Rose Memorial Hospital. The discovery of the cross on the grave and its replacement with a star, however, was only the beginning.

A month after V-E Day, Rabbi Elefant was transferred to Verdun, France. At 2330 hours, one early June night, he was reading when he heard some men asking for a place to sleep. One of the visitors was Lt. Col. Paul Maurer, chaplain of the 3rd Armored Division, and the man who had buried Maurice Rose at Ittenbach under the cross.

During their conversation, Chaplain Maurer told Rabbi Elefant that Rose had attended Protestant services in the field and had never identified himself as a Jew. Colonel Maurer could shed no light on whether Maurice Rose had ever "officially" changed religions. The two men agreed, after some strong statements by the rabbi, to leave the Jewish star in place.[24] But Chaplain Maurer had had another conversation with a Jewish chaplain earlier, and that discussion threatened to be ruinous to the hospital fundraising effort, and indeed to the reputations of those who had supported it in good faith.

Rabbi Sidney M. Lefkowitz had served as a chaplain in combat with "Lightning Joe" Collins' VII Corps during the European Campaign. Because 3rd Armored had no Jewish chaplain on the Continent, it was part of his responsibility to minister to its men and conduct services in the field, which he did regularly. After the Battle of the Bulge at the end of January 1945, he met with General Rose for a half-hour during which time the general never mentioned either his father or his faith. When the rabbi recounted this experience, Chaplain Mauer told him that General Rose had converted to Christianity, married Virginia according to the Episcopal rite, and as a Protestant, was buried properly under a Latin cross.

When news of the hospital fundraising campaign and the use of Maurice Rose as a great "Jewish" symbol reached him six months later, Rabbi Lefkowitz was very upset. Having buried many Jewish boys, and having seen Nordhausen Concentration Camp with his own eyes, he was not inclined to sit idly by while "the attempt to reconvert General Rose to Judaism" went forward, no matter how good the cause. He wrote an impassioned letter to Edward Grusd, editor of B'nai Brith's national journal.[25]

The men running the Rose Hospital fundraising project knew that Rabbi Lefkowitz's letter was potentially very destructive to their efforts if it went unchallenged. They were extremely sensitive, especially since they had enlisted the support of the very editors who were now hearing another side of the Rose story.[26] Max Goldberg, who had single-handedly rallied the press and run the publicity for the project, described the letter as

> ... dynamite and would result only in harm to the General Rose project, to the people who have contributed to it, and would reflect unfavorably upon the Jewish people of America.[27]

Sensitivity to the lingering reality of anti-Semitism, especially surrounding fundraising, also played a part. The counterattack was swift and emphatic.

The substance of the response largely reflected the work of Robert S. Gamzey, the editor of the *Intermountain Jewish News*, who had written extensively about Maurice Rose. He was close to the Rose family and, based on interviews with them, he denied each of Rabbi Lefkowitz's points. The essence of the argument was that in spite of some contrary evidence, Maurice Rose "had remained faithful to the faith of his fathers to the day of his tragic death."[28] Specifically, Maurice Rose was born of Jewish parents, educated in the traditions and rituals of the religion, there was no evidence of a formal conversion, he had his son circumcised, and he was buried in accordance with Jewish Law.[29]

Whatever the truth of the conclusion, the army position would turn out to be that "officially" Maurice Rose was, by his own choice, a Christian. That determination, however, was yet to be made. The controversy was still at a manageable level, but as the leaders began to plan for the groundbreaking ceremony and construction, the implications of Rabbi Lefkowitz's letter were still a threat to their endeavor. If it received widespread distribution, there was no telling what the fallout might be.

Finally, there was no alternative but to try to persuade Rabbi Lefkowitz to back off. Max Goldberg, President of the Denver B'nai Brith chapter, lead spokesman to the press, and a major player in the Hospital Association, took the initiative. He wrote back to Ed Grusd, the man who had originally received Rabbi Lefkowitz's letter.

> I hope you do not think we are presuming too much in requesting Chaplain Lefkowitz to please cooperate with us. Surely nothing can be gained by releasing such information. In the first place, his charges cannot be proven entirely true. Secondly, such information mentioned publicly or privately can only result in bringing incalculable damage to everyone who has boosted, endorsed, or publicized this memorial.
>
> I appreciate ever so much the position you are taking regarding this (*Lefkowitz's*) letter, and want to reassure you again that everything we have done has been with the best of intentions and in the best of faith.[30]

The direct appeal worked. Neither Rabbi Lefkowitz, nor anyone else, stepped up the level of the controversy. By mid November, the crisis had passed and with $800,000 pledged, plans for construction of the hospital proceeded and ground was broken in August 1946.[31] True enough, the public emphasis on Rose as a "Jewish" hero moderated considerably after the scare in favor of a more secular approach.

The cornerstone was laid on August 30, 1948, and Dwight D. Eisenhower delivered the dedication address. For this celebrated event, numerous people connected with Maurice Rose were invited to attend, but sadly two who were ignored were Venice Hanson Rose and her son, 1st Lieutenant Maurice Rose, then serving in the Marine Corps. Arnold Rose was certainly the person responsible for family invitations and this apparently deliberate oversight was unforgivable in the eyes of the twenty-three-year old officer and his mother. More than fifty years later, he still felt the impact of the slight, "I harbored a deep, deep resentment towards the Rose family for not inviting me to the hospital dedication for my

Jewish War Veterans' cartoon celebrating Maurice Rose
(*Source:* Rose Family Album)

father, but I got over it, finally, after many years had passed."[32] The General Rose Memorial Hospital opened its doors on March 1, 1949, and for more than fifty years, through expansions, changes in name and ownership, it has served the Denver community, most recently as the Columbia Rose Medical Center.

As the first anniversary of the death of Maurice Rose approached, it appeared that the hero would rest in peace and glory under a Star of David, forever. That was not to be, but the final scenes of the story were played out not against the glare of public view, but in the private pain of the surviving family members.

Mrs. Virginia Rose left Denver in late May 1945 for Junction City, Kansas, to stay with her mother. It was there that she received her husband's personal effects and final paycheck of $435.50. That, her furniture and other belongings, and her husband's standard $10,000 GI insurance policy, was all the material wealth she had from her nearly eleven years of marriage. **(C)** She faced the prospect of raising her four-year-old son alone and with limited resources.

While in Kansas, Virginia received word that her father-in-law, Rabbi Samuel Rose, had passed away. The *Denver Post* obituary (dated July 10, 1945) mentioned that her husband's first-born son, Maurice, was serving with the Marines. Because of the growing strains in her relationship with brother-in-law Arnold, she contacted her army-appointed liaison officer to obtain the young man's address from the War Department and learned that he was stationed at Quantico, Virginia.

In spite of her own grief, she thought of "the other Maurice" and wrote a heartfelt letter of condolence. As fate would have it, the letter arrived on August 29, 1945, the same day he received his commission as a nineteen-year old 2nd Lieutenant in the U.S. Marine Corps. Her gesture, however, did not elicit a direct response. The requirements of graduation, the round of farewells to fellow classmates, and arranging for his move to his next duty assignment left the young officer with no time for letter writing. He set the note aside, as he had more pressing tasks than replying to a stranger that he had only met once in his lifetime. Even that encounter was filled with ambivalence; that summer day in 1936 was also the single time in his life that he recalled actually being with his father. Even so, such events can have lasting effects and more than fifty-six years later, Maurice

---

C Maurice Rose's will was written when he was stationed at Fort Knox, Kentucky, in 1942. His estate did not require any probate filing.

"Mike" Rose expressed regret that he had not replied to Virginia's letter to thank her for her thoughtfulness and consideration.[33]

When Virginia received the footlockers containing General Rose's souvenirs, decorations, and personal effects, the memories of their life together came flooding back, along with the pain. The physical objects told the story of his life at war and his connection to her. There was the general's typewriter, the instrument of his link to her; the Nazi flag and bust of Hitler taken from Cologne; the medals, insignia, and of course, she had his letters and now also those she had written to him. The bulky stack of V-mails and envelopes, carefully bound together by his hand, contained the written record of her love and passionate longing for him. Almost every day, in spite of combat, exhaustion, and the terrible demands of command, he had written of his love and she had answered with equal fidelity. That written legacy, now complete with her letters, and their photo album, was all that remained of their life together.

But she wanted more; at least, she wanted to be able to visit his grave. During Colonel Smith's visit to the United States in late September 1945, she told him that she wanted the general to be buried at Arlington National Cemetery.[34] More than two years passed before the army began the systematic repatriation of fallen soldiers to the United States. By that time the general's remains had been moved from the cemetery at Ittenbach,

Maurice Rose and son, "Mike," 1936, Salt Lake City, Utah
(*Source:* Colonel Maurice "Mike" Rose, USMC, Retired)

Germany, and temporarily interred at the U.S. Military Cemetery at Margraten, The Netherlands on August 23, 1945, under a temporary wooden Star of David marker.[35]

On November 17, 1947, Virginia, who had by then moved to San Antonio, Texas, received the details of the official Return of World War II Dead Program. On December 2, 1947, she wrote that in accordance with his Last Will and Testament, she wanted her late husband to be buried at Arlington National Cemetery. **(D)** Just as the process of disinterment, shipment, and reburial was about to begin, however, Mrs. Rose abruptly changed her mind. On August 4, 1948, she sent a telegram requesting that her husband be buried permanently overseas.[36]

The reasons for this radical reversal on so sensitive a matter are not known. Perhaps the pain and lingering resentment over how the Jewish community—and the Rose family—had viewed her was still a factor. In fact, Arnold Rose had also made inquiries about the repatriation of her husband's remains, and he knew of her plans to rebury General Rose at Arlington in an Episcopalian ceremony.[37] Perhaps she feared a replay of the controversial "Jewish" issue that had arisen during the hospital campaign, or that her husband's grave would become a kind of symbol that by its very nature would exclude her and her son.

The decision to leave Maurice Rose at Margraten Cemetery, however, was final. On September 27, 1949, she received notification from Major General H. Feldman, the Quartermaster General of the U.S. Army, that her husband had been permanently interred at Margraten. "Customary military funeral services" had been held and a temporary marker—a Star of David—had been placed over the grave.[38] She wondered if she—or Maurice Rose—would ever have peace.

Several days after Mrs. Rose received the letter from General Feldman an official inquiry was initiated by the American Battlefield Monuments Commission—the agency charged with placing a final marker over the graves of the fallen—into the religion of Maurice Rose. **(E)** It didn't take long to find out that Rose had declared himself a Christian on numerous occasions, beginning on September 26, 1918.[39] The original marker over his grave—a Latin cross—had been correctly placed and the replacement by

---

D There is no such request in the Last Will and Testament of Maurice Rose.

E It is not clear what precipitated the inquiry; there is no correspondence in Maurice Rose's Individual Deceased Personnel File (IDPF) requesting such an investigation.

a Star of David (by Rabbi Elefant) had been unauthorized. The temporary re-interment under that symbol, the certification of Rose's religion by the Jewish Welfare Board, and the permanent interment at Margraten in a Jewish ceremony had all been mistakes. On November 29, 1949, the Army wrote to Mrs. Rose one final time.

> A recent review of the official records maintained on the General throughout his Army career shows that on numerous occasions over a period of twenty-three years he had listed his religious preference as Protestant; we are, therefore, in error in having marked his grave with a Star of David.[40]

After all the controversy, the heated words, and the pain, the hero would finally rest in peace. Under the symbol that had united them in marriage, the emblem of the faith that had sustained her through her life, and his death, and under which she would raise their child, he would rest forever. It tempered her grief, if only a small bit. It no longer mattered to Sam Rose and neither Katy nor Arnold would ever visit the grave marked by a religious symbol that was not their own.

The records were changed. A permanent Latin cross was placed over Plot C, Grave #1, Row #1. On the memorial is inscribed the simple legend that marks the World War II graves of those whose names are known:

MAURICE ROSE
MAJ. GEN   3 ARMD DIV
COLORADO   MARCH 30 1945

Appendix I

Panama's Irregular Cavalry

by Captain Maurice Rose, Cavalry

The maneuvers in the Panama Canal Department, probably the most strenuous, comprehensive, and instructive maneuvers that have ever been completed under peacetime conditions by any organization of the United States Army, are over. Organizations had been marched day and night, many day's marches were up to nearly twenty-five miles, food was limited, and hunger and privation were the order of the day, not because the service of supply had failed but because major General Harold B. Fiske placed his command into the field on a war-time basis. War conditions existed, war rations were issued, and the command proved itself ready for—anything.

There was one element which forcibly injected itself into the picture of the Departmental maneuvers, and which through its typical cavalry activities caused Brigadier General John W. Gulick, commander of the provisional Coast Artillery Brigade, to announce in substance at the main critique that the provisional cavalry organization operating under his command had rendered invaluable assistance, convincing him that there should be a detachment of mounted troops in the Department.

It is not my intention to enter into a discussion of the entire maneuver, which lasted between three and four weeks, but rather to mention the operations which our branch is more vitally concerned with (i.e., the operations of mounted troops in the Panama Canal Department).

The enemy, commanded by Major General Lytle Brown, and consisting generally of the 14th Infantry, 33rd Infantry, 2nd Field Artillery, 11th

Engineers, and necessary supply units, had been disgustingly successful and our friendly troops, generally known as the 1st Provisional Coast Artillery Brigade, commanded by General Gulick, had been forced to retire to a position generally along the line extending through Cerro Corozal to the north and south and prepare for a desperate defense. The Department Commander at this time placed at the disposal of the Commanding General of the 1st Provisional Coast Artillery Brigade the facilities of the Panama Pacific General Depot, which under some conditions would not have proven a very serious factor from the standpoint of fire and manpower, but in the Corozal Depot it was a serious factor, because for the past four years the troops of the Depot, under command of Colonel George Williams, Cavalry, have not been known as Depot troops but as the First Provisional Depot Regiment, which were "soldiers first and specialists afterwards." And it was these troops that occupied the "center of the line," bore the brunt of the enemy penetration, and performed their infantry duties in a manner to call for the commendation of the higher commanders.

One other arm remained at Corozal to be utilized for the desperate defense ordered by the Department Commander. The native polo ponies placed under the command of Colonel Williams for exercise, care, and supervision were organized into a provisional troop of cavalry mounted by men of the various services with riding experience, commanded by the author and, with 1st Lieutenant John L. Horner, Jr., of the Quartermaster remount service as second in command, were offered to General Gulick, to assist him in his defense of the Panama Pacific General Depot, the locks at Miraflores, and Pedro Miguel.

The night of March 24th–25th, was a perfect tropical night, especially designed for gay caballeros to whisper sweet nothings into the ears of coy señoritas to the accompaniment of the dulcet strains of strummed guitars instead of the typical phrases so familiar to the cavalry picket line, overheard in the vicinity of the Corozal stables as ponies were saddled, grain packed, and blank ammunition issued to the command which in appearance, closely resembled the aggregation of a Pancho Villa, Sandino, or perhaps even Jesse James.

At five o'clock on the morning of March 25th, the provisional cavalry troop left Corozal charged with the mission of locating and determining the disposition of the enemy force.

The troop moved with its axis generally along the Panama National Highway, and sent an officer's patrol through the Corundu Military

Reservation, via trails, to locate the enemy force whose whereabouts were unknown. At about 9:00 a.m. the point of the enemy advance guard was encountered on the National Highway and captured. Very valuable information was obtained and telephoned to brigade headquarters by utilizing commercial telephones.

The continuation of the reconnaissance along the National Highway led to the enemy in bivouac in the vicinity of Matias Hernandez and, by the use of high-handed methods, the exact location of the various regiments was determined and immediately communicated to the brigade commander.

The next mission assigned the "troop" commander was to "cover the outpost line and act according to your own judgment and training as a cavalryman." This is the sort of an order we all love to receive. Being given a mission and allowed to work out the details is really a perfect "set-up" which we too seldom encounter.

Troop headquarters were established at "stone bridge." Cavalry patrols operated in front of the outpost line of the 1st Coast Artillery. The enemy attempted to take the bridge but was driven back across the river. Covered by the fire of the coast artillery outpost, the "troop" charged across the bridge three times and succeeded in capturing the entire section of the enemy which proved to be a covering detachment sent out to reconnoiter the position in the vicinity of the stone bridge.

Before the end of the maneuvers, the cavalry had captured prisoners from each regiment in the line and, through information brought to the Commanding General of the Coast Artillery Brigade had enabled him to determine the exact formation to be utilized by the enemy in the attack.

The night before the attack, sent on a mission to determine the location of the command post of General Brown and the location of the 2nd Field Artillery, the embryo Cavalry troop was able to gain the information desired, cut the wires leading to the command post of the enemy commander, and capture and bring back, through the city of Panama, the enemy water purification truck and three additional trucks.

On the morning of March 27th, the missions of the Cavalry were independent and they were permitted to operate where they could do the most harm. The enemy attack was launched at 10:00 a.m., but before and during the attack the cavalry made itself felt. Frequent raids were made on infantry, consisting of riding into them while they were deploying and scattering them or causing them to seek cover; but the high point of the entire operation took place when a mounted patrol, commanded by the troop commander and consisting of one other officer, Lieutenant Horner, and six men, while on an independent mission in rear of the enemy line of departure, encountered the commanding officer of the enemy motor convoy and engineer pack train, resting on the bridge over the Corundu River in the vicinity of the Bull ring and about 100 yards from his train, but out of their sight. The commanding officer of the train was immediately captured and forced to surrender his train. Some forty trucks, numerous passenger cars, two trucks equipped with antiaircraft machine guns, and sufficient men to handle them were a part of the spoils of this raid. A discussion with the chief umpire and a brief resume of the circumstances brought forth the welcome information that the capture of the train would be credited to the Coast Artillery Brigade as having been brought in by their mounted patrol.

Since the completion of this maneuver, I have had time to ponder why there is no cavalry in Panama. Of all the places imaginable this is the one where the mounted man should serve. Mechanization is splendid, but cannot operate in the jungles and trails, which exist throughout this isthmus, off the highway. If this small provisional group could have operated in a manner which merited the favorable comments of the Department and Sector Commanders, it is conclusive that a well-trained mounted organization would be highly beneficial to assist in the defense of the canal. The wet season in Panama is extremely prolonged but even in the dry season motors cannot operate off the main trails or highways, and in wet season no wheeled transportation can negotiate most of the trails. But the horse will always go through. We too few cavalrymen in Panama are pleased and enthused with the success of our mounted activities during these maneuvers and have shown higher authority what mounted troops can accomplish here. In every action entered into by the provisional troop, no advantage was taken of the fact that only blank ammunition was used or that we were operating from horseback. Every tactical movement would have the approval of the faculty of the Cavalry School. It was our intention to prove that the use of the horse cavalry in Panama is desirable and we cannot help but feel that we have done so.

An Operation of the 3rd Armored ("Spearhead") Division

by Major General Maurice Rose
Commanding General, 3rd Armored
("Spearhead") Division

The tactical doctrine of the United States Army embodies teachings which caution commanders and staffs against several types of operations. Fortunately this doctrine has not become dogma, for, on occasions, it becomes expedient and necessary to execute certain of these operations. At times the expediency is dictated by a command decision, wherein tactical details are subordinated to the broader strategic perspective. At other times, there is little or no choice afforded the commander, who must accomplish his mission with the forces he has regardless of the type of operation involved. This article proposes to present one case in point taken from the combat experiences of the 3rd Armored Division in France and Belgium.

In order to set this story in its proper time-and-space framework it is well to review briefly the sequence of events leading to the operation with which we are concerned.

While the German Seventh Army was being pummeled to ineffective fragments by the U.S. First Army in the Falaise-Argentan area, the armor of the U.S. Third Army was running almost at will over western France, and by long hops had reached the Seine River south of Paris.

With the mopping up of the Ranes-Fromentel area, the 3rd Armored ("Spearhead") Division completed its part in the Falaise Gap operation on 19 August 1944. Then, after a two-day period of maintenance and refitting, the division moved, without opposition, though Chartres to the vicinity of Corbeil and Melun, arriving on 24 August 1944, and prepared to cross the Seine River. When the 1st and 9th Infantry Divisions closed into assembly areas nearby, the U.S. VII Corps was poised and ready to begin the pursuit that carried from the Seine River to the Siegfried Line in eighteen days.

Spearheading this historic drive, the 3rd Armored Division crossed the Seine River at Tilly and just south of Corbeil on 26 August 1944. Spreading into multiple columns, the division pushed through the shell that the enemy was holding stubbornly around the 4th Infantry Division's bridgehead east of the Seine, and moved swiftly to the east and northeast. The enemy was withdrawing too rapidly to offer strong resistance, but was found on all routes holding road blocks at all favorable points. He opened fire on the armored columns from concealed positions only to find himself quickly overrun or bypassed, contained, and left to be dealt with by the closely following infantry. Parts of the 48th German Infantry Division, the 9th Panzer Division, and an extensive assortment of other enemy troops were encountered. Several enemy columns were overtaken moving in the direction of the 3rd Armored's advance. These columns were engaged, and as a result never reached the predesignated assembly areas of their battered units.

Initially, elements of the 4th Cavalry Group combed a broad front with a reconnaissance screen out in the lead; the 1st and 9th Infantry Divisions followed the 3rd Armored to liquidate pockets of bypassed enemy resistance and to consolidate the gains. Soon, the task force columns of the 3rd Armored, each consisting of a reinforced tank battalion, overtook the reconnaissance elements, and it became apparent that the enemy could not hold, and had no intention of trying to hold, a consolidated defensive line. Whereupon, the cavalry elements side-slipped to the north and south and continued to screen the flanks of the corps' advance. The armored columns moved on at maximum speed, and the 1st and 9th Infantry Divisions followed the "Spearhead" generally abreast of each other, the 1st Division on the left.

On 27 August the 3d Armored ("Spearhead") Division reached the Marne River at La Ferté-sous-Jouarre where both combat commands crossed on existing bridges which were repaired and strengthened by division engineer troops. There was brief fighting for Meaux and Coulommiers. When resistance in these towns was reduced, Combat Command A and Combat Command B started moving again in task force columns toward their respective objectives of Pontarcy and Soissons to seize and secure the crossings of the Aisne River at those locations (see sketch).

Driving at such speed soon brought the 3d Armored into the heart of the enemy's communications zone, where the remnants of enemy combat troops fought in isolated and disorganized groups while other troops attempted to extricate valuable dumps and depots. Near Soissons and Braisne, elements of the division destroyed three railway trains that were evacuating personnel and equipment to move east. Tankers of one armored regiment engaged and destroyed four enemy tanks that were loaded on flat cars and manned by their crews. The attached anti-aircraft artillery battalion stopped one of these trains and raked the troop cars with their multiple .50-caliber machine guns. The countryside was littered with all types of equipment, cosmetics, clothing, and wine bottles, abandoned by the loot-laden German soldiers in their panic.

Passage through the towns and villages, so quickly evacuated by the *Wehrmacht*, was slowed markedly by milling crowds who swarmed on and about the vehicles in delirious exhibitions of their happiness.

On 28 August the Aisne River crossings at both Soissons and Pontarcy were seized intact. (The main highway bridge was destroyed by the enemy, but others to the east were intact.) A few mines had to be lifted from the approaches and the existing spans strengthened. There was increased enemy resistance along the Aisne. In addition to his small arms and mortars, the Germans used a few self-propelled and other anti-tank guns as artillery. In general, the indirect fire of these weapons was inaccurate.

The Aisne bridgehead was expanded and secured on 29–30 August by first seizing the high ground north of the river and then pushing out to the northeast to the line shown on the sketch.

In the left of the division sector on the high ground just across the river from Soissons there were extensive reinforced concrete fortifications. A considerable amount of detailed information concerning these fortifications was furnished by the FFI (Free French of Interior) troops in the area. However, anticipated trouble did not develop. The enemy was not given time to occupy and defend them.

Troops of the 3d Armored ("Spearhead") Division securing Soissons and the river crossings were relieved of these duties early on the morning of

30 August by infantry elements that had come up during the night, but even with this increase in available fighting strength, the 3d Armored ("Spearhead") Division had a rather broad front to cover in securing the proposed bridgehead line. Accordingly, the Division Reserve was committed between Combat Command A and Combat Command B. The bridgehead line was seized on 30 August 1944 and firmly held. The armored reconnaissance battalion patrolled the principal road nets within the zone to keep the small isolated enemy groups from disrupting communications.

Without waiting to be relieved on the bridgehead line by the infantry divisions who were following, the 3d Armored ("Spearhead") Division was assembled in preparation for another push to its new objective, Sedan and Charleville. Five routes (see sketch) were assigned for this advance, which began on the morning of 31 August 1944.

The composition of the columns that started for Charleville and Sedan on 31 August were:

Combat Command A
32 Armd Regt
1st Bn. 36th Armd Inf Regt
Co A, 23d Armd Engr Bn
Co A, 703d TD Bn
Co A, 45th Armd Med Bn
Det Co B, Maint Bn, 3d A. D.
67th Armd FA Bn
54th Armd FA Bn

Combat Command B
33d Armd Regt (-3d Bn)
2d Bn, 36th Armd Inf Regt
Co D, 23d Armd Engr Bn
Co B, 703d TD Bn
Det Co C, Maint Bn, 3d A. D.
391st Armd FA Bn
87th FA Bn

Division Reserve
36th Armd Inf Regt (-1st & 2d Bns)
3d Bn, 33d Armd Regt
703d TD Bn (-A and B Cos)

23d Armd Engr Bn (-A and D Cod)
Co C, 45th Armd Med Bn
Det Co A, Maint Bn, 3d A. D.
991st Armd FA Bn (155 Gun)
183d FA Bn (155 How)

Combat Commands A and B each moved in two columns. Division Reserved moved on the center route in a single column.

As on previous occasions, the enemy used the hours of darkness, while the 3d Armored was halted, to build up a thin screen of resistance with the mission of delaying the advance of the American armor. When the attack started on the morning of 31 August, this initial resistance was quickly overcome and a rapid advance was made throughout the morning.

The reconnaissance battalion advanced in the front of the division, covering the entire line and utilizing the road net to the maximum extent possible. They encountered slight resistance all along the front, much of which they reported and bypassed; even so, the prisoners they took constituted a problem.

Combat Command A crossed their line of departure at 0930 hours and moved rapidly.

Combat Command B was delayed in starting their attack because of having to assemble troops from positions held on the bridgehead line. (This circumstance later proved to be fortunate.) Their attack started at 1224, and moved initially against light resistance.

By 1300 hours the five had encountered resistance, and leading elements of the four columns of Combat Commands A and B were engaged with the enemy. Then, at 1315, a staff officer from VII Corps arrived at the command post of the 3d Armored Division near Laon. He had flown from corps headquarters located at La Rue with instructions to change the direction of attack from east to north. The new objective assigned the 3d Armored was to secure Mons. New routes of advance were through Hirson onto Vervins.

A message was sent by radio from the division command post directing the advancing columns to halt, coil off the roads, and wait further orders. Also, information concerning the change in attack plans was relayed by voice radio to the Division Commander, who was with leading elements of the division near Seraincourt. A staff officer went forward immediately with detailed information concerning the change in plans to join the Division Commander. Combat commanders were also given orders by voice radio to join the Division Commander at Seraincourt.

A meeting of the above column commanders and staff officers was accomplished, and oral orders were given by the Division Commander at 1430 hours, directing a change in routes of advance for the columns, with a change in mission for the division.

When orders directing a change in mission and the route of advance were received by Task Force X of Combat Command A, this force was heavily engaged by the enemy in the vicinity of Novion Porcien. A successful disengagement from the enemy was accomplished by this force, a column reformed, and their route retraced to Hauteville, where a change in direction to the north was made.

Task Force Y of Combat Command A was fighting German rearguard forces just west of the village of Rethel, when orders were received directing the change in route of advance. The column turned northwest on the Rethel–Rozoy road with little or no resistance from the enemy, a complete disengagement with the enemy being accomplished by the change in the route of advance. By dark the forces of Combat Command A had advanced to locations approximately three miles north and northeast of Rozoy, where they bivouacked for the night.

Combat Command B columns, due to a late start on the morning of 31 August 1944, had only reached the towns of Pierrepont and Notre Dame de Liesse even though resistance was light. Their mission had been to protect the left flank of the division while advancing toward Charleville and secure the town of Vervins as an intermediate objective for the day. Consequently, when the order changing the mission for the division was received, no change in direction of the routes of Combat Command B had to be made. By dark the columns of Combat Command B had reached Marle and Hary where they bivouacked for the night.

The Division Reserve, moving in a single column and between Combat Commands A and B, received orders to halt their advance to the east, coil forward with the rear of their column, and wait orders. This halt was made in a wooded area just west of Herbigny. After receipt of orders directing their route of advance be turned north, they proceeded along the secondary road toward Chaumont and Wadimont with an assigned mission of securing Hirson. A well-defended roadblock stopped the advance of the column just north of Wadimont. This block was not reduced prior to dark, so the Division Reserve bivouacked for the night at this location.

When night came the combat commands and Division Reserve were again in contact with even stronger enemy forces than those met during the morning, but had made good progress toward the new objective.

The division's reconnaissance battalion, moving north from the farthest points of advance toward Sedan and Verdun, provided a screen on the right flank of the division. They moved in multiple columns on the secondary road net.

When the advance continued north on 1 September 1944, enemy resistance became more stubborn along the entire front. Combat Command A fought its way to Avesnes, while Combat Command B pushed through Vervins and La Chapelle, reaching a position directly west of Avesnes. Division Reserve reached and held Hirson.

On the following day the attack continued, with Division Reserve moving on the right flank in two columns. By 1900 hours, Combat Command A had reached Mons, and a little later Combat Command B and Division Reserve reached their objectives on the western and eastern sides of the city. A system of roadblocks was established on all routes leading through Mons that night. Enemy pressure from west to east became stronger. The successful change in direction of attack of the 3d Armored ("Spearhead") Division and the speed of execution of this maneuver placed this division directly across the escape route of a retreating German army. The Battle of Mons for World War II had begun.

Correspondence between Rose and General Dwight D. Eisenhower

Dear General Rose:

From time to time I find short stories where some reporter is purportedly quoting non-commissioned officers in our tank formations to the effect that our men, in general, consider our tanks very inferior in quality to those of the Germans. I realize that these sometimes spring from the human tendency to make startling statements in the hope that out of them will come a bit of publicity and self-notoriety. Possibly, also, certain reporters sometimes support their own views on such matters as these by quoting only those statements that support such views.

My own experience in talking to our junior officers and enlisted men in armored formations is about as follows:

Our men, in general, realize that the Sherman is not capable of standing up in a ding-dong, head-on fight with a Panther. Neither in gun power nor in armor is the present Sherman justified in undertaking such a contest. On the other hand, most of them realize that we have got a job of shipping tanks overseas and therefore do not want unwieldly monsters; that our tank has great reliability, good mobility, and that the gun in it has been vastly improved. Most of them feel also that they have developed tactics that allow them to employ their superior numbers to defeat the Panther tank as long as they are not surprised and can discover the Panther before it has gotten in three or four good shots. I think that most of them know also that we have improved models coming out which even in head-on action are not helpless in front of the Panther and the Tiger.

The above, however, are mere impressions I have gained through casual conversations. I am writing you and General White of the 2nd Armored Division identical letters with the request that at your earliest convenience you write me an informal letter giving me: (a) Your own personal convictions about the quality of our tank equipment as compared to the German, and having in mind the necessity of our shipping our materiel over long distances to get it to the battlefield; (b) Your opinion as to the ability of the new T-26 with the 90 mm gun, to meet the Panther on equal terms, and (c) A digest of the opinions of your tank commanders, drivers, gunners, and so on, on these general subjects.

Please do not take the time to make a general staff study out of this matter. If you could include a few quotes from experienced non-commissioned officers it might be helpful to my purpose as I want to tell the truth about these matters to the War Department rather than to allow any misconceptions to prevail.

Please mark the outside of your letter "Personal"

With warm regards,

Sincerely,

Gen. Dwight D. Eisenhower

P.S. Comparison in other types of equipment would be helpful; i.e., half-tracks, light tanks, trucks, guns, bazookas, even clothing.

HEADQUARTERS THIRD ARMORED DIVISION
Office of the Commanding General

A.P.O. #253, U.S. ARMY
21 March 1945

Dear General Eisenhower:

Referring to your letter of 18 March that reached me yesterday, I submit the following information in the form that you have suggested:

a. It is my personal conviction that the present M4 and M4A3 tank is inferior to the German Mark V. I recognize the problem of shipping our equipment over long distances, but am basing my remarks purely from the points of view of comparing our medium tank with the German tank that we are constantly meeting on the battlefield. The fact that the M4 and M4A3 is inferior to the Mark V is borne out by the excessive number of losses we took while fighting in Belgium in December and January. The question naturally arises as to how I can account for the fact that in all of our operations against German armor we have been successful if the statements I have heretofore made are to be accepted. The answer is that we compensate for our inferior equipment by the efficient use of artillery, air support, and maneuver, and in final analysis a great step toward equalizing our equipment is taken by the individual tanker and gunner, who maneuvers his tank and holds his fire until he is in a position most favorable for him. There is no question in my mind but what our gunnery is far superior to that of the Germans, and the instructions that are emphasized in this Division are that our tankers will hold their fire until they are within 800 to 1,000 yards of the enemy tank. This of course is not always possible, and it is often necessary, due to terrain which offers no covered avenues of approach, for our tanks to engage the enemy at greater ranges, and the outcome under those conditions is usually to our disadvantage. A large number of enemy tanks are destroyed by our artillery and also by the fighter bombers, whose efficient operation has always been a material assistance to us. I have personally observed on a number of occasions, the projectiles fired by our 75 and 76mm guns bouncing off the front plate of Mark V tanks at ranges of about 600 yards. Engaging enemy tanks in this manner has been made necessary, due to the canalizing of the avenue of approach of both the German and our tank, which did not permit maneuver.

b. It is my opinion that the new T26 with its 90mm gun is capable of meeting the Panther tank on equal terms. The 90mm gun in the new T26 is still inferior in muzzle velocity. General Barnes, who recently visited us, however, stated that the future arrivals of the T26 would have higher muzzle velocity. We have made limited use of the T26 in combat, and found them highly desirable. We lost one T26 by anti-tank fire, and I know of two Mark V's that were destroyed by fire from this new tank.

c. The following digest of opinions of tank commanders and other personnel in the Division represent, I believe, a good cross-section of the opinions that you have requested:

(1) Lt. Colonel E. W. Blanchard, 0341405, has been a tank battalion commander since "D"-18: "The only Panthers I have seen, not knocked out by our artillery or our air, were either abandoned or destroyed by their

crews, or had been hit by our tanks at very close ranges. Personally, I have seen only one Mark V knocked out by our 75mm. Discounting our air and supporting artillery, we defeat the German tanks by our weight in sheer numbers of tanks and men. The T26s are comparable to the Panther in armor and gun. Its mobility is, I think, superior."

(2) Staff Sergeant Harry W. Wiggins, 37130158, Company "F," 33rd Armored Regiment. This Staff Sergeant has participated in all actions of this Division: "I have seen very few Panthers knocked out by the M4. The air seems to have gotten most of them. I have fired at 150 yards at a Panther (6 rounds—4 APs and 2Hes) without a penetration. This of course was at the front of the Panther, with a 75mm. We manage to get within effective range of German tanks because they are generally hiding or camouflaged, and we try to engage them within a couple of hundred yards. We had more speed than the Panther, but we bog down too easily. I like the 76mm better than the 75, although it still does not have the muzzle velocity that I want. I like the silhouette of the new T26, and the gun impresses me, as it is superior to our 75. All in all, I'd say we could win the war without M4, but it would take a lot of them, and personnel too."

(3) Staff Sergeant William G. Wilson, 36321891, Company "D," 33rd Armored Regiment. This Staff Sergeant has been in all operations of this Division and now commands a T26:

"The Mark V is way out ahead of our M4, in thickness and design of armor, and its gun. I think we have more speed and mobility than the Panther. I have seen M4s knock Panthers out at ranges under 800 yards (firing at the side of the enemy tanks), but it took a lot of nerve to stand there and pump out many rounds before getting a definite penetration. Our new T26 is better. It has a lower outline and good maneuverability. Its gun is better than the Panthers, although I would like more muzzle velocity. We could win this war using our present M4, as we have so many, but I prefer more T26s."

(4) Staff Sergeant Robert M. Early, 17048266, Company "E," 32nd Armored Regiment:

"I am a tank commander and have had nine months' combat experience. I have had a 76 tank for five months, and a 75 tank for three months. I have had a 90 tank about one month. I haven't any confidence in an M4. Jerry armament will knock out an M4 as far as they can see it. If the T26 was armed in weak spots by putting assault tank armor on it, we'd have a tank superior to Jerry. The 90mm gun is far superior to what we have had.

I believe the T26 will make us more equal to the Jerry tank; it has good flotation and maneuverability. I'd like to increase the angle and thickness of the front slope plate on the T26."

(5) Corporal Albert E. Wilkinson, 39402006, Company "F," 32nd Armored Regiment:

"I have been a 75mm gunner for nine months in combat, and have lost one tank by enemy fire. We can't compare with the Jerry tank. We haven't got the armor nor gun. I have fired a ricochet off a Mark IV at 500 yards. Luckily, he had his turret turned the other way. On Jerry armor my gun is ineffective over 500 to 600 yards. We are OK on maneuverability, but Jerry can turn sharper and has more climbing power. He has wider track and can go places we can't. The T26 will put us upon level as far as gun goes; as far as armor goes we are out-classed. I'd like to see a 90 on an assault tank, and a crew would feel it had a chance to fight. When you have fire power that can fight, no matter if you don't have the armor, but when you have neither, you sweat it out.

(6) Private John A. Danforth, 36884252, Company 32nd Armored Regiment:

"I have been a gunner for nine months in combat with a 75 gun. I have had two tanks shot out from under me, and I think we don't have enough gun. The people who build tanks I don't think know the power of the Jerry gun. I have seen a Jerry gun fire through two buildings, penetrate an M4 tank, and go through another building. I like the 90 on the T26, but I want more armor. I'd like to see some sort of reinforcement, perhaps cement, to stop Jerry bazookas."

(7) Tec/4 Jerome O. Hararklu, 36234566, Company "I," 32nd Armored Regiment:

"I have been a driver in combat for nine months and had two tanks disabled by enemy fire. We don't have enough armor plate nor fire power. Tanks with radial engines are unmaneuverable as compared with Ford. I had a penetration on the right side of my tank at about 2,200 yards."

(8) Lt Colonel Matthew W. Kane, 1st Battalion, 32nd Armored Regiment:

"I am a tank battalion commander, and have had six months' combat experience. This battalion has lost 84 tanks through enemy action in nine months of combat. In a tank versus tank action, our M4 tank if woefully lacking in armor and armament when pitted against the super velocity 75mm or 88mm gun of the German tank. Greater maneuverability and speed have failed to compensate for this deficiency, and our tank losses in the Belgian Bulge were relatively high, even when we were in defensive positions. Crews recognized the deficiencies in our tanks, and know that success on the battlefield is attributable to our superiority in numbers of tanks, and resolve to sustain heavy casualties in men and tanks in order to gain objectives.

Relative to the other equipment that you referred to in your "P.S.," I submit the following:

a. Our half-track is a superior vehicle and when utilized as intended, to transport infantry, mounted, in rapidly moving situations, it is highly effective, and I can think of no change that I would like to make in its construction.

b. In my opinion there is no place in an armored division for a light tank whose principal weapon is a 35mm. The new M24 with its 75mm gun is an excellent vehicle for the reconnaissance battalion and the reconnaissance companies within the armored regiments. I would like very much to have my M5 light tanks and the armored cars all replaced by the M24.

c. Our trucks and all general purpose vehicles are far superior to any that I have ever observed being used by the Germans, and are entirely satisfactory for our uses.

d. With the exception of what I have heretofore stated regarding weapons, our guns are excellent and I can think of no point upon which I would fault them.

e. Our bazookas do not have penetrating capabilities that we desire. They are inferior to the German bazooka. Many of our personnel have received instructions and are using the German *Panzerfaust*, and find them much more effective than the bazooka issued to them.

f. Relative to the matter of clothing, I recommend that a uniform similar to our present combat suit, probably more efficiently lined for cold weather, be adopted for all personnel in an armored Division, and that a similar suit, unlined and of lighter texture, be utilized for summer wear. This would standardize the uniform in any armored division. I was astounded to see the many types of garments that are now being worn. At a division assembly held last Sunday for the purpose of decorating members of this division, I was astounded to see the many types of garments that were represented in a formation of some 300 men, and upon inquiry was assured by my Quartermaster that all the garments were issued equipment, and worn in the prescribed manner. I feel that the adoption of this standard type uniform, which would appear the same both in summer and winter, is highly desirable. May I further suggest that a uniform headgear, such as a beret of distinctive color, green is suggested as it is the Armored Force color, be issued to all Armored Force personnel. This would permit personnel to place their helmets on their head, over their beret without its removal, and when the helmet is removed, it would give them a uniform headgear. It would also have the additional beneficial effect of eliminating the wool knit cap. We have long felt a need of a suitable combat shoe for Armored Force personnel. One about 8 to 10 inches high, and designed to be waterproof, would be of great assistance. There are several types of combat shoes, and paratroopers boots now being worn. Paratroopers boots come the closest to being desirable, but they are not available for issue or purchase by Armored Force personnel. The new battle dress is a perfect solution for a Class "A" uniform.

I hope that I have given you the information you desire, and with kind regards, I remain,

Respectfully yours,

/s/ Maurice Rose
/t/ MAURICE ROSE,
Major General, U.S. Army,
Commanding.

GENERAL DWIGHT D. EISENHOWER,
Supreme Commander,
Headquarters SHAEF,
A.P.O. #757, U. S. Army.

DDE/nmr

27 March 1945

Dear Rose:

I am grateful indeed for the trouble you took in answering my recent letter to you so promptly and so intelligently. I feet that your conclusions on
the matter should go at once to the War Department, and I am sending
them on to General Marshall without delay.

If by any chance you have an extra carbon copy of the report you sent
to me, I should like to have it for my own files. On no account, however, are
you to have the work redone as you have already been more than courte-
ous in this matter.

Very sincerely,

Gen. Dwight D. Eisenhower

Acknowledgments

This book would not have been possible without the help and cooperation of many people, the most important of whom are the veterans. Everything begins with them; without their vital input, the pages of military history would be blank.

We are especially indebted to the men of the 2nd and 3rd Armored Divisions who gave their time in responding to letters and sitting for personal interviews. One soldier who must be singled out is Glenn H. Shaunce, General Rose's personal jeep driver. His story of the night of March 30, 1945, has never changed, nor has it ever been embellished. Every moment of that last day of his general's life is indelible and frozen in time for Glenn Shaunce, and as the only living American eyewitness, his testimony and memories are priceless.

The veterans, whose numbers are dwindling faster each day, generously answered our requests for statements covering this important and unforgettable segment of their lives. For some, reliving that period of time and recalling the violent loss of personal friends was a painful ordeal, but they wanted their stories told before they too passed on. Representing the thousands of men who experienced the triumph and tragedy of service with Maurice Rose, we give special thanks to these gallant men who served with the general. The first group are from Brigadier General Rose's headquarters, Combat Command A, 2nd Armored Division: Virgle E. Appleton, Douglas J. Donahue, Philip Geidel, Lawrence A. Hull, Earlie J. Jones, William J. Veno, Philip Reisler; others from 2nd Armored include:

MG Howard Bressler, U.S. Army (Ret.), Ray S. Guistwite, Dr. Norris Perkins, and Henry B. Thompson.

Many veterans of the 3rd Armored Division contributed to this book. They sent photos, letters, newspaper clippings, memoirs (including some that they had never shown to anyone), maps, unit histories, documents, and tapes. They sat for personal interviews at reunions and in visits to their homes. One who deserves special mention is Olin F. Brewster, now gone, who was unstinting in his belief that this story should be told and who lent every available assistance, and whose personal drama runs parallel to the life of Maurice Rose. Others who should be mentioned include: Claude Ball, Jack Boulger, Edward S. Boyden, Angelo Cali, William A. Castille, Belton Y. Cooper, Charlie Corbin, William Edie, William Gaynor, Nate Goldberg, Henry Gosch, Arthur Hauschild, LeRoy Hanneman, Samuel E. Hogan, Syd Johnson, Leonard Mainiero, Walter B. May, Robert L. Milnes, Robert A. Pacios, Richard Raabe, Walter B. Richardson, Robert W. Russell, William Ruth, Clarence Smoyer, Rev. Walter B. Stitt, Wesley A. Sweat, Harley B. Swenson, Jack K. Warden, David Wolf, and Robert Zimmerman. In addition, Elliott Goldstein, Executive Officer, 589th Field Artillery Bn, 106th infantry Division, provided important information about the Baraque de Fraiture action in the Battle of the Bulge. If any have been left out, please accept our apologies.

Among the military historians, librarians, and archivists who provided invaluable assistance, Martin Blumenson deserves special praise. From the beginning, he offered his sage counsel and valued criticism in addition to his constant encouragement and constructive suggestions. As one of the last of the Army's official chroniclers of World War II, he holds a special place in our country's history and his work on Normandy and the Italian Campaign will always be regarded as definitive. LTC Haynes Dugan, US Army (Ret.), wartime Asst. G-2 (Intelligence) on General Rose's staff, and Historian of the 3rd Armored Division Association, was the first to offer encouragement and support and provided a tremendous amount of information that brought to life the general's day to day activities. His introductions to other veterans opened doors that might very well have remained closed to the authors. Dr. Ralph Greene's article in *Armor Magazine* was the first serious work on the life of Maurice Rose and was very valuable for its sources. Donald E. Houston's book on the 2nd Armored Division, *Hell on Wheels*, provided excellent background on Rose's association with that division, especially his time as Chief of Staff and Commanding General, Combat Command A, in Sicily and Normandy.

A number of respected historians—whom we affectionately call "the Colonels"—also offered help and advice including LTC Roger Cirillo, U.S. Army (Ret.), LTC Carlo D'Este, U.S. Army (Ret.), LTC Edward G. Miller, U.S. Army, (Ret.), and LTC Lewis Sorley, U.S. Army, (Ret.).

Dr. Jeanne Abrams, Rocky Mountain Jewish Historical Society; William Hansen, Director of the Army's Armor School Library; William Maher and Maynard Britchford, Archivists at University of Illinois Andrew Barr 3rd Armored Division Archives; Stan Oliner, Colorado Historical Society; Dan Peterson, Curator, 1st AD Museum; and John M. Purdy, Director of the Patton Museum of Armor at Fort Knox all contributed valuable materials and documentation.

While compiling the research for our book, we considered titling the manuscript *In The Heat of Battle—Murder or Misunderstanding* based on the Army Judge Advocate General (JAG) staff's dilemma (and our own) of determining whether or not the shooting of General Rose constituted a war crime. The results of the official investigation lay buried in Army files for more than fifty years, until Senator Dianne Feinstein (California) and Representative Christopher Cox (California, 47th District) were able to secure copies of the JAG files marked "Secret." Our sincere thanks to them for their help. As you read the details of how the shooting occurred, you can decide for yourself if it was murder or misunderstanding.

Don Clark, M.D., of Denver, Colorado, provided valuable technical support. Dr. Clark is among the nation's leading forensic pathologists, specializing in gunshot wounds, and was associated with the Denver General Hospital. His evaluation of the Army's official autopsy, especially in determining the angle and number of bullet wounds, was crucial to our interpretation of how General Rose was killed.

Special thanks to the German veterans, especially Hubert Gees, *275th Infantry Division*, for providing key documentation on the *507th Schwere Panzer Abt* (Heavy Panzer Battalion) and contacts with other German veterans; Sebastian Hupfl, and Dr. Dieter Jahn, both of the *507th Schwere Panzer Abt*, especially the latter for providing the photo of Hauptman Wolf Koltermann obtained from Frau Koltermann. Thanks also to historians Waldemar Becker, Helmet Schneider, and Albert J. Trostorf, especially for their help on the Battle of Paderborn.

We also had important help from the children of some key figures in General Rose's story, including Robert K. Bellinger, son of General Rose's aide, who provided a copy of his father's electrifying memoirs; Finley and Mary, Olin Brewster's children; Lt. General Frederick Brown III, USA (Ret), son of Rose's Artillery Commander and himself a distinguished Armor commander; David J. Fleischer, son of one of the two radio operators in General Rose's M-20 armored car who were captured on March 30, 1945; Linda Lovelady Sharp and Michael Kane, children of legendary 3rd Armored Task Force Commanders; Jeffrey S. Rose, M.D., the general's grandnephew; Maurice Roderick Rose, his son by Virginia Barringer; and Col. Maurice "Mike" Rose, USMC, Retired, his son by Venice Hanson.

Among our numerous supporters, we would like to cite Herb Fine, Robert K. McDonald, Thornton L. Oglove, Arno Lasoe, Scott Schoner, Professor Marion Rapp, Miles Siegel, Arnold Winter, and Ron van Ryjt. Of course, one of our biggest supporters is our agent, Merry Pantano of the Blanche C. Gregory Literary Agency. When we despaired that anyone would take us seriously, she appeared to remind us that we were doing something vitally important with honor and excellence. Similar sentiments apply to our editor, Michael Dorr.

Finally, only the greatest of authors could find the appropriate words for our families, Barbara, Tova, and Jordana—and Phyllis, Judy, Donna, and Gary. The time we spent unraveling the legend of Maurice Rose was time away from them. Their unfailing faith and constant words of encouragement made the hard moments bearable and their pride in our work made the whole journey worthwhile.

All these people—and more—are responsible for what makes this book good. The flaws and limitations are entirely our responsibility.

Notes

Notes for Chapter One

1. Howard Bressler, Phone Conversation with Steven L. Ossad, February 13, 1995.

2. *Spearhead in the West: The 3rd Armored Division In WW II,* Kunst and Wervedruck: Frankfort am Main, 1945 (reprinted by Battery Press, 1990).

3. Leo Kessler, *The Battle of the Ruhr Pocket,* Scarborough House, Chelsea, MI, 1989, pp. 28–29; Lewis Sorley, *Thunderbolt: General Creighton Abrams and the Army of His Times,* Simon & Schuster, NY, 1992, pp. 87–88.

4. Charles B. MacDonald, *The Last Offensive,* Office of the Chief of Military History, Washington, DC., 1973, pp. 350–351.

5. Omar N. Bradley, *A General's Life,* Simon & Schuster, NY, 1983, pg. 420.

6. Kessler, *The Battle of the Ruhr Pocket,* pg. 30.

7. Kessler, *The Battle of the Ruhr Pocket,* pg. 56. Thomas R. Henry, "Masters of Slash and Surprise; 3rd Armored Division," *Saturday Evening Post,* October 19, 1946, pg. 49

8. Russell Weigley, *Eisenhower's Lieutenants, The Campaign of France and Germany 1944–1945,* Indiana University Press, Bloomington, IN, 1981, p. 674.

9. John T. Jones, Personal Experience of John T. Jones, March 30, 1945, undated, (photocopy). In addition to Jones, Sweat and Stephenson, the original passengers in the M-20 included T/4 Wesley D. Ellison, T/4 Neil E. Fleischer, and PFC. William T. Hatry, all of the 143rd Signal Company. PFC James Omand, a motorcycle driver, "hitched" a ride later in the day.

10. Haynes W. Dugan, *Omaha Forward (Sometimes Way Forward): 3rd Armored Division, Division Headquarters in World War II,* unpublished memoir (photocopy), 1987, pg. 51.

11. Elbridge Colby, *The First Army in Europe 1943–1945,* Battery Press, Nashville, TN, 1969.

12. Kessler, *The Battle of the Ruhr Pocket,* pg. 75.

13. *Spearhead in the West,* pg. 143.

14. Huepfl, Sebastian, *Chronik of the Schwere Panzer Abteilung 507*, September 27, 1999 (photocopy); Graves, etc., *Battle of Paderborn*, British Army of the Rhine, 1985, pg. 4.

15. Hubert Gees, Personal Correspondence with Ron van Rijt, October 29, 1999; Schneider, Helmuet, *Chronik der 507th, Kämpfe Gegen U.S. Truppen von Paderborn Bis in Den Harz,* pg. 241.

16. *Das Kriegsende 1945 im Ehemaligen Hochstift Paderborn;* Interview with Wolf Koltermann for the British Army of the Rhine 40th Anniversary study of *The Battle of Paderborn*, 1985, pg. 1.

17. Haynes W. Dugan, Correspondence with Hank Sonderberg, July 4, 1992.

18. Glenn A. Shaunce, Personal Correspondence with Don R. Marsh (postmarked August 28, 1987).

19. Jones, Personal Experience, pg. 2.

20. Robert M. Bellinger, "I Was a General's Aide," 9 pp., unpublished memoir (photocopy), 1965–1966.

21. Toland, *The Last 100 Days*, pg. 321.

22. Graves, *Battle of Paderborn, March/März 1945*, pg. 15.

23. Walter W. May, *Paderborn, Unpublished Memoir*, March 21, 1994, pg. 1–2.

24. Helmuet Schneider, *Chronik der 507th*, pg. 242.

25. May, *Paderborn,* pg. 2.

26. Gees, Personal Correspondence with Ron van Rijt, (photocopy) translated by Professor Marion Rapp; Schneider, Helmüt, *Chronik der 507th, Kaempfe Gegen U.S. Truppen von Paderborn Bis in Den Harz,* pg. 242.

27. Jones, Personal Experience, pg. 3.

28. Graves, *Battle of Paderborn, March/März 1945*, pg. 14.

29. Gees, pg 2; *Chronik*, pg. 243–244.

30. Ibid.

31. Dr. Friedrich G. Hohman *Das Ende des Zweiten Weltkriegs im Raum Paderborn, pg. 369;* Charles Whiting, *The Battle of the Ruhr Pocket*, Ballentine Books, NY; May *Paderborn*, pg. 2.

32. *Spearhead in the West*, pg. 144.

33. T/4 Glenn H. Shaunce, Sworn Testimony of Glenn H. Shaunce, T/4, ASN 37110843, U.S. War Department, War Crimes Office, Judge Advocate General's Office, File No. 12-352A (Rose), HQ, 3rd Armored Division, April 1, 1945 (photocopy).

34. Bellinger, "I Was a General's Aide," pg. 2.

35. Dieter Jähn, Phone Conversation with Don R. Marsh, August 1999.

36. Graves, *Battle of Paderborn, March/März 1945*, pg. 15.

37. T/4 Wesley A. Ellison, Sworn Testimony of Wesley D. Ellison, T/4, ASN 18075906, U.S. War Department, War Crimes Office, Judge Advocate General's Office, File No. 12-407 (Rose), Hilton Hotel, Lubbock Texas, July 3, 1945 (photocopy).

38. L.D. McQuade, Personal Correspondence with Steven L. Ossad, January 13, 1997.

39. Angelo Cali, Phone Conversation with Steven L. Ossad, December 14, 1999.

40. Jones, Personal Experience, pp. 3–4.

41. Francis B. Grow and Alfred, Summers, *A History of the 143rd Armored Signal Company, April 15, 1941/May 8, 1945*, unpublished manuscript (photocopy), Summer 1945, pg. 95–96.

42. Haynes W. Dugan, *A General Dies in Combat as World War II Winds Down: Maurice Rose and the 3rd Armored (Spearhead) Division*, unpublished manuscript, August 17, 1988 (photocopy).

43. James Omand, Personal Correspondence with Glenn A. Shaunce, April 1, 1975 (photocopy).

44. Edward S. Boyden, Personal Correspondence with Don R. Marsh, April 10, 1999.

45. Shaunce, Sworn Affidavit, pg. 1.

46. Frederick A. Brown, Colonel, FA, Div. Arty Cmdr., Sworn Affidavit, April 1, 1945, U.S. War Department, War Crimes Office, Judge Advocate General's Office, File No. 12-352A (Rose).

47. Leonard Y. Kunken, Personal Correspondence with Steven L. Ossad, December 10, 1996.

48. *Spearhead in the West*, pg. 144.

49. John A. Smith, Unpublished Manuscript, Andrew Barr Third Armored Division Archives, (photocopy), pg. 6.

50. Dugan, *Omaha Forward*, 1987, pg. 26.

51. Smith, Unpublished Manuscript, pg. 6.

52. Bellinger, "I Was a General's Aide," pg. 3.

53. Graves, *Battle of Paderborn, March/März 1945*, pg. 15.

54. Grow, *A History of the 143rd Armored Signal Company*, pg. 98.

55. Ibid., pg. 16.

56. Belton Y. Cooper, *Death Traps: Survival of an American Armored Division*, Presidio Press, San Rafael, CA, pg. 256.

57. Schneider, *Chronik der 507th*, pg. 244.

58. Brown, Sworn Affidavit, pg. 2.

59. Bellinger, "I Was a General's Aide," pg. 3.

60. Wesley A. Sweat, Phone Conversation with Steven L. Ossad, April 12, 1996.

61. Bellinger, "I Was a General's Aide," pg. 4.

62. Graves, *Battle of Paderborn, March/März 1945*, pg. 16.

63. Brown, Sworn Affidavit, pg. 2.

64. Jones, Personal Experience, pg. 4.

65. Bellinger, "I Was a General's Aide," pg. 4.

Notes for Chapter Two

1. *Middletown Business Directory*, Middletown, CT, 1900, pg. 140.

2. Jeffrey S. Rose, MD., Personal Correspondence with Steven L. Ossad, February 15, 1999.

3. Robert S. Gamzey, "The Story of General Rose," *The Intermountain Jewish News*, Denver, Colorado, April 19, 1945.

4. Jeff Rose, M.D., Personal Correspondence with Steven L. Ossad, March 30, 2002.

5. Ibid. pg. 139.

6. Haynes W. Dugan, Personal Correspondence with Steven L. Ossad, February 6, 1996.

7. Mrs. Cecil Oppenheim, Personal Correspondence with Steven L. Ossad, April 26, 1996.

8. Fred and Harriet Rochlin, *Pioneer Jews: A New Life in the Far West*, Houghton Mifflin, Boston, 1984, pg. 226.

9. Gamzey, op. cit, April 26, 1945; Maurice Rose, Personal Correspondence to his son, March 24, 1945.

10. Gamzey, op. cit., April 26, 1945.

11. Wesley A. Sweat, Personal Conversation with Steven L. Ossad, April 12, 1996.

12. Dugan, op. cit., February 6, 1996.

13. Jack A. Boulger, Personal Conversation with Steven L. Ossad, October 10, 1998.

14. Ralph C. Greene, MD, *A History of Maurice Rose*, unpublished manuscript, 1990–1991, pg. 3.

15. Gamzey, op. cit., May 2, 1945.

16. Robert M. Cour, "Memorial to a Hero," *Rocky Mountain Empire Magazine*, July 27, 1947, pg. 2.

17. U.S. Army Adjutant General's Office, *Official Army Register*, Government Printing Office, Washington, DC, 1945, pg. 801.

18. *Denver Post*, October 24, 1918.

19. Gamzey, op. cit., May 3, 1945, pg. 11.

20. Ibid, pg. 11.

21. *Denver Post*, January 20, 1918.

22. *Denver Post*, October 24, 1918.

Notes for Chapter Three

1. Col. Leonard P. Ayres, *The War with Germany: A Statistical Summary* (included as Appendix of) *Source Records of the Great War*, Volume VII, The National Alumni, Washington, DC, 1923, pg. 110.

2. Russell F. Weigley, *A History of the U.S. Army*, Macmillan & Co., NY, 1967, pg. 372–373.

3. Donald M. Kingston, "The Plattsburg Movement and its Legacy," *Relevance*, Volume VI, No. 4, Autumn 1997.

4. Ayres, *The War with Germany*, pg ?.

5. Ibid, and Kingston, "The Plattsburg Movement."

6. *Denver Post*, October 24, 1918.

7. Captain Charles F. Dienst, et. al., *History of the 353rd Infantry Regiment*, 353rd Infantry Society, Wichita, Kansas, 1921.

8. Ayres, *The War with Germany*.

9. Carlo D'Este, *Patton, A Genius for War*, pg. 189.

10. Weigley, *U.S. Army*, pg 373.

11. *Intermountain Jewish News*, May 10, 1945, pg. 11.

12. Ibid.

13. *Official Service Record of Maurice Rose, #0-8439*, General Officer Files, April 6, 1945.

14. Lawrence Stallings, *The Doughboys*, New York, 1963, pg. 354.

15. *Summary of Operations of the 89th Division*, American Battlefield Monuments Commission. GPO, Washington, DC, 1944.

16. C.J. Masseck, *Official Brief History of the 89th Division, U.S.A., 1917–1918–1919*, War Society of the 89th Division, 1919, pg. 2.

17. *Intermountain Jewish News*, May 10, 1945.

18. Ibid.

19. *Outline History of the 353rd Infantry, 89th Division, 1917–1918–1919*, U.S. Army, Washington DC, 1919, pg. 2.

20. James Ricci, "Their Eleventh Hour," *Los Angeles Times Magazine*, November 18, 1998, pg. 18.

21. English, *HQ, 177th Infantry Brigade, AEF, Report of Operations of September 12, 1918 (September 30, 1918)*, pp. 334–335.

22. *The Congressional Medal of Honor: The Names, The Deeds*, Chico, Sharp & Dunnigan, 1988.

23. Center of Military History, *Named Campaigns—World War I* (Internet: http://www.army.mil.cmh-pg/reference/wicmp.htm).

24. *89th Division Summary of Operations in the World War*, pg. 20.

25. See chapter 11, pg. 276.

26. "Official Service Record of Maurice Rose, #0-8439; "History of the 89th Division," *Intermountain Jewish News*, May 10, 1945, pg. 11.

27. *Denver Post*, October 24, 1918.

28. *Intermountain Jewish News*, May 10, 1945, pg. 11.

29. Ralph C. Greene, M.D., Personal Correspondence with Don R. Marsh, 1986

30. Wesley A. Sweat, Phone Conversation with Steven L. Ossad, April 26, 1996.

31. Jack A. Boulger, Phone Conversation with Steven L. Ossad, May 26, 1997.

32. Robert Gamzey, Personal Correspondence with Edward Grusd, October 18, 1945.

33. D'Este, op. cit., *Patton*, pg. 171.

34. Martin Blumenson, *Mark Clark: The Last of the Great World War II Commanders*, Congdon & Weed, NY, 1984, pg. 17.

35. See especially Joseph W. Bendersky's *The Jewish Threat: Anti-Semitic Politics of the U.S. Army*, New York, Basic Books, NY, 2000.

36. Haynes W. Dugan, Personal Conversation with Steven L. Ossad, September 17, 1995.

37. James Sawiki, *Infantry Regiments of the U.S. Army*, Wyvern, Dumfries, Virginia, pg. 504–505.

38. "Who's Who in the American Military," *Denver Post, New York Times*, April 3, 1945, etc. Several newspapers also report that Rose won a Silver Star Citation for his actions at St. Mihiel.

39. Samuel C. Kohs and Louis I. Dublin, *American Jews in World War II: The Story of 550,000 Fighters for Freedom*, National Jewish Welfare Board, 1947, pg. 183.

Notes for Chapter Four

1. *Intermountain Jewish News*, May 10, 1945, pg. 11.

2. Ibid.

3. Ibid.

4. MacDonald, *American Military History*, pg. 409.

5. Omar Bradley, *A General's Life*, pp. 54–55.

6. J. Lawton Collins, *Lightning Joe*, pg. 44.

7. See chapter 1, footnote 5.

8. Bradley, *A General's Life*, pg. 54.

9. Ibid., pg. 55.

10. Haynes W. Dugan, Personal Conversation with Steven L. Ossad, September 10, 1995.

11. Col. H.M. Forde, *2nd Armored Division Bulletin*, Issue #3, July–September 1987, pp. 20–21.

12. *Denver Post*, June 30, 1927.

13. MacDonald, *American Military History*, pg. 412.

14. *The Officer's Guide*, Military Book Publishing Company, Tarentum, PA, 1942, pg. 105.

Notes for Chapter Five

1. See especially Mildred H. Gillie, *Forging the Thunderbolt: A History of the Development of the Armored Force*, Harrisburg, PA, 1948.

2. War Department, *Officer's Guide*, pg. 66–67.

3. Martin Blumenson, Personal Correspondence with Steven L. Ossad, July 29, 1999.

4. Lucian K. Truscott, Jr., *Command Missions*, Presidio Press, Novato, CA, 1954, pg. 80.

5. Lucian K. Truscott, Jr., *Twilight of the U.S. Cavalry: Life in the Old Army 1917–1942*, University Press of Kansas, 1988.

6. Thomas R. Henry, "Masters of Slash and Surprise," *The Saturday Evening Post*, 1947, pg. 50; Andy Rooney, "General Rose: One of Tankers' Best," *Stars and Stripes*, April 4, 1945.

7. Ralph C. Greene, M.D., Personal Correspondence with Don R. Marsh, 1991.

8. Captain Maurice Rose, "Panama's Irregular Cavalry," *The Cavalry Journal*, July–August 1935, pg. 26.

9. Ibid., pg. 26.

10. Ibid., pg. 27.

11. Henry, "Masters of Slash and Surprise," pg. 49.

Notes for Chapter Six

1. John Keegan, *Six Armies in Normandy*, Penguin Books, NY, 1982, pg. 24.

2. Lucian K. Truscott, Jr., *The Twilight of the U.S. Cavalry: Life in the Old Army, 1917–1942*, University Press of Kansas, 1988, pg. 138.

3. Christopher R. Gabel, "The Leavenworth Staff College: A Historical Overview," *Military Review*, Volume LXXVII, September–October 1997, No. 5, pg. 98 ff.

4. Thomas Alexander Hughes, Jr., *Overlord; General Pete Queseda and the Triumph of Tactical Air Power in World War II*, Free Press, NY, 1995, pg. 63.

5. Ibid., pg. 63.

6. Truscott, *Twilight of the U.S. Cavalry*, pg. 142.

7. Hughes, *Overlord*, pg. 62.

8. Carlo D'Este, *Patton: A Genius for War*, pg. 331; Truscott, op. cit., pg. 141.

9. D'Este, *Patton*, pg. 141.

10. Hughes, *Overlord*, pg. 60.

11. Gabel, "Leavenworth Staff College," pg. 98 ff.

12. See footnote 6, chapter 1.

13. Hughes, *Overlord*, pg. 62.

14. Ibid., pg. 62.

15. Ibid., pg. 63.

16. Ibid., pg. 63.

17. Allen, Roderick R., "Speech at the Dedication of the *USNS General Maurice Rose* (T-AP126)," February 12, 1947.

Notes for Chapter Seven

1. See chapter 1, footnote 23.

2. See especially Christopher R. Gabel, *The U.S. Army GHQ Maneuvers of 1941*, Center of Military History, U.S. Army, Washington, DC, 1992.

3. Ernest Harmon, *Combat Commander: Autobiography of a Soldier*, Prentice-Hall, Englewood, NJ, 1970, pg. 64

4. Ibid.

5. Lucian K. Truscott, Jr., *Command Missions*, pg. 80.

6. Ibid.

7. Norman Gelb, *Desperate Venture: The Story of Operation Torch*, Morrow & Co., NY, 1995, pg. 302–308.

8. Carlo D'Este, *Patton: A Genius for War*, HarperCollins, NY, 1995, pg. 460.

9. George F. Howe, *The Battle History of the 1st Armored Division*, 1954, pg. 216.

10. Ibid.

11. U.S. War Department, *Maurice Rose #0-8439, General Officer Files*.

12. Omar N. Bradley, *A Soldier's Story*, Henry Holt & Co., NY, 1951, pg. 96.

13. Ibid.

14. "Maj. General Maurice Rose Killed as He Leads Spearhead in Reich," *New York Times*, April 3, 1945.

15. Harmon, *Combat Commander*, pg. 138–39.

16. Bradley, *A Soldier's Story*, pg. 97.

17. "Rose Killed," *New York Times*, April 3, 1945.

18. Harmon, *Combat Commander*, pg. 139.

19. "Rose Killed," *New York Times*, April 3, 1945.

20. Bradley, *A Soldier's Story*, pg. 98.

21. Donald E. Houston, *Hell on Wheels: The 2nd Armored Division*, San Rafael: Presidio, 1977, pg. 148.

22. Committee 4, *The 2nd Armored Division in the Sicilian Campaign*, Advanced Officers Class, The Armored School 1949–1950, (Pamphlet Section, Armor School, Fort Knox, KY), May 1950, pg. 3.

23. Albert N. Garland and Howard M. Smith, *Sicily and the Surrender of Italy*, United States Army in World War II: The Mediterranean Theater of Operations, Office of the Chief of Military History, Washington, DC, 1965, pp. 98–99.

24. Houston, *Hell on Wheels*, pg. 156.

25. Martin Blumenson, *Sicily: Whose Victory?*, Ballantine Books, NY, (Campaign Book #3), 1969, pg. 39.

26. Committee 4, *The 2nd Armored*, pg. 36.

27. Garland, *Sicily and the Surrender of Italy*, pg. 155.

28. Committee 4, *The 2nd Armored*, pg. 38.

29. Allen Jones, "The Sicilian Invasion," *2nd Armored Division Bulletin*, #3, September–December 1993, pg. 30.

30. Houston, *Hell on Wheels*, pg. 159.

31. Dr. Norris Perkins, *North African Odyssey: Adventures in the Mediterranean Theater of War*, Four Mountain Productions, Portland, OR, 1995, pg. 85.

32. Dr. Norris Perkins, "Lessons Learned in the Attack on Canicatti," *Armor Magazine*, May–June 1987, pg. 32.

33. Jones, *The Sicilian Invasion*, pg. 30.

34. Committee 4, *The 2nd Armored*, pg. 39.

35. Garland, *Sicily and the Surrender of Italy*, pg. 199.

36. Perkins, *North African Odyssey*, pg. 113.

37. Garland, *Sicily and the Surrender of Italy*, pg. 199; Committee 4, *The 2nd Armored Division in the Sicilian Campaign*, pg. 40; Houston, *Hell on Wheels*, pp. 160.

38. Jones, *The Sicilian Invasion*, pg. 30.

39. Houston, *Hell on Wheels*, pg. 161.

40. Committee 4, *The 2nd Armored*, pg. 39.

41. Jones, *The Sicilian Invasion*, pg. 30.

42. George S. Patton, *War as I Knew It*, pg. 58–59.

43. Samuel Eliot Morison, *History of U.S. Naval Operations in World War II*, Volume IX, p. 182; Committee 4, *The 2nd Armored*, pg. 53.

44. Garland, *Sicily and the Surrender of Italy*, pg. 254.

45. Jones, *The Sicilian Invasion*, pg. 30.

46. Blumenson, *Sicily: Whose Victory?*, pg. 93.

47. Historical Record, Headquarters, 2nd Armored Division, Office of the Division Commander, *Operations 2nd Armored Division 22 April–25 July 1943*, (Documents Section, Armor School, Fort Knox, KY), 5 August 1943, pg. 9–10.

48. Philip B. Reisler, Personal Conversation with Don R. Marsh (taped), April 4, 1996.

49. Jones, *The Sicilian Invasion*, pg. 30.

50. Blumenson, *Sicily: Whose Victory?*, pg. 93.

51. Historical Record, *Operations 2nd Armored Division*, August 5, 1943, Incl. #10.

52. Reisler, Conversation, April 4, 1996.

53. *Denver Post*, January 5, 1945.

Notes for Chapter Eight

1. E.A. Trahan, et. al., *A History of the 2nd United States Armored Division, 1940–1946*, chapter V, 1946.

2. William A. "Bill" Castille, Personal Correspondence with Steven L. Ossad, July 26, 1996.

3. Don R. Marsh, Letter to his Brother, Tidworth Barracks, England, June 1, 1944.

4. Don R. Marsh, *History of Combat Command "A," 2nd Armored Division 8–15 June 1944*, Unpublished Manuscript, November 5, 1998.

5. Don Marsh, "Achtung! Achtung! CCA—Pyramid Calling," *3rd Armored Division Association Newsletter*, 43rd Series, no. 1, March 1989, pg. 18–19.

6. Ibid, pg. 18–19.

7. Ibid., pg. 19.

8. *CCA after Action Report,* June 1944.

9. Marsh, *History of CCA.*

10. *CCA after Action Report,* June 1944.

11. Trahan, *Chapter V.*

12. Gordon A Harrison, *Cross-Channel Attack,* United States Army in World War II: The European Theater of Operations, Office of the Chief of Military History, Washington, DC, 1950 (reprinted 1973), pg. 187.

13. Clay Blair, *Ridgeway's Paratroopers: The American Airborne in World War II,* William Morrow, NY, 1985, pg. 240.

14. Omar N. Bradley, *A Soldier's Story,* Holt, NY, 1951, pg. 283.

15. Thomas A. Hughes, *Overlord,* pp. 140–144.

16. J. Lawton Collins, *Lightning Joe: An Autobiography.* Baton Rouge, LA, LSU Press, 1979, pg. 205; U.S. War Department Press Summary, "General Officer Casualties," February 1946

17. Collins, *Lighting Joe,* pg. 205; Harrison, *Cross-Channel Attack,* pg. 352.

18. Samuel W. Ketchum, Jr., *Rommel's Last Battle: The Desert Fox and the Normandy Campaign,* Stein & Day, NY, 1986, pg. 96.

19. Collins, pg. 205.

20. "The Battle of the Marshes" (Marker #19, *D-Day: The Onslaught,* railroad station).

21. Roland Ruppenthal, et. al., *Utah Beach to Cherbourg 6–27 June 1944,* The American Forces in Action Series (#13), chapter "The Battle for Carentan," Historical Division, War Department, Washington, DC, 1948 (reprinted by Center of Military History, United States Army, Washington, DC, 1990), pg. 92.

22. Ralph Bennett, *Ultra in the West,* Charles Scribner & Sons, NY, 1979, pg. 71.

23. Bradley, *Soldier's Story,* pg. 293.

24. Omar N. Bradley, and Clay Blair, *A General's Life,* Simon & Schuster, NY, 1983, pg. 260.

25. Bennett, *Ultra,* pg. 71–72.

26. Ibid., pg. 71.

27. Max Hastings, *Overlord: D-Day and the Battle for Normandy,* Simon & Schuster, NY, 1984, pg. 160; *Omaha Beachhead 6 June–13 June 1944,* The American Forces in Action Series, chapter, "Action West of the Vire," Historical Division, War Department, Washington, DC, 1945 (reprinted by Center of Military History, United States Army, Washington, DC,1984), pg. 158.

28. Bradley, *A General's Life,* pg. 260.

29. Bennett, *Ultra,* pp. 71.

30. Ruppenthal, *Utah Beach,* pg. 92.

31. Elbridge Colby, *The First Army in Europe 1943–1945,* Battery Press, Nashville, TN, 1969, pg. 24; Houston, *Hell on Wheels,* op. cit., pg. 201; *Omaha Beachhead,* pg. 158–159.

32. Harrison, *Cross-Channel Attack,* pg. 365.

33. Ruppenthal, *Utah Beach*, pg. 92–93.

34. Don R. Marsh, *History of Combat Command A*, November 5, 1998.

35. Don R. Marsh, *The Man from Colorado,* unpublished memoir, March 30 1987.

36. Trahan, chapter V.

37. Stephen E. Ambrose, *Band of Brothers*, pg. 101; Ruppenthal, *Utah Beach*, pg. 93; *Omaha Beachhead*, pg. 159.

38. Ambrose, *Band of Brothers*, pg. 101.

39. Don R. Marsh, Letter to his Folks; Somewhere in France, June 24, 1944.

40. Rae S. Guistwite, Personal Correspondence with Steven L. Ossad, January 11, 1996.

41. Houston, *Hell on Wheels*, pg. 203; Trahan, chapter V.

42. Ibid.

43. Harrison, *Cross-Channel Attack*, pg. 362.

44. Bradley, *A General's Life*, pg. 260; Trahan, chapter V.

45. Houston, *Hell on Wheels*, pg. 203; Ruppenthal, *Utah Beach*, pg. 92.

46. Houston, *Hell on Wheels*, pg. 204.

47. Ernest Harmon telegram thanking Generals Bradley and Eisenhower for Rose's promotion to Brig. General, June 18, 1943.

Notes for Chapter Nine

1. Martin Blumenson, *Liberation*, Time-Life Books, Alexandria, VA, 1978, pg. 47.

2. Thomas B. Buell, et. al., "Planning & Implementing the Breakout: Operation COBRA," *The Second World War: Europe and the Mediterranean*, Department of History, United States Military Academy, Avery Publishing, Wayne, NJ, 1984, pg. 324.

3. Martin Blumenson, "Escape From Hedgerow Country," *Military History Magazine*, October 1986, pg. 34.

4. Blumenson, *Liberation*, pg. 46.

5. Blumenson, "Escape," pg. 34–35.

6. Kenneth Macksey, *Bocage, The D-Day Encyclopedia CD-ROM*, Simon & Schuster, 1993.

7. Belton Y. Cooper, *Deathtrap: Survival of an American Armored Division*, Presidio Press, San Rafael, CA, 1998.

8. Lt. Col. R.H. Shell, Adjutant General, HQ, Second Armored Division, *Action against Enemy Reports/After Action Reports July 1–31, 1944*, September 21, 1944, Annex 2.

9. Ibid.

10. Cooper, *Deathtrap*, pg. 214.

11. Col. John Collier, HQ, CCA, 2nd Armored Division, Operations Action for Period July 1–31, 1944, (Inclusive), September 24, 1944, pg. 3.

12. David Rushing, "World War II Buddies Reunited Here Recently," *The Tupelo Eagle*, March 25, 1989.

13. Buell, "Operation COBRA," pg. 324.

14. Omar N. Bradley, *A Soldiers Story*, pg. 228; Dwight D. Eisenhower, *The Crusade in Europe*; B.H. Liddell Hart, *History of World War II*, p. 656.

15. Elbridge Colby, *The First Army in Europe 1943–1945*, Battery Press, Nashville, TN, 1969, pg. 54–55; Buell, *Planning & Implementing the Breakout: Operation COBRA*, pg. 324; Martin Blumenson, *Breakout and Pursuit*, United States Army in World War II: The European Theater of Operations, Office of the Chief of Military History, Washington, DC, 1961, pg. 215–217.

16. E.A. Trahan, ed., *A History of the 2nd United States Armored Division, 1940–1945*, 1946, chapter V.

17. Collier, Operations Action for Period July 1–31, 1944, pg. 3.

18. Blumenson, *Breakout and Pursuit*, pg. 224–228; Eddy Bauer, *Illustrated World War II Encyclopedia*, Polus, Monaco, 1966, Volume XIII, Chapter 121, pg. 1683.

19. Blumenson, *Liberation*, pg 53.

20. Shell, *Action against Enemy*, pg. 3.

21. Ernie Pyle, "A Surge of Doom-like Sound; In Normandy, August 8, 1944," reprinted in David Nichols, ed., *Ernie's War: The Best of Ernie Pyle's World War II Dispatches*, Simon & Schuster, NY, 1986, pg. 333.

22. Don R. Marsh, Personal Correspondence with Steven L. Ossad, February 23, 2000.

23. Colby, *The First Army*, pg. 57.

24. A.J. Liebling, "Letter from France August 1944" in *The New Yorker;* "Normandy 1944," reprinted by the permission of Russell & Volkening as agents for the author. Copyright 1944.

25. Blumenson, *Breakout and Pursuit*, pg. 252.

26. Ibid., pg. 254.

27. Ibid., pg. 252.

28. Collins, *Lightning Joe*, pg. 242.

29. Omar N. Bradley and Clay Blair, *A General's Life*, Simon & Schuster, NY, 1983, pg. 278.

30. Colby, *The First Army*, pg. 57.

31. Blumenson, *Breakout and Pursuit*, pg. 252.

32. Ibid. pg. 254.

33. Don R. Marsh, Letter to His Folks, "Somewhere in France," August 5, 1944, pg. 6.

34. Collier, Operations Action for Period July 1–31, 1944, September 24, 1944, pg. 3.

35. Doug Donahue, Personal Correspondence with Don R. Marsh, December 8, 1997.

36. Sgt. Walter Peters, "Taking Off with the Tanks," *Yank Magazine*, Vol. 3, No. 10, August 20, 1944.

37. Blumenson, *Breakout and Pursuit*, pg. 254.

38. Collier, Operations Action for Period July 1–31, 1944, September 24, 1944, pg. 3.

39. Earlie Jones, Personal Correspondence with Don R. Marsh, December 1998.

40. Donahue, Marsh, December 8, 1997.

41. Blumenson, *Breakout and Pursuit*, pg. 252.

42. Alexander, *Overlord*, pg. 219.

43. Ibid, pp. 220–221; Blumenson, *Breakout and Pursuit*, pg. 255.

44. Blumenson, *Breakout and Pursuit*, pg. 255.

45. Don R. Marsh, Personal Correspondence with Lawrence A. Hull, April 6, 1999.

46. Alexander, *Overlord*, pg. 221.

47. Marsh, Letter to His Folks, August 5, 1944, pg. 7–8.

48. Weigley, Russell, *Eisenhower's Lieutenants, The Campaign of France and Germany 1944–1945*, Indiana University Press, Bloomington, IN, 1981, pg. 156.

49. Ibid.

50. Marsh, Letter to His Folks, August 5, 1944, pg. 5–6.

51. Marsh, Hull, April 6, 1999.

52. Ibid.

53. Marsh, Letter to His Folks, August 5, 1944, pg. 2.

54. Weigley, *Eisenhower's Lieutenants*, pg. 156.

55. Don R. Marsh, Personal Correspondence with Steven L. Ossad, March 8, 2000.

56. Philip Geidel, Personal Communication with Don R. Marsh, December 7, 1998.

57. Marsh, Ossad, March 8, 2000.

58. Don R. Marsh, Personal Correspondence with Steven L. Ossad, January 13, 2000.

59. Ibid.

60. Marsh, Letter to His Folks, August 5, 1944, pg. 2–3.

61. Weigley, *Eisenhower's Lieutenants*, pg. 156.

62. Martin Blumenson, Personal Correspondence with Steven L. Ossad, February 9, 2000.

63. Trahan, ed., *A History*, chapter V.

64. Ibid.

65. Shell, Action against Enemy, pg. 8.

66. Trahan, ed., *A History*, chapter V.

67. Shell, Action against Enemy, pg. 8.

68. Marsh, Letter to His Folks, August 5, 1944, pg. 2.

69. Hal Boyle, "Three Times "Hell on Wheels" Division Has Steamrollered Rommel's Best: Second Armored Finally Honored, With the American Forces in France," Associated Press, July 30, 1944.

70. Marsh, Hull, April 6, 1999.

71. Donahue, Marsh, December 8, 1997.

72. Hull, Lawrence A., Personal Correspondence with Don R. Marsh, November 28, 1998.

73. Collins, *Lightning Joe*, pg. 246.

74. Donald E. Houston, *Hell on Wheels: The 2nd Armored Division*, Presideo, Novato, CA, 1977, pg. 241.

75. Colby, *The First Army*, pg. 67.

Notes for Chapter Ten

1. Martin Blumenson, *Breakout and Pursuit*, pg. 676.

2. Haynes W. Dugan, Personal Correspondence with Steven L. Ossad, March 21, 1996

3. 3rd Armored Division, "Call Me Spearhead," *Stars and Stripes*, Paris, 1944, pg. 5; Andrew Barr, et. al., *Spearhead in the West: The 3rd Armored Division [In WW II]*, Kunst and Wervedruck: Frankfort am Main, 1945. (Reprinted by Battery Press, 1991) pg. 66.

4. Barr, *Spearhead in the West*, pg. 196.

5. J. Lawton Collins, *Lightning Joe*, pg. 246.

6. Omar Bradley, *A General's Life*, p. 281.

7. Robert W. Russell, Personal Correspondence with Steven L. Ossad, April 6, 1996.

8. William A. Castille, Personal Correspondence with Steven L. Ossad, July 26, 1996.

9. See chapter 1, footnote 2.

10. Sam Hogan, Personal Conversation with Steven L. Ossad, February 13, 1995.

11. Dugan, Correspondence, March 21, 1996

12. Haynes W. Dugan, Personal Conversation with Steven L. Ossad, September 10, 1995.

13. Castille, Correspondence, July 26, 1996.

14. Mark Reardon, Personal Correspondence with Steven L. Ossad, June 6, 1998.

15. Haynes W. Dugan, *Night Moves (Campaigning with Maurice Rose)*, Unpublished Memoir, June 17, 1993, pg. 4.

16. Dugan, Correspondence, March 21, 1996.

17. Major Haynes W. Dugan, Unpublished Personal Diary, August 25–September 7, 1944, Third Armored Division Andrew Barr WWII Archives, University of Illinois.

18. "An Interesting Excerpt," *3rd Armored Division Association Newsletter*, June 1963, pg. 23.

19. Collins, *Lightning Joe*, pg. 261.

20. Ibid., pg. 264.

21. Major General Maurice Rose, "An Operation of the Third Armored (Spearhead) Division," *Military Review*, March–April 1945.

22. Barr, et. al., *Spearhead in the West*, pg. 209.

23. Collins, *Lightning Joe*, pg. 264.

24. Blumenson, *Breakout and Pursuit*, pg. 684.

25. Committee 14, "Exploitation by the 3rd Armored Division—Seine River to Germany," Advanced Officers Course, The Armor School, Fort Knox, KY, 1949, pg. 21.

26. Ibid, pg. 1.

27. Thomas B. Buell, et. al., *The Second World War: Europe and the Mediterranean*, Department of History, United States Military Academy, Avery Publishing, Wayne, NJ, 1984, pg. 351.

28. Blumenson, *Breakout and Pursuit*, pg. 683.

29. Sam Hogan, Personal Correspondence with Steven L. Ossad, April 1996.

30. Committee 14, Exploitation, pg. 21.

31. Sam Hogan, Personal Correspondence with Steven L. Ossad, March 30, 1996.

32. Thomas Alexander Hughes, *Overlord*, pg. 247.

33. Buell, *The Second World War: Europe and the Mediterranean*, pg. 351.

34. Omar N. Bradley, *A General's Life*, pg. 319.

35. Dwight D. Eisenhower, *Crusade in Europe*, pg. 294.

36. Dugan, Diary, 31 August 1944; Barr, *Spearhead in the West*, pg. 206; Collins, *Lightning Joe*, pg. 261.

37. 3rd Armored Division, *Call Me Spearhead*, pg. 23.

38. HQ, 703rd Tank Destroyer Battalion, Summary of Operations, 1 September 1944–6 September 1944, pg. 1.

39. Francis B. Grow and Alfred Summers, *A History of the 143rd Armored Signal Company, April 15, 1941–May 8, 1945*, unpublished manuscript (photocopy), 1945.

40. Lt. Col. Edward S. Berry, "From the Seine to the Siegfried Line," *Armored Cavalry Journal*, January–February, 1950, pg 38.

41. Committee 14, "Exploitation," pg. 25.

42. Herbert F. Zimmerman, Personal Correspondence with Steven L. Ossad, April 16, 1996.

43. Henry Gosch, Personal Correspondence with Steven L. Ossad, December 30, 1995.

44. Jack Warden, Personal Correspondence with Steven L. Ossad, December 19, 1996.

45. *Call Me Spearhead*, 1944, pg. 24.

46. Dugan, Diary, September 2, 1944.

47. Glenn H. Shaunce, Personal Conversation with Steven L. Ossad, August 18, 1996.

48. Berry, "From the Seine to the Siegfried Line," pg. 38.

49. Claude Lancelet, Letter to the Third Armored Division, n.d., pg. 4.

50. E.A. Roberts, MD, *Five Stars to Victory: The Exploits of Task Force Lovelady (2nd Bn. [Reinf.], 33rd Arm'd Regt., 3rd Arm'd Div., U.S. Army) in the War against Germany 1944-1945*, Atlas Printing & Engraving Co., Birmingham, AL, 1949, pg. 42.

51. Castille, Correspondence, July 26, 1996.

52. Yves Bourdon, Claude Faucon, et. Al., *La Poche de Mons: La Libération, en Septembre 1944, de la région Mons-Borinage,Bavai-Mauberge*, Quorom, Ottignies, 1994, pp. 52–53.

53. Colonel John A. Smith, Jr.,"Draft of a Speech to the Rose Memorial Hospital Ceremony, May 27, 1945," unpublished draft, n.d., pg. 12.

54. Haynes W. Dugan and Dan Peterson, *3rd Armored Division: Spearhead in the West*, Turner Press, Paluckah, KY, 1991, pg. 47.

55. Jack Boulger, Personal Conversation with Steven L. Ossad, May 26, 1997.

56. George Bailey, *Germans: Biography of an Obsession*, Avon Books, NY, 1972, pg. 45.

57. Committee 14, "Exploitation," pg. 44.

58. *503rd Military Intelligence Detachment Unit History*, Unpublished Manuscript, July 8, 1966, pg. 15.

59. Collins, *Lightning Joe*, pg. 261.

60. Ibid, pg. 264.

61 Committee 14, "Exploitation," pg. 41.

62. Ibid, pg. 42.

63. Zimmerman, Correspondence, April 16, 1996.

64. Clarence E. Smoyer, Mons: September 1–2, 1944, Personal Correspondence with Steven L. Ossad, 1998.

65. Syd Johnson, *Recollections of World War II*, Unpublished Manuscript, 1996, pg. 127.

66. Gosch , Correspondence, December 30, 1995.

67. Haynes W. Dugan, *Omaha Forward*, Unpublished Manuscript, 1987, pg. 7.

68. Sam Hogan, Personal Correspondence with Steven L. Ossad, March 30, 1996.

69. Lt. Col. William R. Orr, 1st Battalion, 36th Armored Infantry Regiment, "Action at Mons, Belgium, 2–4 September 1944," January 13, 1945, pg. 1.

70. Warden, Correspondence, December 19, 1996.

71. Orr , *Action at Mons*, January 13, 1945, pg. 2.

72. Johnson, *Recollections*, pg. 128.

73. 1st Lt. Fred L. Hadsel, 2nd Information & Historical Service, VII Corps Team, First U.S. Army, Combat Interview: "The Battle of Mons 1-4 September 1944," March 16, 1945. Interview with Lt. Col. Dale E. Brown, et. al., September 13, 1944, near Stolberg.

74. Ibid, pg. 9

75. Dugan, Diary, September 3, 1944.

76. Grow and Summers, *A History of the 143rd Armored Signal Company*, pg. 50–51.

77. Don R. Marsh, Personal Correspondence with Miles Siegel, March 4, 2000.

78. Thomas R. Henry, "Masters of Slash and Surprise; 3rd Armored Division," *Saturday Evening Post*, October 19, 1946 (reprinted in *3rd Armored Division Association Newsletter,* December 1983, pg. 8–9).

79. Bailey, *Germans*, pg. 42.

80. 503rd Military Intelligence Detachment Unit History, pg. 16.

81. Colonel R.C. Partridge, Headquarters VII Corps, General Orders No. 15 Citation of Unit, March 24, 1945.

82. Committee 14, "Exploitation," pg. 44. See chapter 1, footnote 13, for a description of the Presidential Unit Citation.

83. W.C. Heinz, *The Professional*, NY, 1958, pg. 254.

84. Robert W. Russell, Personal Correspondence with Steven L. Ossad, April 6, 1996.

85. Gosch, Correspondence, December 30, 1995.

86. Barr, *Spearhead in the West*, pg. 87.

87. Hughes, *Overlord*, pg. 247.

88. Iris Carpenter, *No Woman's World*, Houghton Mifflin & Co, Boston, 1946, pg. 128.

89. Zimmerman, Correspondence, April 16, 1996.

90. Haynes W. Dugan, "General Rose and the Railroad Workers," Personal Correspondence with Maynard L. Brichford, Archivist, Univ. of Illinois, January 28, 1986.

91. Russell, Correspondence, April 6, 1996.

92. Ibid.

93. Bourdon, *La Poche de Mons*, pg. 52–53.

94. Committee 14, "Exploitation," pg. 30.

95. Ibid, pg. 44–46.

96. Ibid, pg xiv.

97. Dugan and Peterson, *3rd Armored Division*, pg. 47.

98. Robert Reuben, *From the Seine to Germany, Reuters*, September 15, 1944.

99. Jack Thompson, "Tank Men from Chicago Help Beat Nazi Best, Third Division Feat Wins Name 'Spearhead,'" Chicago Tribune Press Service, August 22, 1944.

100. Wesley A. Sweat, Personal Correspondence with Steven L. Ossad, April 12, 1996.

101. Collins, *Lightning Joe*, pg. 261.

102. Mary Lee Stubs and Stanley Russell Connor, *Armor-Cavalry, Part I: Regular Army and Army Reserve*, Army Lineage Series, Center of Military History, Washington, DC, 1984 (orig. 1969), pg. 279.

Notes for Chapter Eleven

1. Haynes W. Dugan, *Omaha Forward (Sometimes Way Forward); A History of Forward Echelon and HQ Company, Third Armored Division,* unpublished manuscript and related correspondence, 1987, pg. 10.

2. Andrew Barr, Personal Conversation with Frank Koukl, August 15, 1987.

3. Dugan, *Omaha Forward,* pg. 11.

4. Jack A. Boulger, Personal Conversation with Steven L. Ossad, May 26, 1997.

5. Haynes W. Dugan, Personal Correspondence with Steven L. Ossad, March 21, 1996.

6. Headquarters, United States Army, Europe, General Orders 13, "Designation of Rose Barracks," 15 September 1952. The text of the DSC citation was quoted in this barracks rededication order.

7. Don R. Marsh, Personal Correspondence with Steven L. Ossad, May 1, 2000.

8. Charles B. MacDonald, *The Battle of the Hürtgen Forest,* Jove Publications, NY 1963, pg. 28.

9. Ibid., and Collins, *Lightning Joe,* pg. 314.

10. Dugan, Correspondence, March 21, 1996.

11. See especially Edward G. Miller's *A Dark and Bloody Ground.*

12. W.C. Heinz, "A Man of Courage," *New York Sun,* April 1, 1945 (published in the *Third Armored Division Association Newsletter,* August 1970, pg. 31).

13. Sam Hogan, *The Death of a Lieutenant,* Unpublished Memoir, n.d., pg. 3.

14. Thomas R. Henry, "Masters of Slash and Surprise; 3rd Armored Division," *Saturday Evening Post,* October 19, 1946 (reprinted in *3rd Armored Division Association Newsletter,* December 1983, pg. 10).

15. Dugan, *Omaha Forward,* pg. 19.

16. Haynes W. Dugan, "The War Room," *3rd Armored Division Association Newsletter,* June 1983, pg. 10.

17. Dugan, Correspondence, March 21, 1996.

18. Hogan, *Death of a Lieutenant,* pg. 4.

19. Bailey, *Germans,* pg. 51.

20. Ibid, pg. 52; *Intermountain Jewish News,* May 25, 1945.

21. Dugan, Correspondence, March 21, 1996.

22. Bailey, *Germans,* pg. 46–47.

23. Dugan, Correspondence, March 21, 1996.

24. Frank Woolner, "Battle Dress and Chow Line," *3rd Armored Division Association Newsletter,* April 1984, pg. 10.

25. Ibid.

26. Daniel O. Magnussen, Ph. D., "The General Cried at Dawn," *3rd Armored Division Association Newsletter,* December 1988, pg. 9.

27. Boulger, Conversation, May 26, 1997.

28. Jack A. Boulger, Personal Conversation with Steven L. Ossad, 14 June 1997.

29. Ibid.

30. Boulger, Conversation, May 26, 1997.

31. Dugan, Correspondence, March 21, 1996.

32. Boulger, Conversation, May 26, 1997.

Notes for Chapter Twelve

1. Harold Denny, "U.S. Tank Division Honored As Heroic 3rd Wins 'Spearhead' Title for Long Stubborn Fight in 'Battle of Pocket,'" *New York Times*, August 25, 1944.

2. HQ, 3rd Armored Division, *After Action Report 3rd Armored Division, December 1944*, February 1945.

3. Committee 3, "Armor under Adverse Conditions: 2nd and 3rd Armored Divisions in the Ardennes Campaign, December 14, 1944, to January 16, 1945," Advanced Officers Course, The Armor School, Fort Knox, KY, June 1949, pg. 6.

4. Charles R. Corbin, "Memories of Parfondruy, Belgium, December 1944," *3rd Armored Division Association Newsletter*, September 1988, pg. 11ff.

5. Samuel M. Hogan, "The Story of Task Force Hogan (1)," *3rd Armored Division Association Newsletter*, August 1987, pg. 13

6. "General Rose of Denver Has Close Brush with Buzz Bomb," *Denver Post*, December 28, 1944; *Spearhead in the West*, pg. 109.

7. Committee 3, "Armor," pg. 23.

8. 1st Lt. Fred I. Hadsel, 2nd Info and Hist Serv, VII Corps, First U.S. Army, "Combat Interview with Major General Maurice Rose, CG, 3rd AD," Petite Somme, Belgium, January 26, 1945.

9. Hugh M. Cole, *The Ardennes: The Battle of the Bulge*, Office of the Chief of Military History, Washington, DC, 1965, pg. 345.

10. Albert Hemmer, *The Rundstedt Offensive in the Ourthe Valley: The Decisive Battle at Hotton*, Unpublished Manuscript, n.d. pg. 18.

11. Hadsel, Interview with Rose, January 26, 1945.

12. Dugan, *Omaha*, pg. 45.

13. Ibid.

14. Hadsel, Interview with Rose, January 26, 1945.

15. Ibid.

16. Hogan, *Task Force Hogan (1)*, August 1987, p. 13.

17. Hemmer, *Rundstedt Offensive*, chapter I, pg. 31–35.

18. Ibid. pg. 21.

19. Cole, *The Ardennes*, pg. 354.

20. Ibid, pg. 377, Dugan, Correspondence, May 21, 1996.

21. Cole, *The Ardennes*, pg. 354–357.

22. SITW, G-3 Supplement.

23. Hq, 3rd Armored Division, *After Action Report December 1944*, January 1945.

24. HQ, 3rd Armored Division, *S-3 Journal, December 23, 1944,* February 1945.

25. Elliott Goldstein, et. al., *On the Job Training: An Oral History of the Battle of Parker's Crossroads and of the Fate of Those Who Survived,* The 589th Group, Atlanta, GA, 1999.

26. Cole, *The Ardennes.*

27. Goldstein, *On the Job,* pg. 60.

28. Herb Skoog, Reflections #595, Radio Interview with MG. Walter B. Richardson, ret., broadcast New Braunfels, Texas, August 26, 1990, transcript, pg. 19.

29. Committee #1, "The Armored Division in the Defense," Chapter 4, Armor on a Corps Boundary (19–26 December 1944), Advanced Officers Course, The Armor School, Fort Knox, KY, May 1950, pp. 59ff. Olin Brewster considered this study to be the most accurate written account available.

30. Skoog, *Reflections #595,* pg. 20.

31. Ibid, pg. 23. MG Walter B. Richardson, ret., Personal Conversation with Steven L. Ossad, Fort Worth, TX, October 5, 1996.

32. Lt. Colonel Olin F. Brewster (Ret.), "What Really Happened, Belle Haie, Belgium, December 1944 (Task Force Y [Richardson], 3rd Battalion, 32nd Armored Regiment, 3rd Armored Division," *3rd Armored Division Association Newsletter,* Volume XLIV, #3, September 1990, pg. 14–28. The major details of Brewster's account were corroborated by General Richardson at the 1996 Fort Worth, Texas, Reunion.

33. Brewster, "What Really Happened," September 1990.

34. Skoog, *Reflections #595,* pg. 24.

35. Samuel M. Hogan, "The Story of Task Force Hogan (2)," *3rd Armored Division Association Newsletter,* December 1987, pg. 23.

36. Ibid.

37. Ken Dixon (AP), "From Mouth of Hell Came the 400," *Stars and Stripes* (European Edition), 27 December 1944.

38. Ibid, pg. 23–24; Committee 3, Armor, pg. 28–31.

39. Samuel M. Hogan, Personal Correspondence with Steven L. Ossad, March 30, 1996.

40. Iris Carpenter, *No Woman's World,* Houghton Miflin, Boston, 1946, pg. 231.

41. MacDonald, *A Distant Trumpet,* pg. 616.

42. Skoog, Reflections #595.

43. Cole, *The Ardennes,* pg. 589.

44. James I. Robertson, Jr., *Stonewall Jackson: The Man, The Soldier, The Legend,* MacMillan Publishing, NY, pg. 757.

Notes for Chapter Thirteen

1. Grow and Summers, *A History of the 143rd Armored Signal Company,* pp. 80–81.

2. Major General Maurice Rose, Headquarters 3rd Armored Division, Office of the Commanding General, A.P.P #253, U.S. Army, Personal Communication

with General Dwight D. Eisenhower, March 21, 1945, pg. 4 (Copy, Dwight D. Eisenhower Library).

3. Rose, Personal Communication with General Dwight D. Eisenhower, pg. 2.

4. Don R. Marsh, Personal Correspondence with Steven L. Ossad, May 20, 2000.

5. Jack A. Boulger, Personal Conversation with Steven L. Ossad, May 26, 1997.

6. Samuel M. Hogan, Personal Correspondence with Steven L. Ossad, March 31, 1996; *Spearhead in the West* (pg. 122) describes the outcome of the competition with these words: "The fate of the Scotch is not recorded." Colonel Hogan's letter solves that mystery.

7. *Spearhead in the West*, pg. 124.

8. Ibid; *Omaha Forward*, pg. 18.

9. Collins, *Lightning Joe*, pg. 314.

10. Dugan, *Omaha Forward*, pg. 18.

11. Headquarters, 3rd Armored Division, APO #253, U.S. Army, "Action against Enemy, Reports/After/After Action Reports for the Period 1–31 March, 1945, Inclusive, Narrative Battle Report, March 1945," May 4, 1945, pg. 2.

12. Carpenter, *No Woman's World*, pg. 262.

13. See pages 220–221 and 261.

14. Carpenter, *No Woman's World*, pg. 262.

15. "The Desert of Cologne: Germany's fourth largest city is war's biggest ruin," *Life Magazine*, pg. 37–38, March 1945.

16. Clarence E. Smoyer, Personal Correspondence with Steven L. Ossad, October 1998.

17. Ibid.

18. Angelo Cali, Personal Conversation with Steven L. Ossad, May 30, 2000.

19. "The Desert of Cologne," *Life*, pg. 37.

20. Cali, Personal Conversation, May 30, 2000.

21. "The Desert of Cologne," *Life*, pg. 37.

22. Glenn H. Shaunce, Personal Conversation with Steven L. Ossad (taped), August 19, 1996.

23. Maurice Rose, Headquarters 3rd Armored "Spearhead" Division, Office of the Commanding General, Germany, A.P.O. #253, Postmaster NY, Personal Correspondence with Maurice Roderick Rose, March 12, 1945.

24. Nathaniel E. Peavy, Personal Correspondence with Steven L. Ossad, 1996.

25. Don R. Marsh, Personal Conversation with Maurice R. Rose, June 11, 1996.

26. See chapter 2, pg. 42.

27. Grow and Summers, *A History of the 143rd Armored Signal Company*, pg. 86.

28. General Dwight D. Eisenhower, Personal Communication with Major General Maurice Rose, March 18, 1945.

29. Rose, Personal Communication with General Dwight D. Eisenhower, pg. 3.

30. Ibid., pg. 4.

31. Ibid, pg. 1.

32. Ibid, pg. 5.

33. Dugan, *Omaha Forward*, pg. 18.

34. John Thompson, "General's Pistol Helps Rout 30 and Capture 12 Nazis," *Chicago Tribune* (March 27, Delayed), April 1, 1945; Henry, "Masters of Slash and Surprise," pg. 7; Heinz, *A Man of Courage,* pg. 31.

35. Thompson, "General's Pistol," April 1,1945.

36. "General Rose Shoots it Out with Group of 30 Nazis," *Denver Post*, March 31, 1945.

37. Heinz, *A Man of Courage,* pg. 31.

38. Andy Rooney, *My War*, Random House, NY, 1995, pg. 241.

39. Henry, "Masters of Slash and Surprise," pg. 7.

40. Andy Rooney, "Gen. Rose: One of Tanker's Best," *Stars and Stripes*, April 3, 1945.

41. Henry, "Masters of Slash and Surprise," pg. 7.

42 Ibid.

43. Rooney, "General Rose," April 3, 1945.

44. Ibid.

45. Carpenter, *No Woman's World*, pg. 283

46. Heinz, *A Man of Courage,* pg. 31.

Notes for Chapter Fourteen

1. Bellinger, "I Was a General's Aide," pg 4.

2. Shaunce, Tape #3 (May 18, 1996).

3. Shaunce, Sworn Affidavit, pg 1.

4. Brown, Sworn Affidavit, pg. 2.

5. Shaunce, Sworn Affidavit, pg. 2.

6. Brown, Sworn Affidavit, pg. 3.

7. Bellinger, "I Was a General's Aide," pg. 4.

8. Graves, *Battle of Paderborn*, pg. 14.

9. Ibid., pg. 15.

10. Ibid., pg. 16.

11. Brown, Sworn Affidavit, pg. 3.

12. Graves, *Battle of Paderborn*, pg. 14.

13. Brown, Sworn Affidavit, pg. 3.

14. Ibid., pg. 3.

15. Graves, Battle of Paderborn, pg. 16–17.

16. Brown, III (ret.) Lt. General Frederick, Personal Correspondence with Steven L. Ossad, June 4, 1996.

17. Shaunce, Sworn Affidavit, pg. 1.

18. Ibid., pg. 2.

19. Bellinger, "I Was a General's Aide," pg. 6. This account, written more than twenty years after the event, is completely consistent with Bellinger's Sworn Affidavit recorded April 2, 1945.

20. Jones, Personal Experience, pg. 4–5.

21. Francis B. Grow, Alfred Summers, *A History of the 143rd Armored Signal Company*, pg. 97.

22. Glenn Shaunce, Personal Correspondence with Don R. Marsh, August 28, 1987.

23. Shaunce, Tape #2, April 1996.

24. Shaunce, Sworn Affidavit, pg. 1.

25. Bellinger, Sworn Affidavit.

26. Shaunce, Tape #1, October 5, 1987.

27. Bellinger, "I Was a General's Aide," pg. 5.

28. Grow, *A History of the 143rd Armored Signal Company*, pg. 98.

29. Jones, Personal Experience, pg. 5.

30. Wesley A. Sweat, Personal Correspondence with Haynes W. Dugan, March 29, 1988.

31. Wesley A. Sweat, Phone Conversation with Steven L. Ossad, April 12, 1996.

32. James E. Stevenson, Sworn Deposition, taken at Louisville, KY, September 17, 1945.

33. Shaunce, Sworn Affidavit, pg. 2.

34. Glenn Shaunce, Personal Correspondence with Don R. Marsh, August 28, 1987.

35. Shaunce, Tape #1.

36. Don R. Marsh, "CCA — Pyramid Calling," *3rd Armored Division Association Newsletter*, December 1987, pg. 9.

37. L.D. McQuade, Personal Correspondence with Steven L. Ossad, January 13, 1997.

38. Dugan, *Omaha Forward,* pg. 26.

39. Col. John A. Smith, Jr., Unpublished Manuscript, n.d., (photocopy from Andrew Barr Third Armored Division Archives, University of Illinois, Box #2).

40. "Maj. Gen. Maurice Rose Killed as He Leads Spearhead in Reich," *New York Times*, April 3, 1945.

41. Dugan, *Omaha Forward,* pg. 27.

42. S/Sgt. Arthur N. Hauschild, HQ 3rd Armored Division, Sworn Testimony of Arthur N. Hauschild, S/Sgt., ASN 36024152, Hq 1st Bn, 33rd Armd Regt — Rcn Plat Sgt., U.S. War Department, War Crimes Office, Judge Advocate General's Office, File No. 12-352A (Rose), April 2, 1945 (photocopy).

43. Hauschild, Sworn Affidavit.

44. Marsh, Don R., Personal Correspondence with Arthur N. Hauschild, January 30, 1998.

45. Hauschild, Arthur N., "Another Side of the General Rose Story," *3rd Armored Division Association Newsletter*, March 1988, pg. 12.

46. Walter W. May, *Paderborn*, pg. 2.

47. Lt. Col Ellis P. Sylvester, Investigating Officer, I.G.D., HQ, 3rd Armored Division, "Information to Establish Prima Facie War Crimes Case Required by SHAEF, Court of Inquiry, U.S. War Department, War Crimes Office," Judge Advocate General's Office, File No. 12-352A (Rose), April 3, 1945 (photocopy), pg. 2.

48. Don Mahr, "A Medical Soldier's Story," *3rd Armored Division Association Newsletter*, June 1988, pg. 10.

49. Shaunce, Tape #1, Tape #2, April 30, 1996.

50. Shaunce, Sworn Affidavit, pg. 2.

51. Bellinger, Sworn Affidavit.

52. Bellinger, "I Was a General's Aide," pg. 6.

53. Ibid., pg. 7.

54. Ibid.

55. Ibid., pg. 8.

56. Ibid., pg. 9.

57. Brown, Sworn Affidavit, pg. 3.

58. Ibid., pg. 4.

59. Grow, *A History of the 143rd Armored Signal Company*, pg. 100; Omand, James, Personal Correspondence with Glenn A. Shaunce, April 1, 1975.

60. Mahr, *A Medical Soldier's Story*, pg. 10.

61. Ibid.

Notes for Chapter Fifteen

1. "Surrender," *The Reader's Companion to Military History*, Houghton Mifflin Company, New York, 1996, pg. 455–466.

2. Sylvester, Memorandum, pg. 2.

3. Ibid., pg. 2.

4. Shaunce, Sworn Affidavit, pg. 2.

5. Shaunce, Tapes #1, #2, #3, #5 (June 15, 1996).

6. Shaunce, Tape #6 (June 26, 1996).

7. Shaunce, Tape #5.

8. Bellinger, Sworn Affidavit.

9. See chapter 1, footnote 34.

10. Bellinger, "I Was a General's Aide," pg. 6.

11. Robert M. Bellinger, Personal Correspondence with Arnold Rose, February 17, 1946.

12. Col. Leon Jaworski, "Memorandum to Colonel Hall, Subject: File No. 12-352A (Rose)," War Crimes Office, Judge Advocate General Division, June 11, 1945, pg. 1.

13. "Werewolves Claim They Got Gen. Rose," London (AP), *Rocky Mountain News*, April 7, 1945.

14. Col. Melvin Purvis, "Memorandum for Asst. Chief of Staff, G-1," The Pentagon, War Crimes Office, Judge Advocate General Division, April 10, 1945.

15. Andy Rooney, "Maj. Gen. Rose of 3rd Armd Is Captured, Killed in Mixup," *Stars & Stripes* (Paris), April 3, 1945; Don Whitehead (AP), "Gen. Rose Shot by German after Being Captured at Front," *Washington Evening Star*, April 3, 1945; John Thompson (C.T.P.S.), "Greenness of Rose's Captors Blamed for General's Death," *Washington Times Herald*, April 6, 1945; UPI, "Nazis Killed Gen. Rose after He Surrendered," *Washington Daily News*, April 3, 1945.

16. J. Lawton Collins, *Lightning Joe*, pg. 314.

17. Ibid., pg. 2.

18. Ibid.

19. Jaworski, "Memorandum to Colonel Hall," pg. 2.

20. Wesley A. Sweat, Telephone Conversation with Steven L. Ossad, April 12, 1996.

21. Capt. Francis W. McGuigan, QMC, "Memorandum to: Lt. Col. Griffin, Subject: File No. 12-352A, Rose (V)," War Crimes Office, Prosecution Subsection, JAGD.

22. Ibid.

Notes for Chapter Sixteen

1. "Rose Became Great General by Taking Personal Risks," *Intermountain Jewish News*, April 12, 1945, pg. 10.

2. "General Rose Murdered after Capture By Huns; Denver Man is Shot as He Gives Up Gun," *Denver Post*, April 3, 1945 (Afternoon Edition), pg. 1.

3. Ibid.

4. John Stephenson, "Denver's General Rose, 3rd Armored Hero, Is Killed," *Rocky Mountain News*, April 3, 1945, pg. 11.

5. "General's Murder a Passover Symbol, Rabbi Dad Feels," *New York Daily News*, April 4, 1945, pg. 1; "A General Also Dies," *Newsweek*, April 16, 1945, pg. 33.

6. "Rabbi Rose Speaks on NBC V-E Program," *Intermountain Jewish News*, May 10, 1945, pg. 11.

7. "Rabbi Samuel Rose Observes 90th Birthday with Ode to General," *Intermountain Jewish News*, May 17, 1945, pg. 11.

8. Haynes W. Dugan, Don Peterson, et. al, *Spearhead in the West: 3rd Armored Division*, Paluckah, KY, Turner Press, 1991, pg. 74.

9. Telegram of Condolence to Mrs. Maurice Rose, SHAEF FWD, Supreme Commander, to AGWAR, CONFIDENTIAL, Ref. No. FWD-18439, 1720 Hours, April 1, 1945 (Copy from Dwight D. Eisenhower Library).

10. Dugan, *Spearhead*, pg. 74.

11. "Services Held at Synagogue for Gen. Rose," *Denver Post*, April 5, 1945, pg. 30.

12. Robert S. Gamzey, "Rose Memorial Hospital Drive off to Great Start: National Support Coming In," *Intermountain Jewish News*, April 12, 1945, pg. 1.

13. Francis Wayne, "Donations to Rose Hospital Coming from All Over U.S.," *Denver Post*, April 12, 1945.

14. Gamzey, "Rose Memorial Hospital," pg. 11.

15. "Approval of Rose Family Spurs Hospital Drive," *Intermountain Jewish News*, April 26, 1945, pg. 1

16. "Fight Bigots! Says Cantor in NBC Talk," *Intermountain Jewish News*, May 31, 1945, pg. 1.

17. Robert S. Gamzey, "General Rose: His Name Will Live Forever," *Intermountain Jewish News*, September 6, 1945, pg. 9.

18. Phyllis Brill, "Rose Board to Fete General's Men Sept. 11," *Intermountain Jewish News*, September 6, 1945, pg. 8.

19. "The Star of David Graces Grave of General Rose," *Intermountain Jewish News*, June 14, 1945, pg. 1.

20. Brill, "Rose Board"; Gamzey, "General Rose."

21. Rabbi Benjamin J. Elephant, Personal Correspondence with Rabbi & Mrs. Gilbert A. Elefant, April 27, 1945 (photocopy).

22. "The Star of David Graces," pg. 1.

23. Rabbi Gilbert A. Elefant, Personal Correspondence with Maurice B. Shwayder, September 22, 1945 (photocopy).

24. Rabbi Benjamin J. Elefant, Personal Correspondence with Rabbi & Mrs. Gilbert A. Elefant, June 5, 1945 (photocopy).

25. Rabbi Sidney M. Lefkowitz, Personal Correspondence with Edward E. Grusd, September 29, 1945 (photocopy).

26. Edward E. Grusd, Personal Correspondence with Max Goldberg, October 8, 1945 (photocopy).

27. Max Goldberg, Personal Correspondence with Edward E. Grusd, October 18, 1945 (photocopy).

28. Robert Gamzey, Personal Correspondence with Edward E. Grusd, October 18, 1945 (photocopy).

29. Ibid.

30. Goldberg, Correspondence, October 18, 1945.

31. Ben M. Blumberg, Personal Correspondence with Rabbi Gilbert A. Elefant, November 16, 1945 (photocopy).

32. Col. Maurice Rose, USMC (Retired), Personal Conversation with Don R. Marsh, December 9, 2001.

33. Rose, Conversation, December 9, 2001.

34. Lt. Col. B.W. Davenport, Asst. Sec., Gen. Staff, "Memorandum to Director, Bureau Public Relations, re. Return of the Body of General Maurice Rose to the

U.S., War Department," WDCSA 201, Rose, Maj. Gen., Maurice, September 28, 1945 (photocopy).

35. Mulvanity, Chief, Repatriation Records Branch, to Director, Memorial Division, "Memorandum of Telephone Conversation, July 23, 1946, Subject: Burial Place of General Rose and the Marker Covering the Grave," File #GMGYG 293, Rose, Maurice.

36. Virginia B. Rose, Telegram, Office, Quartermaster General, Memorial Division, Washington, DC, August 4, 1948.

37. Arnold Rose, Personal Correspondence with the U.S. War Department, May 27, 1948; Colonel E.V Freeman, QMC, Personal Correspondence with Arnold Rose, June 21, 1948.

38. Maj. Gen. H. Feldman, Quartermaster General, Personal Correspondence with Virginia B. Rose, September 27, 1949.

39. See chapter 3, footnote 37.

40. Colonel E.V. Hinman, QMC, Chief, Memorial Division, Personal Correspondence with Virginia B. Rose, November 29, 1949.

Bibliography

Books

Ambrose, Stephen, *Band of Brothers; E Company, 506th Regiment, 101st Airborne from Normandy to Hitler's Eagle Nest*. New York: Simon and Schuster, 1992.

———. *Citizen Soldiers*. New York: Simon and Schuster, 1998.

Ayres, Col. Leonard P. *The War with Germany: A Statistical Summary, Source Records of the Great War*. Washington, DC: The National Alumni, 1923.

Astor, Gerald. *A Blood-Dimmed Tide: The Battle of the Bulge by the Men Who Fought It*. New York: Dell Publishing, 1992.

Bailey, George, *Germans: Biography of an Obsession*. New York: Avon Books, 1972.

Barr, Andrew and Murray A. Fowler, et. al., *Spearhead in the West: The Third Armored Division [In WW II]*. Frankfort am Main: Kunst and Wervedruck, 1945,

Bennett, Ralph, *Ultra in the West*. New York: Charles Scribner's Sons, 1979.

Blair, Clay, *Ridgeway's Paratroopers: The American Airborne in World War II*. New York: William Morrow, 1985.

Blumenson, Martin, *Battle of the Generals: The Untold Story of the Falaise Pocket— The Campaign That Should Have Won World War II*. New York: William Morrow & Company, 1993.

———. *Breakout and Pursuit*. Washington, DC: Government Printing Office, 1961.

———. *The Duel for France, 1944*. New York: Da Capo Press, 1963.

———. *Liberation*. Alexandria, VA: Time-Life Books, 1978.

———. *Sicily: Whose Victory?* New York: Ballantine Books, 1969.

Bradley, Omar N., and Clay Blair, *A General's Life*. New York: Simon & Schuster, 1983.

———. *A Soldier's Story*. New York: Henry Holt & Company, 1951.

Bourdon, Yves and Claude Faucon et. al., *La Poche de Mons: La Libération, en Septembre 1944, de la région Mons-Borinage, Bavai-Mauberge*. Ottignies: Quorom, 1994.

Buell, Thomas B., et. al., *The Second World War: Europe and the Mediterranean*. Wayne, MI: Avery Publishing, 1984.

Carpenter, Iris, *No Woman's World*. Boston: Houghton Mifflin Co., 1946.

Casey, Robert, *This Is Where I Came In*. New York: Bobbs-Merrill, 1945.

Colby, Elbridge, *The First Army in Europe 1943-1945*. Nashville, TN: Battery Press, 1969.

Cole, Hugh M., *The Ardennes: The Battle of the Bulge*. Washington, DC: Government Printing Office, 1965.

Collins, J. Lawton, *Lightning Joe: An Autobiography*. Baton Rouge, LA: Louisiana State University Press, 1979.

Congressional Medal of Honor: The Names, The Deeds. Chico, CA: Sharp & Dunnigan, 1988.

Cooper, Belton Y., *Deathtrap: Survival of an American Armored Division*. San Rafael, CA: Presideo Press, 1998.

D'Este, Carlo, *Patton: A Genius for War*. New York: HarperCollins, 1995.

Dienst, Captain Charles F., et. al., *History of the 353rd Infantry Regiment*. Wichita, KS: 353rd Infantry Society, 1921.

Dugan, Haynes W., Don Peterson, et. al. *Third Armored Division: Spearhead in the West*. Paluckah: Turner Press, 1991.

Dupuy, Trevor N., et. al. *Hitler's Last Gamble: The Battle of the Bulge, December 1944-January 1945*. New York: HarperCollins, 1994.

———. *Harper Encyclopedia of Military History*. New York: HarperCollins, 1992.

———. *Harper Encyclopedia of Military Biography*. New York: HarperCollins, 1993.

Eisenhower, Dwight. D., *Crusade in Europe*. New York: Doubleday & Co., 1948.

Eisenhower, John S. D., *The Bitter Woods*. New York: Da Capo Press, 1969.

Fighting for America: A Record of the Participation of Jewish Men and Women in the Armed Forces During 1944. Washington, DC: National Jewish Welfare Board, 1944.

Fredman, J. George, and Lewis A. Falk. *Jews in American Wars*. Washington, DC: The Jewish War Veterans of the United States of America, 1963.

Gabel, Christopher R. *The U.S. Army GHQ Maneuvers of 1941*. Washington, DC: Government Printing Office, 1992.

Garland, Albert, and Howard Smith, *Sicily and the Surrender of Italy*.Washington, DC: Government Printing Office, 1965.

Gelb, Norman, *Desperate Venture: The Story of Operation Torch, The Allied Invasion of North Africa*. New York: Morrow & Co, 1992.

Gillie, Mildred H., *Forging the Thunderbolt: A History of the Development of the Armored Force*. Harrisburg, PA: Military Service Publishing Co., 1947.

Harmon, Ernest, *Combat Commander: Autobiography of a Soldier*. Englewood, NJ: Prentice-Hall, 1970.

Harrison, Gordon A., *Cross-Channel Attack.* Washington, DC: Government Printing Office, 1950.

Hastings, Max, *Overlord: D-Day and the Battle for Normandy.* New York: Simon & Schuster, 1984.

Heefner, M. D., and Wilson Allen, *Twentieth Century Warrior: The Life and Service of Major General Edwin D. Patrick,* Shippensburg: White Mane Publishing Co., 1995.

Heinz, H.C, *The Professional,* 1946.

Houston, Donald E., *Hell on Wheels: The Second Armored Division.* San Rafael, CA: Presidio Press, 1977.

Howe, George F., *Northwest Africa: Seizing the Initiative in The West.* Washington, DC: Government Printing Office, 1957.

———. *The Battle History of the First Armored Division,* 1954.

Hughes, Thomas Alexander, *Overlord: General Pete Queseda and the Triumph of Tactical Air Power in World War II.* New York: The Free Press, 1995.

J. Ben Hirsch, *Jewish General Officers.* 1967.

Jacobs, Bruce, *Soldiers: The Fighting Divisions of the Regular Army.* New York: W.W. Norton & Co., 1958.

Johnson, Briard, *A Condensed History of "Hell on Wheels"—Second Armored Division.* Evansville: Unigraphic, Inc. 1980.

Keegan, John, *Six Armies in Normandy: From D-Day to the Liberation of Paris.* New York: Penguin Books, 1982.

Kessler, Leo, *The Battle of the Ruhr Pocket.* Chelsea: Scarborough House, 1989.

Kohs, Samuel C., and Louis I. Dublin, *American Jews in World War II: The Story of 550,000 Fighters for Freedom.* Washington, DC: National Jewish Welfare Board, 1947.

Liddell Hart, B.H. *History of the Second World War.* New York: G.P. Putnum's Sons, 1970.

MacDonald, Charles B., ed. *American Military History.* Washington, DC: Government Printing Office.

———. *A Time for Trumpets: The Untold Story of the Battle of the Bulge.* New York: William Morrow, 1984.

———. *The Battle of the Huertgen Forest.* New York: Jove Publications, 1983 (orig. 1963).

———. *Company Commander.* New York: Bantam Books, 1978 (orig. 1947).

———. *The Last Offensive.* Washington, DC: Government Printing Office, 1973.

———. *The Might Endeavor: American Armed Forces in the European Theater in World War II.* New York: Oxford University Press, 1969.

———. *The Siegfried Line Campaign.* Washington, DC: Government Printing Office, 1963.

Masseck, Major C.J., *Official Brief History of the 89th Division, U.S.A., 1917-1918-1919*. War Society of the 89th Division, 1919.

Mitcham, Jr., Samuel W., *Rommel's Last Battle: The Desert Fox and the Normandy Campaign*. New York: Stein & Day, 1988.

Morison, Samuel Eliot, *Sicily-Salerno-Anzio; History of U.S. Naval Operations in World War II*. Boston: Little, Brown & Company, 1984 (1954).

Officer's Guide. Harrisburg, PA: Military Service Publishing Company, 1942.

Omaha Beachhead 6 June–13 June 1944. The American Forces in Action Series. Washington, DC: Government Printing Office, 1945 (reprinted by Center of Military History, 1984).

Perkins, Norris, MD, *North African Odyssey: Adventures in the Mediterranean Theater of War*. Portland, OR: Four Mountain Productions, 1995.

Roberts, E.A., MD, *Five Stars to Victory: The Exploits of Task Force Lovelady (2nd Bn. (Reinf.), 33rd Arm'd Regt., 3rd Arm'd Div., U.S. Army) in the War Against Germany 1944-1945*. Birmingham, AL: Atlas Printing & Engraving Co., 1949.

Rochlin, Harriet, and Fred Rochlin, *Pioneer Jews: A New Life in the Far West*. Boston: Houghton Mifflin, 1984.

Rooney, Andy, *My War*. New York: Random House, 1995.

Ruppenthal, Roland, et. al., *Utah Beach to Cherbourg 6-27 June 1944*. Washington, DC: Government Printing Office, 1948.

Sawiki, James A., *Cavalry Regiments of the U.S. Army*. Dumfries: Wyvern Publications, 1985.

———. *Infantry Regiments of the U.S. Army*. Dumfries: Wyvern Publications, 1981.

Sorley, Lewis. *Thunderbolt: General Creighton Abrams and the Army of His Times*. New York: Simon & Schuster, 1992.

Stallings, Lawrence, *The Doughboys*. New York: Harper & Row, 1963.

Stanton, Shelby L., *World War II Order of Battle*. New York: Gallahad Books, 1984.

Stubbs, Mary Lee, and Stanley Russell Connor, *Armor-Cavalry, Part I: Regular Army and Army Reserve*. Washington, DC: Government Printing Office, 1969.

———. *Armor-Cavalry, Part II: Army National Guard*. Washington, DC: Government Printing Office, 1972.

Toland, John. *Battle: The Story of the Bulge*. New York: Random House, 1959.

———. *The Last 100 Days*. New York: Random House, 1966.

Trahan, E. A., ed., *A History of the Second United States Armored Division, 1940-1945*. 1946.

Truscott, Jr., Lucian K., *Command Missions: A Personal Story*. Novato, CA: Presideo, 1954.

———. *The Twilight of the U.S. Cavalry: Life in the Old Army, 1917-1942*. Manhattan, KS: University Press of Kansas, 1988.

Official Army Register. Washington, DC: Government Printing Office, 1945.

Wilson, John B., *Armies, Corps, Divisions, and Separate Brigades*. Washington, DC: Government Printing Office, 1987.

Weigley, Russell F., *Eisenhower's Lieutenants, The Campaign of France and Germany 1944-1945*. Bloomington: Indiana University Press, 1981.

———. *The History of the United States Army*. New York: MacMillan Publishing Co., 1967.

Whiting, Charles, *Siegfried: The Nazis' Last Stand*. New York: Stein & Day, 1982.

———. *The Battle of the Ruhr Pocket*. New York: Ballantine Books, 1970.

Williams, Mary H., *Chronology: 1941-1945*. Washington, DC: Government Printing Office, 1959.

Periodicals

"A History of the Third Armored Division, April 1941-July 1958." Darmstadt, *Stars and Stripes*, 68 pp., ill., maps, etc., 1958.

Berry, Lt. Col. Edward S., "From the Seine to the Siegfried Line," *Armored Cavalry Journal*, January-February 1950; (reprinted in September and December 1996, 3AD Association Newletters).

Blake, Tom. "Rifle range's namesake met soldier's ending," *Berlin Observer*, Office of U.S. Commander, Berlin, April 30, 1987, p. 4.

Blumenson, Martin. "Escape from Hedgerow Country," *Military History Magazine*, October 1986, pp. 34-41.

General Rose Memorial Hospital. *Profile of Major General Maurice Rose*. 1995.

Greene, M.D., Ralph C. "The Triumph and Tragedy of Major General Maurice Rose," *Armor Magazine,* March April, 1991, p. 21-29, includes bibliographical notes.

Hammersmark, Mark. "Maurice Rose—the perfect example of the American Soldier," *Colorado History News*, April 1995, p. 1.

Henry, T.R. "Masters of Slash and Surprise; Third Armored Division," *Saturday Evening Post*, October 19, 1946.

Kingston, Donald M. "The Plattsburg Movement and Its Legacy," *Relevance*, volume VI, no. 4, Autumn 1997.

Melrose, Frances. "Remembering a Soldier's Soldier," *Rocky Mountain News Sunday Magazine*, July 23, 1989.

Newsweek. "A General Also Dies," April 16, 1945, pg. 33.

Peters, Sgt. Walter. "Taking Off with the Tanks," *Yank Weekly*, vol. 3, no. 10, August 20, 1944.

Rose, Major General Maurice. "An Operation of the Third Armored ("Spearhead") Division," *Military Review,* June 1945, vol. XXV, no. 3, published by CCGC.

———. "Gen. Rose's Own Story of How He Trapped Huns," *Intermountain Jewish News*, May 24, 1945.

Rose, Captain Maurice. "Panama's Irregular Cavalry," *The Cavalry Journal*, July–August 1935.

Woodson, Dorsey. "Colorado's Fighting General: Maurice Rose," *Empire Magazine, Denver Post*, November 27, 1960.

Unpublished Manuscripts, and Documents

503rd Military Intelligence Detachment Unit History, unpublished manuscript, July 8, 1966 (photocopy).

Appointment of Samuel Rose as Rabbi to Temple Beth Joseph. Jeff Rose Collection, 1925.

Bellinger, Maj. Robert M. "I Was a General's Aide," Robert J. Bellinger Collection, 1966.

Center of Military History, Historical Records Branch, U.S. Army. General Officer Biography files, Washington, DC.

Collins, J. Lawton, Lt. Gen'l. Farewell Address to the Third Armored, 110900 May 1945, at Sangerhausen, Germany. Notes prepared by T/4 Nathaniel Peavy, 3AD Archive.

Committee #1. "The Armored Division in the Defense," Advanced Officers Course, The Armor School, Fort Knox, KY, May 1950.

Committee #3. "Armor under Adverse Conditions: Second and Third Armored Divisions in the Ardennes Campaign, 16 December 1944 to 16 January 1945," Advanced Officers Course, The Armor School, Fort Knox, KY, June 1949.

Committee #4. "The Second Armored Division in the Sicilian Campaign," Advanced Officers Class, The Armored School, Fort Knox, KY, May 1950.

Committee #14. "Exploitation by the Third Armored Division—Seine River to Germany," Advanced Officers Course, The Armor School, Fort Knox, KY, 1949.

Dugan, Haynes W. "Was This How General Rose Died?" *Third Armored Division Association Newsletter*, December 1987.

———. "A General Dies in Combat as World War II Winds Down: General Maurice Rose and the U.S. Third Armored Division." Unpublished manuscipt, Third Armored Division Association Archives, (revised September 3, 1990).

———. "Omaha Forward (Sometimes Way Forward); A History of Forward Echelon and HQ Company," Third Armored Division. Unpublished manuscipt and related correspondence, 1987.

Hadsel, First Lt. Fred. Second Information & Historical Service, VII Corps, First U.S. Army, Combat Interview: "The Battle of Mons 1-4 September 1944," March 16, 1945.

———. Combat Interview with Major General Maurice Rose, CG, 3rd AD, Petite Somme, Belgium, January 26, 1945.

General Rose Memorial Hospital. "Dedication Ceremonies Program," August 31, 1948, 3AD Achives.

Goldstein, Elliott, et. al. *On the Job Training: An Oral History of the Battle of Parker's Crossroads and of the Fate of Those Who Survived.* The 589th Group, Atlanta, GA., 1999.

Graves, Colonel J.R.W., MacLeod, APL Halford, Middleton, GC (British Army of the Rhine). *Battle of Paderborn, March/März 1945,* 1985.

Grow, Francis B., and Alfred Summers. *A History of the 143rd Armored Signal Company, April 15, 1941/May 8, 1945,* unpublished manuscript (photocopy), Summer 1945.

Hemmer, Albert, *The Rundstedt Offensive in the Ourthe Valley: The Decisive Battle at Hotton,* unpublished manuscript, n.d.

KOA-NBC Program. May 27, 1945, *General Maurice Rose Memorial Hospital Program,* transcript, broadcast from the Cosmopolitan Hotel, 10:35-11:00 p.m., draft from 3AD Archives.

Marsh, Don R. "CCA—Pyramid Calling," *Third Armored Division Association Newsletter,* December 1987, pg. 19.

———. "The Man from Colorado," *Third Armored Division Association Newsletter,* December, 1987, pg. 16-17.

———. "History of Combat Command A," *Second Armored Division Association 'Hell on Wheels' Bulletin,* December 1987.

Prue, Bernard. Unpublished manuscript, 1987.

Russell, Robert W. Unpublished manuscript, n.d.

Shaunce, Glenn H. Div HQ, 3AD, tape recordings, October 1987-January 1998.

Smith, Col. John A. Jr. Div HQ, "Draft of a Speech to the Rose Memorial Hospital Ceremony, May 27, 1945." draft, 3AD Archive.

———. Interview conducted in 1972 by Leon Ussery.

Smoyer, Clarence, (33 AR). *Mons, Personal Recollection,* undated, received 10/15/97.

Official Records

World War I

HQ, 177th Infantry Brigade, AEF. *Report of Operations of September 12, 1918 (September 30, 1918).*

Summary of Operations of the 89th Division, American Battlefield Monuments Commission. Washington, DC: Government Printing Office, 1944.

U.S. Army. *Outline History of the 353rd Infantry, 89th Division, 1917-1918-1919,* Washington, DC, 1919.

World War II

1st Armored Division. *After Action Reports.*

2nd Armored Division. *After Action Reports.*

Headquarters, Second Armored Division. *Second Armored Division After Action Report June 1944,* September 9, 1944.

Headquarters, Second Armored Division, Office of the Division Commander. Historical Record, Operations Second Armored Division 22 April-25 July 1943 (Documents Section, Armor School, Fort Knox, KY), August 5, 1943.

Bailey, Jr., Lt. Col. Benjamin M. HQ, CCA, Second Armored Division, CCA, After Action Report, June 1944-July 24, 1944.

Collier, Col. John, HQ, CCA. Second Armored Division, CCA Operations Action for Period July 1-31, 1944 (Inclusive)-September 24, 1944.

Shell, Lt. Col. R.H. Adjutant General, HQ, Second Armored Division, Action Against Enemy Reports/After Action Reports, July 1-31, 1944- September 21, 1944.

3rd Armored Divisions, After Action Reports

HQ, Third Armored Division. *Action against Enemy, After Action Reports for December 1944- February 1945.*

HQ, Third Armored Division. *Action against Enemy, After Action Reports for the Period 1-31 March 1945, Inclusive, Narrative Battle Report, March 1945-4 May 1945.*

HQ, 703rd Tank Destroyer Battalion, *S-3 Journal. 1 Sept 44-6 Sept 44,* 703rd Tank Destroyer Battalion Association Newsletter files (Nathan Goldberg A/703, editor).

HQ, 703rd Tank Destroyer Battalion, *Summary of Operations. 1 Sept 44-6 Sept 44,* 703rd Tank Destroyer Battalion Association Newsletter files (Nathan Goldberg A/703, editor).

Orr, Lt. Colonel William R., First Battalion, Thirty-Sixth Armored Infantry Regiment. "Action at Mons, Belgium, 2-4 September 1944," January 13, 1945.

Correspondence, Conversations, and Tape Recordings

Bellinger, Maj. Robert M, Letter to Arnold Rose, February 23, 1946, Rose Family Collection.

Boulger, ret., Col. Jack, Phone Conversation with Steven L. Ossad, April 12, 1996.

Castille, William A., (CCB), Personal Correspondence with Steven L. Ossad.

Haynes W. Dugan, Personal Correspondence with Steven L. Ossad, 1995–present.

———. Personal Diary, 25 August–17 September 1944.

Gosch, Henry, A., Personal Correspondence with Steven L. Ossad, December 31, 1995.

Hogan, ret., Col. Samuel, Personal Correspondence with Steven L. Ossad, March 30, 1996.

Marsh, Don R. Personal Correspondence, October 1995–present.

Prue, Bernard, Personal Correspondence with Steven L. Ossad, February 1996.

Reisler, Philip B., HQ/CCA, 2AD, "tape recording of April 4, 1996," Don R. Marsh Collection.

Rose, MG Maurice, "Letter to General Eisenhower, March 22, 1945," Eisenhower Library, Abilene, Kansas.

Letter to Mrs. Maurice Rose, March 24, 1945, Jeff Rose Family Collection.

Russell, Robert W., Personal Correspondence with Steven L. Ossad, April 6, 1996.

Skoog, Herb, Radio Interview with MG. Walter B. Richardson, ret. (Reflections #595) broadcast, New Braunfels, Texas, August 26, 1990.

Sweat, ret., Lt. Col. Wesley A., (Div HQ), Personal Correspondence with Haynes W. Dugan, Tuesday AM, March 28, 1988 (Third Armored Division Archives).

———. Personal Conversation with Steven L. Ossad, April 12, 1996.

Warden, Jack B., (36 AIR), Personal Correspondence with Steven L. Ossad, 1996- present.

Zimmerman, Herbert E., (83 Recce), Personal Correspondence with Steven L. Ossad, April 16, 1996.

Index

OTHER TITLES OF INTEREST

'44
In Combat from Normandy
to the Ardennes
Charles Whiting
240 pages, 29 b/w illustrations,
4 maps
0-8154-1214-2
$17.95

ANZIO
The Battle That Failed
Martin Blumenson
224 pp., 4 maps
0-8154-1129-4
$17.95

CANARIS
Hitler's Master Spy
Heinz Höhne
736 pp., 29 b/w photos, 3 maps
0-8154-1007-7
$19.95

CORREGIDOR
The American Alamo of World War II
Eric Morris
560 pp., 23 b/w photos, 4 maps
0-8154-1085-9
$19.95

DEFEAT INTO VICTORY
Battling Japan in Burma and India,
1942–1945
Field Marshal Viscount
    William Slim
New introduction by
    David W. Hogan, Jr.
576 pp., 21 b/w maps
0-8154-1022-0
$22.95

THE DESERT FOX IN
NORMANDY
Rommel's Defense of
Fortress Europe
Samuel W. Mitcham, Jr.
248 pp., 20 b/w photos, 8 b/w maps,
9 tables
0-8154-1159-6
$17.95

GENERAL OF THE ARMY
George C. Marshall, Soldier
and Statesman
Ed Cray
876 pp., 24 b/w photos
0-8154-1042-5
$29.95

THE GI's WAR
American Soldiers in Europe
During World War II
Edwin P. Hoyt
with a new preface
664 pp., 29 b/w photos, 6 maps
0-8154-1031-X
$19.95

GOODBYE, *LIBERTY BELLE*
A Son's Search for His Father's War
J. I. Merritt
Foreword by Samuel Hynes
240 pp., 26 b/w photos and 1 b/w map
0-8154-1231-2
$24.95 cl.

GUADALCANAL
Edwin P. Hoyt
314 pp., 43 b/w photos, 10 maps,
1 diagram
0-8128-8563-5
$18.95

HANGED AT AUSCHWITZ
An Extraordinary Memoir
of Survival
Sim Kessel
New introduction by Walter Laqueur
192 pp., 26 b/w photos
0-8154-1162-6
$16.95

HEROES NEVER DIE
Warriors and Warfare
in World War II
Martin Blumenson
648 pp.
0-8154-1152-9
$32.00 cl.

HITLER
The Survival Myth
Updated Edition
Donald M. McKale
304 pp., 12 b/w photos
0-8154-1128-6
$17.95

HITLER IN VIENNA, 1907–1913
Clues to the Future
J. Sydney Jones
344 pp., 54 b/w illustrations; 16 maps
0-8154-1191-X
$24.95 cl.

THE HITLER YOUTH
Origins and Development, 1922–1945
H. W. Koch
382 pp., 40 b/w photos, 2 maps
0-8154-1084-0
$18.95

HITLER'S COMMANDERS
Officers of the *Wehrmacht*, the
***Luftwaffe*, the *Kriegsmarine*, and the**
Waffen-SS
Samuel W. Mitcham, Jr. and
Gene Mueller
384 pp., 52 b/w photos, 8 maps
0-8154-1131-6
$18.95

HITLER'S FIELD MARSHALS
and Their Battles
Samuel W. Mitcham, Jr.
456 pp., 26 b/w photos, 9 tables, 22
maps
0-8154-1130-8
$18.95

HITLER'S SHADOW WAR
The Holocaust and World War II
Donald M. McKale
504 pp., 39 b/w illustrations
0-8154-1211-8
$29.95 cl.

HITLER'S WAR
Edwin P. Hoyt
with a new preface
440 pp., 60 b/w photos, 4 maps
0-8154-1117-0
$18.95

THE HOUSE OF KRUPP
The Steel Dynasty That Armed
the Nazis
Updated Edition
Peter Batty
360 pp., 17 b/w photos
0-8154-1155-3
$18.95

HUNTERS FROM THE SKY
The German Parachute Corps,
1940–1945
Charles Whiting
with a new preface
240 pp., 12 b/w photos, 8 maps
0-8154-1145-6
$17.95

INFERNO
The Fire Bombing of Japan, March
9–August 15, 1945
Edwin P. Hoyt
188 pp., 10 b/w photos, 2 maps
1-56833-149-5
$24.95 cl.

THE INVASION BEFORE NORMANDY
The Secret Battle of Slapton Sands
Edwin P. Hoyt
212 pp., 22 b/w photos, 4 maps
0-8128-8562-7
$18.95

JAPAN'S WAR
The Great Pacific Conflict
Edwin P. Hoyt
with a new preface
568 pp., 57 b/w photos, 6 maps
0-8154-1118-9
$19.95

THE JEHOVAH'S WITNESSES AND THE NAZIS
Persecution, Deportation, and Murder, 1933–1945
Michel Reynaud & Sylvie Graffard
Introduction by Michael Berenbaum
304 pp., 40 b/w photos
0-8154-1076-X
$27.95 cl.

JULIUS STREICHER
Nazi Editor of the Notorious Anti-Semitic Newspaper Der Stürmer
Randall L. Bytwerk
with a new afterword
264 pp., 31 b/w illustrations
0-8154-1156-1
$17.95

KASSERINE PASS
Rommel's Bloody, Climactic Battle for Tunisia
Martin Blumenson
358 pp., 18 b/w photos, 5 maps
0-8154-1099-9
$19.95

MARSHAL ZHUKOV'S GREATEST BATTLES
Georgi K. Zhukov
Edited by Harrison E. Salisbury
New introduction by David M. Glantz
328 pp., 1 b/w photo; 5 maps
0-8154-1098-0
$18.95

THE MEDICAL CASEBOOK OF ADOLF HITLER
Leonard L. Heston, M.D. and Renate Heston, R.N.
Introduction by Albert Speer
192 pp., 3 b/w photos, 4 graphs
0-8154-1066-2
$17.95

THE MEMOIRS OF FIELD-MARSHAL WILHELM KEITEL
Chief of the German High Command, 1938–1945
Edited by Walter Gorlitz
New introduction by Earl Ziemke
296 pp., 4 b/w maps
0-8154-1072-7
$18.95

MENGELE
The Complete Story
Gerald L. Posner and John Ware
New introduction by Michael Berenbaum
400 pp., 41 b/w photos
0-8154-1006-9
$18.95

MUSSOLINI
A Biography
Jasper Ridley
464 pp., 24 b/w photos, 3 maps
0-8154-1081-6
$19.95